Romancing the Shadow

Romancing the Shadow

Poe and Race

EDITED BY

J. GERALD KENNEDY &

LILIANE WEISSBERG

OXFORD

UNIVERSITY PRESS

2001

OXFORD
UNIVERSITY PRESS

Oxford   New York
Athens   Auckland   Bangkok   Bogotá   Buenos Aires   Calcutta
Cape Town   Chennai   Dar es Salaam   Delhi   Florence   Hong Kong   Istanbul
Karachi   Kuala Lumpur   Madrid   Melbourne   Mexico City   Mumbai   Nairobi
Paris   São Paulo   Shanghai   Singapore   Taipei   Tokyo   Toronto   Warsaw

and associated companies in
Berlin   Ibadan

Copyright © 2001 by Oxford University Press

Published by Oxford University Press, Inc.
198 Madison Avenue, New York, New York 10016

Oxford is a registered trademark of Oxford University Press.

Library of Congress Cataloging-in-Publication Data
Romancing the shadow : Poe and race /
edited by J. Gerald Kennedy and Liliane Weissberg.
    p.   cm.
Includes bibliographical references and index.
ISBN 0-19-513710-8   ISBN 0-19-513711-6 (pbk.)
1. Poe, Edgar Allan, 1809–1849—Political and social views.
2. Race in literature.   3. Literature and society—United States—
History—19th century.   4. Slavery in literature.   5. Afro-Americans in literature.
I. Kennedy, J. Gerald.   II. Weissberg, Liliane.
PS2642.R25 R66   2001
818'.309—dc21   00-031365

9 8 7 6 5 4 3 2 1

Printed in the United States of America
on acid-free paper

ACKNOWLEDGMENTS

This volume is indebted to Toni Morrison's reflections on American literature and received its instigation from her book, *Playing in the Dark*. Morrison's work stands at the center of these chapters.

This book originated in a discussion following a meeting of the Poe Studies Association; we both served as its president at different times. We would like to thank Susie Chang and Elissa Morris from Oxford University Press for turning our project into reality, and the two anonymous readers whose comments helped make this book a much better one. Natalia Vayner's expert technical help transformed a collection of pages into a publishable manuscript.

A longer version of Terence Whalen's chapter appeared in his book *Edgar Allan Poe and the Masses,* and we would like to thank Princeton University Press for permission to publish his essay here. We also gratefully acknowledge all the institutions that have given us permission to publish illustrations included in this volume.

May 2000   J. G. K
                                                                 L. W.

CONTENTS

ABBREVIATIONS

Throughout the present volume, references to works by Edgar Allan Poe are provided parenthetically in the text of each selection.

CW *Collected Writings of Edgar Allan Poe.* Ed. Burton R. Pollin and Joseph V. Ridgely. 5 vols. New York: Gordian Press, 1985–97.
Vol. 1: *The Imaginary Voyages.* Boston: Twayne, 1981; New York: Gordian Press, 1994.
Vol. 2: *The Brevities.* New York: Gordian Press, 1985.
Vol. 3: *Writings in the* Broadway Journal, *Nonfictional Prose.* Part 1, The Text. New York: Gordian Press, 1986.
Vol. 4: *Writings in the* Broadway Journal, *Nonfictional Prose.* Part 2, The Annotations. New York: Gordian Press, 1986.
Vol. 5: *Writings in the* Southern Literary Messenger, *Nonfictional Prose.* New York: Gordian Press, 1997.

Essays *Essays and Reviews.* Ed. G. R. Thompson. New York: Library of America, 1984.

Letters *The Letters of Edgar Allan Poe.* Ed. John Ward Ostrom. 2 vols. 1948. New York: Gordian Press, 1966.

Mabbott *The Collected Works of Edgar Allan Poe.* Ed. Thomas Ollive Mabbott with the assistance of Eleanor D. Kewer and

Maureen C. Mabbott. 3 vols. Cambridge, Mass.: Belknap Press of Harvard University Press, 1969–78.
Vol. 1: *Poems.*
Vol. 2: *Tales and Sketches, 1831–1842.*
Vol. 3: *Tales and Sketches, 1843–1849.*

Works *The Complete Works of Edgar Allan Poe.* Ed. James A. Harrison. 17 vols. New York: Kelmscott Society, 1902.

Introduction

Poe, Race, and Contemporary Criticism

J. GERALD KENNEDY
LILIANE WEISSBERG

Such recent events as the torching of black churches across the South, the hate crime in Jasper, Texas, and threatening, anonymous letters to the heads of minority colleges and universities remind us that racial differences continue to stir fear and loathing in a republic dedicated to "liberty and justice for all." The monstrous paradox embedded in the Declaration of Independence and incompletely resolved by the Civil War haunts the millennial United States with a long legacy of injustice and resentment. In *Faces at the Bottom of the Well*, Derrick Bell has expressed the bleak conclusion that racism is an "integral, permanent, and indestructible component" of American society (ix), and observers such as journalist Carl Rowan have predicted a latter-day "race war." Ostensibly to curb racism, some public officials have called for the elimination of ethnic and racial legal categories and the dismantling of programs such as affirmative action. Labeling efforts to achieve a "color-blind" democracy as misguided, however, Michael Eric Dyson has asserted that "we cannot overcome the history of racial oppression in our nation without understanding and addressing the subtle, subversive ways race continues to poison our lives" (223–24). Dyson insists that "because skin, race, and color have in the past been the basis for social inequality, they must play a role in righting the wrongs on which our society has been built," and he urges Americans to "strive for a society where each receives his or her just due,

xi

where the past in all its glory and grief is part of the equation of racial justice and social equality."[1]

Just how to read "the past" and how such an understanding will produce "racial justice and social equality" Dyson does not undertake to explain, but these compelling questions shape the present volume. While Edgar Allan Poe seems at first glance an unlikely figure around whom to organize a discussion of race and racism in our national culture, the chapters collected here repeatedly bear out Toni Morrison's striking claim that "no early American writer is more important to the concept of American Africanism than Poe" (*Playing in the Dark,* 32). By this phrase (more fully elaborated later), Morrison alludes to a resonant, complex notion of blackness in the Euro-American imaginary that has fueled contemporary notions of racial difference.

In the past two decades, under the rubric of cultural studies, a vast amount of intellectual work has been directed at ways of rethinking race as it influences—and is influenced by—literary production. After the canon wars, debates about political correctness, and deconstructions of identity politics, race and ethnicity remain the source and subject of much American writing, as well as the focus of efforts by critics and theorists to advance understanding of (and respect for) differences of race and culture. Yet the polemical nature of this project also bears scrutiny, and in a real sense the chapters in this volume may be seen as raising several broad, theoretical questions at the crux of current American literary study. These questions concern the public role of the critic/theorist and the objectives of scholarship itself in a politically charged, multicultural society. They bear as well on practical issues of reading, such as what constitutes "evidence," how one assesses authorial "intention," and how (and to what end) one ascertains, historicizes, and evaluates the politics of an author. More specifically, these chapters compel readers to consider the problematic nature of "race," which is neither an essential, invariant set of genetically coded attributes (as racial pseudoscience would contend) nor an entirely arbitrary social construction. They invite reflection on historical changes in racialized thinking and hence on judgments about what constitutes racism at a given historical epoch; they raise the question of what identifies authorial or cultural racism and to what purpose contemporary cultural theory exposes and indicts bygone retrograde attitudes. Finally, the chapters to follow pose the problem of literature's deep relationship to history, economy, and culture and to the concomitant problem of how to balance the difficulties of the text—as well as the ambiguities of the author's "position"—against the pressures of an ideological argument.

It seems indeed curious that Poe should be at the center of this or any debate about the connection between American literature and race in American culture. He is, after all, the quintessential pariah, a lightning-rod figure whose excesses, literary and personal, have long made him both "inescapable" and "dubious" (in Harold Bloom's famous formulation). Excluded from the so-called American Renaissance and from most nationalist critical paradigms from F. O. Matthiessen to Sacvan Bercovitch, Poe has occupied an anomalous position in both the old and new canons of antebellum American writing. Evincing little sustained interest in the frontier, the natural landscape, the Puritan past, the settlement of the colonies, the Revolution, or democracy itself, he seems in many ways the most un-American of our early writers. Many of his narratives (and poems) depict not native scenes but the fantastic, half-remembered landscape of the England he had seen in childhood. Perhaps not coincidentally, Poe has won greater acclaim in Europe, where readers and critics have either detached his work from its historical contexts or assimilated it into Continental intellectual traditions.

Situating Poe's work amid the turbulent cultural developments of the early nineteenth century, and notably amid mounting sectional conflict over slavery, is no simple matter. The geography of his life and career suggests the difficulty of placing him within the regionalized public discourse of the day. Born in Boston, reared in Richmond and London, and educated at Charlottesville and West Point, Poe spent the seventeen years of his career as a publishing magazinist shuttling between the cities of Baltimore, Richmond, New York, and Philadelphia, crossing and recrossing the Mason-Dixon Line, playing the national man of letters in the South and, on occasion, the exiled Southerner in the North. We should note, however, that after leaving Richmond in January 1837, he never again resided in the South and—to judge from his correspondence—retained only a handful of Southern literary connections (including the Baltimore editor and abolitionist Dr. Joseph Snodgrass). Recognizing that his best chance for success as a writer lay in the publishing centers of the North, he cultivated extensive relationships among the literati of Philadelphia and New York. In print Poe remained largely circumspect about the burning political issues that divided not only the North and South but also partisans *within* both regions. Only a few of his farces and satires—pieces such as "Some Words with a Mummy" and "Mellonta Tauta"—reveal flashes of political or social satire, and in those works Poe mainly betrays his contempt for the mob and the gospel of progress. He antagonized the Knickerbocker circle, the Transcendentalists, and the Brahmin admirers of Longfellow but did not venture much into sectional controversy. Despite his professed contempt for the popular audience and his sometimes outrageous lapses of taste or conduct, Poe was in journalistic matters a shrewd pragmatist who courted a national readership. As he traversed the volatile contact zone between North and South, he tended to blink the palpable social and ideological tensions of a Union that would not long endure half slave and half free. Like many of his time and place, that is, Poe endeavored to ignore the terrible contradiction between slavery and the American credo of equality.

Yet for certain critics, Poe has long personified benighted attitudes about race and slavery, and the reasons for such a perception are apparent enough. Three of Poe's tales—"A Predicament," "The Man That Was Used Up," and "The Gold-Bug"—present seemingly ludicrous caricatures of black servants, Jupiters and Pompeys, while his only novel, *The Narrative of Arthur Gordon Pym*, portrays murderous black natives and associates the color white with mystical, even sacred, significance—as epitomized by the huge "shrouded human figure" at novel's end, whose skin is "of the perfect whiteness of the snow" (*CW*, 1:206). Poe also laced several reviews with condescending racial references, and he has been identified repeatedly—and erroneously (as Terence Whalen demonstrates in the present collection)—as the author of a proslavery essay published in the *Southern Literary Messenger* while he was in charge of editorial matters. The perception of Poe as a specifically Southern racist, or (nearly as egregious) a writer insufficiently attuned to political and historical issues has, in an era of cultural studies, negatively affected the volume of critical and scholarly work devoted to his writings—so much so that the annual bibliography *American Literary Scholarship* has lately discontinued its separate Poe chapter, at the very moment when (with Michael Jackson's Poe film in the offing) the author's recognizability in American popular culture has never been greater.

In this paradoxical, revisionary context Toni Morrison has situated Poe where few other critics have, squarely at the center of our literature in its forging of national identity, by insisting that in Poe, "the concept of the American self was . . . bound to Africanism, and was similarly covert about its dependency" (57–58). Hence the African American assumed a subtle, ironic role in Euro-American formulations of American selfhood. "What rose up out of collective needs to allay internal fears and to rationalize external exploitation," Morrison asserts, "was an American Africanism—a fabricated brew of darkness, otherness, alarm, and desire that is uniquely American" (38). In America's fiction, the shadow of the black other has thus frequently served to delineate (as in chiaroscuro) white freedom, equality, and democracy. Morrison's version of cultural history challenges conventional notions of the "American literary tradition" by describing an implicitly Euro-American canon in which racialized blackness signifies in revealing and surprising ways. She revisits classic texts by writers like Melville and Twain to show that the "Africanist presence" provides a "staging ground and arena for the elaboration of [a] quintessential American identity" (44). Recalling an entire tradition she asks, "How did the founding writers of young America engage, imagine, employ, and create an Africanist presence and persona?" (51). Her question thus invites a larger revisionary project that explores the effect of the "Africanist other" (47) on the making of "white" American literature, and that undertaking is indeed well under way.

In her study of Mark Twain's work, for example, Shelley Fisher Fishkin has demonstrated extensive African American sources in the author's vernacular humor; Dana Nelson has traced representations of and ideas about race from early colonial texts to the American literature of the mid–nineteenth century; Eric Lott has examined blackface minstrelsy and its signifying function in white American culture; Eric Sundquist has elucidated issues of race in Melville and Twain; and Teresa Goddu has demonstrated the underlying obsession with slavery and racial difference in American Gothic fiction.[2] These provocative studies and many others sustain Morrison's observation that "reading and charting the emergence of an Africanist persona in the development of a national literature is both a fascinating project and an urgent one, if the history and criticism of our literature is to become accurate" (48).

And astonishingly, Poe himself emerges as the key figure in this project. Morrison points out that beyond his habit of "othering" black characters through "estranging" dialect, fetishized gestures, and blatant stereotypes, Poe's "unmanageable slips" reveal contradictory, suggestive impulses:

> The black slave Jupiter is said to whip his master in "The Gold-Bug"; the black servant Pompey stands mute and judgmental at the antics of his mistress in "A Blackwood Article." And Pym engages in cannibalism *before* he meets the black savages; when he escapes from them and witnesses the death of a black man, he drifts toward the silence of an impenetrable, inarticulate whiteness. (58)

Morrison brilliantly suggests that the Africanist presence in mainstream "white" literature "often provides a subtext that either sabotages the surface text's expressed intentions or escapes them through a language that mystifies what it cannot bring itself to articulate but still attempts to register" (66). Such a perspective opens up an altogether new way of considering the texts of Poe (and other canonical writers) by pushing beyond racist caricature to uncover subversive longings figured through the racial other.

To what degree was Poe outside the social discourse of his time, and to what extent did he participate—albeit covertly—in the contemporary debate on race? Was he really an author "out of Space—out of Time" (to cite the famous line from "Dream-Land"), or do his texts reveal more about his views and about social attitudes in the antebellum period than previously supposed? The present book draws its conceptual inspiration from Morrison's *Playing in the Dark* even as it tests that work's central argument. Each of the pieces gathered here attempts to answer the preceding questions by reflecting on Poe's writing as well as his life. As the reader will see, however, these chapters do not present a one-sided argument but instead implicitly engage each other in a vigorous debate about how to read race in Poe. In a broader sense, they engage issues of critical responsibility and implicitly question the aims of contemporary critical practice. By probing representations of race, class, and ideology within an antebellum cultural context, the contributors may all be said to engage in new historicist readings that seek to unsettle traditional understandings of Poe while foregrounding the historical problem of race (and racism) in America. But these chapters nevertheless differ markedly in purpose and tenor: several are explicitly critical of Poe and his politics, indicting him for unconscionable opinions and values; others regard his social views as historically unremarkable and less interesting than his contradictory representations of otherness. Above all else, the contributors aim to provoke new thinking about the way that race matters and race rules are embedded in American culture and inform the fiction and poetry of its melancholy native son.

While these chapters engage the issue of race in Poe's work in different ways, none present easy answers about Poe's attitudes toward African Americans. In "Average Racism: Poe, Slavery, and the Wages of Literary Nationalism," Terence Whalen provides background for this discussion in his reconstruction of the historical climate of the 1830s. He asks that we acknowledge "multiple racisms and multiple positions on slavery even in the South" and argues that Poe's work must be understood within the context of the literary marketplace. He describes the emerging American publishing industry and its relationship to a nation that depended on, and simultaneously excluded blacks.

Whalen draws a general picture that can serve as an aid for understanding Poe's reviews. Betsy Erkkila and John Carlos Rowe, on the other hand, focus on individual examples of Poe's work. In "The Poetics of Whiteness: Poe and the Racial Imaginary," Erkkila concentrates on Poe's poem "The Raven." In a subtle reading that relates the poem's imagery to the racial discourse of the era, she tries to demonstrate that even a poem as popular as "The Raven" is far from innocent in regard to racial prejudice and anxiety. Erkkila sees Poe supporting dominant Southern views on slavery, as he pictures a universe colored in black and white, and Rowe discovers similar tendencies in Poe's fiction. His discussion of the "Journal of Julius Rodman," *The Narrative of Arthur Gordon Pym*, as well as other narratives, focuses, moreover, on the notion of colonialism. He compares Poe's tales to other, nonfictional narratives of exploration, and Poe's work emerges as part of a general imperialistic discourse that asserts the dominance of white explorers over black slaves and native tribes alike.

Joan Dayan's "Poe, Persons, and Property" likewise begins with a reflection on colonialism, but it then explores the historically linked notion of "property." Why are Poe's heroes so eager to acquire property, whether objects or slaves? "All of Poe's fiction is about property and possession," Dayan writes, "and moves rhetorically back and forth between the extremes of affect (heartfelt devotion or undying love) and dispassion (cold mutilation or self-absorbed insensitivity)." Property and possession are, however, also, and perhaps predominantly, legal terms, and Dayan attempts to integrate Poe's discourse of race within the legal discourse of his time.

If Dayan offers a reflection on the relationship between "race" and "property," Liliane Weissberg's chapter, "Black, White, and Gold," is both a geographic study and an archeological project. She concentrates on Poe's story "The Gold-Bug," and returns it to its setting on Sullivan's Island. To what extent does the tale reflect the history of this island, she asks, and what did Poe have to hide in order to uncover his own mystery of the gold bug? Weissberg not only reintroduces the history of the island as a port of entry for the slaves; in her description of its current landscape, she also depicts what might be called the "Poe-effect," as Poe's work itself is used as an instrument to rewrite the island's history.

The chapters by both Lindon Barrett and Elise Lemire focus on Poe's "Murders in the Rue Morgue." Barrett's "Presence of Mind: Detection and Racialization in 'The Murders in the Rue Morgue'" links Poe's discourse on race to the genre of the detective story, Poe's "tales of ratiocination." To what degree is "Reason" itself, Barrett asks, conflated with whiteness in Poe's tales? Are Poe's tales the exemplification, if not the consequence, of celebrated Enlightenment ideas? Lemire, on the other hand, frames the tale historically by offering information about the race riots of 1838 and their popular reception in the press. In Lemire's reading, Poe's "Murders in the Rue Morgue" appears as a political fable that comments on current affairs, even as it exemplifies contemporary anxieties about "amalgamation."

This contemporary theory of the "mixture" of races also provides the focus of Leland S. Person's chapter, "Poe's Philosophy of Amalgamation: Reading Racism in the Tales." Person examines a number of texts, including *The Narrative of Arthur Gordon Pym* and "The Black Cat," to offer a map of racial anxieties. Like Whalen, Person provides a more general study that concentrates less on Poe the pragmatic journalist than on Poe the raconteur. The final chapter, J. Gerald Kennedy's "'Trust No Man': Poe, Douglass, and the Culture of Slavery," reads Poe's novel, *Pym*, against *The Narrative of the Life of Frederick Douglass* to underscore the reciprical deceptions endemic to a slaveholding culture. Noting that Poe and Douglass briefly inhabited the same Baltimore neighborhood, Kennedy explores the volatility of cities in the upper South in the 1830s as he reconstructs the sociohistorical context that shaped both novel and slave narrative.

The volume thus presents a multitude of perspectives. What is the result, however, of this collective investigation? Was Poe an active promoter of racist ideology, or was he rather a product of his time, repeating generally shared views? If the authors in this volume have reached different answers to such questions, what should be obvious by now is that the racial tensions and differences inscribed in Poe's work have generated a lively discussion of the shadow of race that infuses the nation's unfolding narrative.

Notes

1. See also Leslie G. Carr, *"Color-Blind" Racism.*

2. Shelley Fisher Fishkin, *Was Huck Black? Mark Twain and African-American Voices*; Dana Nelson, *The Word in Black and White: Reading "Race" in American Literature, 1638–1867*; Eric Lott, *Love and Theft: Blackface Minstrelsy and the American Working Class*; Eric Sundquist, *To Wake the Nations: Race in the Making of American Literature*; Teresa Goddu, *Gothic America: Narrative, History, and Nation.*

Romancing the Shadow

CHAPTER I

Average Racism
Poe, Slavery, and the Wages of Literary Nationalism

TERENCE WHALEN

> Public opinion consists of the average prejudices of a community.
>
> Coleridge

> We would therefore propose . . . that history is *not* a text, not a narrative, master or otherwise, but that, as an absent cause, it is inaccessible to us except in textual form, and that our approach to it and to the Real itself necessarily passes through its prior textualization.
>
> Fredric Jameson, *The Political Unconscious* (1981)

In recent years the political and racial meaning of Poe's work has been the focus of intense critical debate, and undoubtedly the positions generated from this debate will have enduring consequences not only for Poe scholars but also for all those investigating the importance of race in American culture. Elsewhere I have argued that Poe's lifelong struggle with the publishing industry constitutes a kind of deep politics that should matter more than his awkward and infrequent forays into partisan rhetoric (*Edgar Allan Poe and the Masses*, 27–39). Poe, that is to say, should be distinguished from the public-spirited intellectuals of his age, for whereas these intellectuals embraced a wide variety of civic and political causes, Poe's political agenda was conspicuously confined to problems of production, ranging from the poverty of authors to the corruption of publishers to the emergence of a vaguely ominous mass audience. To put such a theory to the test, it is necessary to consider what is conventionally seen as the single most important political struggle of antebellum America, namely, the struggle over slavery that divided North from South and that culminated, a dozen years after Poe's death, in a catastrophic civil war. In this chapter I argue that any investigation into Poe's racial views should begin by acknowledging that in the 1830s there were multiple racisms and multiple positions on slavery even in the South. To understand the complex relation between race and literature, moreover, it is also necessary to account for the pressures of literary nationalism and a national literary market because these pressures put constraints on commercial writers in all regions and contributed to the always unfinished formation of what might be called average racism. For Poe and other antebellum writers, average racism was not a sociological measurement of actual beliefs but rather a strategic construction designed to overcome political dissension in the emerging mass audience. In other words, publishers and commercial writers were seeking a form of racism acceptable to white readers who were otherwise divided over the more precise issue of slavery.

Fredric Jameson's admonition about the textual nature of history, cited in the epigraph to this chapter, suggests the general difficulty of unraveling such political intricacies of the past. In the case of Poe and race, this task has been rendered doubly difficult by the texts themselves because most are ambiguous, some are unsigned, and at least one does not even exist. Of all these real and imaginary texts, none is more controversial than the so-called Paulding-Drayton review, an anonymous proslavery essay published in the April 1836 issue of the *Southern Literary Messenger*. On one side of the controversy stand those who attribute the review to Poe and who use it to document his "Southern" attitudes or, more explicitly, his virulent and flagrant racism. Many of these critics share some broad assumptions not only about regionalism and ideology in antebellum America but also about the *aberrance* of discredited doctrines from the past. It is not that they find racism literally unthinkable. Instead, it might be said that for these and other critics, racism is only thinkable as the thought of a Southerner.[1] On the other side of the dispute stand those who attribute the review to Beverley Tucker, law professor at the College of William and Mary and author of the first secessionist novel. The group favoring Tucker's authorship comprises both literary critics who seek to defend Poe from charges of racism and historians who, apparently oblivious to the whole controversy, seek only to clarify Tucker's famous—or infamous—position on slavery and secession. As shall become clear, this ostensibly simple case of attribution raises fundamental questions about the meaning of authorship, questions that no interpretive approach can answer without recourse to history itself.

The nature of the controversy is best illustrated by the glaring contradiction between two literary histories recently issued by Columbia University Press. In "Poe and Writers of the Old South," G. R. Thompson disavows Poe's authorship and then argues that an 1849 review of James Russell Lowell is "the only instance of Poe's taking any kind of stance on the issue of slavery" (269). In "Romance and Race," Joan Dayan identifies Poe as the author of the Paulding-Drayton review, calling it "five of the most disturbing pages Poe ever wrote," and relying on it to expose his "ugly" theory that "the enslaved want to be mastered, for they *love*—and this is the crucial term for Poe—to serve, to be subservient" (98).

In different ways, Thompson and Dayan are both wrong. As I shall demonstrate, Thompson is in error because Poe did make several offhanded statements about slavery, and Dayan is wrong because her interpretation is based almost entirely on a review that Poe did not write.[2] To explore all the relevant evidence, I initially reserve judgment about the legitimacy of "author" and "authorial intent," for by holding the fate of these concepts in abeyance, I am free to pose some basic questions: What can one know about Poe's racial views? In what sense are Poe's expressed views properly his own? What, if anything, can be deduced from Poe's silences? And how should an author's "racism" influence the interpretation of a literary text? Although these questions lead to further inquiries into authorship and literary nationalism, my ultimate aim in this chapter is to lay the groundwork for a more historically informed criticism of race, one that surpasses the prevailing rhetoric of praise and denunciation. In doing so I often find myself contending against those who, like myself, stress the social ramifications of Poe's work, but if political criticism is to be more than politics as usual, it must fulfill a special burden of proof when it turns outward to the unconverted and the undecided.

The Paulding-Drayton Review

In April 1836 the *Southern Literary Messenger* published "Slavery," an unsigned essay purporting to review two recent books: *Slavery in the United States,* by James Kirke Paulding, and *The South Vindicated from the Treason and Fanaticism of the Northern Abolitionists,* an anonymous work generally attributed to William Drayton. The author of the review devotes only a few laudatory sentences to these works, reserving the bulk of the essay to develop an alternative justification for slavery. Instead of treating slavery as a necessary evil, the reviewer defends it as a positively beneficial institution that fulfills God's will by creating a bond of sympathy between the inferior black slave and the superior white master. This bond grows stronger with the master's "habitual use of the word 'my,' used as the language of affectionate appropriation, long before any idea of value mixes with it." In other words, the young master "who is taught to call the little negro 'his,' . . . *because he loves him,* shall love *him because he is his"* (338). As long as "reciprocal obligations" are observed, concludes the reviewer, "society in the South will derive much more of good than of evil from this much abused and partially-considered institution" (339).

After James A. Harrison included the Paulding-Drayton review in *The Complete Works of Edgar Allan Poe* (1902), many literary historians relied on it to document Poe's relation to his social and political surroundings.[3] Later, however, an 1836 letter from Poe to Beverley Tucker raised important questions about the authorship of the review and the validity of interpretations that relied on it. In the letter, dated and postmarked 2 May 1836, Poe refers to "your article on Slavery" and then apologizes for having made some editorial alterations (*Letters,* 1:90–91). First published in 1924 and later reprinted in John W. Ostrom's 1948 edition of Poe's correspondence, the letter seemed to provide conclusive proof that Tucker had written the review and that Harrison had committed a major editorial blunder.

As illustrated by "The Purloined Letter," however, investigators often overlook the most obvious evidence, and many critics continued to attribute the Paulding-Drayton review to Poe long after Ostrom had displayed the letter in plain view. In their anthology *Race and the American Romantics,* for example, Vincent Freimarck and Bernard Rosenthal used the review to prove that Poe was "certainly the most blatant racist among the American Romantics" (3).[4] Later, amid charges that he had perpetuated Harrison's error, Rosenthal defended his choice by claiming that Poe's letter to Tucker must be referring to a still-undiscovered article or pamphlet rather than the Paulding-Drayton review ("Poe, Slavery, and the *Southern Literary Messenger*"). Rosenthal did not provide any definitive proof of Poe's authorship, but he did raise enough doubts to excuse the continued depiction of Poe as a brazen advocate of slavery. In "Romance and Race," Dayan accordingly mentions Rosenthal's "excellent argument for Poe's authorship" and then relies on the Paulding-Drayton review to demonstrate "how much Poe's politics concerning slavery, social status, and property rights owed to the conservative tradition of the Virginia planter aristocracy" (96). Dayan does not explain how this

planter ideology was assimilated by the child of itinerant actors and foster son of a Scottish-born tobacco merchant; like many other literary
critics, she implies that all white Southerners—even transplanted and
temporary ones—held identical views on slavery. But if this is the case,
the position originally derived from Poe's alleged authorship could be
derived—with fewer evidentiary constraints—from Poe's alleged Southernness. John Carlos Rowe has done precisely this, asserting that "Poe
was a proslavery Southerner and should be reassessed as such in whatever approach we take to his life and writings" ("Poe, Antebellum Slavery, and Modern Criticism," 117).[5]

To demonstrate the error of such generalizations, I shall begin by re-
considering the Paulding-Drayton review. My aim is not to produce a
smoking gun, for that already exists in the 2 May 1836 letter from Poe to
Tucker. J. V. Ridgely has recently provided more evidence, and yet the
authorship of the review is still disputed ("Authorship," 1–3).[6] To overcome the resilience of error, something more is required, namely, an interpretive context that allows the letter to be seen as the smoking gun it
most certainly is. So instead of offering a point-by-point refutation of
Rosenthal, I shall focus on the ideological and stylistic similarities between the review and works known to be by Tucker. Even if there were
no other corroborating evidence, these similarities would be enough to
acquit Poe of the accusation, thereby expediting his arraignment on
charges still pending.

Nathaniel Beverley Tucker is today remembered as one of several
proslavery advocates at the College of William and Mary, but he was in
addition a judge, novelist, and active member of the group of Southern
intellectuals that Drew Gilpin Faust has dubbed the "Sacred Circle."
From 1835 to 1837, Beverley Tucker also performed numerous offices
for the *Southern Literary Messenger*, which was published just fifty miles
away from Williamsburg in Richmond, Virginia. Aside from contributing
lectures, poetry, and numerous book reviews, Tucker assisted the magazine by writing favorable notices, selecting appropriate articles for publication, and even correcting proofs. When the Paulding-Drayton review
was published in April 1836, Tucker was also busy writing *The Partisan
Leader*, the first secessionist novel in the United States. Because of his
standing as law professor, Tucker issued the controversial book under a
pseudonym in a vain attempt to conceal his authorship. As Tucker directed the publisher, "Keep dark. I do not wish to be known as the author of these things." In the same letter, Tucker also discussed plans to
secure the assistance of Thomas W. White, proprietor of the *Messenger*:
"I could, if I would, make White praise it to the skies, but I must not give
him any clue to me. He is incapable of secrecy." Given these circum-

stances, it is certainly possible that Tucker turned some of his background reading for *The Partisan Leader* into a hastily written book review
that Poe had to shorten—for either editorial or ideological reasons.[7]

Before examining the most direct evidence, however, it is important
to recognize the strong political affinity between the Paulding-Drayton
review and Tucker's known works, especially since there is no such affinity between the review and texts by Poe. As shall become clear,
Tucker's proslavery writings contain numerous stock arguments and
tropes that are duplicated in the Paulding-Drayton review. These include
sentimental descriptions of sickbed scenes, the use of animal comparisons to explain human racial diversity, charges of Northern meddling
followed by a Southern call to arms, the characterization of slavery as a
positive good rather than a necessary evil, the invocation of divine will
to justify racial subordination, and (sophistical) resolutions of the conflict between equality and difference.[8]

Significantly, some of the most striking correspondences are the ones
between the Paulding-Drayton review and the novel that Tucker was in
the midst of composing. For one thing, both maintain the same hard-
line position. In the review, the author describes "Domestic Slavery" as
"the basis of all our institutions" (337), and in the dedication to *The Partisan Leader*, Tucker refers to a "society whose institutions are based on
domestic slavery" (v). In addition, both the review and the novel attack
the universalizing philosophy that regards human beings "as a unit":

REVIEWER: Such instances prove that in reasoning concern-ing the moral effect of slavery, he who regards man as a unit, the same under all circum-stances, leaves out of view an important consideration. (Review, 339)	TUCKER: If I am put to choose between rejecting the evidence of my own senses . . . or the philosophy which teaches that man is to be con-sidered as a unit, because all of one race, philosophy must go by the board. (*Partisan Leader,* 156)

In both the review and *The Partisan Leader*, there is also an unusual claim
about sentiments in the slave "to which the white man is a stranger":

REVIEWER: [W]e shall take leave to speak, as of things *in esse*, of a degree of loyal devo-tion on the part of the slave to which the white man's heart is a	TUCKER: But [the slave] spoke better than the peasantry of most countries, though he said some things that a white man would not say; perhaps, be

stranger, and of the master's
reciprocal feeling of parental
attachment to his humble
dependent. . . . (Review, 338)

cause he had some feelings to
which the white man is a
stranger. (*Partisan Leader*, 71)

The Paulding-Drayton review goes on to emphasize "the moral influences flowing from the relation of master and slave" (338), which is exactly what Tucker argues in his many signed defenses of slavery.[9] In addition, both writers also claim that the master-slave relationship is essentially familial. The Paulding-Drayton review contends that "the relation between the [white] infant and the [black] nurse" arouses familial sentiments that are then cultivated in the relation between the young white master and his black "foster brother" (338). In *The Partisan Leader*, Tucker likewise emphasizes the relation of the young master to his "black nurse" and "foster-brother." According to Tucker, these slaves "are one integral part of the great black family, which, in all its branches, is united by similar ligaments to the great white family" (*Partisan Leader*, 142). There is one further similarity that does not pertain directly to slavery. In the Paulding-Drayton review, the author uses a comet metaphor to illustrate a cyclical theory of history: "The human mind seems to perform, by some invariable laws, a sort of cycle, like those of the heavenly bodies. . . . Fifty years ago, in France, the eccentric comet, 'public sentiment,' was in its opposite node" (337). In *The Partisan Leader*, Tucker makes a similar argument about the cyclical nature of public sentiment, and he even updates the time line to reflect that the novel is set in the future: "The revolution in public sentiment which, commencing sixty years ago, had abolished all the privileges of rank and age . . . had now completed its cycle" (96).

A survey of other works by Tucker reveals further correspondences in style and phrasing. The Paulding-Drayton review contains a short history of "the war against property" in England and France (337); in an essay on the commercial profession, Tucker declares that "a war against property, in all its forms, has been openly proclaimed" ("Nature and Function," 410).[10] The author of the Paulding-Drayton review contends that "men are always passing, with fearful rapidity, between the extremes of fanaticism and irreligion" (337); in an 1835 review for the *Southern Literary Messenger*, Tucker remarks that at the commencement of the Restoration, the English people "wished no more" of Charles II than that he oppose "irreligion to fanaticism."[11] Two other phrases, common in Tucker's writing and uncommon elsewhere, provide additional evidence. The Paulding-Drayton reviewer starts to make a point about the English Revolution and then declines to pursue it because "with that we have nothing to do" (337). In his verified writings for the *Messenger*, Tucker repeatedly uses the same phrase in the same manner. In one essay he writes that "we have nothing to do with the origin of any particular *mode* of slavery"; in another he protests, "with the philosophy of this we have nothing to do"; and in a third essay he concludes a brief digression by claiming, "with the wisdom or folly of these feelings we have nothing to do."[12] The other phrase, common in Tucker and uncommon elsewhere, is "the march of mind."[13] In the Paulding-Drayton review, the phrase appears in the first paragraph: "'*Nulla vestigia retrorsum*,' is a saying fearfully applicable to what is called the 'march of mind'" (336). Tucker, likewise doubtful of all theories of human perfectibility, later made extensive use of the expression. To indicate his own skepticism toward progress, he generally put the phrase in quotations or italics:

> How long it shall be before the *"march of mind,"* as it is called, in its Juggernaut car, shall pass over us, and crush and obliterate every trace of what our ancestors were, and what we ourselves have been, is hard to say. (review of *A History,* 587)

Tucker wrote this before the publication of the Paulding-Drayton review. Years later, he was still fond of the phrase:

> Where would they now be in the *march of mind*, if, fifty years ago, they could have rooted themselves immovably in the conviction that there were "no secrets in Heaven and earth not dreamed of in their Philosophy." (review of "An Oration, delivered," 44)[14]

Rosenthal's final argument against Tucker's authorship also concerns a matter of style, specifically Tucker's punctuation. Noting that Tucker frequently used colons and semicolons, and that the Paulding-Drayton review contains "not a single colon . . . and only a few semicolons," Rosenthal concludes that the review employs "a mode of punctuation that [Tucker] never used before nor after" (34). Taking into account the customary copyediting practices and the brevity of the review (less than four full pages), such a claim carries little weight. But compare the absence of colons with the presence, again in less than four pages, of these characteristic Tucker phrases: "man as a unit," "feelings to which the white man is a stranger," "fanaticism and irreligion," "the war against property," "with that we have nothing to do," and "the march of mind." The stylistic similarities are so telling that Tucker might as well have signed the review. Combine all of the internal stylistic and ideological evidence with the 1836 letter acknowledging his article "Slavery," and the case for Tucker's authorship is incontrovertible. What Poe said about the novel *George Balcombe* must also be said here, for the author of the Paulding-Drayton review "thinks, speaks, and acts, as no person . . . but Judge Beverley Tucker, ever precisely thought, spoke, or acted before" (*CW,* 5:344).

Poe and Slavery Reconsidered

The resilience of the misattribution raises a number of important issues not only about Poe's racism but also about the peculiar function that the concept of racism plays in critical discourse today. As noted previously, some critics tend to identify racism as a collection of proslavery assumptions held primarily by antebellum Southerners.[15] More recently, critics have emphasized the similarities between antebellum texts and current political struggles, but the discourse on race and literature continues to suffer from several limitations. Due in part to the continuing urgency of the issue, many neglect the historical context of race and instead resort to moralizing apologies, blanket denunciations, or full-blown jeremiads. These approaches, however, present fewer difficulties than the pervasive view of racism as a private sin or psychological malady rather than a long-standing, systemic condition perpetuated by powerful political and economic forces. In keeping with this personalizing tendency, most interpretations of Poe's racism share some common assumptions: that he chose his racial attitudes freely or at least knowingly; that his attitudes could be expressed without constraint; and, by extension, that his expressions constitute a "true" record of his thoughts or feelings. These assumptions are open to attack from many theoretical positions, but I would like to proceed with a more basic investigation of the scene of literary creation. Aside from specifying the social determinants of racism, this investigation should help to clarify one of the most neglected issues in all of Poe criticism, namely, the political and economic constraints on his creative freedom.

To understand these constraints, it is necessary to recall Poe's predicament as editor or editorial assistant for the *Southern Literary Messenger.* Since this was also Poe's first full-time editorial job, it cast a powerful shadow over his entire career in the industry of letters. Thomas Willis White, proprietor of the *Messenger,* conceived of his magazine as both a catalyst and a beneficiary of a mass literary market in the South, but he also worked hard to represent the *Messenger* as a periodical with national significance. Although White probably did not expect to gain much revenue from the Northern market, he nevertheless understood the benefits of cultivating a national image. For one thing, White depended on the North for exchanges, contributions, and editorial favors, which helps to explain why the parsimonious proprietor mailed so many free copies to the offices of Northern newspapers and magazines. Notices in the Northern press enhanced the *Messenger*'s prestige, and since many Southern readers subscribed to Northern journals, this was also an effective (albeit circuitous) way to reach the target audience. For these reasons, White seldom passed up an opportunity to drop intimations of the *Messenger*'s "national" following. During a steamer ride up the James River, for example, White managed to convince antislavery travel writer J. S. Buckingham that although the *Messenger* was published in Richmond, it was "read extensively in every State in the Union" (Buckingham, 2:545).[16]

This marketing strategy sometimes left White straddling both sides of the Mason-Dixon Line. In the *Messenger* prospectus, for example, White first affirms and then denies any sectional bias. On the one hand, he bemoans the lack of Southern periodicals:

> In all the Union, south of Washington, there are but two Literary periodicals! Northward of that city, there are probably at least twenty-five or thirty! Is this contrast justified . . . ? No: for in wealth, talents, and taste, we may justly claim at least an *equality* with our brethren; and a domestic institution exclusively our own, beyond all doubt affords us, if we choose, twice the leisure for reading and writing, which they enjoy.[17]

Immediately after making this oblique and approving reference to slavery, the prospectus disavows all sectional animosity:

> Far from meditating *hostility* to the north, [the editor] has already drawn, and he hopes hereafter to draw, much of his choicest matter thence; and happy indeed will he deem himself, should his pages, by making each region know the other better, contribute in any essential degree to dispel the lowering clouds that now threaten the peace of both, and to brighten and strengthen the sacred ties of fraternal love.

On the surface, these comments seem directed solely toward the North, but sectionalism—not to mention nullification—was also a highly charged issue *within* the South. In other words, White knew that many of his Southern readers were troubled by the growing sectional conflict, and he undoubtedly hoped to mollify these readers with a declaration of nationalist sentiments. The prospectus accordingly exploits fears of Northern dominance, but at the same time it allows liberal or cosmopolitan readers to identify themselves with the image—if not the reality—of a progressive Southern intelligentsia.

To maintain and expand his share of the Southern market, White therefore had to please an audience that was much less homogeneous than generally assumed, at least in regard to political affairs. The *Messenger*'s status as a literary magazine obviously made this task easier, for one of the preeminent ideological attributes of literature is its ability to present itself as a discourse free of ideology. Not surprisingly, White exploited the ostensible neutrality of literature in the prospectus, claiming that "*Party Politics* and controversial *Theology*, as far as possible, are jealously excluded. They are sometimes so blended with discussions in literature or in moral science, otherwise unobjectionable, as to gain admittance for the sake of the more valuable matter to which they adhere; but whenever that happens, they are *incidental* only; not *primary*." White, however, had so little confidence in his literary judgments that he generally deferred to Poe, and when he could not count on Poe, he begged advice from trusted supporters like Beverley Tucker and Lucian Minor. Perhaps because of his uncertainty about literary quality, White often assumed the role of censor, and he paid special attention to inflammatory political issues, which might give offense and thereby drive off subscribers.[18] As White made clear on several occasions, he feared that any involvement in "the strife of party politics" might "jeopardize the fair prospects of the Messenger" (*Richmond Enquirer*, 22 May 1835).

Such fair prospects were imperiled by the growing controversy over slavery. Insofar as it emphasized the fundamental differences between North and South, the struggle over slavery obviously hindered the emergence of a truly national literary market. But as implied earlier, the slavery question also exposed internal divisions within the *Messenger*'s Southern audience. In such a market, economic and ideological forces became fused, and White accordingly attempted to cultivate an average racism that would appeal to a majority of his subscribers. Average racism, however, was easier said than done. White could safely defend the South from the attacks of Northern "fanatics," but he was less certain about whether he should represent slavery as a positive good or a necessary evil, or whether he should take a position on African colonization, that is, on plans to deport American blacks to the African colony of Liberia.

It might have been prudent to avoid such issues altogether, but this was not always possible. In February 1836, for example, Lucian Minor contributed an article purporting to review recent issues of the *Liberia Herald*. In his review, Minor praises the "unparalleled" success of

Liberia, where once "a tangled and pathless forest frowned in a silence unbroken save by the roar of wild beasts," but where today English literature thrives, and with it "those comforts, virtues and pleasures which the existence of Literature necessarily implies" (158).[19] For Minor, literature indicates the overall level of social development, and the newspaper in particular serves as "the most expressive sign of all." Even more expressive than the newspaper itself, however, are the people who produce it. "What heightens—indeed what *constitutes* the wonder," Minor continues, is that the editors, printers, and writers "are all *colored people.*"

By using the *Liberia Herald* as a method of *"instancing* the literary condition of the settlement," Minor was obviously endorsing the work of the American Colonization Society. Founded in 1816, the Colonization Society enjoyed support in both the North and the South for more than a decade. By the 1830s, however, the project of African colonization had come under attack by those maintaining more extreme positions in the debate over slavery. In 1832, for example, abolitionist William Lloyd Garrison and proslavery economist Thomas Dew both denounced colonization as a cruel, unworkable, and prohibitively expensive solution (Tise, 70–74). Minor himself realized that his review might arouse controversy. After praising Liberia effusively, he accordingly disavowed any radical intent: "What we especially had in view, however, when we began this article, was neither rhapsody nor dissertation upon the march of Liberia to prosperity and civilization—unparalleled as that march is, in the annals of civilization—but a notice (a *critical notice*, if the reader please) of the aforesaid newspaper" (158).

The disclaimer was hardly palliative, and this left White in something of a predicament. Since he relied heavily on Minor for articles and editorial advice, he could not simply reject it. But he was also loathe to embroil the *Messenger* in a dispute that might anger his subscribers. Characteristically, White decided to compromise. He ordered Poe to revise or delete the more controversial sections of the review. He also gave Poe the job of informing Minor about these revisions, and Poe dutifully told Minor that "it was thought better upon consideration to omit all passages in 'Liberian Literature' at which offence could, by any possibility, be taken" (*Letters*, 1:83). This incident, it should be noted, suggests another motive behind Poe's "immaterial alterations" of the Paulding-Drayton review. If Poe censored a colonization article to avoid controversy in February, he may have censored Tucker's proslavery article for the same reason in April. In any event, Poe's revision of Minor's article was not entirely successful. In a review of the February *Messenger*, the *Augusta Chronicle* denounced "Liberian Literature" as being "altogether unsuited to our Southern region, and as indicating a dangerous partiality for that most pestiferous and abominable parent of the Abolitionists, the *Colonization Society*."[20] The handling of Minor's article nevertheless reveals something of the ideological constraints that the *Messenger* imposed upon even its most valued contributors.

Significantly, the *Messenger* placed similar constraints on proslavery advocates like Beverley Tucker. These constraints are often overlooked because the *Messenger* later became a forum for proslavery opinion, but Poe's political education occurred during 1835 and 1836. "Notes to Blackstone's Commentaries," one of Tucker's first substantial articles on slavery, appeared in the January 1835 *Messenger*. In the "Editorial Remarks" for this issue, the writer—probably James Heath—takes exception to Tucker's general line of argument. Since these remarks represent the *Messenger*'s official position at its commencement, they are worth quoting at length:

> The able author of the *"Note to Blackstone's Commentaries,"* is enti-
> tled to be heard, even on a subject of such peculiar delicacy. . . .
> Whilst we entirely concur with him that slavery as a political or so-
> cial institution is a matter exclusively of our own concern . . .
> we must be permitted to dissent from the opinion that it is either a
> moral or political benefit. We regard it on the contrary as a great
> evil, which society will sooner or later find it not only its interest
> to remove or mitigate, but will seek its gradual abolition or amelio-
> ration, under the influence of those high obligations imposed by
> an enlightened Christian morality.[21]

White felt obliged to print a more scathing reply to Tucker's article in the next issue. Signed by "A Virginian," the reply begins with a merciless refutation of Tucker's position and concludes by supporting both African colonization and the gradual elimination of slavery.[22] Such incidents demonstrate that White could not prevent the *Messenger* from occasionally becoming "a vehicle of political discussion." Nor could he arrive at an average racism that would satisfy both colonizationists and "positive-good" extremists. He could only attempt to minimize his risks by restricting the number of articles on slavery, by censoring these articles whenever possible, by printing editorial disclaimers, and by encouraging any offended readers to respond with letters rather than canceled subscriptions.

Taken together, the articles by James Heath, Lucian Minor, and Beverley Tucker represent the full range of positions on slavery that could be articulated in the *Messenger* during its early years of operation.[23] During the period of Poe's employment, articles in this Southern magazine did not uphold a single, consistent position on slavery; nor was the *Messenger* a forum for abolitionists and fire-eaters alike. Instead, the political spectrum of the magazine was bounded by gradualists or colonizationists at one extreme and positive-good secessionists at the other. White, moreover, only allowed these extremist positions to be defended by a few privileged contributors, and then only grudgingly. This policy, it should be emphasized, arose not from any moral aversion toward slavery but from White's belief that controversial issues were bad for literary business. As indicated earlier, he had no desire "to jeopardize the fair prospects of the Messenger, by involving it in the strife of party politics."[24]

The strictures on "party politics" applied to Poe as well, especially since he was not a privileged contributor but merely a paid assistant to White. It was Poe's job, moreover, to implement and articulate the *Messenger*'s editorial policies, and on one occasion he found himself explaining that "the pages of our Magazine are open, and have ever been, to the discussion of all general questions in Political Law, or Economy—never to questions of mere party" (Poe, "Editorial," 445). Obviously, then, there were implicit and explicit constraints on what Poe could say about slavery. Even if he had been a ranting abolitionist or a rabid secessionist, he would never have been able to express these views in the *Southern Literary Messenger*. White's fear of political controversy called for positions that were less progressive than Minor's and less reactionary than Tucker's, and in fact all of Poe's remarks on slavery for the *Messenger* fall between these two extremes.

In his review of Anne Grant's *Memoirs of an American Lady*, for example, Poe quotes a romantic description of slavery in colonial New York, claiming that these "remarks on slavery . . . will apply with singular accuracy to the present state of things in Virginia."[25] In the quoted passage, Grant maintains that in Albany, "even the dark aspect of slavery was softened with a smile." Rosenthal sees this as being consonant with "the standard pro-slavery argument" ("Poe, Slavery, and the *Southern Literary Messenger*," 30), but as quoted in the *Messenger*, Grant distances herself from the proslavery position: "Let me not be detested as an advocate of slavery, when I say that I think I have never seen people so happy in servitude as the domestics of the Albanians" (*CW*, 5:234). Less important than the remarks themselves, however, is the regional identification of the speaker. Northern apologies for slavery were highly coveted by Southerners, and for a fledgling magazine such as the *Messenger*, these apologies had the added attraction of mitigating—or appearing to mitigate—sectional differences in the national literary market.

In Joseph Holt Ingraham's book *The South-West. By a Yankee*, Poe found another Northerner who was willing to pardon the peculiar institution. In an account of his travels through Louisiana and Mississippi, Ingraham pauses on several occasions to excuse, if not defend, Southern slavery. After passing a group of slaves purchased in Virginia and bound for a plantation outside New Orleans, Ingraham remarks that "they all appeared contented and happy, and highly elated at their sweet anticipations." "Say not," Ingraham continues, "that the slavery of the Louisiana negroes is a *bitter* draught" (1:190–91).[26] Such pronouncements inspired the following comment, which remains Poe's most explicit statement on slavery:

> The "Yankee," in travelling Southward, has evidently laid aside the general prejudices of a Yankee—and, viewing the book of Professor Ingraham, as representing, in its very liberal opinions, those of a great majority of well educated Northern gentlemen, we are inclined to believe it will render essential services in the way of smoothing down a vast deal of jealousy and misconception. The traveller from the North has evinced no disposition to look with a jaundiced eye upon the South—to pervert its misfortunes into crimes—or distort its necessities into sins of volition. He has spoken of slavery as he found it—and it is almost needless to say that he found it a very different thing from the paintings he had seen of it in red ochre. He has discovered, in a word, that while the *physical* condition of the slave *is not* what it has been represented, the slave himself is utterly incapable to feel the *moral* galling of his chain.[27]

Poe here follows a double strategy. He obviously seeks to defend the South from Yankee "prejudices," but at the same time he attempts to "smooth down" the growing sectional divide by appealing to the liberal opinions of the "great majority of well educated Northern gentlemen." His position on slavery likewise seems directed toward a racist majority. Without advocating any specific policy, he first concedes the "misfortunes" of slavery and then assures his readers that these misfortunes cause little injury to the slaves themselves. In other words, Poe dodges the slavery question by shifting the argument to "common" ground— only what makes the ground common in this case is racism.

In many ways, Poe's statement accords with the "moderate" *Messenger* position articulated in 1835 by James Heath. Unlike Heath, however, Poe failed to advocate even the gradual elimination of slavery. He also seemed hesitant about taking a position on colonization. As editor of the *Messenger*, Poe frequently discussed other monthly magazines, and in the October 1835 *North American Review*, he stumbled upon a long, favorable review of Ralph Gurley's *Life of Jehudi Ashmun, Late Colonial Agent in Liberia*. After quoting a laudatory account of Ashmun's character, Poe admits that he is "willing to believe" this description, and he also concedes that Ashmun "was a noble martyr in the cause of African colonization." But Poe wonders why the reviewer selected this particular book:

> We doubt, however, if there are not a crowd of books daily issuing unnoticed from the press, of far more general interest, and consequently more worthy the attention of our leading Review than even *The Life of Ashmun*. We shall soon, perhaps, have a Life of some Cuffy the Great, by Solomon Sapient; and then the North American will feel itself bound to devote one half of its pages to that important publication.[28]

"Cuffy," derived from an African word for "Friday," was a common given name among American blacks; in this context it may also allude to Paul Cuffee (1759–1817), a black shipowner, Quaker, and political activist who helped establish a colony of African Americans in Sierra Leone.[29] Poe's remarks up to this point therefore suggest a willingness to belittle any text supportive of African colonization. But then, as if stepping back from the threshold of partisan politics, Poe immediately modifies his position: "In expressing ourselves thus, we mean not the slightest disrespect to either Ashmun or his Biographer. But the *critique* is badly written, and its enthusiasm *outré* and disproportionate."

The rest of Poe's reviews in the *Southern Literary Messenger* have little or nothing to add to these brief statements, indicating that he avoided taking a specific position on slavery and instead attempted to embrace an average racism that would appeal to a majority of subscribers. Despite this evidence, many critics nevertheless accuse Poe of sharing the views of the most extreme proslavery advocates. Kenneth Alan Hovey, for example, contends that Poe's social views "are essentially identical" to those expressed by Beverley Tucker in the Paulding-Drayton review (Hovey, 347). Others identify Poe with the proslavery, anticolonization position of Thomas Dew, political economist and president of the College of William and Mary. Joan Dayan notes that Poe corresponded with Dew and wrote the introduction to his "Address" for the *Southern Literary Messenger* ("Romance and Race," 96).[30] John Carlos Rowe refers to Poe's "undisputed admiration" for Dew ("Poe, Antebellum Slavery, and Modern Criticism," 119–20), and Dana Nelson observes that Poe revealed his true sentiments "particularly in his stance on works by the noted Southern defender of slavery, Thomas R. Dew" (91). All of these critics echo

Bernard Rosenthal's claim that "perhaps the most telling fact about Poe's position on slavery is his record of public admiration for Thomas R. Dew, the man most fully identified with the extreme and articulate slavery apologetics of Poe's day" (30).

Aside from insinuating guilt by association, this position rests on a fundamental misconception of Poe's work and work-related constraints at the *Messenger*. Thomas Dew was an important supporter of the magazine, for in addition to contributing articles directly, he was also in a position to influence many other subscribers and potential subscribers. And since he was president of the College of William and Mary, the *Messenger* could not offend Dew without imperiling the substantial patronage of college faculty, students, and alumni. Even if Poe had wanted to express disapproval of Dew, White would never have permitted it. Moreover, the particular text on which this whole argument rests was originally composed not by Poe but by Dew himself, a fact overlooked by nearly everyone. The text in question is Poe's October 1836 review of Dew's welcoming address to the entering class. In order to write the review, Poe asked Dew for a copy of the address (published in the next issue of the *Messenger*) and for general information about the college. Dew responded with what we would today call a press release, and Poe merely revised it for his review. Dew's letter was reprinted in the standard edition of Poe's works, and it is a simple matter to identify the blatant similarities between Poe's review and Dew's press release. In a 1941 dissertation on the canon of Poe's critical works, which Rosenthal explicitly cites, William Hull in fact demonstrates that the six basic points in Poe's review are all derived, nearly verbatim, from the letter by Dew. I list only a few examples.

DEW: The numbers at Wm & Mary have rarely been great, & yet she has turned out more useful men, more great statesmen than any other college in the world in proportion to her alumni. (Hull, "A Canon of the Critical Works of Edgar Allan Poe," 159)

POE: The number has at no time been very great it is true; and yet, in proportion to her alumni, this institution has given to the world more useful men than *any other*—more truly great statesmen. (*CW*, 5:300)

DEW The scenery here, the hospitable population, the political atmosphere all conspire to give a utilitarian character to the mind of the student. Hence the alumni of this college have always been characterized by *business* minds & great efficiency of character. (Hull, "A Canon," 160)

POE: Perhaps the scenery and recollection of the place, the hospitable population, and political atmosphere, have all conspired to imbue the mind of the student at Williamsburg with a tinge of utilitarianism. Her graduates have always been distinguished by minds well adapted to *business*, and for the greatest efficiency of character. (*CW,* 5:300)

DEW: The high political character of old Va. is due to this college. (Hull, 159)

POE: To William and Mary is especially due the high *political* character of Virginia. (*CW,* 5:300)

Rosenthal quotes this final passage to show that Poe "singled out for praise [Dew's] special achievement," namely, his advocacy of an extreme proslavery position. As indicated earlier, however, Poe singled out nothing—he merely made minor stylistic changes in a press release that the *Messenger* was obliged to publish. Clearly, then, the "guilt by association" strategy is subject to abuse and manipulation. Rosenthal claims that Hull's dissertation "gives meticulous evidence establishing Poe's authorship" of the review in question, but Hull in fact gives meticulous evidence that confounds the very concept of authorship by demonstrating Poe's reliance on a text he could not refuse.[31]

Further arguments about Poe's racism have been based on his alleged review of John L. Carey's *Domestic Slavery.* The problem here concerns not authorship but existence, for the review was never published, and no manuscript copy has ever been located. Rosenthal and Nelson nevertheless contend that the review demonstrates Poe's "proslavery sympathies" (Rosenthal, 30; Nelson, 91). This claim merits special consideration because it is one of the most egregious examples of the guilt-by-association strategy practiced by Rosenthal and theoretically justified by Rowe. Reports about the purported content of the review are based on Poe's June 1840 letter to Joseph E. Snodgrass, editor of the *American Museum* and later of the *Baltimore Saturday Visiter.* Snodgrass had sent Poe a copy of Carey's book so that he might review it for Burton's *Gentleman's Magazine.* In a letter to Snodgrass, Poe explained why the review did not appear:

Mr. Carey's book on slavery was received by me not very long ago, and in last month's number I wrote, at some length, a criticism upon it, in which I endeavored to do justice to the author, whose talents I highly admire. But this critique, as well as some six or seven others, were refused admittance into the Magazine by Mr. Burton, upon his receiving my letter of resignation. . . . I fancy, moreover, that he has some private pique against Mr. Carey (as he has against every honest man) for not long ago he refused admission to a poetical address of his which I was anxious to publish. (*Letters,* 1:138)

There are several reasons to question the sincerity of this letter. First, Poe was eager to tarnish the reputation of his former employer; as he later told Snodgrass, "Burton . . . is going to the devil with the worst grace in the world, but with a velocity truly astounding" (*Letters,* 1:152). Second, Poe was caught up in a network of puffing and promotion that included both Carey and Snodgrass. In December 1839, Poe (relying on Snodgrass as a go-between) had sent a copy of *Tales of the Grotesque and Arabesque* to Carey, who was then editor of the *Baltimore American;* shortly thereafter, Carey responded by publishing a favorable review (Thomas and Jackson, 281). In addition, Poe was at this time cultivating Snodgrass as a supporter of his magazine project. When Snodgrass sent Carey's book to Poe, that is, when Snodgrass acted as a go-between in the other direction, Poe may have felt obliged to return Carey's original favor. Given these circumstances, Poe may have felt that a disparaging review would appear ungrateful to both Carey and Snodgrass—editors whose support Poe still wanted. He would have been strongly inclined to express a favorable opinion of Carey's book, and since the review was not published, this approval—whether feigned or genuine—cost him nothing. Finally, it is entirely possible that Poe never reviewed Carey's book at all. If Poe had written a review, Snodgrass would certainly have been willing to publish it in the *Visiter;* as I indicated later, Snodgrass ultimately went on to publish several reviews of Carey's works. In other words, it is entirely possible that conclusions about Poe's racism are being drawn from a review that never existed, for Poe may have responded to Snodgrass's inquiry with a complete, yet plausible, fabrication.

Disregarding these considerations, Rosenthal nevertheless claims that "even a review *mildly* sympathetic to Carey's views would place one in a position of sympathy with the South's pro-slavery orthodoxy" (30). Aside from its scanty foundation in fact, this argument suffers from two additional weaknesses that are characteristic of regionalist reasoning.

First, it collapses the differences between a union-loving colonizationist like Carey and a positive-good secessionist like Tucker. As already demonstrated, in the 1830s several orthodoxies were vying for dominance. Carey himself attempts to sort out these contending positions within the South:

> I take it upon myself to say, that the people of the south have manifested no backwardness in relation to the question of domestic slavery. The time was not long ago, when this subject was discussed with freedom throughout the southern states. It was becoming a matter of anxious solicitude; for it concerned them dearly. The process of effectual reformation was going on in its legitimate way; truth was coming to the minds of the reflecting in the light of their own experience, and was operating upon the unforced will. The evil of slavery was generally acknowledged; for I am persuaded that the sentiments which were declared some time ago, by Gov. McDuffie, of South Carolina, were not held then by the intelligent portion of southern people. (Carey, 99)[32]

In the conflicted political environment of Baltimore, Carey concocts a position that mixes racism with a mild form of antislavery activism. On the one hand, he contends that two distinct races cannot peacefully coexist unless "the one be in subjection to the other" (34), and that abolitionists have only caused a hardening of Southern attitudes. On the other hand, he advocates colonization as a "safe and effectual system" capable of "delivering this country from the evil of slavery, with security at once to both races, and with a prospect of final good to the blacks" (112–13). It is therefore unclear what Poe might have said in his attempt to "do justice to the author" of *Domestic Slavery*, if he made the attempt at all.

Second and most important, images of a monolithic South falsify the true political terrain of the region. We have already seen some of the ideological dissension and diversity that characterized the *Messenger* in the 1830s; this diversity was even more pronounced in border states such as Maryland. Joseph Evans Snodgrass, for example, was actually attempting to encourage an antislavery movement within the South. The *Baltimore Saturday Visiter* had been marketed as a family newspaper devoted to art and literature, but by 1843, Snodgrass was publishing articles that defended *and* attacked slavery. In 1845 he used another book by John Carey (*Slavery in Maryland, Briefly Considered*) to solicit controversial reviews, two of which he later published separately as pamphlets. In the first of these (*A Letter on Slavery, Addressed to John L. Carey*), Dr. R. S.

Steuart describes slavery as a kind of "tutelage" that prepares savages for civilization and that—in due time—should be gradually eliminated. Later that year, however, Snodgrass published *Slavery in Maryland: An Anti-Slavery Review*, which attacks Steuart's gradualist approach on moral and religious grounds. The author of this second pamphlet disputes the benevolence of slavery and further contends that colonization, or any plan to remove blacks from Maryland, would prove both cruel and un-workable. In the concluding section, the author refuses to apologize or temporize:

> It is in vain for the advocates of slavery to throw themselves into the breach that had been made in their bulwarks; their efforts will be powerless to arrest the progress of liberal opinions. . . . Can we allow our liberties to be wrested from us in order to perpetuate an institution that has been a blighting mildew on every land it has ever touched from the creation of the world? With a slow and al-most imperceptible progress it has overshadowed the whole land, obscuring the moral vision of the people, and infecting the atmos-phere of the mind. . . . [U]nless its progress can be arrested, we shall be reduced to a feeble and degenerate people, crouching among the mighty works erected by our fathers.[33]

Signed by "A Virginian," the pamphlet has been attributed to none other than James E. Heath, novelist, Virginia state auditor, and sometime edi-tor of the *Southern Literary Messenger*.

Poe's "associations," then, exposed him to diverse positions on slav-ery, but even this does not mean that such positions could be freely cho-sen or freely advocated, especially in the Southern literary market. In his "Anti-Slavery Review," for instance, Heath counsels against establishing a newspaper devoted exclusively to emancipation, for he believes that a general publication with a few articles on slavery would reach more Southern readers:

> [The question] cannot be investigated effectually without some organ of public communication by which information may be dif-fused and the various plans brought forward, and fully discussed before the people. It, however, appears to me that a newspaper devoted to this especial object, would not effect so much as the introduction of suitable essays into the columns of papers already established. A paper devoted to emancipation would probably have but a limited circulation in the South, and that chiefly among persons already convinced. (4)

Snodgrass himself used similar arguments to solicit financial contributions from such notable abolitionists as Wendell Phillips, E. G. Loring,
and Maria Weston Chapman. In an unpublished 1846 letter to Chapman,
Snodgrass discusses the cost of sending his paper to "slave-holders and
pro-slavery men in their feelings." According to Snodgrass, he and other
progressive Southern editors will succumb to the "cash rule" unless he
can convince "the friends of Reform to do their [financial] duty." "We
are," he concludes, "too few and too feeble to stand alone as yet."[34] Circumstances proved him right. By discussing plans for the abolition of
slavery, Snodgrass damaged both his reputation and the circulation of
his paper. According to Dwight Thomas, many residents of Baltimore
regarded Snodgrass as "a dangerous radical," and journalist Jane Swisshelm, a dangerous radical herself, remembered Snodgrass as "a promi-
nent Washington correspondent, whose anti-slavery paper had been
suppressed in Baltimore by a mob" (D. Thomas, 635).[35]

As Poe learned in New York, pressure could also be exerted in the
other direction. In 1845, Poe had become one of the editors of the
Broadway Journal. For the March 22 issue, he wrote an extremely favorable
notice of the *Southern Literary Messenger*, claiming that under his editorship it had enjoyed "a success quite unparalleled in the history of our
five dollar Magazines." The *Messenger's* subscribers, Poe continued, "are
almost without exception the *élite*, both as regards wealth and intellectual
culture, of the Southern aristocracy, and its corps of contributors are
generally men who control the public opinion of the Southerners on *all*
topics."[36] Poe's 1845 notice raised doubts about the political neutrality of
both the *Messenger* and the *Broadway Journal.* It also aroused the anger of
antislavery activists, who were disturbed to see such a notice in a paper
that was supposedly friendly to their cause. Writing for the *Liberator*,
Robert Carter responded with a full-scale attack. According to Carter,
many other reformers had hoped that the *Broadway Journal* would support "the cause of Human Rights" by "properly rebuking evil and evil-
doers." Instead, Carter complained, the *Broadway Journal* had entered into
an unholy alliance with a Southern magazine whose "principles are of
the vilest sort" and whose aims are "to uphold the peculiar institution, to
decry the colored race," and "to libel the abolitionists."[37]

Carter was under the mistaken impression that the notice of the *Messenger* had been written by coeditor Charles Briggs, so Poe escaped from
the incident relatively unscathed. Briggs's reaction, however, reveals
much about the predicament of a magazine attempting to circulate
among subscribers with diverse and conflicting views toward slavery.
Briggs claimed to be "unqualifiedly opposed to slavery in every shape,"[38]
but despite constant prodding from his friend James Russell Lowell, he

was unwilling to turn the *Broadway Journal* into an abolitionist paper. If the paper were to espouse such a position, openly, reasoned Briggs, it would lose the very readers most in need of reform:

> In the little time that our Journal has been going, we have received considerable countenance from the south and yesterday a postmaster in the interior of North Carolina wrote to solicit an agency. Now we should turn the whole people south of the Potomac from us if in our first number we were to make too strong a demonstration against them; and all my hopes of doing good by stealth would be frustrated.[39]

Briggs, however, had other motives. When Lowell pressed him to take a more daring stand, Briggs invoked financial necessity: "You know that publishers and printers judge of propriety by profit . . . and my publisher and printer took alarm at the outset at my manifest leaning toward certain horrifying because unprofitable doctrines." After Carter's attack appeared in the *Liberator*, Briggs stated the case more bluntly: "I cannot afford to publish a radical reform paper, for I could get no readers if I did."[40] The lesson in political neutrality first given at the *Messenger* was therefore repeated at the *Broadway Journal*, and Poe seems to have learned his lesson well. With the exception of the laudatory notice of the *Messenger*, Poe was as willing as Briggs to measure "propriety by profit."

After this period, Poe made only two conspicuous statements about slavery, and unfortunately the context of these statements has been universally neglected. The references to slavery appear in reviews of Longfellow and Lowell, but in each case Poe made the remarks anonymously or under cover of what we would today call plausible deniability. The first statement occurs in an unsigned review of Longfellow published in the April 1845 *Aristidean*, just one month after the attack of the *Liberator*. Importantly, this review was published in the midst of the so-called Longfellow War, which Poe instigated when he accused the esteemed New England poet of being a self-promoter and a plagiarist. The *Aristidean* review begins by disparaging Longfellow's Boston supporters, a group identified as "the small coterie of abolitionists, transcendentalists, and fanatics in general," or, more pointedly as "the knot of rogues and madmen" (*Essays*, 760). Then commences an attack on Longfellow's latest poetic works. Referring specifically to *Poems on Slavery*, the reviewer accuses Longfellow of pandering to "those negrophilic old ladies of the north" with "a shameless medley of the grossest misrepresentation." Noting how easy it was for a Northern professor to "write verses instructing the southerners how to give up their all with a good grace," the reviewer charges that Longfellow has confused slavery in the South with the treatment of slaves in Cuba. Longfellow, the reviewer continues, has "no right to change the locality, and by insinuating a falsehood in lieu of a fact, charge his countrymen with barbarity" (*Essays*, 762, 763).

In an apparent attempt to do "evil by stealth," the anonymous writer turns Briggs's strategy on its head. This review, however, must be used with caution, for it is evidently a collaborative production by Poe and Thomas Dunn English, editor of the *Aristidean*. Most passages seem to come directly from Poe, but there are enough inconsistencies to indicate the work of a second author. In all likelihood, Poe provided a rough draft, which English altered to suit his own design.[41] This arrangement apparently satisfied both parties, for Poe wanted the piece to look as if it had been written by another hand. The Longfellow review contains many third-person references to "Mr. Poe," and in a subsequent notice of the *Aristidean*, Poe with some impudence attempts to maintain this illusion:

> There is a long review or rather running commentary on Longfellow's poems. It is, perhaps, a little coarse, but we are not disposed to call it unjust; although there are in it some opinions which, by implication, are attributed to ourselves individually, and with which we cannot altogether coincide. ("The Aristidean," 285)

It is therefore difficult to decide whether to blame Poe or English for such phrases as "negrophilic old ladies of the north."[42] But two points are clear. First, the defense of the South is presented as a reaction to a Northern attack, specifically an attack by a Boston gentleman who could—without financial risk—turn poetry into a vehicle for political criticism. Second, whether or not Poe "coincided" with the *Aristidean* review, he certainly recognized that it might arouse some outcry, and he accordingly sought to distance himself from any "horrifying because unprofitable doctrines."

Poe repeated this strategy in his 1849 attack on James Russell Lowell's *Fable for Critics*. In a review written expressly for the *Southern Literary Messenger*, Poe denounces Lowell as "one of the most rabid of the Abolition fanatics." Posing as a guardian of Southern sensibility, he attempts to shield prospective readers from Lowell's "prejudices on the topic of slavery." "No Southerner," Poe warns, "who does not wish to be insulted, and at the same time revolted by a bigotry the most obstinately blind and deaf, should ever touch a volume by this author" (*CW*, 5:376).

As with the Longfellow review, Poe intended this to be anonymous.

On several occasions, the writer refers to "Mr. Poe" in the third person, and in his private correspondence, Poe stresses that he had the review published "editorially" (*Letters*, 2:449). For the first time in years, then, Poe was in a position to write anonymously for a Southern audience. But instead of unleashing a pent-up defense of slavery, Poe uses the opportunity to discuss the perils of fanaticism in general:

> His fanaticism about slavery is a mere local outbreak of the same innate wrong-headedness which, if he owned slaves, would manifest itself in atrocious ill-treatment of them, with murder of any abolitionist who should endeavor to set them free. A fanatic of Mr. L's species, is simply a fanatic for the sake of fanaticism, and *must* be a fanatic in whatever circumstances you place him.

In other words, fanaticism is a national problem that merely expresses itself differently in different regions. But as indicated in the succeeding paragraph, what most disturbs Poe is the power of fanaticism to aggravate the cultural division between North and South, for this effectively deprives Southern writers of access to the national literary market: "It is a fashion among Mr. Lowell's set to affect a belief that there is no such thing as Southern Literature. Northerners—people who have really nothing to speak of as men of letters,—are cited by the dozen. . . . Other writers are barbarians and are satirized accordingly—if mentioned at all" (*CW*, 5:377). Even when writing anonymously, Poe found it easier to denounce abolitionism than to justify slavery, and when he did defend the South, he showed greater concern for Southern writers than for Southern institutions.

There are other stray references to race, ranging from a comment on African American speech in his review of Sedgwick's *The Linwoods* to a matter-of-fact description of a slave uprising in his review of Bird's *Sheppard Lee*.[43] But given the vast bulk of his writings, these references are conspicuously few. Unable and unwilling to bear the risks of political speech, Poe succumbed to the pressures of a national literary market either by falling silent on controversial issues or by searching for an average racism that could take the place of unprofitable doctrines about slavery. There were of course writers who rejected this strategy and profited nevertheless, but as G. R. Thompson has pointed out, Poe generally shied away from the literary sectionalism of such writers as Simms, Longfellow, and Harriet Beecher Stowe.[44] Of Poe's sixty-five tales, only two—"The Gold-Bug" and "A Tale of the Ragged Mountains"—are set in the South, and many of the rest seem to be set nowhere at all. Thompson attributes this antiregional stance to Poe's professionalism, but it should be noted that professional calculations are not always honorable or just. For Poe, admission to the national literary market meant turning his back on the momentous political and social struggles of the day, except when such struggles impinged directly on the material interests of a commercial writer. So if there is relatively little cause to denounce Poe for his statements on slavery, there is certainly no reason to praise him for his professional silence. Patriotism may be the *last* refuge of scoundrels, but professionalism is often the first.

Conclusion: The Wages of Nationalism

All of this suggests that Poe, far from being "the most blatant racist among the American romantics," was arguably among the most discreet. Illuminating in this regard is the case of Ralph Waldo Emerson. Following what is now a familiar pattern, the critic Kun Jong Lee has recently attempted to "unmask" Emerson's racism by assembling an extremely partial and incriminating selection of his journal entries.[45] In 1822, for example, Emerson reported that he saw "a hundred large lipped, low-browed black men who, except in the mere matter of languages, did not exceed the sagacity of the elephant." Emerson also described blacks as being "preAdamite" and marked for extinction: "It is plain that so inferior a race must perish shortly." In 1848, Emerson even wrote that "it is better to hold the negro race an inch under water than an inch over" (K. J. Lee, 334).[46] These journal entries are more blatantly racist than anything in Poe's private correspondence or anonymous reviews. And yet, such a collection of quotations should not be taken as proof that Emerson was more "racist" than Poe. The kind of selective citation used to denounce Emerson and even Lydia Maria Child as racists, I would argue, crosses the boundary from political criticism into sheer character assassination. Critical approaches based on character assassination, or on any ahistorical diagnosis of racism, may possess some marginal pedagogical and heuristic value, but these approaches also project current stalemates into both the past and the future. In other words, the fervent hunt for some blatant racist utterance reveals less about antebellum literature than about the contemporary practice of endlessly unmasking racism as a scandal, as an unsurpassable and perversely cathartic spectacle.

To those in search of spectacle, Poe's reticence is especially frustrating because, unlike Emerson, he left no incriminating private manuscripts. Curiously, Poe's most virulent pronouncements on race are contained in *The Narrative of Arthur Gordon Pym*, a book more or less

consciously written for a national audience. The book was published by
the New York firm of Harper and Brothers in 1838. Two years prior to
publication, James Kirke Paulding had quietly urged Poe to "lower himself a little to the ordinary comprehension of the generality of readers."
In another letter, Harper and Brothers advised Poe that "readers in this
country have a decided and strong preference for works (especially fiction) in which a single and connected story occupies the whole volume."[47] In response to this advice about the national literary market,
Poe composed what would be his only novel; at the end of this book,
Poe describes the black natives of Tsalal as "the most wicked, hypocritical, vindictive, bloodthirsty, and altogether fiendish race of men upon
the face of the globe" (*CW*, 1:201). Modern critics have pointed to the
political implications of this description, but in the rush to denounce
Poe's racism, the peculiar formal and historical determinants of *Pym*
have been obscured. First, Poe clearly borrowed from widely circulated
travel narratives of Africa and the South Seas, many of which contain
similar denunciations of the ignorance and backwardness of "barbarous" non-Western peoples, including the dark-skinned aborigines of
Australia, New Zealand, and Tasmania. Second, the natives on Tsalal
take on an allegorical quality because of their extreme blackness, a blackness that includes not only the eyes and teeth of the natives but also
much of the natural environment. As the fictitious "editor" emphasizes,
"Nothing *white* was to be found at Tsalal, and nothing otherwise in the
subsequent voyage to the region beyond" (*CW*, 1:208). Third, there is no
obvious link between this racist representation and a specific position on
slavery, especially since abolitionists and colonizationists were themselves prone to accept and repeat racist stereotypes.[48]

These points are crucial to understanding why Poe, whose personal
and editorial writings seem relatively muted on the issue of slavery,
should make what now appears as his most blatant statement in the most
public—and the most national—forum he could find. At the *Messenger*,
Poe had learned to avoid controversial political issues, especially those
likely to elicit complaints from Southern readers. When composing a
novel for a New York publisher and a national audience, Poe would have
paid even closer attention to divisive issues, and if *Pym* had contained
"horrifying because unprofitable doctrines," the Brothers Harper undoubtedly would have objected. The lurid description of Tsalal therefore
demonstrates the difference between a racist representation—especially
one conforming to the orders of average racism—and a statement calling for a specific action on slavery. But this is only part of the story. As
suggested at the start of this chapter, average racism arose less from an
essential American bigotry than from the historically specific conjunc-

tion of an emerging national culture and an emerging national market. In this regard the example of Poe is particularly revealing, for his attempt to construct or exploit an average racism was in many ways a deliberate strategy designed to unify sections divided by slavery. Antebellum nationalism, far from being a simple expression of solidarity, should instead be seen as a product of the growing antagonism between North and South, and Poe's literary nationalism should likewise be understood as an attempt to escape from the realm of unprofitable political strife into the more lucrative *neutral territory* of mass culture.

Once again, then, the concept of average racism helps to explain Poe's writing. As suggested earlier, average racism was not a simple set of beliefs and practices but rather an ongoing attempt to invoke—without specifying too precisely—the imaginary foundation for political consensus. And the best way to protect this consensus was to keep it out of play, insulated from the contentious fray of what was called "partisan politics." Lest we judge antebellum America too harshly, we should also acknowledge the possibility that modern orthodoxies about race suffer from similar shortcomings. I think it is possible, for example, to imagine a future that would question our sacred image of diversity, namely, the posed multiracial group that pervades television commercials and college recruiting brochures. It is possible, in other words, to imagine a future where our image of racial diversity would be derided as the "master mix" that inadvertently circumscribed both the breadth of individual difference (by treating members of a racial group as interchangeable) and the scope of social progress (by assuming that the mere existence of a multiracial group solved all problems and conflicts). As illustrated by *Moby-Dick* and *The Narrative of Arthur Gordon Pym*, a multiracial crew does not guarantee a successful voyage. The canoe at the end of Poe's narrative, it should be recalled, carries the white Pym, the black Nu-Nu, and the mixed Peters. Needless to say, it is not clear what we should make of this crew or of the death of Nu-Nu, since for Poe even death is an ambiguous condition. But if Poe is making a statement about slavery, he seems wary of being labeled a *partisan*.

Poe's wariness toward slavery is further demonstrated by "A Predicament" and "The Gold-Bug," the only tales containing extensive depictions of African Americans. In "A Predicament," the companion piece to "How to Write a Blackwood Article," Poe parodies the affection between a black servant and white mistress in order to disparage both characters. But although the description of the servant relies heavily on racist stereotypes, Poe eludes the slavery controversy by setting the tale in the North (first Philadelphia and then Scotland). "The Gold-Bug" presents more problems because it is expressly set in South Carolina. Once again there is something vaguely comical about the master-servant relationship, although in this case there is no question of improper affections, at least not on the part of Legrand. The black servant Jupiter, however, seems to embody "the staunch loyalty and heart-felt devotion" celebrated by Beverley Tucker (*Partisan Leader,* 142). Aside from his extreme devotion to Legrand, Jupiter's speech is apparently intended to represent a black dialect influenced by Gullah, a creole spoken by blacks on the coastal islands of South Carolina and Georgia.[49] Indeed, in his review of Sedgwick's *The Linwoods,* Poe objects to "the discrepancy between the words and the character of the speaker," particularly in cases where the character is black. After quoting a rousing speech by an African American character named Rose, Poe asks, "Who would suppose this graceful eloquence . . . to proceed from the mouth of a negro woman?" (*CW,* 5:64). Poe evidently sought to correct this alleged discrepancy in "The Gold-Bug," and in his unsigned review of himself, he in fact singles out the "accurate" depiction of Jupiter:

> The characters are well-drawn. The reflective qualities and steady
> purpose, founded on a laboriously obtained conviction of
> Legrand, is most faithfully depicted. The negro is a perfect pic-
> ture. He is drawn accurately—no feature overshaded, or distorted.
> Most of such delineations are caricatures. (*Essays,* 869)

In what sense is Jupiter a "perfect picture"? Presumably, Poe is referring to his dialect, his superstition, and perhaps his inability to tell right from left. In addition, Jupiter is "obstinate" and physically strong—at one point he even considers beating Legrand with a stick to cure his gold fever. But as indicated already, Jupiter's most important trait is his loyalty to Legrand. Significantly, this loyalty determines the narrator's response to Legrand's apparent madness: "Could I have depended, indeed, upon Jupiter's aid, I would have had no hesitation in attempting to get the lunatic home by force; but I was too well assured of the old negro's disposition, to hope that he would assist me, under any circumstances, in a personal contest with his master" (*CW,* 3:822).

Taken in isolation, such behavior seems derived from plantation narratives, and some critics have accordingly described Jupiter as a "black slave."[50] But as Poe carefully specifies at the beginning of the story, Jupiter is actually free:

> [Legrand] was usually accompanied by an old negro, called Jupiter,
> who had been manumitted before the reverses of the family, but
> who could be induced, by neither threats nor promises, to aban-

don what he considered his right of attendance upon the foot-
steps of his young "Massa Will." (*CW,* 3:807)

Recognizing the political divisions in the national audience, Poe
shrewdly tries to have it both ways. On the one hand, he exploits conventions about the intimate, loyal bonds between white masters and
black servants. On the other hand, he attempts to evade any outcry over
such a portrayal by making Jupiter free, and although Legrand is referred
to as "master" on several occasions, never once in the entire story does
Poe use the word *slave.* In other words, Poe capitalizes on the average
racism of his audience while neutralizing the sectional conflict over slavery. Through a crucial yet subtle change in Jupiter's legal status, Poe attempted to create a sanitized South that could circulate freely in the national literary market.

At the end of his life, Poe made one last statement about blackness
that underscores how ideological and economic forces combined to
determine the *salability* of racism. In a 26 June 1849 letter to George
Eveleth, Poe discusses *Eureka* (recently published) and his still unful-
filled plans for the *Stylus.* In the course of the letter, Poe also mentions
the review in which he chastises Lowell for being an "Abolition fanatic" and for treating writers outside of Boston—especially Southern
writers—as "barbarians" (*CW,* 5:377). This induced Poe to recall a
"Monk" Lewis anecdote, which he must have read about years earlier.[51]
Lewis's play *The Castle Spectre* was first performed in 1797; though popular, it was criticized for its fantastic elements, including the presence of
black servants in a Welsh castle. In the published version of the play,
Lewis justified his audacity:

> That *Osmond* is attended by *Negroes* is an anachronism, I allow; but
> . . . I by no means repent the introduction of my *Africans*: I
> thought it would give a pleasing variety to the characters and
> dresses, if I made my servants black; and could I have produced
> the same effect by making my heroine blue, blue I should have
> made her. (Lewis, 101–2)

In Poe's version, there are some revealing distortions:

> Monk Lewis once was asked how he came, in one of his acted
> plays, to introduce *black* banditti, when, in the country where the
> scene was laid, black people were quite unknown. His answer was:
> "I introduced them because I truly anticipated that blacks would
> have more *effect* on my audience than whites—and if I had taken it

into my head that, by making them sky-blue, the *effect* would have been greater, why sky-blue they should have been." To apply this idea to "The Stylus"—I am awaiting the *best opportunity* for its issue. (*Letters,* 2:449–50)

How should we account for Poe's revisionary memory? Do the changes constitute a sort of racist slip that reveals his true sentiments? Or do the changes reflect an appreciation of Lewis's willingness to exploit the shock value, or salability, of racial difference? The letter, after all, discusses plans to arouse interest in a new magazine project, and although Poe's claim about deliberately postponing the *Stylus* is dubious, he did place great emphasis on the conscious and sometimes manipulative creation of a specific *effect*—not only within a literary text but also within an entire literary market. The distortions or slips in his recollection could therefore be attributed to an ongoing negotiation between racist ideologies and the pressures of a mass publishing industry. As a commercial writer, Poe had to produce a text that could transcend competing ideologies of racial difference—one might call them dueling racisms—to achieve a uniform literary effect among a divided national audience.[52] Unlike "horrifying because unprofitable doctrines" about slavery per se, however, representations of racial difference—whether sentimental or sensational—remained viable in all segments of the American market. For this reason, racism exerted an economic influence over both literary and commercial calculations, and it also encouraged the kind of distortions manifested in the misquotation of Monk Lewis. Poe accordingly omits the blue heroine, substitutes a single "effect" for a "pleasing variety," and, in his most revealing distortion, transforms the black "servants" into "black banditti." Not incidentally, the transformation of servants into bandits precisely duplicates the events in *Pym,* where seemingly friendly natives turn into murderous black savages.

Poe's calculating approach to the mass literary market complicates the political meaning of *Pym* and his other fictional writings. Based on what we know of these calculations, it is misguided to conceive of his racism as an attitude or sentiment somehow separable from the constraints and pressures of the prevailing modes of production, especially in a nation that suffered antagonistic modes to coexist until the advent of civil war. By extension, it is misguided to conceive of literary creation as occurring in some fantastic realm of freedom apart from the ideological and material forces that sustain a social formation. If nothing else, the recognition of these forces makes it possible to move beyond interpretations that are informed by hindsight but not by history. For example, the paucity of comments about race in Poe's private correspondence, along

with the offhanded disparagement of abolitionist poets in his anonymous critical reviews, should cast doubt on interpretations of the final
chapters of *Pym* as divine retribution for "the known offense of slavery"
(Dayan, "Romance and Race," 109). I must also question Dayan's claim
that "Poe remained haunted, as did Jefferson, by the terrible disjunction
between the ideology of slavery . . . and the concrete realities of mutilation, torture, and violation" (102). If anything, Poe seems to have conjured up the haunting portrait of blackness as a means of appealing to
multiple segments of the white literary audience. And as soon as the audience is described in these terms, it becomes clear that his racist representations have less to do with black-white relations than with the way
white people relate to each other.

The way white people relate to each other: this is what haunts Poe,
this is what motivates his fantasies of a neutral culture, and this, to an extent seldom acknowledged, is what burdens the current critical discourse
on race. What matters about Poe is not so much his reticence on slavery,
nor even his use of racist stereotypes—which are as infrequent as they
are offhanded. Instead, the case of Poe matters because both his utterances and his silences were part of a coherent strategy to expel politics
from the literary commodity. This is why attempts to read politics back
into Poe's work have proven so vexing. To make this task easier, critics
still turn to the Paulding-Drayton review as the smoking gun that will
convict Poe once and for all. When this does not succeed, blame is
sometimes placed on conspiratorial Poe scholars, who are seen as with-
holding or covering up incriminating evidence.[53] This chapter is not designed to comfort the vexed, but I do hope that I have demonstrated
two things. First, although Poe left behind a clear trail of what might be
called circumstantial racism, he avoided—by habit and design—the kind
of political speech practiced by fire-breathing secessionists like Beverley
Tucker and by antislavery moralists like James E. Heath (both of whom
Poe knew during his connection with the *Southern Literary Messenger*).
From this follows the second point, namely, that the "depoliticized" Poe
is only partly the work of his interpreters. Observing the dictates of the
"cash rule," Poe sometimes played to the average racism of the national
audience, but more frequently he avoided altogether those "horrifying
because unprofitable doctrines" about slavery. In other words, Poe's
work was not simply depoliticized by modern critics; it was in many ways
depoliticized from the start. This, I would suggest, must be the basis for
all future political criticism of Poe. Significantly, the acknowledgment of
Poe's apolitical predicament would not preemptively exclude the ideological interpretations of Poe that I have been disputing throughout this
chapter. Although there may be flaws in the evidence and assumptions

of critics such as Rosenthal, Nelson, and Rowe, the case of Poe never-theless demonstrates the importance of race in determining what litera-ture *is*—the form and meaning of its sentences, the form and meaning of its silences.

Taken in context, the example of Poe reveals the error of viewing racism as a private demon to be exorcised through simple denunciation, or as a Southern disease to be eradicated through a liberal dose of en-lightenment. All too frequently, such views lead to the creation of an interpretive framework that merely diagnoses texts as being racism-positive or racism-negative. When the texts themselves resist such a diagnosis, critics sometimes resort to ad hominem arguments that re-solve textual ambiguity by invoking the alleged beliefs of the alleged au-thor. Given the divergent political agendas of such writers as Tucker, Emerson, and even Lydia Maria Child, it is at least necessary to consider the motives and pressures determining their respective representations of race. And given the peculiar circumstances surrounding Poe, it is also worthwhile to recall that the relation between literature and politics is it-self historically determined—so much so that a strategy originally de-signed to avoid controversy now provokes it. To resolve the current tan-gle of error and simplification, it is necessary to step back from the purity of ahistorical criticism and to delve into the complexities of a painful and uncompleted past. In the case of Poe and other antebellum writers, such an approach reveals a world of Orwellian complicity far be-yond the explanatory reach of praise and denunciation. In that world—and perhaps in our own—all racisms are equal, but some racisms are more equal than others.

Notes

1. I am turning a phrase from Stephen Greenblatt, who writes, "I am not ar-guing that atheism was literally unthinkable in the late sixteenth century but rather that it was almost always thinkable only as the thought of another" (22).

2. Neither Thompson nor Dayan, I hasten to add, is completely culpable for these mistakes. Thompson was making a quick point with a bit of hyperbole, and Dayan was basing her arguments on a persuasive but flawed article by Bernard Rosenthal, "Poe, Slavery, and the *Southern Literary Messenger*: A Reexami-nation." In addition, both writers were prevented from qualifying or justifying their arguments in footnotes. For complete texts, see G. R. Thompson, "Poe and the Writers of the Old South," and Joan Dayan, "Romance and Race."

3. Arthur Hobson Quinn, for example, sees the review as proof that Poe did take an interest in contemporary politics and that his "knowledge of the ac-tual conditions [of slavery] was much more accurate than that of Emerson or Whittier" (*Edgar Allan Poe: A Critical Biography*, 249). In his influential piece "Poe

as Social Critic," Ernest Marchand gives a less tolerant account of Poe's complicity with the Old South. Drawing heavily from the Drayton-Paulding essay, Marchand argues that Poe "brings to the defense of the South's peculiar institutions the same rationalizations that issued from a thousand Southern pulpits every Sunday, and from a thousand Southern presses every day of the week for more than twenty years" (37). F. O. Mathiesson also relied on the Paulding-Drayton review for the chapter on Poe in the *Literary History of the United States,* 321–27. 3rd. ed., ed. Robert E. Spiller et al., New York: Macmillan, 1963.

4. Rosenthal selected and introduced the material on Poe.

5. Many critics dubious of the Paulding-Drayton review espouse similar positions. See, for example, Kenneth Alan Hovey, "Critical Provincialism: Poe's Poetic Principle in Antebellum Context," 347, 353 n. 40; and A. Robert Lee, "'Impudent and Ingenious Fiction': Poe's *The Narrative of Arthur Gordon Pym of Nantucket,*" 128. For further speculations on Poe's racial fears, see Louis D. Rubin Jr., *The Edge of the Swamp: A Study in the Literature and Society of the Old South.*

6. Ridgely's argument is summarized in *CW,* 5:153-54.

7. This conjunction of factors explains many inconsistencies noted by Rosenthal. On Poe's possible ideological motives for altering the review, see the account of Lucian Minor's "Liberian Literature," later in this chapter. For Tucker's comments on *The Partisan Leader,* see Tucker to Duff Green, 20 April 1836, Duff Green Papers, Library of Congress. Typescript in Noma Lee Goodwin, "The Published Works of Nathaniel Beverley Tucker, 1784–1851," unpublished M.A. Thesis, Duke University, 1947, 212–15.

8. For sickbed scenes, compare "Slavery" (338) and "Blackstone" (230); on animal metaphors, compare "Slavery" (338) and *The Partisan Leader* (156); on Northern meddling and Southern defense, see "Slavery" (339) and "Blackstone" (228); on slavery as a positive good, see "Slavery" (339) and "Blackstone" (227); for appeals to divine will, see "Slavery" (338) and "Effect" (330, 333); on the paradox of equality and difference, see "Slavery" (338) and "Effect" (330).

9. See, for example, Tucker's "An Essay on the Moral and Political Effect of the Relation between the Caucasian Master and the African Slave," 332.

10. Tucker makes similar claims in "The Present State of Europe." There, he notes that "first and last, property is the real object of controversy in strife between the orders of society" (285); and that "property, then, of old, as now, was at the bottom of all the revolutionary movements of England" (286).

11. Tucker, review of "An Oration on the Life and Character of Gilbert Motier de Lafayette," by John Quincy Adams and rev. of "Eulogy on La Fayette," by Edward Everett, 309.

12. All these writings appear in the *Messenger:* "Note to Blackstone's Commentaries . . ." 228; "Bulwer's New Play," 92; "A Discourse on the Genius of the Federative System of the United States," 768.

13. For more about this connection, along with some good observations on the larger issues, see J. V. Ridgely in "The Authorship of the 'Paulding-Drayton Review,'" 2.

14. See also Tucker's "The Present State of Europe," 294, 279, 286.

15. For a fine analysis of this and other matters, see Teresa A. Goddu, *Gothic America: Narrative, History, and Nation,* 73–93.

16. For further information on the *Messenger,* see David K. Jackson, *Poe and the "Southern Literary Messenger."*

17. This version of the prospectus appeared on the cover of the December 1838 *Messenger.*

18. For White's desire to maintain full editorial control, see his 2 March 1835 letter to Lucian Minor, in David K. Jackson, "Some Unpublished Letters of T. W. White to Lucian Minor," 227. For White's wariness about political writing, see, in addition to the material below, White's letter to Minor, 31 March 1840: "If I was to insert my personal, and at last my political, friends' addresses, I should raise at once a hornet's nest about my head and ears, that I should not soon get clear of." Reprinted in Jackson, Continuation of "Some Unpublished Letters of T. W. White to Lucian Minor," 48.

19. It is worth noting, in this context, that Lucian Minor had several (Southern) relatives who opposed slavery. His grandfather, Major John Minor of Topping Castle, had introduced a bill for the emancipation of slaves in the Virginia legislature shortly after the Revolution. And Lucian's cousin Mary Berkeley Minor Blackford denounced both slavery and secession. Between 1832 and 1866, she kept a journal called "Notes Illustrative of the Wrongs of Slavery." See L. Minor Blackford, *Mine Eyes Have Seen the Glory,* 5, 46, 263 n. 2.

20. 6 March 1836. Cited in Dwight Thomas and David K. Jackson, 193. Poe called the *Chronicle* reviewer a "scoundrel," and in a personal correspondence he assured Minor that his article on Liberian writing had been "lauded by all men of sense" (*Letters,* 1:88).

21. *Southern Literary Messenger* 1 (January 1835): 254.

22. "I had supposed before, that no gentleman of any intelligence could be found within the four corners of our state, who would seriously undertake to maintain that our domestic slavery, which is obviously the mere creature of our own positive law, is so right and proper in itself, that we are under no obligation whatever to do any thing to remove, or lessen it, as soon as we can. I had thought, indeed, that it was a point conceded on all hands, that, wrong in its origin and principle, it was to be justified, or rather excused, only by the stern necessity which had imposed it upon us without our consent, and which still prevented us from throwing it off at once. . . . And, at any rate, I had imagined that all of us were fully satisfied, by this time, that [slavery] was an evil of such injurious influence upon our moral, political, and civil interests, that we owed it to ourselves as well as to our subjects, to reduce, and remove it, as soon, and as fast as possible. . . . In all this, however, it seems, I was reckoning without my host, the author of the article before me, who has come forward, at this late hour, to assert the absolute rectitude and utility of the system. . . ." (A Virginian, "Remarks on a Note," 266).

23. In the 1840s and especially in the 1850s, the *Messenger* published many more articles defending the South against Northern "fanaticism." A change in editorial policy is signaled in the opening article of volume 5; see "To Our Friends and Subscribers," *Southern Literary Messenger* 5 (January 1839): 1–2.

24. *Richmond Enquirer*, 22 May 1835.

25. Poe, review of *Memoirs of an American Lady* by Anne Grant, *CW*, 5:234. The review originally appeared in the *Southern Literary Messenger* 2 (July 1836): 511.

26. Like Grant, Ingraham apologizes for slavery without advocating it: "Do not mistake me: I am no advocate for slavery; but neither am I a believer in that wild Garrisonian theory, which, like a Magician's wand, is at once to dissolve every link that binds the slave to his master, and demolish at one blow a system that has existed, still gaining in extent and stability, for centuries" (2:33).

27. Poe, review of Joseph H. Ingraham's *The South-West. By a Yankee*, *CW*, 5:93. The review was originally published in the *Southern Literary Messenger* 2 (January 1836): 122.

28. Poe, review of the *North American Review*, *CW* 5:68. The commentary originally appeared in the *Southern Literary Messenger* 2 (December 1835): 59.

29. "Cuffies" is the common transliteration of the African name; it was a common practice to name children after days of the week. See Peter Wood, *Black Majority*; Gary Nash, *Forging Freedom* 301 n. 26; and David DeCamp, "African Day-Names." My thanks to Ted Pearson and Kathy Brown for this information.

30. Dayan insinuates that Poe is guilty by association. She does not, of course, insinuate that Poe was an abolitionist because he corresponded with Lowell and Longfellow, or because he favorably reviewed the work of Lydia Maria Child. In addition, Dayan erroneously identifies Dew as author of *Vindication of Perpetual Slavery*. Dew actually wrote an essay called "Abolition of Negro Slavery" (1832); this was later expanded and published by Thomas W. White as the *Review of the Debate in the Virginia Legislature of 1831–1832* (1832) and subsequently reprinted many times, most notably in a collection called *The Pro-slavery Argument* (1852).

31. Rosenthal continues the guilt-by-association argument when he identifies Poe with the brief extract of Dew's address that appeared in the October 1836 *Messenger*. Rosenthal fails to mention that Poe breaks off the extract in midsentence and thereby avoids printing a more explicit statement on slavery. In the three sentences following the extract (not quoted by Poe), Dew calls upon students to defend the slave South:

> I hope—yes, I know, that at this moment a worthier and a nobler impulse actuates every one of you. And you must recollect too, that you are generally members of that portion of our confederacy whose domestic institutions have been called in question by the meddling spirit of the age. You are slaveholders, or the sons of slaveholders, and as such your duties and responsibilities are greatly increased. ("An Address," 765)

32. George McDuffie had declared in 1835 that slavery was "the cornerstone of our republican edifice" (Tise, 100).

33. A Virginian [James E. Heath], *Slavery in Maryland: An Anti-slavery Review*, 20–21.

34. Letter to Maria Weston Chapman, 25 November 1846 (134). See also letter to Chapman, 17 March 1846 (31). Some of the money donated by Chapman
was used to pay for *Slavery in Maryland: An Anti-slavery Review*.

35. See also 896–99; Jane Swisshelm, *Half a Century*, 132. Significantly, Snodgrass persisted in his antislavery activism into the next decade. In 1852, for example, he ran as an elector at large (Maryland) for the ill-fated Free Soil Presi-
dential ticket of John P. Hale and George W. Julian. See the "Free Democratic"
handbill, 370.

36. *Broadway Journal* 1 (22 March 1845): 183.

37. R. C. (Robert Carter), "The Broadway Journal."

38. Briggs to Lowell, 22 January 1845 (quoted in Weidman, 106).

39. Briggs to Lowell, 22 January 1845 (quoted in Weidman, 107). The line
about doing "good by stealth" comes from Alexander Pope, *Imitations of Horace*,
"Epilogue to the Satires," Dialogue I, l. 135.

40. Briggs to Lowell, 19 March 1845 and 10 April 1845 (quoted in Weidman,
108, 110).

41. For a more conservative estimate of Poe's contribution to the review, see
Thomas and Jackson, 529.

42. Silverman speculates that English may be the author of the phrase because he spoke derogatorily of blacks on other occasions (254, 491). To my ear,
however, the alliterative slur sounds like the work of Poe, and the rest of the review seems perfectly consistent with Poe's other critical writings.

43. Poe's review of *The Linwoods* appeared in the *Southern Literary Messenger* 1
(December 1835): 57–59; reprinted in *CW*, 5:62–64. His review of Robert
Montgomery Bird's *Sheppard Lee* appeared in the *Southern Literary Messenger* 2
(September 1836): 662–67; reprinted in *CW*, 5:282–86.

44. Thompson argues that Poe lacked the "regionalist sentiment" of other
Southern writers ("Poe and the Writers of the Old South," 268–69). Stowe's
Uncle Tom's Cabin was of course a phenomenal success, but a Boston publisher,
accepting the logic of political and regional neutrality, turned it down because
"it would not sell in the South" (Charvat, 301).

45. Lee disputes Philip Nicoloff's characterization of Emerson as "a relatively mild racist" (Nicoloff, *Emerson on Race and History*, 124; quoted in K. Lee,
334).

46. In Emerson's defense, it should be noted that many of these statements
appear to be fragmentary or even experimental. In addition, Lee sometimes
quotes Emerson totally out of context, as with an entry concerning the fate
of blacks to "serve & be sold & terminated" (K. Lee, 334). The rest of the
passage—omitted by Lee—argues for the opposite position:

> But if the black man carries in his bosom an indispensable element of a
> new & coming civilization, for the sake of that element no wrong nor
> strength nor circumstance can hurt him, he will survive & play his part.
> So now it seems to me that the arrival of such men as Toussaint if he is
> pure blood, or of Douglas [*sic*] if he is pure blood, outweighs all the En-

glish & American humanity. . . . Here is the Anti-Slave. Here is Man; &
if you have man, black or white is an insignificance. Why at night all men
are black. (*The Journals and Miscellaneous Notebooks of Ralph Waldo Emerson,*
9:125)

In my view Lee also unfairly belittles the antislavery efforts of Lydia Maria
Child (343 n. 7). This condemnation of Child makes use of the evidence,
though not the complete argument, of George M. Frederickson (*The Black Image
in the White Mind: The Debate on Afro-American Character and Destiny,* 37).

47. The advice about Poe "lowering himself" comes from Paulding to
T. W. White, 3 March 1836. Harper and Brothers June 1836 letter to Poe is reproduced in A. H. Quinn, 250–51.

48. Consider, for example, the comments of black historian and novelist
William Wells Brown:

> History shows that of all races, the African was best adapted to be the
> "hewers of wood, and drawers of water." Sympathetic in his nature,
> thoughtless in his feelings, both alimentativeness and amativeness large,
> the negro is better adapted to follow than to lead. His wants easily sup-
> plied, generous to a fault, large fund of humor, brimful of music, he has
> ever been found the best and most accommodating of servants. (179)

Brown is also the author of the important antislavery novel *Clotel* (1853).

49. On Jupiter's use of Gullah, see Marc Shell, *Money, Language, and Thought:
Literary and Philosophical Economies from the Medieval to the Modern Era,* 5–23.

50. See, for example, Toni Morrison, *Playing in the Dark,* 58.

51. Poe may have known that his mother, Eliza Poe, played the part of An-
gela in *The Castle Spectre* on 18 August 1810 in Richmond. See J. H. Whitty,
"Memoir," in *The Complete Poems of Edgar Allan Poe,* xx.

52. Though readers do not respond uniformly in reality, the assumption of a
uniform or at least average response necessarily informs most attempts to appeal to the widest possible audience. Wordsworth effectively acknowledged that
as a dramatist, Monk Lewis was more adept than he was at anticipating the average response. After seeing a performance of *The Castle Spectre,* Wordsworth
equivocally noted that the play "fitted the taste of the audience like a glove"
(quoted in Peck, 75).

53. John Carlos Rowe, for example, accuses Poe critics of repressing "the
subtle complicity of literary Modernism with racist ideology," and Dana Nelson
complains of "the recent trend to sweep Poe's politics under the rug" (Rowe,
"Poe, Antebellum Slavery, and Modern Criticism," 136; Nelson, 91). Curiously,
Rowe himself is one of the critics Nelson accuses of depoliticizing Poe, although she bases her argument on *Through the Custom House,* published ten years
before "Poe, Antebellum Slavery, and Modern Criticism."

C H A P T E R   2

The Poetics of Whiteness

Poe and the Racial Imaginary

BETSY ERKKILA

I am not a spook like those who haunted
Edgar Allan Poe.

Ralph Ellison, *The Invisible Man*

In his now classic study *Charles Baudelaire: A Lyric Poet in the Era of High Capitalism*, Walter Benjamin observes: "In *l'art pour l'art* the poet for the first time faces language the way the buyer faces the commodity on the open market. He has lost his familiarity with the process of its production to a particularly high degree" (105). In this chapter, I want to look at the concept of the aesthetic as a production within rather than outside of history. Focusing in particular on the poetry and poetics of Edgar Allan Poe, I want to connect what Poe called the "poem written solely for the poem's sake" (*Works,* 14:272) and the emergence of aestheticism more generally with the social, political, and specifically racial struggles of his time and ours. I want to suggest the relation between the emergence of the aesthetic as a distinct mode of organizing and isolating the subjective experience of beauty in art and the simultaneous emergence among scientists and philosophers of notions of racial difference and racial purity grounded in an Enlightenment metaphysics of whiteness. Rather than begin with the theories of racial difference that frame Immanuel Kant's *Observations on the Feeling of the Beautiful and the Sublime* (1764), I would like to begin closer to home with Thomas Jefferson's *Notes on the State of Virginia* (1787).

Skin Aesthetics

Written while the American Revolution was still being fought, *Notes on the State of Virginia* was central to the early national formation of American culture and society: it is one of the first works to define an American sublime; it is the locus classicus of the myth of the virtuous American republic; it defends the American continent and its native inhabitants against the degenerative theories of Count Buffon; it advances it "as a suspicion only" that blacks "are inferior to the whites in the endowments both of body and mind" (143); it argues that to preserve the "dignity and beauty" of "human nature," blacks must be colonized elsewhere, "beyond the reach of mixture" (143); and, under the pressure of the contradiction between the revolutionary rhetoric of American liberty and the historical reality of black enslavement, it is spooked, over and over again, by the fear of black insurrection and the specter of the "extirpation"of the white "masters" (163).

Jefferson's racial hierarchies and his social fears translate into and shape his judgment of beauty and art. His phobia about the black body, "that eternal monotony, which reigns in the countenances, that immoveable veil of black which covers all the emotions of the other race," leads him to assert skin color, the difference of white from black, as "the foundation of a greater or less share of beauty in the two races" (138). Even blacks prefer the "superior beauty" of whites "as uniformly" as "the Oran-ootan" prefers "black women over those of his own species" (138). This erotically charged skin aesthetics becomes the ground for a series of artistic judgments in which black painting, sculpture, music, and writing are consistently excluded, along with the passions and the body, from the realm of true beauty and true art.

In one of the earliest instances of the politics of white canon formation, Jefferson writes:

> Among the blacks is misery enough, God knows, but no poetry.
> Love is the peculiar oestrum of the poet. Their love is ardent, but
> it kindles the senses only, not the imagination. Religion indeed has
> produced a Phyllis Whately [*sic*]; but it could not produce a poet.
> The compositions published under her name are below the dignity
> of criticism. The heroes of the Dunciad are to her, as Hercules to
> the author of that poem. (140)

In Jefferson's skin aesthetics beauty and the imagination are, like his ideal American republic, by definition white. And yet, whiteness needs blackness to establish its own cultural precedence. To solicit our admiration for white poetry and white art, Jefferson must simultaneously cast out from the realm of the aesthetic a black body capable of no more than animal creation. Here, as in Kant's *Observations on the Feeling of the Beautiful and the Sublime* and other eighteenth-century writings on aestheticism, the social subordination of blacks to whites develops in tandem with the cultural valorization of aesthetic beauty. Jefferson's aesthetic hierarchies are driven by the social logic of slavery: If "Phillis Whately" was in fact Phillis Wheatley the revolutionary poet, if her poetry was worthy of comparison with the poetry of Alexander Pope, if blacks were as capable of imaginative creation as whites, then the justification of black enslavement and the "enlightened" social ground of white America would begin to erode, as it subsequently did, under the pressure of its own contradictions.

What is racially marked in Jeffersonian aesthetics becomes less so in the nineteenth century. Gesturing toward "a wild weird clime that lieth, sublime, / Out of SPACE—out of TIME," the poetic theory and practice of Edgar Allan Poe would appear to be completely removed from the devastating cruelty of black enslavement and the sordid reality of whips, rape, blood, violence, and the torture of black bodies. And yet Poe was raised in the South and spent the formative years of his life there. He was brought up in a slaveholding family in Richmond, Virginia: "You suffer me to be subjected to the whims & caprice, not only of your white family, but the complete authority of the blacks," Poe complained to his foster father, John Allan, in 1827 (*Letters,* 1:8). In at least one instance, Poe appears to have sold a slave, "a negro man named Edwin aged twenty one years . . . to serve until he shall arrive at the age of thirty years no longer."[1] As in Jefferson's writings, the presence and labor of blacks in the social landscape, a simultaneous identification with and revulsion against the figure of the slave, the specter of slave insurrection, fear of a reversal of the master-slave relation, and an apocalyptic vision of the domination of blacks appear to energize and propel Poe's aestheticization of whiteness, his attempt to create forms of white beauty, white art, white writing, and white culture against and beyond time, history, the body, the black, the other.

Despite, or perhaps because of, Poe's Southern roots, the mainstream of American criticism has tended to treat him as an exotic alien, a strange and otherwordly purveyor of pure poetry, fractured psyches, and un-American gloom. To Vernon Parrington, in *Main Currents in American Thought* (1927), Poe was an "aesthete and a craftsman" who "lies quite outside the main current of American thought" (2:57, 56). The primarily linguistic emphasis of modernist and postmodernist critics, from T. S. Eliot and Paul Valéry to John Irwin and Jacques Lacan, has also tended to locate Poe's writings outside of time and history. This ahistorical and un-American face of Edgar Allan Poe has been vigorously challenged in the last few years, most notably by Toni Morrison's extended meditation on what she calls "a real or fabricated Africanist presence" in white American writing in *Playing in the Dark: Whiteness and the Literary Imagination* (6). Commenting on the "shrouded human figure" whose skin "was of the perfect whiteness of snow" at the end of Poe's *Narrative of Arthur Gordon Pym* (1838), Morrison asserts uncategorically: "No early American writer is more important to the concept of American Africanism than Poe" (33).[2]

But while Morrison and others have offered a useful corrective to the erasure of race in past approaches to Poe, there is a tendency among recent critics to reduce Poe to his proslavery sentiments and American literature to American Africanism. "It was this Africanism," writes Morrison, "deployed as rawness and savagery, that provided the staging ground and arena for the elaboration of the quintessential American identity" (44). This exclusive focus on the shaping presence of "American Africanism" in the constitution of American national identity seems much too simple. For one thing, there were other races, cultures, and nationalities that vied for geopolitical space and presence in writing and naming America. Moreover, blackness and Africanism cannot be separated from a whole complex of personal and cultural phobias and fetishes around the body, nature, women, race, the Orient, and the democratic masses that haunt and spook the American imaginary. To reverse the hierarchical relation of white to black by claiming black precedence risks reinstating the exclusions of the white literary tradition; it also isolates blackness and Africanism from the complicated network of religious, cultural, historical, economic, and ultimately transnational relations in which they were involved. Morrison's focus on the shaping presence of Africanism in creating a distinctively American literature keeps both "American" and "African American" neatly contained within a nationalist and exceptionalist frame and thus tends to erase the crosscurrents of international exchange, economic as well as cultural, imperial as well as textual, in which the figure of Edgar Allan Poe and the writing of the United States more generally have played a commanding role.

While there has been a renewed interest in the historical and racial contexts of Poe's work, critics have also tended to focus almost exclusively on Poe's prose rather than his poetry. Thus, for example, in his important work on Poe and the masses, Terry Whalen turns to Poe's tales as a "privileged" site of his social and economic analysis ("Horrid Laws," 398). Given the constitutive role that Poe's notions of supernal Beauty, art for art's sake, pure poetry and poetic craft have played, both nationally and internationally, in the emergence of nineteenth-century aestheticism, New Critical formalism, postmodern texuality, and the ongoing struggle to claim or reclaim the social being of language and literature, it is important that we not repeat Poe's own ahistorical gestures in seeking to grant poetry a special status outside history and beyond the reach of cultural analysis.

Tamerlane, *the Orient, and American Indian Policy*

The ways in which Poe's work intersects with a complex network of international relations is particularly evident in his first two volumes of poems, *Tamerlane and Other Poems* (1827) and *Al Aaraaf, Tamerlane, and Minor Poems* (1829). In these volumes the shaping presence is not Africanism but Orientalism. Published during the years when Andrew Jackson came to power bearing a public rhetoric (if not reality) of democracy and the common man and a nationalist vision of westward expansion and progress, Poe's early volumes of poetry, which were printed and circulated in limited editions, suggest his aristocratic refusal, as gentleman and poet, to write for the masses or the market. Both volumes assert the integrity of private, subjective, and ultimately poetic desire against the debased imperatives of the public sphere. In the preface to *Tamerlane and Other Poems*, Poe writes that in his title poem "he has endeavoured to expose the folly of even *risking* the best feelings of the heart at the shrine of Ambition" (Mabbott, 1:22). Traditionally, "Tamerlane," like much of Poe's poetry, has been interpreted as personal lyric inscription: "Poe took little from historic and dramatic sources," writes Thomas Mabbott, "his poem is largely a personal allegory, based on his unhappy love for his Richmond sweetheart, Sarah Elmira Royster" (Mabbott, 1:24). But while Poe appropriates the fourteenth-century Mohammedan ruler for the expression of his own "agony of desire" as both lover and poet, "Tamerlane" cannot be separated from the broader politics, at once national and global, of imperial conquest.

Like "Al Aaraaf" and other Poe poems and tales, "Tamerlane" participates in and is shaped by the Orientalism of Byron's *Giaour*, Thomas Moore's *Lala Rookh*, and Chateaubriand's *Itinéraire de Paris à Jérusalem, et de Jérusalem à Paris*, all of which were themselves engaged in what Edward Said calls the "Orientalist" struggle of Britain and France to extend their empire and their dominion to the Near and Far East in the nineteenth century.[3] Although the United States had not yet emerged as a power in the Orient, it is simply not true to say, as Said does, that the United States did not emerge as a major power in the struggle for empire until after

World War II. From the time of the First Continental Congress in the Revolutionary period to the Monroe Doctrine, the Indian "removal" policy, the Mexican War, and the politics of Manifest Destiny in the nineteenth century, the United States struggled to extend its territories and its empire in North as well as South America.[4]

Like James Fenimore Cooper's *Last of the Mohicans* (1826), which prophesies the doom of the Indian at the same time that it celebrates the eventual triumph of American empire over the British and the French in North America, Poe's *Tamerlane* provides an early cultural instance of the ways American writers participated in the broader politics of imperial struggle in the nineteenth century. Written at a time when Poe had himself enlisted in the United States Army, "Tamerlane" is on the most fundamental level a poem about the lust for empire. "I was ambitious," Tamerlane asserts: "A cottager, I mark'd a throne / Of half the world as all my own" (Mabbott, 1:57). In a note to the 1827 version of the poem, Poe further observes: "The conquests of Tamerlane far exceeded those of Zinghis Khan. He boasted to have two thirds of the world at his command" (Mabbott, 1:37). Although the narrative sets Tamerlane's desire for woman, love, and beauty against his "unearthly pride" and ambition for fame, conquest, and "the crush / Of empires" (Mabbott, 1:55) in a manner that suggests Poe's own historical resistance to the Jacksonian rhetoric of Western conquest and imperial advance, as in other writings by Poe, the poem also participates in the structures of knowledge, the Orientalist relation of West to East, white to other, that would frame Jackson's Indian removal policy in the 1830s and, more broadly, that had framed and would continue to frame the Western strife for empire in the Orient and elsewhere.[5]

As a signifier of the Orient, Tamerlane is a split figure, an embodiment at once of white desire and white fear. Tamerlane is, on the one hand, a "kingly" figure, whose love for a woman is represented as a version of white pastoral, a utopian scene of purity, beauty, and light. Within this "holy grove," Tamerlane remembers:

> I wandered of the idol, Love,
> Who daily scents his snowy wings
> With incense of burnt offerings
> From the most unpolluted things,
> Whose pleasant bowers are yet so riven
> Above with trellic'd rays from Heaven
> No mote may shun—no tiniest fly—
> The light-ning of his eagle eye—
>   (Mabbott, 1:61)

On the other hand, as an embodiment of the passionate excess of the desert—"where the grand— / The wild—the terrible conspire / With their own breath to fan his fire" (Mabbott, 1:58)—Tamerlane is also ruled by Eblis, the Mohammedan prince of evil spirits and darkness, who creeps into the "unpolluted" bower of love in the form of Ambition:

> I do believe that Eblis hath
> A snare in every human path—
>
> .   .   .   .
>
> [Else how] was it that Ambition crept,
>   Unseen, amid the revels there,
> Till growing bold, he laughed and leapt
>   In the tangles of Love's very hair?
>   (Mabbott, 1:60–61)

Taken over by Ambition, Tamerlane becomes, in this concluding passage of the poem, the Oriental as fiery figure of passion and excess who pollutes and destroys the "holy grove" of "snowy" whiteness signified by woman, beauty, and love. As a topos of pure woman, pure beauty, and pure love, Poe's "holy grove" suggests the ways his aestheticization of whiteness becomes bound up with a deep cultural fear of mixture with and pollution by the racial other. In the concluding image of Eblis tangled in the "very hair" of pure love, Orientalism intersects with Africanism and a whole complex of white cultural fears about mixture with and violation by the dark other, whether black, red, or Mohammedan.

In Poe's early poems, the Orientalist story of "Tamerlane" is dispersed and refigured in a symbolic dialectics of East versus West. In "Sonnet—To Science," which serves as an introduction to "Al Aaraaf" in *Al Aaraaf, Tamerlane, and Minor Poems* (1829), the Orient becomes the emblem of an exotic otherworld of the imagination that is opposed to the Western world of time, change, and history, signified by the "peering eyes" and "dull realities" of reason and science. As in "Romance," in which the "idle" and dreamy world of romance, "lyre and rhyme," signified by the "painted paroquet," is set against the "eternal Condor years" and "tumult" of the present, in "Sonnet—To Science" the poet rejects Western history and progress in favor of a timeless and Orientalized world of mythological creatures and "jewelled skies" where he can pursue "[t]he summer dream beneath the tamarind tree" (Mabbott, 1:91).

In "Al Aaraaf," the Orient is both figure and locus of poetry itself. Poe explains his use of the title "Al Aaraaf," which is drawn from the Koran, in a note to the poem: "With the Arabians there is a medium between Heaven and Hell, where men suffer no punishment, but yet do not attain that tranquil and even happiness which they suppose to be characteristic of heavenly enjoyment" (Mabbott, 1:111–12). According to George Sale, the English translator of the Koran, the term *al Araf* derives from "the verb, *arafa,* which signifies to *distinguish* between things, or to *part* them" (94). Poe was not so much interested in the Koran or the religious beliefs of the Arabs as he was in "the Arabians" as figures of romantic *apartness* and otherworldliness. Located in a distant star, beyond the reach of earthly "dross" and the passions of the body, Al Aaraaf represents the otherworldly space of beauty and pure poetry, a place of purely aesthetic experience where flowers speak "in odors" and language is closer to "silence" than to our "world of words" (Mabbott, 1:102, 104). As Poe writes of the spirit world of "Al Aaraaf" in the opening of the poem:

> O! nothing earthly save the ray
> (Thrown back from flowers) of Beauty's eye,
>
> . . . .
>
> O! nothing earthly save the thrill
> Of melody in woodland rill—
>
> . . . .
>
> Oh, nothing of the dross of ours—
> Yet all the beauty—all the flowers
> That list our Love, and deck our bowers—
> Adorn yon world afar, afar—
> The wandering star.
>
> (Mabbott, 1:99–100)

Within the Orientalist frame of "Al Aaraaf," Poe conducts what is, in effect, his most radical experiment in pure aestheticism, his attempt to invent a language of pure musicality, rhythm, spirit, and sound. He also anticipates in figurative and poetic form the "Idea of Beauty" and the idea of poetry as a realm of purely aesthetic experience apart from both bodily passion and intellectual knowledge that he would begin to articulate in his prose introduction to *Poems of Edgar A. Poe* (1831). In "Al Aaraaf" as in his 1831 poem "Israfel," it is finally because Poe's "Arabians" lack bodies and historical being that they can be consigned to the realm of pure aestheticism.

A few months earlier, in an address to Congress on 6 December 1830, Jackson announced the near completion of the Indian removal policy, which was initiated by Jefferson, supported by James Monroe and John Adams, and passed by Congress in 1830:

It gives me pleasure to announce to Congress that the benevolent policy of the Government . . . in relation to *the removal of the Indians beyond the white settlements* is approaching to a happy consummation. . . . To follow to the tomb the last of his race and to tread on the graves of extinct nations excites melancholy reflections. But true philanthropy reconciles the mind to these vicissitudes as it does to *the extinction of one generation to make room for another.* . . . What good man would prefer a country covered with forest and ranged by a few thousand savages to our extensive Republic, studded with cities, towns, and prosperous farms . . . ? (quoted in Blum et al., 232; emphasis added)

For all Poe's efforts to locate poetry and "the Arabians" in a world elsewhere, they are part of a social formation that includes U.S. Indian policy, the literary and pictorial convention of the dying Indian from Cooper's *Last of the Mohicans* (1826) to Tompkins H. Matteson's painting *The Last of the Race* (1847), and a more global imperial movement that requires that the wandering tribes of the East die off in order to, as Jackson says, "make room for" the advance of "white" civilization. Whether it is a site of pure love, pure passion, or pure poetry, the Orient has no contemporary reality in Poe's early poems: it is not so much a place as it is a space for the imaginative figuration of white fear and white desire. As in Cooper's *Last of the Mohicans* and Jackson's "melancholy" reflection on the Indian as "the last of his race," Poe's Orientals are figures of the past and myth with no historical presence or agency in the ongoing struggles of the present and the future.

Poe Spooks

"I am not a spook like those who haunted Edgar Allan Poe," says the protagonist in the opening of Ralph Ellison's *Invisible Man.* Drawing on Ellison's pun on the double meaning of "spook" as the ghostly specters that haunt Poe's writings and the vernacular meaning of spook as a black person, in this section I want to examine the ways Orientalism intersects with Africanism and a whole series of social subordinations—of black to white, female to male, nature to spirit, body to mind, democratic mob to genteel aristocrat—in the formation of Poe's poetics of whiteness. More specifically, I want to argue that Poe's poetics of whiteness is, in effect, shaped and spooked by the historical presence of enslaved and laboring black bodies in the social landscape of America. Whereas Poe's Arabs existed as distant and bodiless figures of the past and myth, blacks had an immediate corporeal presence not only in the plantation economy of the South but also in the periodic acts of violent resistance, the ongoing fear of slave insurrection, and the state of public and private crisis, North as well as South, provoked by the institution of slavery in America.[6] Like Poe's *Mob*, "a giant in stature—insolent, rapacious, filthy" and "a foreigner, by the by" ("Mellonta Tauta," Mabbott, 3:1300), blacks were a part of the democratic and specifically racial history that his poetics of whiteness was formed against.[7]

Poems by Edgar A. Poe (1831), which was sold by subscription to West Point cadets and dedicated "To the U.S. Corps of Cadets," is introduced by a "Letter to Mr. ———— ————" in which Poe seeks for the first time in prose to articulate his theory of poetry as a realm of purely imaginative activity: "A poem," he asserts, "is opposed to a work of science by having, for its *immediate* object, pleasure, not truth; to romance, by having for its object an *indefinite* instead of a *definite* pleasure, being a poem only insofar as this object is attained" ("Letter to B——," 503). Written at a time when Poe was being disinherited from his expectations as Southern gentleman by his foster father, John Allan, Poe's "Letter," which is dated West Point, 1831, seeks to defend poetry and the poet as part of a cultural elite—a kind of aristocracy of the mind—against both the masses and his own diminished status as the son of actors. Against "the world's good opinion," as it is represented by the masses and the market, Poe sets what he calls "the Andes of the mind," a hierarchy of critical judgment and good taste that rises "ascendingly" from the fools on the bottom to "a few gifted individuals" and "the master spirit," the poet, who stands at the top ("Letter to B——," 501).

The dialectical relation between the "master spirit" of the poet and the body of the dark other in Poe's poetics is suggested by the oppositional structure of his "Letter." As in Poe's poetic dreamlands, poetry is defined against all that is corporeal, animal, dark, earthly: "Think of all that is airy and fairy-like," Poe writes, "and then of all that is hideous and unwieldy; think of his huge bulk, the Elephant! and then—and then think of the Tempest—the Midsummer Night's Dream—Prospero—Oberon—and Titania!" ("Letter to B——," 503). In Poe's Shakespearean definition of the purely imaginative space of poetry, the aesthetic becomes a line that marks the boundary between light and dark, Prospero and Caliban, civilization and its others. And yet, in the very process of marking this boundary, Poe simultaneously produces the fantasies of mixture and seepage, doubling and impurity, that are the obsessive subject of his work.

While *Poems* is still framed by an Orientalist structure, with "Romance" at the beginning, "Al Aaraaf" and "Tamerlane" at the end, and a new poem, "Israfel," added, in this volume Poe begins to accentuate three motifs that would become increasingly central to his poetry and poetics: the idealized figure of woman as emblem of pure beauty, pure love, and pure poetry in "To Helen"; fantasies of female violation by figures of darkness and dissolution in "Irene" (later "The Sleeper") and "A Paean" (later "Lenore"); and the specter of dark apocalypse in "The Doomed City" (later "The City of Sin" and "The City in the Sea"). I want to suggest that the increasing emphasis on these racially inflected motifs in Poe's 1831 *Poems*—which was published the same year that William Lloyd Garrison began publishing *The Liberator,* a weekly newspaper dedicated to the immediate abolition of slavery and universal enfranchisement of blacks—represents, at least in part, a response to the growing state of crisis provoked by the "hideous" presence of enslaved and potentially unruly black bodies within the virtuous and putatively white body of the American republic. During this "new post-1830 era in proslavery ideology," writes Drew Faust, "the slavery controversy not only became a matter of survival for the southern way of life; it served for Americans generally as a means of reassessing the profoundest assumptions on which their world was built."[8]

In "To Helen," Poe presents the ideal woman who is at the center of his aesthetics of whiteness. Associated with artifice, stasis, light, soul, distance, and "statue-like" perfection, Helen is not a flesh-and-blood woman but a dead woman—light, bright, white, and dead:

> Helen, thy beauty is to me
>   Like those Nicéan barks of yore,
> That gently, o'er a perfumed sea,
>   The weary, way-worn, wanderer bore
>   To his own native shore.
>
> On desperate seas long wont to roam,
>   Thy hyacinth hair, thy classic face,
> Thy Naiad airs have brought me home
>   To the glory that was Greece,
>   And the grandeur that was Rome.
>
> Lo! in yon brilliant window-niche
>   How statue-like I see the stand,
> The agate lamp within thy hand!
>   Ah, Psyche, from the regions which
>   Are Holy-Land!
>   (Mabbott, 1:165–66)

With its varied metrics, intricate patterns of rhyme and alliteration, and exquisite use of language, phrase, and image, "To Helen" is, in the words of Mabbott, "often regarded as the finest of Poe's lyrics" (Mabbott, 1:163). But what gets written out of critical assessments of the poem is that Helen, as a metonymic figure of ideal woman, beauty, and art, is also a representative of the Western ideal of whiteness as signified by the classical culture of Greece and Rome. This meaning is more evident in the 1831 version of the poem, in which the poet is brought home

> To the beauty of *fair* Greece
> And the grandeur of old Rome
> (Mabbott, 1:166; emphasis added)

Although critics continue to speculate about which woman inspired Poe's poem, Helen lacks any particular historical embodiment. With her "hyacinth hair," "classic face," and "Naiad airs," she is a representative of all women as white woman. As a perfect emblem of the Western ideal of white beauty, white value, and white art, Helen is the prototype of the impossibly pure, fair-haired, and blue-eyed maidens who begin to proliferate in Poe's poems and tales of the 1830s and 1840s.

In a specifically American context, "To Helen" marks an increasing fetishization of whiteness and purity—of woman, of beauty, of culture, of skin color, of blood—that comes in response to the growing historical fear of mixture, violation, and encroaching darkness. And yet, for Poe, as for the proslavery apologists, the ideal of white womanhood—of what W. J. Cash has called "the South's Palladium . . . Athena gleaming whitely in the clouds" (86)—breeds fantasies of defilement, mixture, and reversal that appear to undermine the sexual and racial taxonomies he seeks to enforce.[9] What is socially forbidden and excluded returns as an obsessive set of imaginative representations—the ghosts and spooks and black phantasms that haunt Poe's work.

Whereas Helen is located in a "Holy-Land" beyond the reach of bodily mixture and mortality, in "The Sleeper" (originally "Irene"), the "lady bright," as a figure of "All beauty," is exposed to the ghostly hauntings of darkness and night:

> Oh, lady bright! can it be right—
> This window open to the night?
> The wanton airs, from the tree-top,
> Laughingly through the lattice drop—
> The bodiless airs, a wizard rout,
> Flit through thy chamber in and out,

And wave the curtain canopy
So fitfully—so fearfully—
Above the closed and fringéd lid
'Neath which thy slumb'ring soul lies hid,
That o'er the floor and down the wall,
Like ghosts the shadows rise and fall!
Oh, lady dear, hast thou no fear?

(Mabbott, 1:187)

Like the threat of violation by worms ("Soft may the worms about her creep!") and the "Triumphant" figure of the "black / And wingéd pannels" of the family vault "fluttering back" to engulf the female corpse at the end of the poem (Mabbott, 1:188), the "wanton airs," "wizard rout," and ghostly "shadows" of night are associated with bodily dissolution and the earthly processes of time, change, mortality, and death. Along with the terrorization of women and the specter of bodily dissolution, the fear of mixture, penetration, violation, and domination by harrowing figures of blackness and death is at the very sources of the mechanics of horror in Poe's work and, not surprisingly, at the symbolic center of the American cultural imaginary in the mid–nineteenth century.[10]

In "Lenore" (originally "A Paean"), the poet needs to kill off the "fair and debonair" heroine with "her yellow hair" in order to save woman, beauty, and the ideal of whiteness from the "fiends" of "damnéd Earth." The aristocratic lover, Guy de Vere, sings the death of his young bride as a "flight" away from earth into a "golden" world of "high estate," without history, without bodies, without blacks:

"Avaunt!—avaunt! to friends from fiends the indignant
    ghost is riven—
From Hell unto a high estate within the utmost Heaven—
From moan and groan to a golden throne beside the King
    of Heaven:—
Let *no* bell toll, then, lest her soul, amid its hallowed mirth
Should catch the note as it doth float up from the damnéd
    Earth!"

(Mabbott, 1:337)

Poe's fantasy of a spirit world beyond the reach of color or mixture is underscored in the 1831 version of the poem, in which the heroine's soul is lifted to the "untainted mirth" of angels in heaven. More explicitly than other dead-woman poems, "Lenore" suggests the relation between aesthetics and social desire in Poe's work: between the poet's desire for a pure white space of beauty and pleasure, signified by the death of woman, and the aristocratic desire for an alternative social order, signified by the "high estate" and "untainted mirth" of "utmost Heaven."

Like other Southern writers, Poe associated the ideal of fair womanhood with the social ideals—and health—of Southern culture. "The glory of the Ancient Dominion is in a fainting—is in a dying condition," he wrote in 1835, in a comment that suggests the relation between the dying women of his poems and the failing plantation economy of the South. Virginia had become "a type for 'the things that *have been*'" (*Works*, 8:119). Although critics have tended to read Poe's lyrics as forms of merely personal or perverse psychology, the tone of mournfulness in his poetry and its thematics of disintegration might also be read as a melancholic response to the loss of a whole way of Southern life, grounded in what Poe called "the laws of *gradation*," under the pressure of democratic and specifically Northern industrial transformation. This elegiac tone is particularly evident in "The Colloquy of Monos and Una" (1841), in which the poets as "master-minds" set themselves against Enlightenment reason, science, knowledge, and "the progress of civilization":

> [T]hese men, the poets, pondered piningly, yet not unwisely upon the ancient days . . . holy, august, and blissful days, when blue rivers ran undammed, between hills unhewn, into far forest solitudes, primaeval, odorous, and unexplored. . . . Meantime *huge smoking cities arose, innumerable.* Green leaves shrank before the hot breath of furnaces. *The fair face of Nature was deformed as with the ravages of some loathsome disease.* (Mabbott, 2:609–10; emphasis added)

Whereas in the poem "The Valley of Unrest" (originally "The Valley Nis") the poet's mournfulness about "the ancient days" is associated more generally with an "unquiet" landscape of "restlessness" and "perennial tears"—"Nothing there is motionless" (Mabbott, 1:195–96)—in "The City in the Sea" (originally "The Doomed City"), as in "The Colloquy of Monos and Una," this melancholia is associated more specifically with the city, "the ravages" of the "fair face of Nature," and a hellish vision of modern apocalypse.

Drawn originally from a passage in an early version of "Al Aaraaf" describing the fallen city of Gomorrah, the landscape of death in "The City in the Sea" is represented in Orientalist images of "shrines and palaces and towers" and "Babylon-like walls":

> Lo! Death has reared himself a throne
> In a strange city lying alone

Far down within the dim West,
Where the good and the bad and the worst and the best
Have gone to their eternal rest.
There shrines and palaces and towers
(Time-eaten towers that tremble not!)
Resemble nothing that is ours.
Around, by lifting winds forgot,
Resignedly beneath the sky
The melancholy waters lie.

                              (Mabbott, 1:201)

Critics have usually identified the city with the legendary ruined cities of
the Dead Sea, but Poe's reference to "a strange city" in "the dim West"
also suggests the spiritual destiny of America as "a city upon a hill"
(Winthrop, 49) and Enlightenment notions of the advance of civilization westward, which Poe associated with the rise of industry, the city,
republican government, "omni-prevalent Democracy," and the emancipation of slaves (Mabbott, 2:610). Although the city lacks specific historical reference, here, as elsewhere in Poe's writings, the association of
figures of blackness ("the long night-time of that town") with the vision
of apocalyptic doom that closes the poem ("Down, down, that town
shall settle hence. / Hell, rising from a thousand thrones") registers a
widespread—and still prevalent—cultural fear of the fall of the West
that will come as a result of some sort of catastrophic uprising of the
dark other, associated with blackness, the satanic, the Orient, the city,
and death. In 1845, Poe underscored the prophetic dimension of his
poem when he published it under the title "A City in the Sea: A
Prophecy." Unlike the apocalyptic warnings proliferated in other mid-
century works, including most notably "the wrath of Almighty God"
that closes Harriet Beecher Stowe's *Uncle Tom's Cabin* in 1852 (629), Poe's
prophecy is grounded not in fear of punishment *for* the contradiction of
slavery in the American republic but rather in his fear that the logic of
the American republic—founded on "the queerest idea conceivable . .
. that all men are born free and equal" ("Mellonta Tauta," Mabbott,
3:1299)—would lead to the emancipation of slaves or, even worse, as
Jefferson had predicted, to the extirpation of the white masters.

Nat Turner, Slave Insurrection, and Pure Poetry

Only a few months after Poe published "The Doomed City" in his 1831
Poems, his fear of some sort of apocalyptic uprising of blacks assumed

palpable bodily form when, in August 1831, Nat Turner led the bloodiest
slave insurrection in United States history in Southampton County, Virginia. "Whilst not one note of preparation was heard to warn the devoted inhabitants of woe and death," wrote Thomas R. Gray of Turner's
revolt, "a gloomy fanatic was revolving in the recesses of his own dark,
bewildered, and overwrought mind, schemes of indiscriminate massacre
to the whites—schemes too fearfully executed as far as his fiendish band
proceeded in their desolating march" (Gray, 4). The insurrection, which
resulted in the death of sixty whites, the torture and execution of scores
of innocent blacks, and a widespread hysteria about the possibility of
further uprisings, led to a tightening of slave laws and an increasingly
vigorous defense of the institution and culture of slavery throughout
the South. Emancipation would lead to the South's "relapse into darkness, thick and full of horrors," wrote the proslavery apologist Thomas
Dew in his influential defense of the institution of slavery following the
debates about the future of slavery in the Virginia legislature in 1831–32
(Dew, "Abolition of Negro Slavery," 57).

It was into this heightened atmosphere of panic about the possibility
of bloody slave insurrection and hysteria about the security and survival
of the institutions and culture of the Old South that Poe entered when
he returned to Richmond, where he would serve as editor of the *Southern
Literary Messenger* between 1835 and 1837.[11] In a much-disputed review of
two proslavery books, *Slavery in the United States* by J. K. Paulding and *The
South Vindicated from the Treason and Fanaticism of the Northern Abolitionists*
by William Drayton, which appeared in the *Southern Literary Messenger*
under Poe's editorship in April 1836, the reviewer asserts the relation between the logic of progressive history, as signified by the French Revolution and the rights of man, and the specter of black emancipation, violent or otherwise.[12] Commenting on the irreligious fanaticism of the
French Revolution, he warns: "[I]t should be remembered now, that in
that war against property, the first object of attack was property in
slaves; that in that war on behalf of the alleged right of man to be discharged from all control of law, the first triumph achieved was in the
emancipation of slaves" (*Works,* 8:269). Alluding to the violent slave insurrection in San Domingo (Haiti), where blacks rose up, killed their
white masters, and, in the name of liberty and individual rights, set up as
an independent black nation in 1804, the reviewer calls attention to the
"awful" significance of progressive history for the South: "The recent
events in the West Indies, and the parallel movement here, give awful importance to these thoughts in our minds" (*Works,* 8:269). The South is
haunted by "despair," "apprehensions," foreboding "superstitions," and
"vague and undefined fears" in response to these "awful" events (*Works,*

8:269), which appear to include the San Domingo slave insurrection, the "triumph" of Haiti against the French empire in 1804, Nat Turner's insurrection in 1831, the emancipation of slaves in the British West Indies in 1834, the rise of the abolition movement in the 1830s in the United States, and the attack on "Domestic Slavery," which is "the basis of all our institutions" (*Works*, 8:269). Whether this review was written by Poe, as some believe, or by his friend Beverley Tucker, as a defense of "all our institutions" and "all our rights" written from the collective point of view of the South—and presumably reflecting the views of the *Southern Literary Messenger* and its editor—it shares Poe's own grim vision of democratic history as a triumph of blacks, blood, and dark apocalypse.

Haunted by similarly "vague and undefined fears" in response to "recent events in the West Indies, and the parallel movement here," Poe's poetry and tales of the 1830s and 1840s continue to be spooked by the terrifying logic of progressive history, the fear of black emancipation, the specter of blood violence, the ongoing atttack on the institution of slavery, an apocalyptic vision of the triumph of "blackness," and a flight away from history into fantasies of whiteness and purity: pure white woman, pure white beauty, pure white art, pure white poetics. *The Narrative of Arthur Gordon Pym* (1838) makes explicit the phobia about the dark other, the fear of black insurrection, and the flight into an otherworldly space of pure whiteness that remain just beneath the surface in several of Poe's poems. Influenced by the specter of blood violence in both San Domingo and the American South, the "massacre" of whites by the natives of the all-black island of Tsalal leads Pym to assert: "In truth, from everything I could see of these wretches, they appeared to be the most wicked, hypocritical, vindictive, blood thirsty, and altogether fiendish race of men on the face of the globe" (*CW*, 1:201). Referred to interchangeably as savages, barbarians, desperadoes, and "warriors of the black skin" (*CW*, 1:186), the natives of Tsalal suggest the ways antiblack feeling intersects with a more generalized phobia about the racial other—Indian, Mexican, African, or other—in the American cultural imaginary.[13] Here as elsewhere in Poe's poems and tales, the narrative underscores the ways the terror of what Pym calls "the blackness of darkness" (*CW*, 1:175) drives the imaginative leap toward an otherworld of pure whiteness: Faced with the prospect of "brute rage," "inevitable butchery," and "overwhelming destruction" in the concluding passages of the story, the protagonists rush into the milky white embrace of a "shrouded human figure": "And the hue of the skin of the figure was of the perfect whiteness of the snow" (*CW*, 1:206). But while the ending appears to promise entrance into a utopian world of "perfect whiteness," as the multiple and conflicted readings of *Pym*'s conclusion sug-

gest, the precise nature of this "shrouded human figure" is at best ambiguous: Is it biblical apocalypse or metaphysical sign, utopian dream or
perfect terror, pure race or pure hoax? It might be the "White Goddess,"
or mother, but it might also be the ghost of the all-black Nu-Nu returned from the dead.[14]

As in *The Narrative of Arthur Gordon Pym,* Poe's seemingly stable taxonomies of black and white would continue to be spooked by fantasies
of mixture, seepage, revenge, and reversal. In "The Haunted Palace,"
which was initially published in April 1839 and incorporated a few
months later into his story "The Fall of the House of Usher," the poet's
dream of "perfect whiteness" is corroded by the "encrimsoned" spectacle of invasion and dark apocalypse that closes the poem. Associated
with "the monarch Thought's dominion," the palace is, in its unsullied
form, an emblem of white mind: it is fair, yellow, golden, pallid, lu-
minous, wise, harmonious, beautiful, and, in the original version of
the poem, "Snow-white" (Mabbott, 1:315, 317). The poem enacts the
compulsive dream-turned-bad of mid-nineteenth-century American
fantasy—the fall of white mind to the dark and "hideous throng":

> But evil things, in robes of sorrow,
>   Assailed the monarch's high estate.
>
> . . . .
>
> And travellers, now, within that valley,
>   Through the encrimsoned windows see
> Vast forms that move fantastically
>   To a discordant melody,
> While, like a ghastly rapid river,
>   Through the pale door
> A hideous throng rush out forever
>   And laugh—but smile no more.
>   (Mabbott, 1:316–17)

By the palace, Poe wrote Rufus Griswold in 1841, he meant "to imply a
mind haunted by phantoms—a disordered brain" (*Letters,* 2:161).
Whether "The Haunted Palace" is an allegory of individual mind or the
haunted mind of America or the West, the "phantoms" that haunt it
conjoin a terror of the dark other and the democratic mob with the
specter of insurrection and blood violence and a more generalized fear
of madness, dissolution, and the fall of Western civilization. In fact, the
connection between Poe's "Haunted Palace" and the threat posed by the
"hideous throng" of Negroes and lower classes in the American city was
made quite explicitly by one of Poe's contemporaries, Henry B. Hirst,

who parodied Poe in "The Ruined Tavern," a poem about a brawl in a Philadelphia tavern frequented by "tough Negroes," which includes the lines: "Never negro shook a shinbone / In a dance-house half so fair."[15]

Against this apocalyptic vision of the blackness and blood of progressive history—a vision that gets powerfully enacted in the story of the collapse of "the last of the ancient race of the Ushers" into "a black and lurid tarn" in "The Fall of the House of Usher" (Mabbott, 2:404, 398)—Poe seeks to define poetry as a separate and purer realm, grounded in an ethos of social subordination, of men over women, imagination over body, and white over black. The "sentiment of Poesy" is, he wrote in a review of 1836, linked with the sentiment of reverence and the hierarchical "relations of human society—the relations of father and child, of master and slave, of the ruler and the ruled" (CW, 5:165). In other words, the "sense of the beautiful, of the sublime, and of the mystical" is "akin" to the slave's reverence for the white master: to aspire to Beauty is to aspire to God and thus affirm the "primal" subordination of slave to master (CW, 5:166). As in later modernist manifestos, including Ezra Pound's *Patria Mia* (1912) and the Southern Agrarians' *I'll Take My Stand* (1930), in Poe's "Colloquy of Monos and Una" (1841), aesthetic judgment and the poet's craft become forms of social salvation: "taste alone could have led us gently back to Beauty, to Nature, and to Life" and thus "purify" the "Art-scarred surface of the Earth" from the ravages of Enlightenment "knowledge," "progress," "universal equality," and "omni-prevalent Democracy" (Mabbott, 2:610, 611–12).[16]

In his essays and reviews of the 1830s and 1840s, Poe is on a kind of rescue mission to save both poetry and criticism from the "daily puerilities" of public opinion and the popular press (CW, 5:164), as well as from the black facts and blood violence of American history. The social and specifically racial shaping of Poe's aesthetics is particularly evident in his reviews of Longfellow and other abolitionist poets of New England. As Kenneth Hovey has argued, "Poe attacked Longfellow and the poets of the Northeast unsparingly for their double error of didacticism and progressivism." "Fearing the advancing truth of what he called 'fanatic[ism] for the sake of fanaticism,' he advocated a beauty no truth could invade, the 'poem written solely for the poem's sake'" (350, 349).

In an 1845 review of Longfellow's *Poems on Slavery* (1842), Poe cites the following lines from "The Warning" as an instance of "absolute truth":

> There is a poor, blind Sampson in this land,
>   Shorn of his strength and bound in bonds of steel,
> Who may, in some grim revel, raise his hand,

And shake the pillars of the common weal,
Till the vast temple of our Liberties,
A shapeless mass of wreck and rubbish lies.

(Aristidean, 133)

Poe blames Northern abolitionist poets for the "grim" prospect of
blood violence against the white masters: "One thing is certain:—if this
prophecy be *not* fulfilled, it will be through no lack of incendiary doggrel
on the part of Professor LONGFELLOW and his friends" *(Aristidean,*
133).[17] At a time when there was an increasing emphasis on the social
power of the word, especially the black word, in bringing about an end
to the historical contradiction of slavery in the American republic, Poe
seeks to strip poetry of its moral imperative, its "truth" claims, and its
historical power by establishing "the radical and chasmal difference
between the truthful and the poetical modes of inculcation" (Poe, *"Ballads,"* 248). And yet, for all Poe's emphasis on the formalist and proto-
modernist values of "pure beauty" and unity of poetic effect—as opposed to "instruction" or "truth"—as the sole legitimate province of
poetry (Poe, *"Ballads,"* 250), his aestheticism cannot be separated from
his political judgment that Longfellow, like James Russell Lowell, is part
of a Boston "junto" "of abolitionists, transcendentalists and fanatics"
whose writings are "intended for the especial use of those negrophilic
old ladies of the north" *(Aristidean,* 130, 131). It is, he writes, "very comfortable" for the professor "to sit at ease in his library chair, and write
verses instructing the southerners how to give up their all with good
grace, and abusing them if they will not" *(Aristidean,* 132). Poe's attack on
the didacticism of Longfellow, Lowell, and others was not only a defense
of pure poetry and the sanctity of art: it was also a defense of whiteness,
slavery, and a whole way of Southern life against the increasing threat of
Northern and particularly black defilement.

The Croak of the Raven and the Poetic Principle

"The croak of the raven is conveniently supposed to be purely lyric,"
wrote Hervey Allen in 1927 of the contemporary lack of concern with
"what Mr. Poe had to say of democracy, science, and unimaginative literature" (xi). While recent critics have turned with renewed attention to
the historical and specifically Southern contexts of Poe's writing, there is
still a tendency to pass over Poe's poems as sources of "purely lyric" expression. And yet, as I have been trying to suggest, whether they are read
as forms of aesthetic resistance or as perverse symbolic enactments that

ooze darkness and death over the American dream of progress, freedom, and light, Poe's poems are deeply embedded in the sociohistorical
traumas of his time. This is particularly true of his most popular poem,
"The Raven," one that, in the words of Arthur Hobson Quinn, "made
an impression probably not surpassed by any single piece of American
poetry" (439). What does it mean, I want to ask, in the context of the
heightening social, sexual, and racial struggles of the United States in the
1840s, for a dead white woman to come back as an "ominous" and am-
biguously sexed black bird? While critics have tended to follow Poe in
"The Philosophy of Composition" in interpreting the raven as an emblem "of *Mournful and Never-ending Remembrance*" (*Works*, 14:208), I want
to suggest that the "ghastly" figure of the black bird "perched" upon
"the pallid bust of Pallas" also evokes the fear of racial mixture and the
sexual violation of the white woman by the black man that was at the
center of antebellum debates about the future of the darker races in
white America.[18]

In the July–August 1845 issue of the *Democratic Review*, which had
published Poe's essay "The Power of Words" only a month before, John
O'Sullivan declared that it was the "manifest destiny" of Anglo-Saxon
America "to overspread the continent allotted by Providence for the free
development of our yearly multiplying millions" (5). Critical of those
who opposed the annexation of Texas because it would lead to the increase and perpetuation of the institution of slavery in America, O'Sullivan argued that, on the contrary, the "Spanish-Indian-American populations of Mexico, Central America and South America" would provide a
kind of national sewage system to "slough off" emancipated Negroes in
order to leave the United States free and pure to realize its white Anglo-
Saxon destiny: "Themselves already of *mixed and confused blood*," writes
O'Sullivan,

and free from the "prejudices" which among us so insuperably *for-
bid the social amalgamation which can alone elevate the Negro race out of a
virtually servile degradation* even though legally free, the regions occupied by those populations must strongly attract the black race in
that direction; and as soon as the destined hour of emancipation
shall arrive, will relieve the question of one of its worst difficulties, if not absolutely the greatest. (7; emphasis added)

In O'Sullivan's formulation, the United States will, in effect, expel the
degraded and "servile" bodies of "the black race" in order to "relieve"
the country of the prospect of "social amalgamation."

Although "The Raven" was published before O'Sullivan's article, I want to suggest that the figure of Poe's "grim, ungainly, ghastly, gaunt, and ominous" black bird registers symbolically and more pessimistically some of the same national anxiety about "mixed and confused blood" that O'Sullivan expresses in his famous declaration of America's white Manifest Destiny. Moreover, I want to argue that in "The Raven," as elsewhere in Poe's writings, the dead white woman and the ominous black presence are foundational to Poe's poetics, his attempt to achieve "that intense and pure elevation of the *soul*" that he associates with "Beauty" as "the sole legitimate province of the poem" (*Works*, 14:197). In fact, the poem's dramatic contrasts of black and white are productive of its scene of terror and the melancholy tone of sadness, which is Beauty's "highest manifestation" (*Works*, 14:198).

While "The Raven" is not explicitly about race, like Poe's use of the orangutan in "The Murders in the Rue Morgue" to commit "*excessively outré*" acts of violence against two white women, his idea of using "a *non-reasoning* [black] creature capable of speech" in writing "a poem that should suit at once the popular and the critical taste" (*Works*, 14:200, 196) evokes popular notions of blacks as parrots incapable of reason: its story of a dead white woman coming back in the form of an "ominous" black bird of prey who penetrates the heart and overtakes the mind and soul of the white speaker registers the simultaneous fear of and fascination with penetration, mixture, inversion, and reversal that emerges alongside of (and as part of) an increasingly aggressive nationalist insistence on sexual, social, and racial difference, white superiority, and Anglo-Saxon destiny. Perhaps better than other antebellum American writers, Poe reveals the linked processes of demonization, mixture, and reversal in the national imaginary.[19] In "The Raven," as in other Poe poems and tales, the expelled other of American national destiny—the dark, the corporeal, the sexual, the female, the animal, the mortal— returns as an obsessive set of fantasies about subversion, amalgamation, and dark apocalypse.[20]

Like O'Sullivan's essay on Manifest Destiny, "The Raven" is all about boundaries—and the horror of their dissolution. Associated with the name Helen and its derivatives Ellen, Elenore, Lenore—which mean, in Poe's terms, "light" and "bright" (Mabbott, 331)—Lenore is another of those "rare and radiant" maidens whose death enables both poetry and beauty. As Poe famously wrote in his scientific analysis of "The Raven" in "The Philosophy of Composition" (1846): "[T]he death, then, of a beautiful woman is, unquestionably, the most poetical topic in the world" (*Works*, 14:201). In the poem, however, the "lost Lenore," like Ligeia and Madeline Usher, refuses to stay dead. Although her radiant whiteness is at first set against the darkness of time, history, and the colors of the body, in the course of the poem she is confused with, and indeed replaced by, the darkly foreboding and sexually ambiguous black bird of prey. Expecting to find Lenore at his bedroom window, the protagonist opens the shutter to find, "with many a flirt and flutter," an uppity black bird in human drag, which collapses the boundaries between animal and human, black and white, female and male, body and spirit, real and supernatural, dead and undead:

> In there stepped a stately Raven of the saintly days of yore;
> Not the least obeisance made he; not a minute stopped or stayed he;
> But, with mien of lord or lady, perched above my chamber door—
> Perched upon a bust of Pallas just above my chamber door—
>   Perched, and sat, and nothing more.
>   (Mabbott, 1:366)

While the raven's hypnotic croak—"Nevermore," "Nevermore," "Nevermore"—appears to have a "purely lyric" reference to the death of the "sainted maiden" and the futility of joining her in another world, the "ebony" bird's physical location on "a bust of Pallas" suggests a broader reference to the negation of whiteness: not only the death of white beauty and white art but also the death of white mind and an entire regime of classical and Enlightenment order, reason, and knowledge associated with Pallas Athena. Although Poe does not say so in "The Philosophy of Composition," the black bird's physical presence in the bedroom "perched" on the "bust of Pallas," a locale that is marked by the bereaved lover's obsessive repetition—"upon the sculptured bust," "on the placid bust," "on the pallid bust of Pallas"—also evokes the specter of sexual violation, racial mixture, and a reversal of the master-slave relation.[21]

At issue is not only the prospect of black domination but also, as in *The Narrative of Arthur Gordon Pym* and "Instinct vs Reason—A Black Cat," the question of black intelligence. "Startled" by the apparent prescience and wisdom of the bird's "aptly spoken" reply, the speaker assumes that it is merely parroting the words of "some unhappy master":

> "Doubtless," said I, "what it utters is its only stock and store
> Caught from some unhappy master whom unmerciful Disaster
> Followed fast and followed faster till his songs one burden bore—"
>   (Mabbott, 1:367)

The speaker's words link the "croak" of the raven with the master-slave relation and an entire Western philosophical defense of white mastery.

"There scarcely ever was a civilized nation of any other complexion than white," wrote David Hume in 1748 in a defense of the superiority of white, and especially English, civilization. "In JAMAICA, indeed," he writes, "they talk of one negroe as a man of parts and learning; but 'tis likely he is admired for very slender accomplishments, *like a parrot, who speaks a few words plainly*" (Hume, 86; emphasis added). Edgar Allan Poe, or at least the sorrowful white scholar of "The Raven," would "doubtless" agree.

If "The Raven" aspires toward "that pleasure which is at once the most intense, the most elevating, and the most pure" through "the contemplation of the beautiful" (*Works*, 14:197), it is, paradoxically, a pleasure and a beauty that are achieved through the death of the female body and the cultural terror of the black body. This bodily terror is perhaps most startlingly figured in the fluid interpenetration of light and dark in the concluding passage of the poem:

And the Raven, never flitting, still is sitting, *still* is sitting
On the pallid bust of Pallas just above my chamber door;
And his eyes have all the seeming of a demon's that is dreaming,
And the lamp-light o'er him streaming throws his shadow on the floor;
And my soul from out that shadow that lies floating on the floor
   Shall be lifted—nevermore!

                     (Mabbott, 1:369)

More than a "purely lyric" expression of "*Mournful and Never-ending remembrance*," the demonic and shadowy figure of the black bird sitting "[o]n the pallid bust of Pallas" also projects some of the culture's deepest fears about the sexual violation of the white woman (or man) by the dark other, a possible reversal of the master-slave (or male-female) relation, and the apocalyptic specter of the end of Western wisdom and civilization in unreason, madness, and the bodily domination of black over white.

In "The Poetic Principle," which was delivered as a lecture on several occasions in 1848 and 1849, Poe gives more explicit critical formulation to the racially inflected poetics of whiteness that frames his poems.[22] Against "the heresy of *The Didactic*," the notion that the object of poetry is truth or the inculcation of a moral, Poe asserts the absolute value of the "poem *per se*—this poem which is a poem and nothing more—this poem written solely for the poem's sake" (*Works*, 14:272). Recapitulating in slightly revised form many of the same notions of poetic purity that Poe had originally set forth in his 1842 review of Longfellow's *Ballads and Other Poems*, this foundational text in the history of modern aestheticism represents, at least in part, a historical response to the moral imperative and abolitionist politics of New England poetry.[23]

But while "The Poetic Principle" is shaped by national and race-centered debates about "true Beauty" and true Americanism, it also participates in and makes a distinctive contribution to broader philosophical and political contests about the meaning of the aesthetic. Against the Emersonian definition of the poem as "a meter-making argument" (Emerson, "The Poet," 450) and the abolitionist emphasis on literature as a form of moral action, Poe follows Kant's *Critique of Judgment* (1790) in seeking to distinguish between the good, the true, and the beautiful.[24] Focusing on the aesthetic subject rather than the aesthetic object, Poe argues that "a work of art" is to be judged "by the impression it makes, by the effect it produces" in creating "that pleasurable elevation or excitement, *of the soul,* which we recognize as the Poetic Sentiment, and which is so easily distinguished from Truth, which is the satisfaction of the Reason, or from Passion, which is the excitement of the heart" (*Works,* 14:268, 275). He reiterates the notion of a tripartite division of the mind that he had originally set forth in his 1842 review of Longfellow:

> Dividing the world of mind into its three most immediately obvious distinctions, we have the Pure Intellect, Taste, and the Moral Sense. I place Taste in the middle, because it is just this position, which, in the mind, it occupies. . . . Just as the Intellect concerns itself with Truth, so Taste informs us of the Beautiful while the Moral Sense is regardful of Duty. (*Works,* 14:272–73)

Drawing on eighteenth-century constructions of the individual mind and subject and the effort to discover what Burke had called "the logic of Taste" (11), Poe's attempt to carve out a separate space of pure pleasure and pure beauty might be read as a radical affirmation of human being and spirit in the face of the theoretical abstractions of Enlightenment rationalism, the dehumanizing technologies of modern science, and the increasingly mechanistic and self-alienating effects of the industrial marketplace. "An immortal instinct, deep within the spirit of man, is thus, plainly, a sense of the Beautiful," Poe writes. "It is at once a consequence and an indication of his perennial existence. It is the desire of the moth for the star. It is no mere appreciation of the Beauty before us—but a wild effort to reach the Beauty above" (*Works,* 14:273). Whereas in the work of Alexander Baumgarten and other early philosophers of the aesthetic, the *aesthetic* was meant to designate perception *through* the body and the senses in opposition to abstract reason and immaterial thought, in Poe, as in Kant, the aesthetic represents an effort to climb out of the body to attain what Poe calls "but brief and indeterminate glimpses" of the beauty beyond.[25]

And yet, for all Poe's effort to lay claim to a separate space of pure beauty, pure art, and pure pleasure beyond empirical knowledge and the passions of the body, the subject he seeks to affirm and the pure space of beauty toward which he aspires continue to be shaped by the racial codes, hierarchies, and values of Western, and specifically Anglo-American, culture. Poe's emphasis on what he calls "radical and chasmal differences between the truthful and the poetical modes of inculcation" (*Works*, 14:272), his desire to distinguish and differentiate the aesthetic as a separate realm of activity, participates in, even as it seeks to surmount, an emergent scientific discourse of racial difference, purity, and distinction that grounds both modern "white" subjectivity and Western aestheticism. Thus, for example, in Kant's *Observations on the Feeling of the Beautiful and the Sublime* (1764), his attempt to distinguish Beauty as a purely subjective and disinterested realm of aesthetic activity is grounded in his assertion of fundamental national and racial difference. In a section of *Observations* entitled "Of National Characteristics, so far as They Depend upon the Distinct Feeling of the Beautiful and the Sublime," Kant writes that there is a "fundamental difference" between the black and white "races of man, and it appears to be as great in regard to mental capacities as in color" (111). The aesthetic is, in effect, color-coded in Kant's cultural taxonomy: blacks are not only different from and inferior to whites; they are also incapable of experiencing or producing beauty. "The Negroes of Africa have by nature no feeling that rises above the trifling," Kant writes in support of Hume's observation that "not a single [Negro] was ever found who presented anything great in art or science or any other praise-worthy quality" (Kant, 110–11).

Poe's "Poetic Principle" is similarly grounded in the bodily presumption of white over black. In the passages he cites from Percy Bysshe Shelley, Thomas Moore, Thomas Hood, Lord Byron, Alfred Tennyson, and Edward Coote Pinckney to exemplify his aesthetic theory, beauty and poetry are associated with whiteness, purity, love, and fair womanhood; blackness is associated with "muddy impurity," corporeality, pain, horror, and the "stain" of mortality. And yet, as in Poe's "The Raven," in which the whiteness of the marble bust of Pallas necessitates the blackness of the raven, and the desire for beauty and the beauty-effect are intensified by the physical presence and social horror of blackness, in Poe's aesthetic theory, as in Kant's, beauty paradoxically incorporates blackness as part of its own self-definition and its subjective "effect."

In its most utopian form, Poe's theory of "Supernal Beauty" represents an attempt to unite a fractured nation and an increasingly atomized world on the common ground of culture. But while Poe seeks in "The Poetic Principle" to establish a kind of science of aesthetic value as a means of bridging the apparent division between the poet-critic, the popular press, and what he calls "the mass of mankind' (*Works,* 14:278), his desire to locate pure beauty "Anywhere, anywhere / Out of the world!" (*Works,* 14:286) is also linked with his lifelong ambition to establish an aristocracy of taste and intellect that will decide—against the debased judgment of the masses and the moral pieties of the New England literary establishment—what counts as true art. This is particularly evident in Poe's ongoing dream of founding his own magazine. In 1848 Poe wrote to Helen Whitman requesting her aid in financing the *Stylus*: "Would it not be 'glorious,'" he asked, "to establish, in America, the sole unquestionable aristocracy—that of intellect—to secure its supremacy—to lead & to control it?" (*Letters,* 2:410). Here, as elsewhere in Poe's writing, culture becomes the ground at once of "unquestionable aristocracy" and social control. For Poe, no less than for Jefferson, this cultural aristocracy and its ideals of pure beauty cannot finally be separated from the question of race and the ongoing historical struggle over the color of American skin. Emerging out of the broader taxonomies of the Western Enlightenment, the aesthetic is itself a historically marked signifier that would continue to play a key role in national and international efforts to fix the boundary not only between races and nations but also between civilized and uncivilized, culture and its others.

Poe in Blackface

In his review of Poe scholarship in *Eight American Authors,* Jay Hubbell observes: "Poe was the one black sheep in the American literary flock, and very black indeed he seemed when placed beside the great New Englanders" (8). Associated with the South, the city, the masses, excess, dissolution, and the terror of blackness, Poe may have been written out of the American tradition precisely because he so nearly touched the trauma of race and the crisis of national identity at the center of nineteenth-century American culture. From Rufus Griswold's representation of Poe as a figure of "morbid excess" with "a face shrouded in gloom" (Griswold, 33–34), to Walt Whitman's evocation of Poe as "a dim man" with "an incorrigible propensity toward nocturnal themes, a demoniac undertone behind every page" (Whitman, 873–74), to Henry James's observation that "an enthusiasm for Poe is the mark of a decidedly primitive stage of reflection" (James, 76), critical responses to Poe have had at their center debates about American national identity conducted in a racially in-

flected language of black and white, demon and angel, primitive and civilized. If Poe's aesthetic theory was driven, as I have tried to suggest, by an
imaginative flight away from the historical presence of blacks in the social
landscape of America, it is ironic that following his death, he himself became the dark other, the demon, the "one black sheep in the American literary flock," who needed to be expelled from the social body to make way
for the New England–centered moral and spiritual imperatives of American national destiny as they came to be embodied by what F. O.
Matthiessen called the "American Renaissance."[26]

It was not until Poe went to France, where he was in some sense
cleansed of his blackness and his history, that he could reenter American
literature in the cold war period in the name of art for art's sake, aesthetic formalism, otherworldly metaphysics, and *la poésie pure*. Although
Edmund Wilson had invoked the French response to Poe as early as
1926 in calling on Americans to focus on "Poe's absolute artistic importance" rather than "his bad reputation as a citizen" (Wilson, 145, 143), it
was the "French face" of Poe in T. S. Eliot's *From Poe to Valéry* (1948) and
Allen Tate's "The Angelic Imagination: Poe as God" (1953) that prepared for his emergence in the post–World War II period as an icon of
modernist and new critical method and sensibility.[27] Whereas Tate urged
a philosophical rather than a merely personal or psychological approach
to Poe as the anticipator of "our great subject, the disintegration of personality" (60), Eliot emphasized the importance of Poe's theory of the
"poem written solely for the poem's sake" for an aesthetic tradition that
focuses with "increasing consciousness of language" on "what we may
call *la poésie pure*" (26). Looking at Poe "through the eyes of Baudelaire,
Mallarmé and most of all Valéry" (32), Eliot underscores Poe's lack of
relation to his time: "There can be few authors of such eminence who
have drawn so little from their own roots, who have been so isolated
from any surroundings" (9). Although Eliot concedes that the language
of Poe's poetry is not pure, he argues that Poe represents the origin of
the French symbolist theory of *la poésie pure* in the sense that "the subject
is little, the treatment is everything" (29). This evacuation of the subject and history from the terrain of writing—an evacuation that anticipates the linguistic and nonreferential emphasis of poststructuralist
criticism—is commonly regarded as the defining characteristic of symbolist theory and practice from Poe to Valéry.

And yet, if we return for a moment to the three seminal essays that
Baudelaire wrote on Poe between 1852 and 1857,[28] what is striking is the
extent to which they are embedded in Baudelaire's own historical and
racially marked attack on "democracy, progress and *civilization*" ("New
Notes," 124). "Nature produces only monsters, and the whole question is

to understand the word *savages*," he wrote in response to the "rising tide of democracy," "modern philosophy," and "misguided equalitarians" ("New Notes," 128, 124, 125, 126). Baudelaire was, in fact, one of the first to draw attention to the relation between Poe's pursuit of "pure beauty" and "pure poetry" and the racial turmoil of "a country in which slavery exists" and "chained Negroes" are burned ("New Notes," 135, 132). "Aristocrat by nature even more than by birth," Poe was "the Virginian, the Southerner," the "true poet . . . who does not wish to be elbowed by the crowd and who runs to the far east when the fireworks go off in the west" ("New Notes," 125). To Baudelaire, Poe was himself the exotic other of the West—the Orientalized "Arab" and "savage" who bodied forth "the primordial perversity of man" ("New Notes," 126) at the same time that he wrote poetry that was "carefully wrought, pure, correct, and as brilliant as a crystal jewel" ("Edgar Allan Poe," 67).[29]

The word *pure* figures at the center of a similarly marked racial aesthetics of black and white, primitive and civilized, "bawling" mass and pure signifier in Mallarmé's famous sonnet "Le Tombeau d'Edgar Poe," which was written to commemorate the dedication of Poe's tomb in Baltimore in 1876. Against the detestable "hydra" of his age and time, Poe is evoked as a purifying "angel" who cleanses language and poetry of their darkness and their history to give "a purer meaning to the words of the tribe" ("un sens plus pur aux mots de la tribu"). Fallen from some "obscure disaster" and surrounded by darkness, Poe's tomb will stand, Mallarmé suggests, as a barrier against the "black flights of Blasphemy" ("noirs vols du Blasphème") that will circle about it in years to come (Mallarmé, "Le Tombeau d'Edgar Poe," 70).[30]

The racially inflected response to Poe in the work of Baudelaire and Mallarmé, who both contributed to the development of a symbolist aesthetics of the "poem itself" and a language purified of the "words of the tribe" during the very years when France emerged as a major imperial power, suggests the more transnational histories, racial as well as textual, in which Poe's aesthetics of purity has played a role. In the history of Poe criticism, however, as in T. S. Eliot's *From Poe to Valéry*, the French response to Poe has served as a kind of aesthetic purifier, cleansing Poe's face of the marks of race and history to save him for the transcendence of art. This tradition, and its various permutations among decadents, modernists, postmodernists, and proponents of art for art's sake, has continued to be one of the main traditions of Poe criticism. Whether the approach is archival or theoretical, aesthetic or psychoanalytic, formalist or poststructuralist, until quite recently, critics have tended to focus on the primarily textual, linguistic, and psychological meanings of Poe's art. By seeking to locate Poe's poetic theory and practice within rather than outside history, I have attempted to suggest the ways that even calls for a purely aesthetic appreciation of Poe cannot finally be removed from the historical and racial struggles of the nineteenth and twentieth centuries. T. S. Eliot and Paul Valéry notwithstanding, there is no such thing as a pure poem.

Notes

1. The bill of sale, dated 10 December 1829, indicates that Poe acted as an agent in the sale of a slave named Edwin to Henry Ridgway, who may also have been a person of color (quoted in Miller, 52). See Kennedy, Chapter 9, figure 2, this volume.

2. For earlier discussions of *Pym* as racial allegory, see Sidney Kaplan and Beaver. See also Campbell, "Poe's Treatment of the Negro," and Marchand. Recent discussions of Poe and race include Hovey; Dayan, "Romance and Race" and "Amorous Bondage"; Rowe, "Antebellum Slavery"; Nelson, *The Word in Black and White*; Whalen, "Subtle Barbarians"; and Goddu, "The Ghost of Race."

3. According to Mabbott, Poe read Chateaubriand's *Itinéraire* (1810–11) in F. Shoberl's translation *Travels in Greece, Palestine, Egypt, and Barbary* (1813). For a discussion of Orientalism, see Said.

4. For a discussion of the imperial contours of American history, see William Appleman Williams. In "'Left Alone with America,'" Kaplan traces the ways American historiography has denied American empire.

5. See, for example, Rowe's discussion of the ways "the racial hierarchies recognizable in nineteenth-century British imperialism" are shifted to African Americans and native Americans in Poe's "Tale of the Ragged Mountains" and "The Journal of Julius Rodman" (chapter 6, this volume).

6. In 1832, the proslavery advocate Thomas Dew observed with some alarm that blacks were everywhere "intertwined" with whites in Southern society: "a race of people differing from us in colour and in habits, and vastly inferior in the scale of civilization, have been increasing and spreading—'growing with our growth and strengthening with our strength'—until they have become intertwined with every fibre of society" ("Abolition of Negro Slavery," 23).

7. For a discussion of the relationship between the "needs of an alienated Southern intellectual class" (6), the defense of Southern culture, and the proslavery argument, see Drew Gilpin Faust, "A Southern Stewardship." See also Donald, who argues that the defenders of slavery sought to escape the national and regional crisis by fleeing to some "bygone pastoral Arcadia" that had been lost.

8. In *The Black Image in the White Mind*, Frederickson also notes that after 1830, in response to growing attacks by Northern abolitionists, Southerners began to articulate an increasingly coherent proslavery ideology grounded in notions of African savagery and inferiority and the socially good effects of Southern enslavement (45).

9. Although Stallybrass and White do not explicitly address the question of the racial body in *The Politics and Poetics of Transgression*, their comments on the social ideal of the pure classical body are relevant to the entangled dependencies of whiteness and blackness in Poe's work: the "closure and purity [of the classical body] are quite illusory and it will perpetually rediscover in itself, often with a sense of shock or inner revulsion, the grotesque, the protean and the motley, the neither/nor, the double negation of high and low which is the very precondition of its social identity" (113). See also Dayan's splendid discussion of the ways "Poe's unlinked Great Chain completely mixes men, nature, women, reason, and dreams" ("Amorous Bondage," 246).

10. Fiedler notes that Poe was one of the first "to express a peculiarly American dilemma of identifying the symbolic blackness of terror with the blackness of the Negro and the white guilt he embodies" (378). Although the black and white symbolism in Poe's work cannot be reduced to race, it cannot be entirely separated from race either. As critics from Levin and Fiedler in the 1950s and 1960s to Toni Morrison in the 1990s have noted, given the racial struggles of the nineteenth century and the Judeo-Christian and Enlightenment symbology of darkness and lightness, it would be difficult to separate Poe's pervasive use of black and white symbolism from any racial reference. In a comment on the "esthetic effect" of blackness in Poe's work, Levin observes: "[S]uch effects do not pre-exist in a vacuum, although the artist may obtain them subconsciously; he chooses one shade, rather than an alternative, because it bears some connotation for him and for others" (28–29). Whether slavery caused the cultural denigration of blackness or the cultural denigration of blackness caused African enslavement, as Winthrop Jordan observes: "Blackness had become so thoroughly entangled with the basest status in American society that at least by the beginning of the eighteenth century it was almost indecipherably coded into American language and literature" (*White Over Black*, 258). Moreover, in the history of Western aestheticism, blackness had a longstanding association with dark skin. Thus, for example, by the mid–eighteenth century, the association of the horror of darkness with horror of dark skin had become so pervasive that in his *Philosophical Enquiry into the Origin of our Ideas of the Sublime and the Beautiful* (1757), Burke equates sublime terror with terror at the first sight of a Negro. Citing William Cheselden's account of a boy who had been born blind and regained his eyesight at age thirteen or fourteen, Burke notes that "the first time the boy saw a black object, it gave him great uneasiness; and that some time after, upon accidentally seeing a negro woman, he was struck with great horror at the sight" (131).

11. As editor of the *Southern Literary Messenger,* Poe wrote a laudatory review of one of Dew's speeches that concludes with the following excerpt on the "awful conflict" of the times: "Never were the opinions of the world more unsettled and more clashing than at this moment. Monarchists and democrats, conservatives and radicals, whigs and tories, agrarians and aristocrats, slave-holders and non-slave-holders, are all now in the great field of contention. What will be the result of this awful conflict, none can say" (quoted in Rosenthal, 30).

12. The review was included in Harrison's *Complete Works of Edgar Allan Poe* (8:265–75). In a 1941 doctoral dissertation, Hull argued that it was written not by Poe but by Poe's proslavery friend, Judge Beverley Tucker. Hull's conclusions were later challenged by Rosenthal. Although some critics continue to argue that the review was written by Poe (see, for example, Dayan, "Amorous Bondage"), the current critical consensus seems to be that it was written by Tucker; see, for example, Ridgely; and Whalen, "Average Racism" (chapter 1, this volume). In making the case against Poe's authorship, Ridgely notes that "the issue here is not the fact of Poe's racist attitudes": "Poe shared in the racism and proslavery sentiment of his time and place; he also expressed contempt for abolitionists" ("Authorship," 2).

13. In *The Confessions,* Gray also refers to Nat Turner's insurrection as a "massacre" committed by "a band of savages" (4).

14. Bezanson reads the final scene as Pym's return home: "Home to mother through a warm cosmic milk bath. . . . Or, if one prefers older conventions, welcomed into his dream of oblivion by the White Goddess" (173). Goddu, on the other hand, notes, "Given the timing of Nu-Nu's death, it is possible to see the shrouded figure at the end as the spiritual revivification of Nu-Nu. Pym might be embracing precisely what he hopes to evade" ("The Ghost of Race," 246).

15. See Mabbott, 2:317; Woodberry 2:420. A version of Hirst's parody published in *Sartain's Magazine* in 1852 substitutes the following lines: "Never negro took a nip in / Fabric half so black and bare" (434). In "Abolition of Negro Slavery" (1832), Dew uses the term *fairy palace* to describe the luxurious world of whiteness to which black people are denied access. See also, "The Murders in the Rue Morgue" (1841), where the *"excessively outré"* murder and mutilation of an old woman and her daughter are committed by a "large fulvous Ourang-Outang," which, as in Jefferson, is associated in the popular imagination with the "imitative propensities" and apelike inferiority of blacks (Mabbott, 2:559). For a discussion of the racial sources of Poe's orangutan in a contemporary newspaper account of the violent and "atrocious murder" of a black woman by a black man, see Kopley.

16. For a discussion of the relation between Poe's theory of taste and his "philosophical" attack on Enlightenment rationalism, see Tate. See also, Jacobs, "Poe and the Agrarian Critics."

17. In his proslavery essay "Abolition of Negro Slavery," Dew similarly notes that "schemes of emancipation . . . are admirably calculated to excite plots, murders, and insurrections" (57).

18. If slaves were emancipated, wrote Dew in 1832, "The whites would either gradually withdraw, and leave whole districts or settlements in their possession, in which case they would sink rapidly in the scale of civilization; *or the blacks, by closer intercourse, would bring the whites down to their level"* ("Abolition of Negro Slavery," 57; emphasis added).

19. Stallybrass and White's discussion of "the contradictory and unstable representation of low-Others" is relevant here. "A recurrent pattern emerges," they observe as,

the "top" attempts to reject and eliminate the "bottom" for reasons of prestige and status, only to discover, not only that it is in some way frequently dependent upon that low-Other (in the classic way that Hegel describes in the master-slave section of the *Phenomenology*), but also that the top *includes* that low symbolically, as a primary eroticized constituent of its own fantasy life. The result is a mobile, conflictual fusion of power, fear and desire in the construction of subjectivity: a psychological dependence upon precisely those Others which are being rigorously opposed and excluded at the social level. It is for this reason that what is *socially* peripheral is so frequently *symbolically* central. (5)

20. Poe makes recurrent use of animals in racially inflected contexts in his writings: the orangutan that is provoked to acts of "frightful mutilation" by its master's "use of a whip" in "The Murders in the Rue Morgue" (Mabbott, 2:547, 565); the "perverse" relation between black cat and master in "The Black Cat"; the ape that is worshiped and the "wild beasts" that periodically rise up against their masters in "Four Beasts in One—The Homo-Cameleopard"; the black cat capable of reason in "Instinct vs Reason—A Black Cat"; and the figure of the condor as ominous black bird of prey in the poems "Sonnet—To Science" and "The Conqueror Worm." In these and other poems and tales, such as "The Haunted Palace," *Pym*, "Ligeia," "The Fall of the House of Usher," "The System of Dr. Tarr and Professor Feather," and "Hop-Frog," Poe returns over and over to fantasies of revenge and reversal of the master-slave (or male-female) relation. See also Poe's 1836 review of Robert Bird's *Sheppard Lee*, in which he praises a sequence in which the ghost of the white man, Sheppard Lee, assumes the body of a black man, Nigger Tom: "In his character of Nigger Tom, Mr. Lee gives us some very excellent chapters upon abolition and the exciting effects of incendiary pamphlets and pictures, among our slaves in the South. This part of the narrative closes with a spirited picture of a negro insurrection, and with the hanging of Nigger Tom" (*CW*, 5:285).

21. See also John F. Adams, who observes: "Classical mythology has Pallas, the embodiment of wisdom, as the raven's original master, a tradition Poe evidently drew upon in perching his raven on her white bust" (53).

22. Poe delivered his lecture "The Poetic Principle" in Providence, Rhode Island, on 20 December 1848; in Richmond, Virginia, on 17 August and 24 September 1849; and in Norfolk, Virginia, on 14 and 17 September 1849 (Thomas and Jackson). The lecture was published posthumously in 1850.

23. In response to Poe's lecture in Richmond on 17 August 1849, John M. Daniels in the *Semi-Weekly Examiner* praises Poe for exploding "the poetic 'heresy of modern times'" by insisting that poetry should have no "'end to accomplish beyond that of ministering to our sense of the beautiful.—We have in these days poets of humanity and poets of universal suffrage, poets whose mission is to break down the corn laws and poets to build up workhouses" (Thomas and Jackson, 827).

24. Whereas earlier critics, including Woodberry, Campbell (*The Mind of Poe*),

Stovall, and Laser, have emphasized the determining influence of Coleridge on Poe's aesthetic ideas, Omans argues convincingly that Poe's tripartite division of the mind derives not from Coleridge but from Kant's *Critique of Judgment* (1790): "Not only are Poe's three faculties, pure intellect, taste, and the moral sense, translations of Kant's German terms, *Verstand, das Geschmacksurteil,* and *Vernunft,* but also Poe, like Kant, places the faculty of taste between those of the intellect and moral sense and emphasizes its function as a 'connecting link in the triple chain'" (128). For a discussion of Poe in relation to eighteenth-century moral sense philosophers, see Jacobs, *Poe: Journalist and Critic,* especially 3–34.

25. Baumgarten's two-volume *Aesthetica* was published in Germany in 1750 and 1758. For a discussion of the historical emergence of the term *aesthetic* in Germany and England in the eighteenth and nineteenth centuries, see Raymond Williams, 31–32. In *The Ideology of the Aesthetic,* Terry Eagleton argues: "Aesthetics is born as a discourse of the body" (13).

26. In a footnote to his discussion of "Method and Scope" in *American Renaissance,* Matthiessen says that he excluded Poe from his study because he "was bitterly hostile to democracy" and lacked "the moral depth of Hawthorne and Melville" (xii).

27. See also Patrick F. Quinn.

28. *Edgar Allan Poe: Sa vie et ses ouvrages* (1852); *Edgar Poe: Sa vie et ses oeuvres* (1856); *Notes nouvelles sur Edgar Poe* (1857).

29. In his first published essay on Poe, Baudelaire wrote: "He went through life as if through a Sahara desert, and changed his residence like an Arab" ("Edgar Allan Poe," 63). Given the racially marked nature of Baudelaire's response to Poe, it is significant that his interest in Poe was aroused by a reading of "The Black Cat," a story that he discusses at length as a fable of human perversity in his 1852 essay on Poe.

30. In his own pursuit of technical perfection and a poetic language purified of all social reference, Mallarmé regarded Poe as "my great master" (quoted in Mondor, 104). Claiming that he learned English in order to translate Poe, he published translations of several of Poe's poems. See Mallarmé, *Les Poèmes d'Edgar Poe.*

CHAPTER 3

Edgar Allan Poe's Imperial Fantasy and the American Frontier

JOHN CARLOS ROWE

> Such are the fluctuating fortunes of these savage nations. War, famine, pestilence, together or singly, bring down their strength and thin their numbers. . . .
> There appears to be a tendency to extinction among all the savage nations; and this tendency would seem to have been in operation among the aboriginals of this country long before the advent of the white men.
>
> Washington Irving, *Astoria* (1836)

Poe's fictional representations of racialized "savages" as threatening figures, often associated by Poe with mass murder and mob rule, are not just evidence of his identity as a Southern regionalist. Poe's rhetorical uses of non-European peoples should also be interpreted in relation to late eighteenth- and nineteenth-century imperialism and the discursive practices employed by the imperial powers to rationalize their subjugation and, in many cases, destruction of native peoples. In making this argument, I do not wish to distract scholars from the important work of reinterpreting Poe's writings in relation to the ideology of the antebellum Southern slavocracy. We must never forget that slavery is an instance of the fundamental violence of colonialism: the conscious effort to take from others their very means of survival. Southern slavery and westward expansion in the United States have often been treated differently from the colonial institutions of other nations because the former are assumed to be acts of "internal colonization." Yet the slave trade in the United States caused political, social, and economic instabilities in Africa and the Caribbean that should be understood as "colonial," and the domination of African Americans in the antebellum South was accomplished with the familiar colonial instruments of economic, political, legal, and psychological control.[1]

In the reassessment of how U.S. imperialism took shape in the eighteenth and nineteenth centuries, providing in many cases foundations for twentieth-century foreign policies and cultural attitudes toward other nations and peoples, we should consider the similarities between the Southern colonization of Africans and more general U.S. efforts to colonize the frontier by subjugating its native peoples. The cultural histories of Southern slavery and westward expansion are complicated by the tendency of U.S. politicians and intellectuals to emulate the authority and cultural superiority of Great Britain, in whose vast imperial shadow the United States continued to live as its leaders developed its imperial "destiny." Besides the antebellum South's notable imitation of English culture, westward expansion often was rationalized as a continuation of the migratory and conquering nature of the "Anglo-Saxon." Such Anglophilia in the United States was complicated in the nineteenth century by the general U.S. effort to achieve economic, political, and cultural independence from its former colonial ruler and by the mounting anti-English feelings of the Southern slavocracy in response to the effective antislavery movement in Great Britain.

Reginald Horsman neatly sorts out U.S. Anglophilia and Anglophobia in the 1840s by observing how frequently in public discourse the "English people" were "respected as fellow Anglo-Saxons," whereas the British government was typically condemned for its interference with U.S. expansionist aims, notably in this period in the Oregon Territory (22). Popular contempt for British economic, territorial, and military meddling in North America did not disturb the strong identification so many citizens felt with the English, in part because many Americans still believed that the British government represented older aristocratic powers that had been eliminated in the United States. Horsman cites Representative James B. Bowlin (Missouri), who argued in 1845 that "destiny had arranged for Americans to check in Oregon England's drive for universal dominion" and that the "English were in trouble in Oregon . . . , because they were meeting free representatives of the same Anglo-Saxon race" (221). Matching his own rhetoric to this popular discourse in the 1840s, Poe imaginatively retravels English routes of trade and colonial expansion with American characters, and he appropriates for these characters what he judges to be the best qualities of British culture and imperial power.

Cultural apologists for Southern slavery and westward expansion worked diversely in the first half of the nineteenth century to develop what might be viewed as homegrown defenses of our colonial practices, even if the sources in English policies were often still readable. In this chapter, I interpret the ways Edgar Allan Poe developed an "American" rhetoric of imperial power that reinstates many of the racial hierarchies recognizable in nineteenth-century British imperialism. Shifting the racial hierarchies from the "peoples of color" in British India, Africa, and the Pacific to African Americans and Native Americans, Poe ostensibly rejects the hereditary class system of the English aristocracy for a meritocracy that still relies on racial hierarchies and frequent appeals to the tests of reason and its complement, rhetoric. In this regard, too, he differs little from the prevailing public discourse in the United States in the 1840s regarding Anglo-Saxon racial "purity," especially as it was invented to contrast with the mestizos of Mexico and thereby provide legitimacy for our aggression toward Mexico in the Mexican-American War (1846–48) (Horsman, 208–48).

In "The Journal of Julius Rodman" and "A Tale of the Ragged Mountains," Poe's model for imperial power in North America and India, respectively, is Great Britain, but there is a strange doubling of Great Britain and the United States in these two narratives that works out what I will call Poe's *imperial fantasy*. What Poe imagines in these two fantastic travel narratives is achievable only in and through his own poetic authority; it is a fantasy of imperial power and authority vested in the literary author and by no means realizable in what Poe considers the increasingly decadent politics of democracy. Fantastic as such poetic authority may thus remain, it is by no means harmless or trivial; it remains very much a part of the neocolonial practices that can be traced from the late eighteenth century to the present and are uniquely influential in the development of U.S. imperialism in this same modern period.

Poe's unfinished "Journal of Julius Rodman," which was published anonymously in *Burton's Gentleman's Magazine* from January to June 1840, when Poe left the editorial staff of the magazine, has justifiably received little attention (A. H. Quinn, 293). As previous scholars have pointed out, much of the narrative is paraphrased or directly plagiarized from actual frontier narratives, including his major sources —Washington Irving's *Astoria* (1836) and its sequel, *The Adventures of Captain Bonneville* (1837), and Nicholas Biddle's *History of the Expedition under the Command of Lewis and Clark* (1814)—and lesser borrowings from John K. Townsend's *Narrative of a Journey across the Rocky Mountains to the Columbia River* (1839), the journals of Sir Alexander Mackenzie, and "other accounts of American exploration" by "Flagg, . . . Samuel Parker, and others" (A. Quinn, 293).[2] Grandly subtitled, "Being an Account of the First Passage across the Rocky Mountains of North America ever achieved by Civilized Man," and beginning with the sort of hyperbole that typifies Poe's parody of other travel narratives and affirmation of his own poetic ambitions in *The Narrative of Arthur Gordon Pym* (1838), the six chapters published in *Burton's Gentleman's Magazine* never make it across the Rocky Mountains, leaving the reader hanging at the end of the frontier party's conventionally sensational combat with two hostile brown bears.

Left unfinished by Poe, never published by him in book form, and not even acknowledged by him as his own work, "The Journal of Julius Rodman" has rarely been interpreted in relation to the chief themes of Poe's other writings, with the exception of the evidence it gives of Poe's interest in grounding such "imaginary voyages" as *Pym* in the facts of actual narratives of exploration.[3] To be sure, there is virtually nothing of aesthetic value in "Julius Rodman," but there is much of political relevance for the current reevaluation of Poe as a Southern writer, including my own interest in expanding Poe's Southern regionalism to include his contributions to the culture of U.S. imperialism. In his biography of Poe, Kenneth Silverman comments on the "manumitted black servant Jupiter" in "The Gold-Bug" and the slave, Toby, in "Julius Rodman" as evidence that "Poe opposed abolition, and identified with slaveholding interests in the South, whom he felt Northern writers misrepresented" (207).[4] In his brief but perceptive remarks on "Julius Rodman" in "The Literature of Expansion and Race," Eric Sundquist takes seriously what other critics have considered the hoax of Poe's invention of a character, Julius Rodman, who crossed the Rocky Mountains *before* any other European:

> Poe's temporal dislocation of the narrative of Julius Rodman into the past has a multiple significance. . . . It corresponded to contemporary efforts by Parkman and others to displace the conquest of the continent and the "doom" of the American Indian into an earlier century. At the same time, it accentuated Poe's own obsession with America's futurity as expressed in his short science fiction tales or in the philosophical dream tract *Eureka* (1848), in which boundless cosmic space appears in part as a figure for the unfolding destiny of the nation. (146)

Sundquist's discussion of Poe's unfinished "imaginary voyage" is included in a section of the new *Cambridge History of American Literature* entitled "Exploration and Empire," in which he focuses on the ideological function of frontier narratives in the racialization of Native Americans that served the emerging Myth of the Vanishing American and the larger imperial ambitions of the United States in the era of Manifest Destiny. The ideological purposes of "The Journal of Julius Rodman" may appear unexceptional when understood in the context of other frontier writings, full of the same ethnocentrism and racial demonization of Native Americans abundantly evident in "Julius Rodman," but it is finally the significance of this conventional ideology of Manifest Destiny for the otherwise uniquely elite Edgar Allan Poe that deserves critical attention.

Julius Rodman is introduced as a native of England, from a good family and well educated, who emigrated to the United States in 1784 at the age of eighteen with "his father, and two maiden sisters" (*CW,* 1:522).[5] From New York City, the family traveled to Kentucky, then to Missouri, where they "established themselves, almost in hermit fashion, on the banks of the Mississippi, near where Mills' Point now makes into the river" (*CW,* 1:522). After his father and his sisters conveniently die, Rodman sells the family's "plantation" and sets out on a fur-trapping expedition in the spring of 1791, returning in 1794 to take up residence in Abingdon, Virginia, where he "married, and had three children, and where most of his descendants now live" (*CW,* 1:522). Burton Pollin points out that Kentucky in 1784 was a rough frontier region, where most settlers lived on small farms, feared Indian raids, and sought protection in military stockades: "In short, Poe's use of the term 'plantation' is anachronistic for 1792, but not for 1840" (*CW,* 1:585–86 n. 1.2B). The anachronism that troubles Pollin, however, is easy to explain: Poe imagines the expansion of the slave economy into the frontier territories, citing Kentucky as one historical example. In a period when public debate revolved around how the question of slavery would be decided in the new territories, Poe follows proslavery Southern leads in extending the plantation system and slaveholding to the new frontier.

The direct line connecting the Southern and obviously aristocratic Rodmans with their good family in England is typical of Poe's Southern pretensions. The region that Rodman proposes to explore in the course of his fur-trapping expedition is in 1791 "the *only* unexplored region within the limits of the continent of North America," and it seems to encompass basically the same route as Lewis and Clark's—up the Missouri River from St. Louis through the Midwest, then across the Rocky Mountains eventually to reach the Columbia River and the Pacific coast (*CW,* 1:521). Poe's unfinished narrative stops at the Rocky Mountains, but the completed narrative would have represented two regions crucially contested by the European colonial powers: the French territory between the Mississippi and Missouri Rivers sold to the United States as the Louisiana Purchase and the Oregon Territory.[6] Thomas Jefferson arranged for Meriwether Lewis to explore the territory up the Missouri River and as far as the Pacific not only in hopes of finding a water route across the continent "for the purposes of commerce" but also to discover what "commerce . . . may be carried on with the people inhabiting" the regions explored.[7] Although formal disputes between the United States and Great Britain over the Oregon Territory would not become public issues until 1811, Jefferson probably had in mind as early as 1803 the idea of a U.S. expedition from St. Louis to the Pacific Ocean as a means of establishing a commercial and then political claim to these two frontier territories.[8]

Under the French, the territory of what became the Louisiana Purchase (1803) had been open to French trappers and traders throughout the eighteenth century, even though at the end of the French and Indian War France ceded Louisiana, west of the Mississippi, to Spain by the terms of the Treaty of Fontainebleau (1762). Lewis and Clark encounter several posts operated by venturesome French traders along the Missouri, as well as ruins of previous sites of early commerce with native peoples. With some regularity, they pass French traders' rafts carrying furs acquired from Native Americans farther up the river. Some of this French trade in the area of the Louisiana Purchase is, of course, a consequence of the relatively recent retrocession of the territory from Spain to France, under the terms of the secret Treaty of San Ildefonso (1800) that Napoleon signed with the Spanish. But much of the French influence in the Louisiana Territory traveled by Lewis and Clark, then by Poe's Rodman, represents the continuous presence of French trappers, voyageurs, and small entrepreneurs who succeeded under either French or Spanish colonial rule. Both the Oregon Territory and Louisiana from the 1790s (the time of Rodman's travels) to 1840 (publication of the "Journal") are areas of intense international political and commercial competition with several different Euro-American powers trying to take permanent possession of them.[9]

As Poe knew from Irving's *Astoria*, that public relations book John Jacob Astor had commissioned Irving to write about the failed settlement of Fort Astor at the mouth of the Columbia River, between 1811 and 1846 the Oregon Territory was a special region of "free-trade imperialism," in which commercial ventures of the Canadian North West Company, the British Hudson's Bay Company, U.S. merchants like Astor, and Russian commercial interests virtually governed their respective and often conflicting trade territories. Like British India under the East India Company, the disputed Oregon Territory was a colonial region ruled primarily by commercial rather than governmental masters. This confusion of private commercial ventures and U.S. government efforts to foster commerce is typical of these early ventures into territory west of the Mississippi. The rugged individualism of the frontiersman often thinly disguised a governmental plan, as Lewis and Clark's expedition demonstrates, and the "entrepreneurial spirit" of early capitalists, like John Jacob Astor, often succeeded thanks to generous political, military, and financial support from the government.

After the death of his father and sisters, Rodman takes "no farther interest in [his] plantation" and sells it "at a complete sacrifice," choosing instead to go "trapping up the Missouri . . . and try to procure peltries. I believe that much more property might be acquired in this way." (*CW*, 1:529). Like so many of Poe's poetic characters, particularly Roderick Usher, Rodman suffers from romantic melancholia, in this case named "hereditary hypochondria," for which he hopes to find some cure on his expedition. Burton Pollin suggests that Poe draws on Meriwether Lewis's well-publicized hypochondria, especially as recounted by Jefferson in his "Memoir of Meriwether Lewis," as the basis for Rodman's melancholia (*CW*, 1:522, 583 n. 1.1F). Given Poe's heavy reliance on Jefferson's memoir and the 1814 history of the Lewis and Clark expedition, as well as public fascination with Meriwether Lewis's mysterious death or suicide in 1809, this is a reasonable speculation. But Rodman's hypochondria and melancholia are also typical qualities of many of Poe's other characters. When these characters head into the natural world to discover some cure, they find instead the unconscious causes of their illnesses exposed. Bored, distracted, and mournful in his Missouri home, Rodman becomes vital, energetic, and interested on his frontier journey. For Poe, Rodman's unconscious poetic and romantic inclinations reveal themselves to the reader on the frontier. For us, the civilization of Rodman's settled life on his Missouri plantation is exposed as another version of the trapper's savage and violent life on the frontier: both are versions of Rodman's colonial will to power.

In his account of the settlement at Astoria, Irving makes clear how Astor imagined his American Fur Company and its post at Astoria as a commercial "empire" within the democratic United States:

> He was already wealthy beyond the ordinary desires of man, but he now aspired to that honorable fame which is awarded to men of similar scope of mind, who by their great commercial enterprises have enriched nations, peopled wildernesses, and extended the bounds of empire. He considered his projected establishment at the mouth of the Columbia as the emporium to an immense commerce; as a colony that would form the germ of a wide civilization; that would, in fact, carry the American population across

the Rocky Mountains and spread it along the shores of the Pacific,
as it already animated the shores of the Atlantic. (*Astoria*, 23)

The complicity of the U.S. government with large American corpora-
tions in the work of what some have termed *free-trade imperialism* is recounted by Irving: "[Astor] was aware of the wish of the American government . . . that the fur trade within its boundaries should be in the
hands of American citizens, and of the ineffectual measures it had taken
to accomplish that object. He now offered, if aided and protected by the
government, to turn the whole of that trade into American channels"
(15–16).[10] Astor's commercial ambitions are, not surprisingly, international, stretching beyond the continental United States and disputed
Oregon Territory to encompass what he envisioned as a chain of islands
across the Pacific controlled by the American Fur Company to secure
the route to China, the largest buyer of North American furs.[11]

Unlike Astor, Rodman receives no offers of help from the U.S. government for his 1791–94 expedition, but Poe makes it clear that the earliest explorations of this region were motivated by commercial interests
that had international ambitions. Referring to Jonathan Carver's (1710–
80) exploration of the Northwest Territory in search of the elusive
Northwest Passage, Poe summarizes Carver's ambitions: "A settlement
in this neighborhood would disclose new sources of trade, and open a
more direct communication with China, and the British possessions in
the East Indies, than the old route afforded, by the Cape of Good Hope.
He was baffled, however, in his attempt to cross the mountains" (*CW*,
1:525). In many respects, Jefferson imagined Lewis and Clark's expedition as the ultimately successful effort to find such a water passage west
to the Pacific, but within territory Jefferson expected the United States
would soon control. After he returns from his travels, however, Rodman
is contacted by André Michaux (1746–1802), the French botanist whom
Thomas Jefferson had asked in 1792 to explore the territory subsequently charted by Lewis and Clark; Michaux urges Rodman to write out
in detail an account of the expedition, which Rodman originally
recorded as "an outline diary." In this regard, Rodman's diary seems
modeled on Meriwether Lewis's diary of the 1804–6 expedition and
William Clark's copy of it, together with Clark's additional comments,
both of which were used by Nicholas Biddle for the 1814 *History* and
subsequently revised by Elliott Coues in a four-volume edition published
in 1893 and considered the authoritative nineteenth-century account of
the Lewis and Clark expedition.[12] Indeed, Poe's fictional use of Michaux
is but a thin paraphrase of what Jefferson himself recounts in his 18 August 1813 "Memoir of Meriwether Lewis" of Michaux and Lewis's early

plans to "explore [the] region . . . by ascending the Stony [Rocky] mountains, and descending the nearest river to the Pacific" (1:xix).[13] In keeping with the usual Poe complications regarding missing, misplaced, and missent manuscripts, Rodman's revised "MS. when completed, however, never reached M. Michau [sic], for whose inspection it had been drawn up; and was always supposed to have been lost on the road by the young man to whom it was entrusted for delivery at M. M[ichaux]'s temporary residence, near Monticello" (CW, 1:523).[14]

Poe quickly abandons any pretense of describing an actual commercial expedition, however, in his account of the travels of Julius Rodman. Except for some early descriptions of beaver and techniques of beaver trapping, reminiscent of the technical digressions on the "drying" of bîche de mer in Pym, Poe's narrative quickly swerves in the direction of a loosely constructed ode to the sublimity of nature that Rodman encounters—a thinly disguised metaphor for the *supernatural* dimension that Poe likely would have added to the finished narrative. Yet what assures us that this narrative belongs with those "free-trade imperial" narratives of westward commercial expansion are the unmistakable class and racial hierarchies that Rodman's journal so clearly establishes.

Leaving the slave economy of the Missouri plantation behind, Rodman is nonetheless accompanied by a representative slave, "a negro belonging to Pierre Junôt, named Toby." Toby is probably based on the "black servant" York, "belonging to Captain Clark," who joined the Lewis and Clark expedition and is the only member of the expedition *not* granted a military title as part of his service (Jefferson, "Memoir of Meriwether Lewis," 1:2). Poe characterizes Toby as "a faithful negro" who "was rather too old to accompany such an expedition as ours; but Pierre was not willing to leave him. He was an able-bodied man, however, and still capable of enduring great fatigue" (CW, 1:532). In respect to age and physical abilities, Toby differs markedly from Captain Clark's servant, York, who is described as "a remarkably stout, strong negro," who will entertain the Arikaras with "feats of strength" and find special sexual favor with the Arikara women (Jefferson, "Memoir of Meriwether Lewis," 1:159, 164). Was Poe afraid to attribute sexual powers to an African American, as Lewis and Clark quite openly do, in keeping with Poe's Southern fears of miscegenation? Whatever the reason, Poe's change of York from the physically able and youthful man to the aged, feeble, and thus dependent Toby seems curious, given Poe's heavy reliance on Lewis and Clark's York as a model for Toby. One possible explanation is in the name "Toby," which Poe may have borrowed from the name Lewis and Clark give to the Shoshone, "our old guide Toby and his son," who leads them over the Rocky Mountains (Jefferson, "Memoir of

Meriwether Lewis," 2:1008).[15] In conflating the Shoshone guide and the African American servant, Poe departs from Lewis and Clark's tendencies in their diaries to distinguish between Native American and African American racial characteristics and thus conforms to the popular discourse of the period that deliberately combined and confused Native American, African American, and Mexican.

Poe must have had greater plans for Toby in the extended narrative because he claims that Toby "was not the least important personage of our party," even though he will play only one part in the subsequent six chapters—a stereotyped performance of exotic negritude for a band of Assiniboins who venture upon the expedition and with whom Rodman makes friends by virtue of Toby's display. "Struck with sudden amazement at the sooty appearance of our negro, Toby," the Assiniboins request "a good look at Toby," and Rodman agrees to let them examine him in exchange for a boat they have seized. He thus sends the old slave ashore "*in naturalibus*, that the inquisitive savages might observe the whole extent of the question." Toby's nakedness recalls the slave auction, as does his body as an item of exchange, even though in this case it is merely his display that is exchanged for the pirogue. What *is* displayed is Poe's racism, as the Assiniboins express their astonishment at the features of Toby, which Poe describes according to the pseudoscientific racism of the early nineteenth century: "Toby . . . was as ugly an old gentleman as ever spoke—having all the peculiar features of his race; the swollen lips, large white protruding eyes, flat nose, long ears, double head, pot-belly, and bow legs" (*CW,* 1:569).

Toby's racialized physical characteristics are an amalgam of those Poe used for Dirk Peters and Nu-Nu in *The Narrative of Arthur Gordon Pym*, incompletely serialized three years earlier (1837) and published in book form two years earlier (1838). The physically powerful Peters, who will survive the tale to live out his days in Illinois, is introduced as a "half-breed"—"son of an Indian woman of the tribe of Upsarokas [Absarokas]" and "a fur-trader . . . connected in some manner with the Indian trading-posts on the Lewis river"; he is described as having "arms, as well as legs, . . . *bowed* in the most singular manner" and a "head . . . equally deformed, being of immense size, with an indentation on the crown (like that on the head of most negroes)" (*CW,* 1:87). Late in *Pym,* only paragraphs before he expires, Nu-Nu displays his "black" teeth, prompting Pym to reflect: "We had never before seen the teeth of an inhabitant of Tsalal" (*CW,* 1:205). These and other racialized descriptions of the Tsalalian natives in *Pym* suggest affinities with the "swollen lips" of Toby. In contrast, Peters's "lips were thin" and "the teeth . . . exceedingly long and protruding, and never even partially covered, in any instance, by the lips," giving him the look of "a demon" (*CW*, 1:87). The African American York on the Lewis and Clark expedition seems a possible model for *Pym*'s Dirk Peters, whereas Nu-Nu's physical deterioration, admittedly in response to the tabooed "white," seems to anticipate the physical decrepitude of Toby in "Julius Rodman." And yet Dirk Peters shares physical characteristics with Poe's black characters, such as the "bowed" legs and "deformed" head.

Poe's confusion of different racial characteristics is not unusual in this period. Pseudo-ethnographies, legal judgments, publications in the natural sciences, and many other discourses confirm the prevailing ideology of "white" as designating the U.S. "citizen" and a wide range of peoples of color constituting "the opposite of 'white.'" The preceding quotation is from the 1854 Supreme Court of California decision in the case of the *People v. George W. Hall*, in which Hall had appealed his murder conviction on the grounds that "the testimony of Chinese witnesses" should not have been allowed.[16] Citing such odd and contrary evidence as Columbus's confusion of Native Americans and Chinese ("Mongolians," in the language of the Court) and Cuvier's "scientific" classification of "the human species" into "three distinct types," the Court not only "excludes black, yellow, and all other colors" from the "citizenship" available to "Caucasians" but also treats peoples of color as "a distinct people, . . . recognizing no laws of this State, . . . a race of people whom nature has marked as inferior, and who are incapable of progress of intellectual development beyond a certain point" (*People v. Hall*).[17] Thus when Poe mixes and matches characteristics of Teton Sioux, Tsalalian islanders, and African Americans to suit his fictional purposes, he merely typifies the prevailing racial ideology in the nineteenth-century United States.

Poe's account of Toby's antics follows in many respects Lewis and Clark's diary entries about York's performances for the Arikaras (the "Ricaras" in the diaries). Lewis and Clark's accounts represent unmistakably early nineteenth-century U.S. racism regarding both Native Americans and African Americans, but with important differences from Poe's racism in "The Journal of Julius Rodman." Unlike Poe, Lewis and Clark do not stress York's ugliness, focusing instead on his color as the source of the Arikaras' fascination:

The object which appeared to astonish the Indians most was Captain Clark's servant York, a remarkably stout, strong negro. They had never seen a being of that color, and therefore flocked round him to examine the extraordinary monster. By way of amusement he told them that he had once been a wild animal, and caught and tamed by his master; and to convince them showed them feats of strength which, added to his looks, made him more terrible than we wished him to be. (Jefferson, "Memoir of Meriwether Lewis," 1:159)

What attracts the Arikaras to York is precisely his difference from their own appearance, and York's novelty is what Lewis and Clark conclude cause the Arikaras to encourage him to engage in sexual intercourse with their women: "[T]wo very handsome young squaws were sent on board this evening, and persecuted us with civilities. The black man York participated largely in these favors; for, instead of inspiring any prejudice, his color seemed to procure him additional advantages from the Indians, who desired to preserve among them some memorial of this wonderful stranger" (Jefferson, "Memoir of Meriwether Lewis," 1:164).[18]

Toby's physiological markers of race are accompanied for Poe by the behavioral qualities familiarly identified with African Americans in proslavery propaganda of the period. Once he has been examined by the Native Americans, Toby performs "a jig dance" for them, and Rodman notes that "had Toby but possessed a single spark of ambition he might then have made his fortune for ever by ascending the throne of the Assiniboins, and reigning as King Toby the First" (CW, 1:569). Pollin points out that "jig" dances in the United States probably originated with late eighteenth-century Irish immigrants and that the "earliest dated references to Negro jigs . . . are to blackface impersonators doing 'jigs and clogs of English and Irish origin' on the American stage in 1810" (CW, 1:639 n. 5.17C). In other words, Poe is once again conflating 1840, when African American jigs were popular entertainments, with his imaginary "1791–1794," when Rodman pursues his explorations of the West. Lewis and Clark pause to comment on York's importance among the Arikaras, especially as a figure of sexual interest, and the Native Americans' relative lack of racial prejudice. On the other hand, Poe repeats racist clichés about African American "laziness" in close conjunction with his accounts of Native Americans described elsewhere in "The Journal of Julius Rodman" as similarly lacking in industry and prone to theft. Whereas the white Southern aristocrat Rodman diligently finds more beaver than he had expected on this voyage, so that he may devote extended periods to mere contemplation of nature to the neglect of trapping, Toby is associated with the racial stereotypes of "laziness," good humor at his own humiliation, and entertainment.

The final connection made in the narrative between the Assiniboins and Toby, between Native Americans and African Americans, is by no means a casual identification. Different as Toby may appear to these Native Americans, he shares with them the racial degradation that Poe has elsewhere identified with the hostile and "thieving" "rascals," the Lakota Sioux. From the beginning of his journal, Rodman claims to know little about Native Americans. Nevertheless, before having encountered *any* tribal peoples on his journey, Rodman judges the Sioux "as, in the main, a treacherous race, not to be dealt with safely in so small a party as ours" (*CW*, 1:536). Indeed, Rodman's obsession with the Sioux is such that even the "editor" of the journal feels compelled to comment: "The Sioux, indeed, appear to have been Mr. Rodman's bugbears *par excellence*, and he dwells upon them and their exploits with peculiar emphasis" (*CW*, 1:550). Among the "warlike" Sioux, Rodman (by way of the editor's summary) distinguishes the Tetons as "most renowned for their violence." One tribe of the Tetons, the Bois-Brulé, turn out to be lying in ambush for Rodman's expedition as it passes "near the White and Teton" Rivers' confluence with the Missouri (*CW*, 1:551). Not surprisingly, then, when Rodman finally does encounter these fierce Bois-Brulé, he "discovers" the physiological markers of racial inferiority he also finds in old Toby: the Sioux are described as "an ugly ill-made race, their limbs being much too small for the trunk, according to our ideas of the human form—their cheek bones are high and their eyes protruding and dull" (*CW*, 1:551).

Poe's language in this passage is a paraphrase of Lewis's diary entry for 26 September 1804 (Jefferson, "Memoir of Meriwether Lewis," 1:138). This rhetoric of racial classification is, of course, typical of frontier writing published in the first half of the nineteenth century. Nevertheless, there are important differences between Lewis and Clark's and Poe's descriptions of these "Indians." Lewis and Clark distrust the Teton Sioux whom they initially feared and with whom they have an encounter that nearly deteriorates into a violent confrontation that threatens to end the expedition prematurely. Although Lewis and Clark comment on various aspects of Teton Sioux tribal life they obviously consider primitive, such as dancing and music they do not understand, they also note social practices, such as policing tribal behavior, that they consider equivalent to their own state of civilization (Jefferson, "Memoir of Meriwether Lewis," 1:136–37, 141). For Poe, however, the physical ugliness of the Sioux is matched by their stupidity, and Rodman easily convinces them that the expedition's deck cannon is a "Great Spirit" who is "displeased" with the Sioux warriors who have insulted it by misnaming it "a great green grasshopper." Justifying his act of firing this cannon into a crowd of a hundred Sioux warriors, killing six men and seriously wounding eighteen more, Rodman goes among the wounded giving them small presents, only to spend a sleepless night and part of a paragraph reflecting how "[h]uman blood had never, before this epoch, been shed at my hands; and although reason urged that I had taken the wisest, and what would no doubt prove in the end the most merciful course, still conscience, refusing to hearken even to reason herself, whispered pertinaciously within my ear—'it is human blood which thou hast shed'" (*CW,* 1:558–59). The next morning Rodman has recovered fully, his thoughts of charity and morality apparently sufficient to justify such murder. In contrast, Lewis and Clark's diaries make much of the explorers' good fortune in being able to avoid firing the "swivel-gun" mounted on the bow of their keelboat, not out of any regard for their Teton antagonists but for the sake of continuing their journey without fear of reprisals and attacks from local inhabitants (Jefferson, "Memoir of Meriwether Lewis," 1:133, 133 n. 1).

Both Poe's literary and Lewis and Clark's historical accounts stress the warlike qualities of the Native American tribes they encounter for the sake of justifying U.S. removal and destruction of native peoples. In the epigraph to this chapter, I quote Washington Irving's sentiments regarding the "tendency to extinction" of native peoples that Irving is convinced antedates the arrival of Euro-American colonists. In a similar manner, Lewis and Clark describe their own "peacemaking" efforts with the perpetually "warring" tribes of Native Americans to be part of the process of civilization and progress over the inherent violence of supposedly less "civilized" peoples. Never does it occur to Lewis and Clark that the consequence of Euro-American colonization has been the displacement of native peoples that has directly resulted in conflicts among different tribes over basic resources. In sum, both Poe and Lewis and Clark shape the Myth of the Vanishing American by means of historical revisionism: displacing the violence of Euro-American colonization onto the "inherent" tribal violence of "primitive" native peoples.

What is unique in Poe's racially constructed narrative of the frontier is his insistence that African Americans and Native Americans are "unnatural" presences in a landscape that meets all his requirements for aesthetic sublimity. When the Bois-Brulé first appear, they do so in a "landscape of the soul" reminiscent of the ravines in which the "treacherous" natives ambush Pym and Dirk Peters on the island of Tsalal in *Pym:* "The region infested by the tribe in question" is

> deeply cut by gorges or ravines, which in the middle of summer
> are dry, but form the channels of muddy and impetuous torrents
> during the season of rain. Their edges are fringed with thick
> woods, as well at top, as at bottom; but the prevalent aspect of the
> country is that of a bleak low land, with rank herbage, and with-

out trees. The soil is strongly impregnated with mineral substances
in great variety . . . which tinge the water of the river and im-
part to it a nauseous odor and taste." (*CW,* 1:552–53)

In contrast, Rodman contemplates vast prospects and Edenic delights
on his journey that are deliberately, if conventionally, literary. It is sublimity for which Rodman yearns and which the narrative suggests may
be the proper "cure" for his "hereditary hypochondria." He is "possessed with a burning love of Nature; and worshipped her, perhaps,
more in her dreary and savage aspects, than in her manifestations of
placidity and joy" (*CW,* 1:524). These are typical Poe sentiments, as are
Rodman's descriptions of this nature in its cultivated, often Asiatic, aspects: "The prairies exceeded in beauty any thing told in the tales of the
Arabian Nights. On the edges of the creeks there was a wild mass of
flowers which looked more like Art than Nature" (*CW,* 1:542). The aura
of romance in the nature Rodman encounters is elsewhere described as
a landscape that "rather resembled what I had dreamed of when a boy,
than an actual reality" (*CW,* 1:543). And of an island in the Platte River,
Rodman writes: "The whole bore a wonderful resemblance to an artificial flower garden, but was infinitely more beautiful—looking rather like
some of those scenes of enchantment which we read of in old books"
(*CW,* 1:543). Such romantic passages depart notably from the plain style
of Lewis and Clark, as well as of their sergeant, Gass, in their descriptions of the country traversed on the expedition.[19] Lewis and Clark
comment repeatedly on the "vanishing" Native American, usually attributing the diminution of certain tribes and disappearance of others to
warfare among tribal peoples, rather than to the effects of French,
British, and U.S. colonialism disrupting Native Americans and provoking
warfare. But Lewis and Clark's early version of the Myth of the Vanishing American never suggests that the Native American's "savagery" is
"unnatural" within the paradise of North American wilderness. Poe's romanticism adds another dimension to an ideology that had indeed developed in perverse sophistication, albeit of a very fantastic sort, in the
thirty-five years separating these historic and fictive expeditions.

Like Patrick Quinn's reading of *Pym* as "imaginary voyage" and Jean
Ricardou's reading of it as a *textual voyage,* so "The Journal of Julius Rodman" appears to be headed in the direction of some unrealized poetic
displacement of the "factual" voyage. In the course of this displacement, Rodman must pass *through* the primitive "nature" represented by
Toby and the Sioux, as well as the treacherous landscapes with which the
latter are identified, to reach the poetic domain that would be fully under
his control (and the poetic authority of his true master, Edgar Allan

Poe). Such a poetic will to power is very much the equivalent of an emerging commercial power over new territories, such as John Jacob Astor's, which Poe clearly admires both for its progressive qualities and for its refunctioning of an older, feudal hierarchy. The happy jig danced by the guileless and powerless Toby is matched by the inability of the Teton Sioux to read signs properly, like that of the bronze deck cannon that destroys one quarter of their number in punishment for their igno-rance. The enforced illiteracy of the African American and the predomi-nantly oral cultures of Native Americans exclude them from the appre-ciation of that higher Nature available only to Poe and his educated readers.

Some evidence of this narrative intention to move from a treacher-ous, primitive nature toward a poetic, transcendental Nature is provided by the "remarkable cliffs" Rodman encounters in the last chapter of the unfinished "Journal." Like the chasms on the island of Tsalal, these western cliffs are "of the most singular appearance" and possess "a very regular artificial character." Composed of "very white soft sandstone, which readily receives the impression of the water," the face of these cliffs "is chequered with a variety of lines formed by the trickling of the rains upon the soft material, so that a fertile fancy might easily imagine them to be gigantic monuments reared by human art, and carved over with hieroglyphical devices" (*CW*, 1:573). For Rodman, they "had all the air of enchanted structures, (such as I have dreamed of,) and the twitter-ing of myriads of martins, which have built their nests in the holes, . . . aided this conception not a little" (*CW*, 1:573). Not surprisingly, these cliffs affect Rodman with emotions of sublimity: "It left upon my mind an impression of novelty—of singularity, which can never be effaced" (*CW*, 1:574). The projection of romantic fantasies on the actual land-scape of the West is typical of frontier writing from the earliest explor-ers to the present day, so I do not wish to single out Poe as unique in this regard.[20] Nevertheless, Poe's romantic extremity, especially as it mani-fests itself in exotic Middle Eastern and Asiatic imagery and settings, contributes to the tendencies of explorers, frontier writers, and natural scientists to exoticize, romanticize, and Orientalize the West.

These dreamlike, psychic topographies are familiar in Poe's writings, of course, but they have rarely been connected with what I have termed Poe's *imperial fantasy*. When reread in terms of the colonial and racial rhetoric in "The Journal of Julius Rodman," these features become far more visible in Poe's poetic landscapes. In "A Tale of the Ragged Moun-tains," which Poe published in *Godey's Magazine* in April 1844, the narra-tor sets Bedloe's experience of the transubstantiation of souls in the hills southwest of Charlottesville, Virginia—in the region "where [Poe] had lived as a student at the University of Virginia"—and uses rhetoric remarkably similar to that in "The Journal of Julius Rodman" (Silverman, 207). Loaded up with his morning dose of morphine, still under the hypnotic suggestion of his physician, Dr. Templeton, Augustus Bedloe strolls into the "chain of wild and dreary hills . . . dignified by the title of the Ragged Mountains," which legend associates with "the uncouth and fierce races of men who tenanted their groves and caverns" (Mabbott, 3:942, 943). Like Julius Rodman, Bedloe is a wealthy young Southerner, who betrays all the personality traits of the imaginative and poetic character. Like Pym and Rodman, Bedloe enters a dreamlike region where he is "the very first and sole adventurer who had ever penetrated its recesses" (Mabbott, 3:943). What Bedloe discovers in this "singular" and "novel" place is a spiritual and temporal passage from Virginia to the mysterious Orient. Stumbling on a "wild man" pursued by "a huge beast . . . a hyena," Bedloe next finds himself gazing down upon "an Eastern-looking city, such as we read of in the Arabian Tales, but of a character even more singular than any there described" (Mabbott, 3:943–45). This place turns out to be the holy Indian city of Benares on the Ganges, and Bedloe has been transubstantiated into the spiritual place of a British officer, Oldeb, who fought on the side of Warren Hastings, the East India Company's governor of Bengal from 1771 to 1784, against Cheyte Singh, the raja of Benares (the modern city of Varanasi).

Poe's description of the dreamscape of Benares is a conventional Orientalist fantasy in nineteenth-century Western literature, including "wildly picturesque" houses, "millions of black and yellow men," a "wilderness of balconies, of verandahs, of minarets," abundant "bazaars," turbans, beards, graceful maidens, "idols," and "elephants gorgeously caparisoned" (Mabbott, 3:945). The fantastic appearance of Benares in the hills southwest of Charlottesville condenses the "wildness" of primitive peoples of the North American continent, including Native Americans and African Americans, with the European fantasy of the "sensuous riot" of the "mysterious" East.[21] The coincidences between this Orientalism and Rodman's "first" expedition across the Rocky Mountains are instructive because they involve the connection between colonial and racial issues. Bedloe's South, like Rodman's West, is contaminated by people of color—red, yellow, and black—who are immediately recognized as natural enemies by both characters. Just as Rodman fires on the Sioux without any real provocation (they have demanded his stores of whiskey and tobacco, but they are waving spears at Rodman and his men, who are floating in the middle of the Missouri River), so Bedloe finds himself magically transported into the combat of

British officers and sepoys against a "rabble pressed impetuously upon us, harassing us with their spears, and overwhelming us with flights of arrows" (Mabbott, 3:947).[22]

Bedloe's soul mate, Oldeb, whose name the narrator will learn is the mirror image of Bedloe's (without the *e*), dies fighting in a remote and apparently obscure Indian colonial skirmish that nonetheless has considerable significance for the United States, in which Poe has fantastically resituated this battle. When France allied itself with the colonies in the American Revolution against Great Britain, there were global consequences. In India, Warren Hastings took over the direction of military affairs in Bengal and virtually eliminated French influence in India by consolidating British holdings. To finance what amounted to a series of local wars, Hastings demanded contributions from Bengali rajas, especially Chait Singh, the raja of Benares, who was deposed by Hastings after resisting such colonial extortion. In his dream, Bedloe finds himself with the British troops and sepoys "driven to seek refuge in a species of kiosk," from which he "perceived a vast crowd, in furious agitation, surrounding and assaulting a gay palace that overhung the river. Presently, from an upper window of this palace, there descended an effeminate-looking person, by means of a string made of the turbans of his attendants" (Mabbott, 3:947). This episode is described in the manner of a story out of *The Arabian Nights*, the source both for Bedloe's vision of the Eastern-looking city in the Ragged Mountains and for Rodman's sublime vision of the western prairies along the upper reaches of the Missouri. Bedloe's personal physician, Dr. Templeton, will soberly explain to him that his dream has its solid basis in historical fact and that his double, Oldeb, was in fact Dr. Templeton's dear friend, killed in "1780 . . . during the administration of Warren Hastings." As Dr. Templeton reconstructs the history of that battle in which Bedloe "dies" again:

> You have described . . . the Indian city of Benares, upon the Holy River. The riots, the combats, the massacre, were the actual events of the insurrection of Cheyte Sing, which took place in 1780, when Hastings was put in imminent peril of his life. The man escaping by the string of turbans, was Cheyte Sing himself. The party in the kiosk were sepoys and British officers, headed by Hastings. Of this party I was one, and did all I could to prevent the rash and fatal sally of the officer who fell, in the crowded alleys, by the poisoned arrow of a Bengalee. (Mabbott, 3:949)

The "poisoned arrow" of the East Indian is doubled by the "poisonous sangsue" that Dr. Templeton mistakenly applies as a "medicinal leech" in his effort to cure Bedloe of the illness induced apparently by his dreamy struggles in Benares of 1780. In typically pseudoscientific manner, Poe provides us with a "Nota Bene," in which he explains: "The poisonous sangsue of Charlottesville may always be distinguished from the medicinal leech by its blackness, and especially by its writhing or vermicular motions, which very nearly resemble those of snake" (Mabbott, 3:950). Apparently playing on the Hindu belief that to die in Benares assures a Hindu release from endless rebirths, Poe has Bedloe and Oldeb "die" two deaths, one in Benares and the other in Charlottesville, that apparently close the cycle of this very Western version of the Hindu transmigration of souls.

Poisoned arrows and poisonous snakes, "millions of black and yellow men," beards, turbans, temples, and colonial skirmishes fill out Poe's Orientalist fantasy, but the precision of his historical events is unusual amid the huge volume of xenophobic Western writings about the exotic and mysterious Orient. Like the counterrevolution I have argued elsewhere that Dupin stages in "The Purloined Letter," so the dramatic action of "The Ragged Mountains" revolves around the very precise efforts of Warren Hastings to secure British colonial mastery in India over France in the period of the French alliance with the American Revolutionaries, offering a further explanation for why Poe substitutes the Anglo-American Rodman for the more characteristic French trappers of the 1790s in the region of North America described in "The Journal of Julius Rodman" (Rowe, *At Emerson's Tomb*, 48–62). Poe clearly represents Hastings as a heroic figure, victimized by the "insurrection" of the raja of Benares, when in fact Hastings's effort to extort financial support from the Bengali rajas for his colonial ventures in India would be a major cause of his impeachment by the House of Commons in May 1787 on charges of oppression, cruelty, bribery, and fraud while he was the governor of Bengal.[23] Just as Rodman identifies himself with the commercial or "free-trade imperialism" of John Jacob Astor and the American Fur Company, so Hastings is associated with the East India Company's rule of India. Whether or not Poe connects consciously the colonialism of Rodman and Astor with that of Bedloe/Oldeb and Hastings, there are clear thematic connections that establish what I would term an *imperialist unconscious* in Poe's writings. Horsman points out that despite the anti-British sentiments in the United States of the 1840s, fueled in part by conflict over the Oregon Territory, British imperialism *outside* North America was often viewed favorably in U.S. popular culture. In such contexts, "British imperial power could be viewed" not as "resistance to American desires but [as] a general triumph of the Anglo-Saxon race" (Horsman, 227).

Three other significant details link "A Tale of the Ragged Mountains" with the unfinished "Journal of Julius Rodman." First, the near-"hieroglyphic" markings in the cliffs toward the end of the "Journal" suggest the usual poetic transmigration Poe typically effects in his pseudofactual narratives, such as *The Narrative of Arthur Gordon Pym*. In a similar fashion, the mirror image of the two names, "Bedloe" and "Oldeb," suggests that the *real* transmigration of souls is effected by means of the *poetic journey* that the "educated" author, always from a "good family" and properly descended from his European (usually English) forebears, directs for his grateful readers. Second, the name "Bedloe" is not significant just for its reversal of "Oldeb"; it also is the name of the island in New York Harbor where Fort Wood was established in 1841, only three years before Poe published "A Tale of the Ragged Mountains."[24] The fortifications of the British East India Company and those of an ideal United States are rhetorically linked in the name, suggesting a "destiny" for an American imperium that would follow the racist and aristocratic values represented by Rodman and Bedloe. Hindu reincarnation and the migration of souls are mere superstitions typical of "primitive" peoples of color, whether red or yellow or black. Poe's repeated judgment that these peoples are variously deformed, ignorant, or effeminate is obviously part of the racial and gender hierarchies of nineteenth-century Western culture, typified in its extreme form by the proslavery rationalizations and xenophobia of white Southerners. History "repeats itself" only by that appeal to "tradition" that is best achieved by the "culture" sustained by authors who represent such ruling-class values. In such contexts, it is difficult, if not impossible, to distinguish Poe's verbal plays, his literary hoaxes, his outright plagiarisms, and his unreliable narrations from the mystification and rationalization of racial and imperial ideologies of the period.[25]

Third, Dr. Templeton's role in "treating" both Bedloe's body and his soul recalls the entanglement of romantic and scientific interests in Rodman's response to the sublimity of the prairies. This combination of science and poetry pervades Poe's writings, inspiring and organizing *Eureka: A Prose Poem* (1848), whose bizarre mixture of astronomy, astrophysics, and poetic fantasy constitutes Poe's unique response to the conflict between empiricism and idealism in romantic philosophy. It is also characteristic of Dupin, that "algebraist of Paris," whose triumphs over the police prefect demonstrate the superiority of Poe's ratiocinative poetics over empiricism. Soberly declaring that Bedloe's experience is not merely "a dream," Templeton concludes, "'Let us suppose only, that the soul of the man of to-day is upon the verge of some stupendous psychal discoveries'" (Mabbott, 3:948). Mabbott claims that Templeton is referring here to metempsychosis, as if the transmigration of souls might be possible if the combination of morphine, hiking, physical conditioning (or lack of it), and storytelling were somehow just right! (Mabbott, 3:952 n. 18). More relevant to my thesis is the conclusion that Bedloe's "fantasy" assumes a pseudoscientific credibility by way of Dr. Templeton, who thus legitimates for the first-person narrator, and thus for Poe's ideal reader, the claims to imperial superiority worked out in the historical precedent and its poetic representation.

It is thus not just the conventionality of Poe's racist and imperialist fantasies that we should condemn but also the extent to which Poe has employed his undisputed powers as a creative writer to weave such fantasies into what has for so long been appreciated for its aesthetic qualities. Dr. Templeton is a conventional delegate of the canny Poe, and the reader's experience of Poe's manipulation of him or her is not that different from a dose of Dr. Templeton's morphine. To be sure, "The Journal of Julius Rodman" has never been judged as "great art," even by Poe's most dedicated readers, but "A Tale of the Ragged Mountains" enjoys a modest reputation as a "realistic treatment of the supernatural [that] was rarely done better by Poe" (A. H. Quinn, 401). What should interest us are the ways Poe's enthusiasm for racism and imperialism, especially as he finds his own poetic way to participate in their new forms, infects even his most famous tales. In "Poe, Antebellum Slavery, and Modern Criticism," I suggested how the racism and colonialism in *Pym* may be read as well in "The Purloined Letter" and "The Man of the Crowd." I will conclude this chapter by suggesting that the same rhetoric may be found in "The Murders in the Rue Morgue," which appeared just a year after "The Journal of Julius Rodman," in *Graham's Magazine*, of April 1841, and in "Hop-Frog" (1849).

Kim Hall has shown how seventeenth-century European narratives of travel to Africa frequently identify African peoples with apes and both people and apes with their predilections for theft and mimicry. In works like Edward Topsell's *History of Four-Footed Beasts and Serpents* and Thomas Herbert's *Account of the Cape of Good Hope*, we find early formulations of "racial traits" based on fantasies of the identification of humans with animals that would be elaborated in the pre-Darwinian evolutionary theories proposed by Baron Cuvier in the first two decades of the nineteenth century (Hall, 120–44).[26] Hall points out that these identifications are by no means exclusively *African*, although they are all linked in her argument with an incipient European colonial ideology; Herbert, for example, compares Africans "both with Apes and [with] the already colonized Irish" (125). Topsell also describes human features that resemble those of apes in terms that reflect moral and behavioral qualities: "Men that have low and flat Nostrils are Libidinous as Apes that attempt Women, and having thicke lippes the upper hanging over the neather, they are deemed fooles, like the lips of Asses and Apes" (Topsell, 4). Topsell calls particular attention to the "lustfull disposition" of the various kinds of apes and monkeys he includes in his seventeenth-century "history" (13). Interestingly, he attributes the power of speech to apes, even though it appears to be merely linguistic imitation without rational understanding:

> And as the body of an Ape is ridiculous by reason of an indecent likeness and imitation of man, so is his soule or spirit. . . . A certaine Ape after a shipwracke swimming to lande, was seene by a Countrey man, and thinking him to be a man in the water, gave him his hand to save him, yet in the meane time asked him what Countrey man he was, who answered he was an *Athenian*: well, saide the man, Doost thou know *Piraeus* (which was a Port in *Athens*) very well saide the Ape, and his wife, friends and children, whereat the man being moved did what he could to drowne him. (4)[27]

In her discussion of the racial implications of the orangutan in "The Murders in the Rue Morgue," Loisa Nygaard points out that the ape is not merely "the perfect suspect, the ultimate 'foreigner' with whom no one need identify"; she also suggests "distant echoes of the slave trade," insofar as the orangutan was "then believed to be one of the closest relatives of the human race" (251). As Nygaard points out, Dupin's "role in this story is not to bring a criminal to justice, . . . but instead to restore the runaway ape to its proper owner, who promptly sells it for a large sum just as he had planned. Poe, himself a Southerner and a supporter of slavery, defended it on the basis of the private individual's right to undisturbed enjoyment of his property."[28] Although he draws no conclusions regarding the ideological consequences of Poe's use of the orangutan in "Murders in the Rue Morgue," Shawn Rosenheim interprets the ape as Poe's "own myth of human origins, which condenses within itself both individual and evolutionary history" (*The Cryptographic Imagination,* 83). Combining Nygaard's and Rosenheim's observations, I would conclude that Poe enacts in "Murders in the Rue Morgue" his own myth of human, linguistic, and social origins by *distancing* himself, his art, and his fictional double, Dupin, from the racialized savagery and animality of the orangutan.

Dupin's solution of the mystery depends crucially on his ability to resolve the disagreement among those overhearing voices in the hall at the time of the crime about the language spoken by the party responsible for the "shrill voice." As it turns out, those overhearing the voices of the French sailor and his orangutan are respectively English, Dutch, French, German, Spanish, and Italian, suggesting the cosmopolitanism of Paris as a new global capital, and they variously identify the language of the "shrill voice" in terms of languages with which they are respectively unfamiliar. Dupin himself entertains the possibility that the "foreign language" misidentified by these witnesses might in fact be a non-European language, "the voice of an Asiatic—of an African" (Mabbott, 2:550). But Dupin quickly sidesteps this reasonable possibility by claiming: "Neither Asiatics nor Africans abound in Paris; but, without denying the inference, I will now merely call your attention to three points. The voice is termed by one witness 'harsh rather than shrill.' It is represented by two others to have been 'quick and *unequal.*' No words—no sounds resembling words—were by any witness mentioned as distinguishable" (Mabbott, 2:550).

Once again, the "solution" to a Poe mystery revolves around language use, and the specific solution begins with Dupin commanding the narrator: "Read now . . . this passage from Cuvier," in which a "minute anatomical and generally descriptive account of the large fulvous Ourang-Outang of the East Indian Islands" is given, including the animal's "gigantic stature, . . . prodigious strength and activity, . . . wild ferocity, and . . . imitative propensities" (Mabbott, 2:559). Nygaard contends that neither Cuvier nor the American translation of Cuvier by Thomas Wyatt that Poe most likely used mentions the "orangutan's alleged 'ferocity' or 'prodigious strength'" (254).[29] Rosenheim argues that "in Poe's version the description of the orangutan virtually reverses Cuvier's actual claims," concluding from this that "Poe's intellectual allegiance to Cuvier was subservient to his need to magnify the melodramatic and gothic aspects of the murders" (*Cryptographic Imagination,* 74). In McMurtrie's abridgment and translation of Cuvier, the orangutan "when young, and such as he appears to us in his captivity, . . . is a mild and gentle animal, easily rendered tame and affectionate" (Cuvier, *The Animal Kingdom,* 44). Despite Poe's liberties with Cuvier, however, the latter provides plenty of pseudoscientific "evidence" to suggest superficial affinities between the orangutans and human beings: "Of all animals, this Ourang is considered as approaching most nearly to Man in the form of his head, height of forehead, and volume of brain" (44). Unlike earlier naturalists, Cuvier makes no claim for the orangutan's powers of speech, but he does stress its propensity to imitate human behavior: "[H]e is enabled by his conformation [to human physical characteristics] to imitate many of our actions, but his intelligence does not ap-

pear to be so great as is reported, not much surpassing that of the Dog"
(44). What Poe borrows from Cuvier are just those "primitive" and
"savage" qualities that he would attribute to the Teton Sioux and to the
"millions of black and yellow men" in his fictional India. Rosenheim
concludes that "Poe finds in [Cuvier's] mode of analysis an analogue to
his own technique of detection," thereby establishing a connection between Poe's verbal and Cuvier's zoological analyses (*Cryptographic Imagination*, 73). What links Cuvier's natural and Poe's semiotic sciences, finally, is their shared commitment to Enlightenment rationality and its
inherently imperialist imaginary.[30] What appeals to Poe is Baron Cuvier's
pseudo-evolutionary classification of human types in the manner of animal species, as well as the flagrant Eurocentrism of his taxonomies of
the human.[31]

With remarkable frequency, Poe racializes masters and servants, even
when no strictly regional or realistic purpose is served. In "Hop-Frog"
(1849), Poe appears to identify with the dwarf, Hop-Frog, who rebels
against the tyrannical king and his ministers after the king abuses Trippetta, a female dwarf and Hop-Frog's "sworn friend." Hop-Frog's ingenious and apparently just rebellion involves disguising the king and his
seven ministers as "eight chained ourang-outangs," in part by covering
them with tar and simulating fur with flax (Mabbott, 3:1350–51). Although Poe normally associates mob actions, such as tar and feathering,
with the breakdown of reason and thus proper class hierarchies, in
"Hop-Frog" he justifies rebellion by means of a fictional masquerade, in
which false rulers are made to reveal their true natures—dark beasts—
and suffer appropriate punishment. By the same token, Poe compares
Hop-Frog with a monkey on several occasions and announces the climax of the dramatic action with the grinding noises made by his "fang-
like teeth" (Mabbott, 3:1353).

The secret savagery of illegitimate rulers differs, however, from the
monkey-like mimicry of their fool, Hop-Frog. Identifying his own poetic wit with the dwarf's ingenious and implacable revenge, Poe *appropriates* antimonarchical sentiments and open rebellion to serve his own profoundly authoritarian values. Like Dupin in open competition with
Minister D——, Poe usurps another's formal power by turning his own
trickery against him. In the end, the king and his ministers have been
doubly blackened, both by the tar and by the fire Hop-Frog sets to them,
leaving "eight corpses" swinging in "their chains, a fetid, blackened,
hideous, and indistinguishable mass" (Mabbott, 3:1354). What Hop-Frog
has properly "mimicked" in his monkey-like fashion is just the "hideous" moral "blackness" and "savagery" of the tyrannical king. The
"masquerade" staged to testify to the king's authority (for "some grand

state occasion—I forget what") becomes instead testimony to the power of artistic disguise, thus rendering the nominal ruler "savage" in comparison with the artist and his delegates, Hop-Frog and Trippetta (Mabbott, 3:1347). Yet, for such an imaginary usurpation to occur, Poe must "blacken" his antagonist, as well as disguise him as a orangutan, whose figurative significance for Poe is worked out in even greater detail in "The Murders in the Rue Morgue."

The razor-wielding, imitative, ferocious, and prodigiously strong orangutan of "The Murders in the Rue Morgue" acts out a racist fantasy regarding civilized women—Madame and Mademoiselle L'Espanaye—brutalized by "savages" incapable of "proper speech," lacking the linguistic competence of those "Caucasians" classified by Cuvier as the group that "has the most highly civilised nations" (Cuvier, *The Animal Kingdom*, 40). At the end of his classification of the orangutan, Cuvier distinguishes the "*Simia troglodytes*" of Linnaeus, or "The Chimpasé," to which Cuvier attributes very human social organization and behavior: "It inhabits Guinea and Congo, lives in troops, constructs huts of leaves and sticks, arms itself with clubs and stones, and thus repulses men and elephants; pursues and abducts, it is said, negro women, etc."[32] Like the black cook in the mutiny in *Pym*, the orangutan in "The Murders in the Rue Morgue" enacts a fantasy of slave insurrection loosely tied to Southern white hysteria regarding Nat Turner's Southampton insurrection in 1831 and the more general anxiety of antebellum Southerners that the immoral system of slavery might well provoke bloody revolution.[33] In "Hop-Frog," this overt racism is more subtly shifted to include false authority, such as the tyrannical king represents, and in Poe's imitations of frontier narratives, such as "The Journal of Julius Rodman," such poetic racism includes Native Americans who "contaminate" the otherwise romantic moonscape of the West.

The racial connotations of Poe's rhetoric are today perfectly readable, despite the neglect of them by several earlier schools of scholarship, and they have cultural significance not only for Poe's Southernness but also for the emerging imperial ambitions of the young nation, which frequently imitated the British imperium even as the United States was already trying out variations of its own "free-trade imperialism." Poe's writings do not restrict racial hierarchies to the antebellum South or to class and caste systems of nineteenth-century British imperialism. Poe's nominally fantastic, Gothic narratives actually help destabilize racial categories, even as these narratives rely on many conventional pseudo-scientific accounts of racial identity. Yet by confusing the customary referents for racial superiority and inferiority on the American frontier, in the British Empire, and in the slaveholding South, Poe helped popularize

the sort of ambiguity of racial difference that would enable new hierarchies to emerge in the aftermath of slavery as complements in the "conquest" of the West, U.S. imperial ventures in the Caribbean and the
Philippines, and even the assimilative work of modern immigration. Of
course, racism does not in and of itself constitute imperialism, but Poe's
representations of racial differences generally refer to hierarchies of
peoples and cultures that help legitimate historically specific ventures of
U.S. territorial expansion and cultural appropriation or removal.

Many frontier writers commonly relied on racial hierarchies, as well as
flexible racial stereotypes, to rationalize U.S. imperialism, but in his aesthetic practice Poe more ingeniously dramatizes the rhetorical superiority that allows his concept of the modern author to be prototypical of
Euro-American superiority over "savage" mimicry. Some critics might
argue that Poe effectively parodies the rhetoric of exploration and conquest, thereby escaping the taint of imperial legitimation associated with
the rhetoric of the frontier and detective narratives in his era. To be sure,
Poe did not invent the conventions of such narratives: they derive from
a pervasive and diverse ideology of conquest and racial superiority. But
Poe's apparently harmless parodies and hoaxes actually allow such popular discourses to recirculate in high culture, often relying on the original's
racial hierarchies. Like so many racial or ethnic jokes, Poe's parodies do
not mitigate the stereotypes on which they rely for their laughter but
deepen them.

Lacanian and other poststructuralist interpretations of Poe's writings
have interpreted them ingeniously as narratives that anticipate modern
psychoanalytic accounts of the linguistic differences essential to psychic
experience. Yet these same critics miss the ideological consequences of
the psychic and linguistic origins Poe has offered us. Long before the
modern psychiatrist promised to cure patients by understanding the psychic logics of their stories, Poe played with the gendered and racialized
"bodies" he believed were effects of the language of which he was master. Crucial for any imperial authority was the establishment of racial and
gender hierarchies that increasingly would be judged by one's relative
command of a "linguistic competency," whose arbitrary standard and
curious genealogies were maintained by such heralds of the American
Empire as Edgar Allan Poe.[34]

Notes

1. See Rowe, *At Emerson's Tomb: The Politics of Classic American Literature,*
where I argue that the historical issue of Poe's position on slavery and the poststructuralist interpretation of Poe as modernist are related questions. Poe's an-

ticipation of modernist conceptions of the ironic, canny, and masterful "author" may well be motivated by his own ambitions to control words, narrative, and readers in the ways antebellum Southern aristocrats controlled cultural traditions, property, and slaves.

2. See also Sundquist, "The Literature of Expansion and Race," 145–46; Pollin, "Introduction" to "The Journal of Julius Rodman," writes: "'Rodman' . . . more nearly resembles a verbal collage than any other work by Poe" (*CW,* 1:512), but as I shall argue in this chapter Poe uses his sources to attain recognizably distinct Poe effects. In his "Notes and Comments" to "The Journal of Julius Rodman," Pollin provides an authoritative account of just which passages Poe used from these sources, and it is clear that the principal sources, in order of their frequency and length are the 1814 *History* of the Lewis and Clark expedition, Irving's *Astoria,* and Irving's sequel, *The Adventures of Captain Bonneville.* See also Kime, "Poe's Use of Irving's *Astoria* in 'The Journal of Julius Rodman.'"

3. Pollin, "Introduction" to "The Journal of Julius Rodman," points out that there were to be twelve chapters and each chapter was equivalent to a monthly installment of *Burton's* for 1840. Only six chapters were published in the January through June 1840 issues of the magazine. The chapters were to follow a "predetermined route: to the West across the Rockies, up to the Yukon, and back to the starting point of Kentucky or Missouri" (*CW,* 1:508–9).

4. Silverman also points out that while "editing *SLM* [*Southern Literary Messenger*]—which published several defenses of slavery during his editorship—Poe several times commented incidentally on slavery, in one case praising the antiabolitionist strain in Robert Montgomery Bird's novel *Sheppard Lee*" (484 n.).

5. Pollin, "Notes and Comments," "The Journal of Julius Rodman," points out that 1784 is exactly the date John Jacob Astor emigrated to the United States as recounted in Irving's *Astoria* (*CW,* 584–85 n. 1.2A). For connections between Rodman and Astor, as well as between Poe's "Journal of Julius Rodman" and Irving's *Astoria,* see later discussion.

6. Pollin argues plausibly that the "area which Poe designates [as unexplored] corresponds roughly to what is today the Yukon Territory," and the plan for the final chapters of "The Journal" included the extension of Rodman's travels all the way to the Yukon, improbable as this plan was in light of the fact that Poe has not managed to get Rodman and his party past the Rocky Mountains by the end of chapter 6 (*CW,* 1:590 n. 1.7–8A). Nevertheless, it would be absurd to take Poe too literally in regard to what he means by "unexplored territory" in this work. Like his other imaginary voyages and literary hoaxes, "The Journal of Julius Rodman" merely plays with such historical "facts" for the sake of rhetorical and poetical effects. To be sure, the Yukon Territory would have served Poe reasonably well to pit U.S. and British interests against each other, but the Oregon Territory, mentioned frequently in the "Journal," is far more relevant to the actual struggles for British or U.S. hegemony in Poe's 1830s.

7. Thomas Jefferson, "Memoir of Meriwether Lewis," in Meriwether Lewis and William Clark, *The History of the Lewis and Clark Expedition,* ed. Elliott Coues, vol. 1 (1893; Rpt. New York: Dover Publications, Inc., 1950), pp. xv–

xxxiii, which includes Jefferson's original instructions to Lewis, pp. xxiii–xxxiii. Further references to the Coues edition in the text.

8. The Oregon Territory was not established formally until President James K. Polk signed a bill to organize the vast area between the forty-second and forty-ninth parallels, the Rockies and the Pacific, on 14 August 1848, two years after the border dispute had been settled with Canada.

9. Pollin notes that Poe "appears to be forgetful or heedless of the Spanish hegemony in the 1790s over . . . Louisiana, which was trying to divert all trade, including that in furs, to New Orleans" (*CW*, 1:599 n. 2.1C). It is hard to imagine that Poe would "forget" something so obvious to U.S. citizens in the first decades of the nineteenth century as Spanish colonial influence in Louisiana up to 1800 and in the other areas of the Western Hemisphere. I think Poe is simply *ignoring* the Spanish, much in the manner that other Americans between 1830 and 1850 would judge Spanish colonialism in the Americas to be "decadent"—as Melville does in *Benito Cereno* (1855)—and thus doomed to be overtaken by the English and the United States, with the French playing a supporting role. For a fuller account of this demonization of Spanish colonial rule in the Western Hemisphere in this period, see Horsman, 229–48.

10. The term *free-trade imperialism* was developed by Ronald Robinson and John Gallagher in "The Imperialism of Free Trade" and is discussed at length as "the theory of free-trade imperialism" in Wolfgang J. Mommsen's *Theories of Imperialism,* 86–93.

11. Irving mentions this plan in *Astoria*, although he trivializes it: "It was a part of the wide and comprehensive plan of Mr. Astor to establish a friendly intercourse between these islands [Hawaiian Islands] and his intended colony [Astoria], which might, for a time, have occasion to draw supplies thence; and he even had a vague idea of, some time or other, getting possession of one of their islands as a rendezvous for his ships, and a link in the chain of his commercial establishments" (47).

12. Elliott Coues expanded the 1814 Biddle edition of Lewis and Clark's journals, relying on many sources unavailable to Biddle, but Coues included in brackets the original pagination of the Biddle edition and termed his own version "A New Edition" of Biddle's *History of the Expedition under the Command of Lewis and Clark to the Sources of the Missouri River, thence across the Rocky Mountains and down the Columbia River to the Pacific Ocean, performed during the Years 1804–5–6, by Order of the Government of the United States.* Like some character in a Poe story, Meriwether Lewis died in 1809 under mysterious circumstances, either murdered or a suicide, while on his way to Washington, D.C., having done little since his return from the West to prepare his much-awaited journals of the expedition for publication. Rodman's "melancholic hypochondria" may be modeled after Lewis's manic-depressive personality.

13. Interestingly, Jefferson first proposes the expedition by Michaux and Lewis to "the American Philosophical Society" as a "subscription," rather than a publicly funded enterprise. Pollin points out that Michaux was prevented from accepting Jefferson's mission, not because of what Jefferson terms "'botanical

inquiries' pursued 'elsewhere'" but because he was "given (with Stephen Drayton) charge of the filibustering expedition organized by 'Citizen' Genêt, minister of France, in 1793, against the Spanish government of Louisiana" (*CW*, 1:587–88 n. 1.3A). Unfortunately for my argument, Poe seems utterly ignorant of Michaux's paramilitary, colonial ventures in Louisiana Territory.

14. The references to Jonathan Carver, André Michaux, and Washington Irving are part of Poe's effort to transform the physical journey into a literary voyage. Carver's exploration of the old Northwest Territory was less important than his popular *Travels through the Interior Parts of North America in the Years 1766, 1767, and 1768*, which was published in London in 1778 and went through four translations and more than thirty editions. Michaux's botanical works were also well known in the early nineteenth century: *Histoire des chenes . . . de l'Amerique septentrionale* (1801) and *Flora boreali-americana . . .* (1803).

15. Pollin suggests rather improbably that Laurence Sterne's "Uncle Toby" influences Poe's choice of name, but Pollin acknowledges that Toby's "grotesque appearance and whimsical behavior" are typical of what Poe "usually associated with blacks and even with the 'hybrid' Dirk Peters" in *Pym* (*CW*, 1:604 n. 2.9A). Pollin also notes Poe's use of the name for "Toby Dammit," the foolish character who loses his head in Poe's satire of Transcendentalism, "Never Bet the Devil Your Head" (1841), but this seems less probable as an affinity with the African American Toby, despite Poe's racialization of Toby Dammit's response to violent abuse as a child: "he grew so black in the face that one might have mistaken him for a little African" (Mabbott, 2:623).

16. *The People, Respondent, v. George W. Hall, Appellant*, Supreme Court of California, 4 Cal. 399; 1854 Cal. LEXIS 137. I am citing the text of this decision from the electronic legal archive: (http://lexis-nexis.com). I am grateful to Kay Collins, U.S. government information librarian at the University of California, Irvine, for helping me obtain a transcript of this 1854 decision.

17. It should not be forgotten that the irrational and contradictory racist arguments of the Supreme Court of California were used to reverse the judgment of murder against George Hall on grounds that the Chinese witnesses' testimony could not be admitted in a "white" court, leaving Hall's "cause remanded."

18. In a long footnote to the 1893 edition, Coues connects York and his gossip back in St. Louis after the expedition, when he was freed, with the "famous old hoax of a nation of bearded, blue-eyed, and red-haired Indians on the Upper Missouri," which is traceable at least back to the 1760s (1:159 n. 31). Poe gives no indication that he was familiar with such myths, but it is unlikely he would have introduced them in his narrative in any connection with the obviously degraded African American character of Toby.

19. Sergeant Patrick Gass kept his own journal of the Lewis and Clark expedition, which he published in 1807. Coues characterizes Gass as "an intelligent and observant person of very limited education," and his journal as "a plain, straightforward, and connected account" (Coues, "Bibliographical Introduction," 1:cxvii).

20. For example, in the 1880s John Wesley Powell's chief geologist, Clarence Edward Dutton, lavished Oriental names on significant landmarks in the Grand Canyon, as Wallace Stegner points out in *Beyond the Hundredth Meridian: John Wesley Powell and the Second Opening of the West*: "The fixed binoculars at the lookout points will, for a dime, bring you close up to the Hindoo Ampitheater, the Ottoman Ampitheater, Vishnu's Temple, Shiva's Temple, the Temples of Isis and Osiris, . . . the Tower of Set, named by Moran on Dutton's example, . . . and Krishna Shrine and Rama Shrine" (196).

21. For Betsy Erkkila's complementary reading of Poe's Orientalism in his poetry, see chapter 2, this volume. The locus classicus in Western thought for such Orientalism is Hegel, whose interpretation of Hinduism and its social and artistic representations stresses the essential anarchy and failure of abstract thinking in this religion's panoply of gods. See Hegel, 1:332–70.

22. The rhetoric of "The Journal of Julius Rodman" is replete with references to Sioux "infesting" the landscape and other terms suggestive of disease and natural deterioration, as in the passage quoted earlier regarding the "foul-smelling" waters in the vicinity of the Sioux. To be sure, the Teton tribe lived in the vicinity of the geothermal marvels of Yellowstone, but Poe's purpose here seems hardly to be to take notice of such natural wonders but instead to provide a psychic landscape for these demonic, warlike, and dangerous "freebooters." Irving also treats the native peoples of the West as thieves and "pirates," commenting that the "Sioux Tetons were at that time a sort of pirates of the Missouri, who considered the well freighted bark of the American trader fair game" (*Astoria*, 141). Irving also repeatedly refers to the Plains in oceanic metaphors to reinforce the reader's impression that the frontier resembles the oceans by which modern America will pursue "free trade."

23. Hastings was eventually acquitted on 23 April 1795, although he had been financially ruined by the long-running trial. He was, however, given an annuity by the East India Company that allowed him to live comfortably for the rest of his life.

24. Now known as Liberty Island, where Frédéric A. Bartholdi's Statue of Liberty was placed in 1885.

25. Loisa Nygaard makes this same point at the beginning of her essay: "But the problem with Poe's works goes beyond the unreliable narrator to the unreliable *author*. Poe as a writer was fascinated by what he called 'mystification,' by duplicity, obfuscation, manipulation" (223).

26. I am grateful to Kim Hall for discussing her research with me during her lecture on this topic at Irvine.

27. Elsewhere, describing the baboon, Topsell writes: "They cannot speake, and yet they understand the *Indian* language" (11).

28. Nygaard footnotes here the infamous review of James Kirk Paulding's *Slavery in the United States* and *The South Vindicated from the Treason and Fanaticism of the Northern Abolitionists (Southern Literary Messenger*, April 1836), as if this review were indisputably the work of Poe. For my discussion of this controversy and

its relevance to the discussion of race and imperialism in Poe's writings, see *At Emerson's Tomb,* 42–51.

29. Mabbott identifies Wyatt's 1839 compilation of Cuvier as the text that Poe read (Mabbott, 2:573–574 n. 35).

30. Horsman claims that Johann Friedrich Blumenbach's "fivefold division" of the human species was "the basis of the work of most influential writers on race in the first half of the nineteenth century," but he notes that Cuvier's "threefold division" also had "great importance" and influence (47–48).

31. Cuvier's classification is hierarchical, and "The First Order of Mammalians" is "Bimana, or Man," which he organizes in order of the "three races . . . very distinct—the *Caucasian* or white, the *Mongolian* or yellow, and *Ethiopian* or negro" (40). The Caucasian has given rise to "the most highly civilised nations, and those which have generally held all others in subjection," whereas "great empires have been established by" the Mongolian, but its "civilisation . . . has always remained stationary" (40). For Cuvier, the "Negro race" is composed of "hordes" that "have always remained in the most complete state of utter barbarism" (40). In his reading of Poe's tale, Rosenheim in no way connects Poe's uses of Cuvier's natural science with their ideological consequences for nineteenth-century European and U.S. conventions regarding race.

32. The McMurtrie edition and abridgment of 1834, cited earlier, does not include the passage regarding chimpanzees' tendencies to "abduct" women. I am citing here from Baron Georges Cuvier, *The Animal Kingdom, Arranged after its Organization; Forming a Natural History of Animals and an Introduction to Comparative Anatomy*, trans. and adapted to the present state of science by W. B. Carpenter and J. O. Westwood, 44.

33. On antebellum Southern hysteria regarding slave insurrections around the world, see Sundquist, *To Wake the Nations,* 146–51, 210–20.

34. On the relation between gender and racial hierarchies in Poe, see Dayan, "Amorous Bondage," (109–43). On Poe's biographical and literary fantasies of dismembered women, see Silverman, 515 n.

CHAPTER 4

Poe, Persons, and Property

JOAN DAYAN

> For when it is now clear beyond all dispute, that the
> criminal is no longer fit to live upon the earth, but is to
> be exterminated as a monster and ban to human so-
> ciety, the law sets a note of infamy upon him. . . .
> He is then called attaint, *attinctus*, stained, or blackened.
> William Blackstone, *Commentaries on the Laws of England*

In an unforgettable passage of *Discourse on Colonialism* (1955), Aimé Césaire, obsessed by the fecal motives implicit in the rule of law, reflected on the colonies as a safety valve for modern civil society. But he warned that, inevitably, the pristine locale purged of barbarism turns into "a receptacle into which there flow all the dirty waters of history" (45). Edgar Allan Poe's preoccupation with what is pernicious, dark, and deadly might be qualified somewhat more cautiously as his attempt to make his tales those circumscribed places that would contain what his society deemed monstrous and unfit. Let us take Césaire's dirty flood and all-encroaching dunghill as an apt image for theorizing Poe's recycling of persons and property, the way his characters portray again and again the waste products, the residue, the outcasts excluded from the privileges and immunities granted citizens in the nation's legal order.

Which Poe character enjoys life and liberty, and at what cost? Who in Poe's tales pursues and obtains happiness and safety, and for how long? What kinds of property are acquired and possessed, and for what purpose? I do not intend to answer these questions point by point, but rather to offer a reading of Poe that depends on understanding the particular kind of degradation and defilement that mattered to him, the sense of crime and punishment that made his writing an alternative version of life and death in antebellum America.[1] Emancipated, or rather ejected, from the circle of citizenry, disdained, wandering, and known by a baptismal or false name only, these narrators generally suggest that we recognize how persons and privilege might be compromised or threatened by forbidden love, perverse will, or other kinds of disabilities made literal in tales of disease, domination, and duress: "The Masque of the Red Death" (1842), "The Pit and the Pendulum" (1842), "The Man That Was Used Up" (1839), "The Tell-Tale Heart" (1843), "Ligeia" (1838), and "Berenice" (1835), to name just six of Poe's meditations on incapacitation.

Both "The Masque of the Red Death" and "The Pit and the Pendulum" are fictions of containment, depending for their effects on what Poe praised in "The Philosophy of Composition" (1846) as "a *close circumscription* of space." Both were published in 1842, the same year that Charles Dickens made his visit to Eastern Penitentiary in Philadelphia. Known popularly as "Cherry Hill," the prison was immortalized by Alexis de Tocqueville and Gustave de Beaumont in their *On the Penitentiary System in the United States* (1833) as the locale for "absolute solitude," which "destroys the criminal without intermission and without pity; it does not reform, it kills" (5). The "Philadelphia System," operating according to the prescripts of utter seclusion, justified separate confinement as the method most certain to protect criminals "from mutual pollution" or "fatal contamination" (23). No doubt the severity of this penal reform, which depended for its effectiveness on a Gothic architecture both costly and imposing, led Beaumont and Tocqueville to conclude: "Whilst society in the United States gives the example of the most extended liberty, the prisons of the same country offer the spectacle of the most complete despotism" (47).

On 8 March 1842 Dickens visited Eastern Penitentiary. He had written Poe two days earlier, answering positively Poe's request for an interview. Whether they met before or after Dickens's visit to the prison he would later describe in *American Notes* (1842) as a monument to "solitary horrors," where men are "buried alive; to be dug out in the slow round of years; and in the meantime dead to everything but torturing anxieties and horrible despair," remains uncertain (Dickens, 101).[2] What can be argued, however, is that Poe's decors of lavish, medieval ornament, gates of iron, crenellated towers and picturesque effects, premature burials, and the singular torments of narrators who experience unnatural solitude and dark phantoms owe their force to his knowledge of the excesses of the Pennsylvania System of prison discipline. Living in Philadelphia from 1838 to 1844, a city infatuated with prisons and the numerous theories concerning them, Poe had ample evidence of the material apparatus that both guaranteed and maintained the phantasm of criminality essential to the American project.[3] The restraints of continuing solitude proved to be more corrective than corporeal punishment. Though critics of the Pennsylvania "separate system," popularly known as "the discipline," called it inhumane and unnatural, numerous Quaker reformers argued that criminality called for expiation and that only secret punishment and ignominy could compel repentence. In his "Letter on the Penitentiary System," Roberts Vaux, chief spokesman for the Philadelphia Prison Society and later on the Board of Commissioners that erected Eastern State, insisted that separation and silence were the only cures for the polluting threat of those whose "unrestrained licentiousness renders them unfit for the enjoyment of liberty."[4]

Sites of crime and corruption regulated by varying containment strategies would figure in tales as disparate as "The Fall of the House of Usher" (1839), "The Tell-Tale Heart," "The Black Cat" (1843), and "The System of Doctor Tarr and Professor Fether" (1844). The Gothic locale of the last is a cross between a plantation and a madhouse, with patients thinking themselves teapots, donkeys, cheese, frogs, or pinches of snuff—delusions of depersonalization that Poe knew to have their source in the thorny legal discourse of slaves as chattel. For Poe, prison, madhouse, and plantation were synonymous in "treating" those who, once branded as nonpersons, have forfeited all claims to individual rights.

I am less interested, however, in Poe's fictions of containment and architectures of surveillance than in his reimagination of civil life in the nineteenth-century United States, which for him meant disclosing how the law operates both forward and backward along a temporal continuum to exclude, subordinate, and annihilate. Whether depicting orangutan, prosthetic general, Parisian grisette, mummy, corpse, or criminal, Poe uses these materials to reflect on the status of persons and property. In other words, in fictions of law Poe expressed the stigma or taint that deviously could be made the cause of negative personhood: the "captive" whom Orlando Patterson, quoting Claude Meillassoux in *Slavery and Social Death* (1982), described as "marked by an original, indelible defect which weighs endlessly upon his destiny" (38). For Poe, the law engendered the stigma that became an indelible truth, a mandate for perpetual incapacity, while the cunning violence of legal inquiry ensured that these marks were something other than—and somehow unrelated to—the laws that stigmatized them.[5]

Poe's fiction frames a particular understanding of the law, which, like his "Poetic Principle," is the ideal construct, the place of beauty, harmony, and consistency. But, as happens throughout Poe's stories, that form is eroded from below by something akin to the atmosphere of Usher's domain—a "pestilent and mystic vapor" (Mabbott, 2:400). This power of defilement yields a way to discuss "race," one that complicates an easy alliance of race with blackness, as if the mere mention of the term *race* means we have darkness in tow. For Poe's ability to complicate the issues of human servitude lies not in any narrow delineation of slavery, which was broad and variously applied in the nineteenth century, but in his portrayal of the slippage between degrees of color, gradations of personhood, and the bounds of civility and savagery.

If we begin to look at Poe's characters as legal personalities, we can read many of his tales as concerning (1) the existence of actual as opposed to civil or legal facts, for example, the physical person (solely body and appetite) and personhood (the social and civic components of personal identity); the fact of natural death and the fiction (or metaphor) of civil death; and (2) the supernatural relation of the believer to the dead who do not die, as opposed to the natural and daily relation of the living who are dead, those who have undergone "civil death."[6] Indeed, what has been called "supernatural" might better be termed "intralegal." By invoking the twofold condition of the undead, Poe tackled the problematic status of human materials, the uncertainty in defining a "person legally." In cordoning off certain humans from the bounds of empathy or, more precisely, treating humans as if not accorded the rights or status of persons, but rather as entities located at the margins of civilization, Poe moved the realm of myth or religion into the place of law.[7]

Creatures of Law

In May 1841 a case came before the Columbia, South Carolina, Court of Errors on appeal from the judgment of the circuit court. The question before the court was whether Joyce, a young female slave, had to be returned bodily to the plaintiff or whether the defendant could replace her by paying money damages as remedy for her loss. The decision turned on whether slaves are to be regarded as chattels—things personal and movable, mere merchandise, perishables in the market—or real estate, affixed to or growing upon the land. In this case, Joyce is argued to be no "mere toy" or "snuff-box" but a valuable entity.

> Is there anything in a barren sand hill that could attach a purchaser
> to it, and give it a peculiar and special value that may not be found
> in an able, honest, and faithful slave. It is answered that with the

value of the slave in money, recovered as damages, you may buy
another. Is this true? Can you go into market, daily, and buy one
like him, as you might a bale of goods, or a flock of sheep? (*Young
v. Burton,* 162)

Suddenly infused with nonfungible attributes, Joyce's body became a
new kind of property in law. In law a slave had no legitimate will of her
own and belonged bodily to her owner. As property, a slave could be
bought and sold. As animated property, she could be forced to work like
a domestic animal, but one needing special restraints and care.

What, then, is this species of property? If, in regard to civil rights and
relations, slaves are what constitutional and statute law makes them and
nothing more, then once we enter the realm of feeling or attachment,
these objects of law undergo strange metamorphoses. For on one hand
they must be kept in their proper place of absolute civil nonentity, and
on the other they must be deemed, when it served the needs of the
owner, as a peculiar kind of property: a "creature" that engenders sentiments of friendship, affection, and esteem. To create this special legal
creature, the courts had recourse to fantastic fictions—for example, in
transport a slave "resembled a passenger, and not a package of goods,"
but even this comparison had to be qualified. Slaves were like "dogs,
cattle, wild animals," over which "the carrier has not and cannot have
the same absolute control as over a common package" (*Bailey & als v.
Poindexter's Ex'or,* 148). When lost or stolen, an irreplaceable slave would
be like "'a cherry-stone very finely engraved'" or "'an extraordinary
wrought piece of plate,'" rather than "'diamonds,'" where "'one may be
as good as another. (*Summers & al. v. Bean* 411)'"[8]

Poe returned to Richmond, Virginia, in 1835, after an absence of
eight years. In 1831, Nat Turner, called "General Nat" and compared
with the rebel slave and founder of Haiti Jean-Jacques Dessalines, had
led a failed insurrection some seventy miles below Richmond. The revolt
produced what became known as the Great Southern Reaction, which
ended all talk of emancipation and instead increased the control and disenfranchisement of slaves. Poe knew the chains and coins that accompanied the peculiar institution. In passing by slave auctions in the market
two blocks away from the offices of the *Southern Literary Messenger,* Poe
witnessed the frequent sale of bodies, for the profit in this brand of
property had increased sharply in the 1830s.[9]

In rethinking Poe's highly stylized descriptions of law's power to create new, paradoxical, and often unnatural entities, I recall how, in numerous cases regarding slaves, there were moments when that legal nonde-
script, who had no civil rights to lose, could nevertheless gain qualities

like devotion or attachment at the hands of the definers. The law could, when necessary, create a person out of a thing or, more precisely, give extra-added value and uniqueness to the property item. What kind of being is created by the law when that entity is a slave? Worked at from the outside in: What kind of external world can exist for the object of law? Is lacking the ability to perform a civil act, to count in terms of civil rights and relations, something like losing a soul and keeping only a body, with or without limbs, as the law sees fit?

In *Creswell's Executor v. Walker* (1861), the court considered whether or not slaves, upon the death of their master, had a legal capacity to elect freedom or servitude, having inherited the right to election in testamentary trust. Deciding that a master could not "by his will" give his slaves the power to change by an act of their will their own civil status, Justice Joshua D. Clarke engaged in an alternating process of decreation and reconstitution. In Clarke's primary retraction of personhood, slaves are uncreated insofar as their effects in society:

> So far as their civil status is concerned, slaves are mere property, and their condition is that of absolute civil incapacity. Being, in respect of all civil rights and relations, not persons, but things, they are incapable of owning property, or of performing any civil legal act, by which the property of others can be alienated. (*Creswell's Executor v. Walker,* 233)[10]

In this diagnosis of a state of society, the court announces that the will of the dead master cannot, or can no longer, be given. For the slave cannot choose or elect freedom; if these actions were allowed, the slave would thereby gain a legal personality. For the court this is impossible: "No man can create a new species of property unknown to the law" (233).

But this rhetoric of divestment can be retracted, and in this secondary operation, the slave moves from property to person. What is known to the law, hence, what is possible, is that slaves can be declared human only insofar as they err. The accretion of positive or human qualities, yoked as it is to the fact of property, outfits slaves for one thing only: crime. Their only possible act, recognized by society, is a negative one.

> So far as civil acts are concerned, the slave, not being a person, has no legal mind, no will which the law can recognize. But as soon as we pass into the region of crime, he is treated as a person, as having a legal mind, a will, capable of originating acts for which he may be subjected to punishment as a criminal. (*Creswell's Executor v. Walker,* 236)[11]

As an object of possession or a criminal, this body becomes the vessel for an oddly additive procedure, a surfeit of qualities that juridically make or unmake the idea of the person, who is actually nothing more than a "creature of law."

All of Poe's fiction is about property and possession and moves rhetorically back and forth between the extremes of affect (heartfelt devotion or undying love) and dispassion (cold mutilation or self-absorbed insensitivity). But this engagement with the alternating themes of legally ordained deprivation and recompense gains authority because of his confrontation with the undeniable claims of civil life. Poe plays with the working dichotomy that construes both persons and privilege: not only the opposition between natural (read physical) death and unnatural (read legal) death but also the strategic agenda implied in the distinction between natural rights and civil rights. One can, hypothetically, retain natural rights but still be disabled by statutory abridgment, condemned by societal (or civilized) needs. In the arena of law and rights, the claim for personal rights, like the very meaning of personhood, becomes shifting and tentative, even paradoxical.

The concept of the legal person obsessed Poe, as did similar philosophical inquiries into the constitution of personal identity (Dayan, *Fables of Mind,* 133–84). But he is ultimately concerned with the law, both as an ideology so powerful that it can announce apocalypse in *Eureka* (1848)—that day when matter folds into oneness, or, in his words, the "condensation of *laws* into *Law*"—and as an actuality so pervasive that terror, the raw material of authority, becomes synonymous with the legal instruments of punishment: incarceration, dismemberment, and torture. Legal thought relied on a set of fictions to sustain such precepts as the absolute concept of property and the alternating distinction of slaves as things or persons, depending on whether the context was civil action (as an article of property, utterly deprived of civil capacity) or criminal action (as capable of crime, recognized as a rational being). In both cases, what is legally possible or impossible demands the give-and-take between categories such as contract or tort, public or private, thing or self, physical or incorporeal.

Poe's criminals dabble in the convertibility between or, rather, pursue alternative ways of seeing tangible and intangible, bodies and spirits, persons and property, and, finally, natural and unnatural death. Whether we turn to the ultimate conversion of wife into object in "The Oval Portrait" (1842) or to the many narrators involved in varying kinds of immurements, dismembering, cutting, or turning body parts into fungible commodities, we encounter the perils of possession. Control and enjoyment implicate personhood and will.[12] In "Morella" (1835), "Ligeia," and "Berenice" (1835), the most hallowed days of love and attachment end in hate and repulsion, as these feelings usher in reflections on bodies that return as the living dead. These memoirs of the will to possess become paradigmatic of loss: the dissolution of self, identity, and mind. Berenice, once disabled by mysterious illness, makes inevitable the narrator's obsession and the consequent violation that transforms a once idealized beloved into personal property. Once her person is reduced into nothing but overvalued teeth, those things are taken and boxed, as her body is buried. Poe's women, then, though adored or treasured, are never quite human. Indeed, Poe's obsession with possession, personal identity, and the will—as Ligeia's "will," which is or is not lost with death—is no empty philosophizing or haunting but an appeal to the paradoxes necessary to sustain slavery, to its specific forms of degradation and figurative death. Poe's tales about women enact what it means legally to disable, kill off, or nullify the person in the slave body.

In drawing our attention to legal philosophy and practice, Poe yet demands a way of reading that escapes the binary bind of the racist or nonracist Poe, which, like all antinomies applied to Poe, delimits and distorts his writings. I suggest another kind of analysis, one that moves us into a model of reading embodiment into what otherwise might remain a specter of law, a means by which degradation can be envisioned and imagined, that is to say, interpreted. When I argued that we read "Poe's romantic fictions as bound to the realities of race," I concentrated on the necessary connection for proslavery apologists between ladies, "those rarified vessels of spirit," and brutes, "the negro" ("Amorous Bondage," 243–44). For Poe understood more than any other writer of the American Renaissance that the very separation of these two specimens of "person" said much about how the cult of sentiment allowed the radical denaturing of both women and blacks. I wanted to suggest how deeply Poe understood the terrible knot of complicity, the reciprocity between one who calls him- or herself master and one who responds as slave. Whether or not Poe wrote what has become known as the "Paulding-Drayton" review in the April 1836 issue of the *Southern Literary Messenger* is not my point here, since, in the course of his life, he complicated what might first have seemed his regionalist or apparently proslavery sentiment.[13] As Poe confirmed in "The Black Cat," perfect submission, a black pet loved and owned by an increasingly cruel master, effects a damning conversion: the once benevolent owner utterly bestialized, reduced by the very thing he brutalized.

In 1849, during the last year of his life, Poe wrote his most horrible tale of retribution, "Hop-Frog; or, The Eight Chained Ourang-Outangs." Here, the orangutan murder in the Rue Morgue gets mind and

motive in the person of the enslaved dwarf "from some barbarous region . . . no person ever heard of" (Mabbott, 2:1346). Hop-Frog and
his female companion dwarf Tripetta are war loot, captives turned into
gifts for the cruel king of the story. The king, who likes nothing better
than a good joke, usually at Hop-Frog's expense, underestimates the reasoning powers of his chattel. To the king's joyous "'Hop-Frog! I will
make a man of you,'" Poe invites readers to observe Hop-Frog's literal
dehumanizing of the king and his seven privy councillors. Poe creates a
pseudo-Africa within the sumptuous artifice of the masquerade, setting
the scene for the conversion of masters into slaves. The chained tar-
saturated, flax-covered king and ministers, once turned into orangutans,
"very rarely . . . seen in any part of the civilized world," are hoisted up
between the skylight and the floor, torched, and burned to "a fetid,
blackened, hideous, and indistinguishable mass" (Mabbott, 3:1354).[14]

Disabled but Not Dead

Although Poe recognized the marks of inferiority and degradation im-
pressed upon blacks, he never forgot that racial imperatives like bondage
or servitude did not occupy a place cordoned off from civil society. The
indelible mark of infamy remained a threat to certain individuals no matter their color or the abstract claims for individual rights. In fact, until
ratification of the Fourteenth Amendment, the Constitution nowhere
defined the term *citizen* (Graham, 502–4). Into the same society that
sanctioned the accumulation of money, goods, and land seeped the rot
of surfeit, captured in the stink of the tarn into which the Great House
of Usher ultimately falls. If we take Blackstone's stunning embrace of
property as the "sole and despotic dominion which one man claims and
exercises over the external things of the world, in total exclusion of the
right of any other individual in the universe" (2:2),[15] we find a key not
only to Poe's monomaniacal narrators but also, and more important, to
his obsession with investment, inheritance, descent, and lineage.

A conceptual apparatus that complicates the racial paradigms of
black and white, offering a way of reading race into Poe, should not
oversimplify the tangled plot of Poe's fiction. Let me put it another way:
the forms of law energized the unconditional maintenance of a servile
order, sometimes anchored in but more often unmoored from its racialized episteme in order to resurface, transmuted and terrible, under the
guise of an essentialized criminal agency: socially excluded and civilly
dead.[16]

In a ritual of banishment, William Wilson announces that his real

name has become "an object for the scorn—for the horror—for the de-
testation of my race," describing himself as guilty of "infamy," "outcast
of all outcasts most abandoned!" and utterly dead "to the earth, . . . to
its honors, to its flowers, to its golden aspirations" (Mabbott, 2:426). His
self-abnegation is more than mere hyperbole, for he has portrayed himself as suffering the curse of "civil death," the status of a person who,
having violated societal or positive laws, has been deprived of all civil
rights: *civilter mortuus*, or "dead in law" (Blackstone, 4:374). William Wilson dies not once but twice, as if Poe felt compelled to redouble this fiction of law, to make a fiction twice over, as captured in the doublet
William Wilson. First, he is severed from his family ties and ousted from
organized society; second, facing off his adversary—portrayed as consummate will—he plunges his sword into the breast of his antagonist,
only to see his own blood-dabbled image in the mirror, dying as he murders his shadow self.

The use of this unusual fiction of law to produce the juridical nonex-
istence of the person raised the specter of natural versus artificial.
"Natural persons are such as the God of nature formed us," Blackstone
argued, while "artificial are such as created and devised by human laws
for the purposes of society and government" (1:119).[17] In "Loss of
Breath," Poe's natural man dies many deaths—losing his breath, breaking his neck, being hanged and dissected—but he remains intact as a
civil creature who recalls, records, and constructs his story, as do other
Poe narrators who write their narratives after what should be their natural death.

Existing as a good citizen, however, does have its costs. In "The Man
That Was Used Up," Brevet Brigadier General John A. B. C. Smith has
lost his natural body and voice fighting the Kickapoo Indians. Although
he has lost his natural body, he is remade as artificial public hero, fit icon
of the body politic. Civilly reconstructed each day, all his synthetic body
parts put together by Pompey, his black valet, he literalizes just what it
means to sacrifice the natural and gain those privileges that, though unnatural, yet garner for him life, limbs, body, and reputation (Blackstone,
1:119, 125–28). With each successive body part replaced in pursuit of
something suggestive of a "more perfect union," the general further articulates and ordains his place in civil society, regaining the right to enjoy
his property (both his body and his servant) with each command, with
each insult to the "old negro" on whom he utterly depends. Replete now
with life, liberty, and possessions, Poe's consummate gentleman becomes the person who, in repossessing his body, repossesses the right to
kill, enslave, and dispossess.

With living men regarded as dead, dead men returning to life, and the same man considered alive for one purpose but dead for another, the realm of legal fiction compels us to reconsider the nature of Poe's particular brand of Gothic: a supernatural grounded in the materials, habits, and usages of society, the debates, whether philosophical, historical, or legal, that defined and amplified the claims of the bodies politic. Slaves were judged things: "the slave, not being a person, has no legal mind" for all purposes of civil identity. But, as I have noted, "in the region of crime, he is treated as a person, as having a legal mind" (*Creswell's Executor v. Walker*, 236). Criminals were held alive for the purpose of being sued or charged in execution, but dead insofar as transmitting their estate to their heirs.

How did civil death affect rights of property and privilege at common law? There were three principal incidents consequent upon an attainder for treason or felony: forfeiture, corruption of blood, and the extinction of civil rights, more or less complete. Of Saxon origin, forfeiture was part of the punishment of crime by which the goods and chattels, lands and tenements of the attainted felon were forfeited to the kin. According to the doctrine of corruption of blood, introduced after the Norman Conquest, the blood of the attainted person was deemed to be corrupt, so that he could not transmit his estate to his heirs, nor could they inherit. The incident of civil death attended every attainder of treason or felony (Blackstone, 4:373–81).

The fiction of civil death depends on the belief that so powerful are the rules of civilization and the prescripts of law that one can be dead when alive. Law can make one dead-in-life; further, the law can determine just how dead one is, and when and if one can be resurrected. For William Wilson, once identified as pollutant of what had been a pure and legitimate pedigree inherited through blood, nothing is left to him but his written testament of crimes, debt, degradation, and banishment. Before institutionalized slavery and its codes that depended on the stain or drop of black blood for the biological ignominy that stigmatized persons, thus justifying their status as mere property, there had already existed a grid for producing noncitizens outside the bounds of civil society.

In suggesting that "civil death" juridically sustained the potent image of the servile body necessary to the public endorsement of dispossession, I am aware of the possible caveat that whereas the person declared civilly dead had property to lose, and once convicted of a crime was condemned to a loss of civil rights, the slave never had property, was in fact property, and could never have any relation to property. I am arguing, however, that Poe, in collapsing the two conditions of being or, more precisely, rendering them in tandem, moves us into a model of reading that attends both to the artifices of law and the imperatives of fiction.

There are correlations to be made in these narrations: the thematization of legal authority with unlimited resources at its disposal, those of affirming and negating, acknowledging and ignoring, giving and taking away. It is almost as if with each realization of the legal demand for disability, for certain groups or persons in society—and the juridical redefinition of status and personhood—Poe felt the need for more ingenious expressions of derangement.

Civil death sustained itself through two ruling metaphors: "corruption of blood" or "forfeiture of property." The English common-law fiction of strict civil death, to be "dead in law"—forfeiting property as well as personal rights—though generally rejected as a rule of American common law, was adopted by some states. The U.S. Constitution specifically prohibits forfeiture and corruption of blood except during the life of a person convicted of treason. In addition, civil death was declared not to exist in the absence of an express statute. Yet in the United States civil disabilities—and civil death more or less extreme—continued to play a significant role in the treatment of criminals.

On 29 March 1799, a New York statute was enacted that changed the language of "civil death" from the more lenient common-law wording "shall thereafter be deemed civilly dead" to the more severe "be deemed dead to all intents and purposes in the law" (*Troup v. Wood*, 299; *Platner v. Sherwood*, 127).[18] What are the limits of civil death? "How much of the convict is civilly dead, and how much civilly alive?" as dissenting Judge Earl put it in *Avery v. Everett* [1888], 335. In both *Troup v. Wood* (1819) and *Platner v. Sherwood* (1822), death exists on a continuum: on one extreme, you are alive but have no status at all, a mere cipher; on the other, you are not "dead in fact," as if naturally dead, for you can will your property. In the same Act of 29 March that recast statutory law on civil death as the utter decimation of all civil rights, the legislature set up a system of laws for the gradual abolition of slavery in New York State. Not only is there a structural relation between slavery and civil death, but also, I would argue, civil death statutes became harsher, and more necessary, as the system of domestic slavery was ameliorated.[19]

The idea of civil death remains crucial to our understanding just how monstrous would be the legal annihilation of will, the incapacitation by fiat, the juridical decimation of personhood understood as domestic slavery. For what had been forfeiture of property and corruption of blood—indeed, those few circumstances in which civil death was coextensive with physical death—understood by Blackstone as caused by profession (as in a monk professed), abjuration from the realm (deportation for crime), and attainder and banishment (for treason), became the terms out of which came a new and terrible rendition of legal incapacity.

As Blackstone explained: "The civil death commences if any man be banished the realm by the process of the common law, or enters into religion; that is, goes into a monastery, and becomes there a monk professed: in which cases he is absolutely dead in law, and his next heir shall have his estate" (1:128).

Civil death and the consequent representation of the criminal imprisoned for life as the living dead set the terms for a new understanding of punishment. Though slavery had ended, incarceration had not. I distinguish civil death from other legal sanctions, since this concept and its attendant disabilities maintained both a strictly hierarchical order and the race defilement on which that order depends. Corruption of blood thus operated practically as a severing of blood lines, cutting off inheritance, but also metaphorically as an extension of the "sin" or "taint" of the father visited on his children. If we treat *blood* and *property* as metaphors crucial to defining *persons* in civil society, then it is easy to see how "corruption of blood" and "forfeiture of property" could become the operative components of divestment. By a negative kind of birthright, bad blood blocked inheritance, just as loss of property meant disenfranchisement. Yoked together as they are, these terms loosely but powerfully define types of slavery. Whether applied to the slave or the criminal, both are degraded below the rank of human beings, not only politically, but also physically and morally. How this project of incapacitation continued to threaten the weak and socially oppressed, as well as how old rhetorical strategies initiated new forms of containment is what matters here.[20]

Transmissible Blood

The vestiges of slavery kept civil death alive in the United States. At least, its terms could be easily forced into the service of the ideology that underwrote the complex network of images for civility or savagery, ability or deficiency, naturalness or unnaturalness, slavery or freedom—the very rules for a modern concept of race. It was as easy to deem the extinction of civil rights and legal capacities as punishment for or as socially necessary consequence of the crime of color as it was for the conviction of crime—even easier, perhaps. For color, this appearance of moral essence or transmissible evil, could stand in society as both a threat and a curse or, finally, as justification for the subjugation of those so tainted.

If we make slavery in the Americas our hypothetical still point, we can move back and forth through varying considerations of what kinds of persons would end up being redefined or rendered as dead in law.

The materiality of the slave, analogous to that of the civilly dead felon, links both in their status as unredeemed corporeality.[21] As vessels of corrupt blood, neither houses inheritable blood. In seeking out an idiom of servitude, Poe understood, as did Herman Melville, how the raw material of legal authority could become the stuff of literary fiction. Poe moves us back to a time when a myth of blood conferred an unpolluted, legitimate pedigree ("The Fall of the House of Usher" or "William Wilson," both 1839) and forward to an analytics of blood that ushered in a complex of color: the ineradicable stain, the drop that could not be seen but must be feared ("Ligeia," "The Masque of the Red Death," or *The Narrative of Arthur Gordon Pym* [1838]).

As late as 1864, *Webster's* noted that "[b]y the constitution of the United States, no bill of attainder shall be passed; and no attainder of treason (in consequence of a judicial sentence) shall work corruption of blood or forfeiture, except during the life of the person attainted." How did corruption of blood come to equal forfeiture of property in attainder? When justifications for slavery were needed, no doubt this mysterious conjunction (influenced by its erroneously assumed relation to "taint," hence the idea of "corruption of blood") was appropriated illiberally and indiscriminately. When an innate quality (the unseen blood stain) could result in the conversion of person into property, a genetic trait (seen or unseen) could be substituted with a criminal deed, and the loss and humiliation that followed.

Let me recall the ruses of color in colonial Saint-Domingue, a fiction that has occupied me for some time now. By 1773, the number of *gens de couleur*, especially free women of color, had steadily increased. The necessity to separate materially what had been constituted as two races—and in more extreme cases fantasized as two species—even as they mixed, meant that the very idea of *free* or *freed* had to be transformed or, more precisely, degraded. That intermediate class of persons freed and "lightened" by interbreeding threatened the cause of white identity. New laws were needed to regulate their behavior and thus redefine their status as persons. Further, the curse of color, the sin of the flesh, had to be made indelible through time. In *The History of Jamaica* (1774), Edward Long refers to the Dutch method of experimentation to clarify the perpetuity of a drop of black blood:

> They add drops of pure water to a single drop of dusky liquor,
> until it becomes tolerably pellucid. But this needs the apposition
> of such a multitude of drops, that, to apply the experiment by
> analogy to the human race, twenty or thirty generations, perhaps,
> would hardly be sufficient to discharge the stain. (Long, 2:261)

But "whites" also could be "degenerated" or "disabled." The numerous whites who married women of color were accused of *misalliance* and
hence formed yet another intermediate category, now deployed as that
between whites and people of color. Once descended into the purgatory
assigned to free coloreds, they suffered excommunication from public
life. The lawyer Hilliard d'Auberteuil explained the reasoning behind this
judgment of indelible contagion:

> A white who legitimately marries a mulâtresse descends from the
> rank of whites, and becomes the equal of the affranchis [free
> coloreds]; even they consider him their inferior: in effect this man
> is despicable. Anyone who is so low as to fail himself, is even
> more sure to fail the laws of society, and one is right not only to
> scorn, but furthermore, to suspect the probity of [him] who by in-
> terest or by thoughtlessness, descends so low as to misally himself.
> (2:77–78)[22]

No gift of liberty could remove the contamination of blood, the "ineradicable stain," as Hilliard d'Auberteuil called it.

The rules for turning a person into a thing were thus already prepared
for by a terminology that had assured the connection between the condition of *being attainted* and *having in law stained and corrupted blood*. Once "attainted" was mistakenly derived as if from "taint," corruption of blood
became articulated as the essence of attainder; for example, lawyers
identified the stain or blood taint of a criminal capitally condemned.
This working strategy of domination and control, once materialized in
the taxonomies that quantified blood on a scale of white to black, would
prove too powerful an apparatus to lose. And Poe knew it.

At this point, the metaphorical terrain thickens. I want to offer that
complex ground as a way to reconsider Poe's own "close circumscription
of space" and "predetermined effect." For once declared civilly dead,
the person becomes grotesquely unrecognizable, the inexact or inelegant
but nonetheless effective icon of brute matter. Within the bounds of
numerous tales, Poe dramatizes the barbarism and waste so keenly assured and masked by the claims of civilization. Who gets to be human,
and who gets to be brute? Poe's stories about taint, disability, corruption
of blood, and dispossession are relevant not only to the Fourth and
Fifth Amendments that protect "persons" and "property"—yoked in
the language of each amendment—but also to the extension of a model
of possession that appears in Poe's turns on dislocation, immurement,
and detention.

Poe's fantasies of degeneration or disability, then, are never *only* about the enslavement of the African American, for then he would indeed be guilty of what Theodore W. Allen, in *The Invention of the White Race,* has called "White over Black, innate, ineradicable—a Calvinism of the genes, a Manifest Destiny of the White Soul" (9).[23] Instead, Poe set himself a riskier goal of puzzling over the mysteries of identity, the riddle of bodies and minds that lived during a generation that proclaimed perfectibility and progress but that he knew was steeped in disaffection, servility, and destitution. The rituals of blood accomplished by slavery, the metaphor of stain and corruption so handily embodied in the criminal, were not racially particular. How could they be when Poe understood so well that the legal terminology of disability and blood taint extended the terms of civil death, upward, downward, and for all time? Once surcharged with racial prejudice and market greed, the terms could remain so much a part of the deployment of power that anyone could become a creature of law, something like a synthetic or artificial slave: incapacitated and hence barbaric. For the dead-alive body in flesh and bones cannot forget that blood is everywhere: oozing out of pores in "The Masque of the Red Death," dropping from the ceiling in "Ligeia," and coloring the swamp in "Silence—A Fable" (1832–35).

Notes

An earlier version of this chapter was published in *American Literary History* (Vol. 11, no. 3, fall 1999). I first presented parts of this work at the Tudor and Stuart Club, Johns Hopkins University; the Center for the Study of Black Literature and Culture, University of Pennsylvania; and the Barker Center, Harvard University. In each case, I benefited from stimulating discussions; and I thank the graduate students of Johns Hopkins and also Ronald Paulson, Houston Baker, Doris Sommer, and Randy Matore for making these encounters possible. I thank Dana Nelson and Sharon Cameron for being such sharp critics and demanding interlocutors.

1. Poe often mocks faith in human perfectibility, equality, and progress. In *Democracy in America,* Tocqueville described the rights of private persons subsumed by what he called the "democratic community," "the state," or "modern society": "As the conditions of men become equal among a people, *individuals* seem of less and society of greater importance" (290). As Tocqueville warned that in modern society "everything threatens to become so much alike that the peculiar characteristics of each individual will soon be entirely lost in the general aspect of the world" (328), so Poe complains in both his fiction and his criticism of "the generalizing spirit" or the great and imposing "mass." In "Mellonta Tauta" (1849), from atop a balloon, the blustering Pundita travels through space and time to survey "the habitation of Man," reveling in Poesque ironic

distance: "I rejoice, my dear friend, that we live in an age so enlightened that no such thing as an individual is supposed to exist. It is the mass for which the true humanity cares" (Mabbott, 3:1293). In *Democracy and Punishment: Disciplinary Origins of the United States*, Thomas Dumm describes the discourse of "liberal humanism" and "democratic equality" as preludes to a dangerous, if indirect, subjugation. Although much of Dumm's text is overly dependent on Foucault's cult of discipline, he challenges his readers to rethink how punishment and incarceration not only became critical to the ideology of democracy but also shaped a genealogy of property and possession essential to what he calls "the American project" (6).

   2. Dwight Thomas and David K. Jackson's *The Poe Log: A Documentary Life of Edgar Allan Poe, 1809–1849*, notes 7 March as a possible date: "Poe has 'two long interviews' with Dickens, presumably at the United States Hotel." Dickens's scathing description in "Philadelphia and Its Solitary Prison" and the effects of "this slow and daily tampering with the mysteries of the brain . . . immeasurably worse than any torture of the body" appeared in *American Notes* (99). I am indebted to the work of my student Donald McNutt on Poe, urban space, and incarceration in "Fictions of Confinement: Poe, Dickens, and Eastern State Penitentiary" (in progress).

   3. Finally completed in 1836, this solitary prison with towers, massive front building, and gigantic walls resulted in extravagant expenditures. The walls alone cost $200,000. Before completion, the prison would cost Pennsylvania around $772,000, which raised the price of each cell to more than $1,800. Contemporary descriptions of the prison treated the architectural design as a necessary symbolic reminder of the austerity and grimness of the regimen that awaited the prisoner who entered its walls. The layout owed much to experiments with Jeremy Bentham's panopticon design, where the radial plan (at least hypothetically) made possible total surveillance.

   4. Roberts Vaux, "Letter on the Penitentiary System of Pennsylvania, addressed to William Roscoe, Esquire" (Philadelphia: Jesper Harding, 1827), 9.

   5. In *Dred Scott v. Sanford* (1857), the Supreme Court ultimately ruled that since freed blacks were not citizens within the meaning of the U.S. Constitution, they were not entitled to the privilege of suing in the U.S. courts under Article 3. Chief Justice Roger Brooke Taney asked: "Can a negro, whose ancestors were imported into this country, and sold as slaves, become a member of the political community formed and brought into existence by the Constitution, and as such become entitled to all the rights, and privileges, and immunities, guaranteed by that instrument to the citizen? One of which rights is the privilege of suing in a court of the United States in the cases specified in the Constitution." Although rendered after Poe's death, Taney's argument depends on the collapse of a superior "state of feeling" into a fact of law that proves the degradation of those felt to be so degraded. Freed blacks are not members of the political community of the United States, Taney argues, for an externally imposed stigma is derived from and remains integral to an inherent feature or type. In other words, what René Depestre, in *Bonjour et adieu à la négritude*, called a "somatic semi-

ology" converted a stigma of the skin first into an imaginary essence or racial substance of inferiority, and second into a legal status. Although incomplete as a description of practice, judicial logic is integral as a description of thought, and Poe knew legal artifice as necessary not only to maintaining slavery but also to preserving a social order itself dependent on the ruses of civility and decency. For a discussion of how "a racialized conception of property implemented by force and ratified by law" produced "a peculiar, mixed category of property and humanity," see Harris.

6. I am indebted here to Patterson's discussion of "liminal incorporation" in *Slavery and Social Death*: "Although the slave might be socially dead, he remained nonetheless an element of society. So the problem arose: how was he to be incorporated? Religion explains how it is possible to relate to the dead who still live. It says little about how ordinary people should relate to the living who are dead" (45). In attempting to link what Patterson calls the slave's "social death" to the felon's "civil death" in my analysis of Poe's fiction, I stress how both conditions when brought into relation encode forms of historical memory, the residue of which remains with us still. In October 1998, Human Rights Watch and the Sentencing Project published *Losing the Vote: The Impact of Felony Disenfranchisement Laws in the United States*, explicitly linking "slavery," "civil death," and contemporary disenfranchisement laws "that may be unique in the world": "In fourteen states even ex-offenders who have fully served their sentences remain barred for life from voting." The impact of these laws reminds us that we now face the most radical redefinition of persons and property since slavery in the Americas: "An estimated 3.9 million U.S. citizens are disenfranchised, including over one million who have fully completed their sentences. . . . Thirteen percent of African American men—1.4 million—are disenfranchised, representing just over one-third (36 percent) of the total disenfranchised population" (1–2).

7. I use the term *law* generally here and assume throughout that Poe not only knew Blackstone's *Commentaries*, which appeared in America in 1771–72, but also used his fictions to dramatize the artificial identities construed in such legal fictions as civil death, human property, and the mind, will, and reason of the slave that can be decimated in law. A favorite text in the antebellum South, Blackstone's *Commentaries* appeared in a new edition by St. George Tucker in 1803. According to Robert M. Cover, in *Justice Accused: Antislavery and the Judicial Process*, "More than 1,000 textual footnotes updated the law, and more than 800 pages of appendices, consisting of essays, refuted or supplemented the *Commentaries* on major issues" (37). For a discussion of the demand for Blackstone's work and its influence on American law, see Anthony F. Granucci, "'Nor Cruel and Unusual Punishments Inflicted': The Original Meaning": "In 1775 Edmund Burke is reported to have told the House of Commons that almost as many copies of the *Commentaries* had been sold in America as in the whole of England." For a lengthy discussion of Poe's knowledge of Blackstone, see Alterton, 55–60.

8. The court here cites an English case, *Pearne v. Lisle* (19 October 1749).

9. For a lengthy discussion of Poe's return to Virginia and his "racialized gothic," see Dayan, "Amorous Bondage."

10. See also Justice Story in *Emerson v. Howland et al.* (1816): "The owner of the slave has the most complete and perfect property in him. The slave may be sold or devised, or may pass by descent, in the same manner as other inheritable estate. He has no civil rights or privileges" (636).

11. During Reconstruction, with the advent of convict-lease and the chain gang, this logic of control and subordination defined the law of the New South, taking to the extreme the production of nonpersons, now shorn of even the moral and intellectual qualities sometimes granted them as property. No longer the master's creatures, they were criminals newly defined as "slaves of the state." See *Ruffin v. Commonwealth*, 796.

12. The legal relation of master and slave turned on the question of will, as do such Poe tales as "Ligeia," "Morella," "William Wilson," "The Imp of the Perverse," and "The Black Cat," the last of which begins with a discussion of "the spirit of PERVERSENESS" and the longing "to violate that which is *Law*, merely because we understand it to be such." Since civil status referred to property—the power of holding it, using it, acquiring it—as the singular right of the master, the slave remained unknown in law except as the subject of property owned by another. What kind of being, asked the North Carolina Judge Thomas Ruffin in 1829 (*State v. Mann*), could be "doomed in his own person, and his posterity, to live without knowledge, and without the capacity to make anything his own"? Ruffin answered: "Such services can only be expected from one who has no will of his own; who surrenders his will in implicit obedience in the consequence only of uncontrolled authority over the body" (quoted in Cover, 77n, and in Patterson, 3–4).

13. One of the more disappointing developments in Poe studies is the increasingly racialized delimiting of Poe's exploration of the ambiguities of servitude and bondage (something like the unfortunate assignation of "postcolonial" to whatever is not white, not "first world," not Europe). When I argued that Poe wrote the Paulding-Drayton review, I did not mean to assign Poe to the stagnant role of proslavery apologist. Instead, I stressed that Poe, throughout his fictions, especially those written later in his life, sought to question the sureties of both Northern abolitionists and Southern proslavery advocates. For Poe is obsessed with blurring the strategic categorizations that leave, to paraphrase Toni Morrison in *Beloved* (1987), definitions in the hands of the definers. Poe instead analyzes the disabilities—and the codification—that link "the white male writer, the white woman of his dreams, and the ungendered, unmentioned black" (Dayan, "Amorous Bondage," 249).

14. In nineteenth-century America, "to be tarnished with the tar-brush" or "have a touch of the tar-brush" meant having black blood. In the climax of "Hop-Frog," Poe takes the "black drop" of blood and materializes it in the extravagant conversion of persons into property: the masters into a lump of foul matter.

15. If no physical thing was possessed, for example, as with an incorporeal

hereditament, one had to be fictionalized. Throughout the nineteenth century, this set of fictions sustained Blackstone's absolutist and physicalist conception of property.

16. Blackstone's "private self is swallowed up in the public," and this substitution of the "artificial" for the "natural" person is the hinge on which his fiction of civil life turns. Yet the rights protected by law can be curtailed by the death of the person, which can be either civil or natural. For a superb meditation on the fiction of civil death and the demands it makes on interpretation, see Kim Lane Scheppele, "Facing Facts in Legal Interpretation," which came to my attention after I had completed this chapter. Meditating on how the fiction of being dead in law gives the ordinary term *death* a technical meaning that creates a new state, Scheppele clarifies the stakes of law language (especially for those who are the recipients of legal judgments): "What makes fictions *different* from other descriptive terms is that the technical, legal description created by the fiction overrides another ordinary description that is directly contrary to the fictional one. The civilly dead person is actually alive" (58).

17. For an exhaustive discussion of citizenship and social compact theory, and the characters and capacities of citizens from *Dred Scott v. Sanford* to the Fourteenth Amendment, see Douglas G. Smith.

18. See *Troup v. Wood,* 299, and *Platner v. Sherwood,* 127.

19. The Thirteenth Amendment to the Constitution, announced in December 1865, clarifies what I have suggested as a connective tissue linking criminality and race. A discursive link between the civilly dead felon and the slave or social nonperson, it embodied exclusion through a kind of disembodiment, a realm of redefinition where criminality could be racialized and race criminalized. The Thirteenth Amendment outlawed slavery and involuntary servitude "except as punishment of crime where of the party shall have been duly convicted." During the second session of the Thirty-ninth Congress (12 December 1866–1867), debates centered on the meaning of the exemption in the antislavery amendment. Charles Sumner warned that what had seemed "exclusively applicable" had now been "extended so as to cover some form of slavery." He asked that Congress "go farther and expurgate the phraseology from the text of the Constitution itself" (Avins, 258). The legal exception became the means of terminological slippage: those who were once slaves were now considered criminals. Under the guise of apprentice, vagrant, and contract regulations, various states kept blacks in servitude. Thus the burdens and disabilities that constituted the badges of slavery took powerful hold on the language of penal compulsion. A criminal punished with "civil death" became the "slave of the state," enduring both the substance and the visible form of disability, as if imaginatively recolored, bound, and owned. See *Ruffin v. Commonwealth* (1871). This doubling transaction back and forth between prisoner and the ghosts of slaves past allowed that the entity called "citizen" alone be granted the fundamental privileges and immunities guaranteed in Section 1 of the Fourteenth Amendment. Attention to the too-often ignored Thirteenth Amendment would demonstrate how uncertain is the notion of a "constitutional person." Legal practice, as Jus-

tice John M. Harlan understood in his dissent in the *Civil Rights Cases* (1883)—
which analyzes the Thirteenth Amendment at length—depends on this conceptual uncertainty in order to continue to grant only a minimum bundle of constitutional rights to certain categories of persons.

20. For a charting of the trajectory of the concept "corruption of blood"
and the slippage of blood into racial categories, see Dayan, "Legal Slaves and
Civil Bodies," in *Materializing Democracy,* eds., Dana Nelson and Russ Castronovo
(Durham: Duke University Press, forthcoming 2001). Crucial to my concept of
the *"disabled citizen"* remains the process whereby imprisonment became a way
to recreate an image of servility, just as statutory law ensured that the "badges
and incidents of slavery" might continue to exist under cover of civil death.

21. In the slave codes—especially the 1645 Code Noir in the French
colonies—the attention to the limits of physical or bodily punishment and to
the minimal needs of daily survival, food, clothing, and lodging bear an unsettling resemblance to the way the U.S. courts have traditionally interpreted the
cruel and unusual punishments clause in the Eighth Amendment to the Constitution. As Granucci notes in " 'Nor Cruel and Unusual Punishments Inflicted' ":
"It is indeed a paradox that the American colonists omitted a prohibition on excessive punishments [punishment should not be disproportionate to the offense charged] and adopted instead the prohibition of cruel methods of punishment, which had never existed in English law" (847). In recent conditions of
confinement cases, the Supreme Court has adopted the corporal punishment
paradigm: attending to the body, not the intangible qualities of the convicted
criminal. Like the slave whose servile, brute body had yet to be protected
against unnecessary mutilation or torture, the criminal is reduced to nothing but
the physical person, suggesting that the term *human* in the phrase "a single, iden-
tifiable human need such as food, warmth, or exercise" (*Wilson v. Seiter* [1991])
juridically redefines what we mean by human when applied to the incarcerated.
Bodily suffering or the needs of bare survival have become the standards for
Eighth Amendment cases, not psychological pain or the social and civil components of confinement that are responsive to the needs of personhood.

22. See my discussion of codes of law and bodies of color in *Haiti, History,
and the Gods* (219–37).

23. See also Fanon: "[T]he black soul is a white man's artifact" (14).

CHAPTER 5

Black, White, and Gold

LILIANE WEISSBERG

> Two men and blackfella servant, applying human inge-
> nuity, measured paces, and plumb line, crack third-level
> mystery and uncover wealth beyond their wildest
> dreams. Only at story's end does he emerge to shake
> off the fictional spell. "Gold Bug" is the ticket all right;
> he has come to the right place.
>
> Richard Powers, *The Gold Bug Variations*

Coming to the Right Place

Ben Sawyer Boulevard, S.C. 703, connects the mainland with Sullivan's Island, one of several islands located east of the city of Charleston. It is a small stretch of land, a narrow sandbar really, named after a sea captain who made it his home in the late seventeenth century. Now Sullivan's Island boasts a major east-west route, Middle Street, as well as a brief extension of route 703 to the Isle of Palms to the northeast. A number of narrower streets lead to vacation homes facing the intercoastal waterway or the Atlantic Ocean. Toward the Isle of Palms, slightly newer homes appear, built by wealthier vacationers (figure 5.1). The western end, bordering Charleston Harbor, offers a slightly denser street pattern and suburbanized housing for year-round residents. The town hall is located here, and Fort Moultrie, a fortification that had served Charleston Harbor until the end of World War II (figure 5.2).

The western end of the island has been its strategically important part. The fort was first built of sand and palmetto logs in 1776 to shield Charleston from British invaders. Due to hurricane damage, as well as

FIGURE 5.1. Isle of Palms, vacation homes

FIGURE 5.2. Sullivan's Island, Fort Moultrie

the development of new war technologies, it was rebuilt and enlarged several times and was in active use until the mid–twentieth century. Today Fort Moultrie is a museum operated by the National Park Service and the U.S. Department of the Interior; it offers self-guided tours and houses a gift shop with books and other items relating to American warfare. Private homes adjoin the site, as well as a public beach that bears signs warning visitors against littering (figure 5.3). Sunbathers, not battleships, settle today under Fort Moultrie's flag (figure 5.4).

These vacationers may, indeed, continue an older tradition. Already in the late eighteenth century, Sullivan's Island gained significance both as a military outpost and as an escape from the urban summer heat. Tourist brochures available at Fort Moultrie advertise the island as a "summer retreat for Charlestonians since at least 1791" and continue to evoke its history: "At that time the island was accessible only by water and moving

FIGURE 5.3. Sullivan's Island, beach near Fort Moultrie

FIGURE 5.4. Sullivan's Island, sunbather at the beach; Fort Moultrie's flag

families for three months or more was quite an undertaking. Food, linen, silver, clothing, carriages, animals including cows, chicken, etc. . . . had to be loaded into the ferry boat that crossed between Charleston and Sullivan's Island."[1]

Not many traces of this time remain. The denser streets on the western end offer smaller but permanent homes now, and the streets themselves—numbered from north to south, named from west to east—seem newly christened, if not newly planned. Thus, a street bordering Fort Moultrie has been named after a soldier who was stationed here for one brief year, from November 1827 to December 1828, and is called Poe Avenue. Through the middle of the island run roads that memorialize a poem and a story written by this same soldier, Edgar Allan Poe: the idyllic Raven Drive and the much longer Goldbug Avenue (figures 5.5 and 5.6).

Goldbug Avenue divides Sullivan's Island into north and south; like a traffic route mimicking the Mason-Dixon Line, it transverses the dunes. In Poe's tale "The Gold-Bug," it is east and west, however, that separate the island into contrasting spheres. In the west, Poe situates the more densely populated area around Fort Moultrie, but in the east, he describes a mere wilderness. The eastern and western parts that Goldbug Avenue connects show little resemblance to the areas that Poe depicts in his story. His eastern island landscape offers its heroes a sense of isolation that was hardly experienced by travelers in his time, but it also reflects a geography and vegetation more dramatic than that of the actual place. Poe renders his vision in great detail:

This Island is a very singular one. It consists of little else than the sea sand, and is about three miles long. Its breadth at no point exceeds a quarter of a mile. It is separated from the main land by a scarcely perceptible creek, oozing its way through a wilderness of reeds and slime, a favorite resort of the marsh-hen. The vegetation, as might be supposed, is scant, or at least dwarfish. No trees of any magnitude are to be seen. Near the western extremity, where Fort Moultrie stands, and where are some miserable frame buildings, tenanted, during summer, by the fugitives from Charleston dust and fever, may be found, indeed, the bristly palmetto; but the whole island, with the exception of this western point, and a line of hard, white beach on the seacoast, is covered with a dense undergrowth of the sweet myrtle, so much prized by the horticulturists of England. The shrub here often attains the

FIGURE 5.5. Sullivan's Island, Raven Drive

FIGURE 5.6. Sullivan's Island, Goldbug Avenue

height of fifteen or twenty feet, and forms an almost impenetrable coppice, burthening the air with its fragrance. (Mabbott, 3:806–7)

In his notes to Poe's tales, Thomas Ollive Mabbott insists on the existence of an indigenous kind of myrtle (Mabbott, 3:845 n. 3), although Poe's description of the flora and fauna here and elsewhere in the tale does not quite agree with any possible firsthand experience: "[H]e took liberties with fact in his description," Mabbott allows (Mabbott, 3:845 n. 2). Whereas Mabbott tries to correlate the actual geography or information available about Poe's stay on the island to the narrated scenery, and synchronizes his perspective with that of Poe and of his narrator and hero, Jean Ricardou insists on a wide gap between the real and the imagined, textual landscape. In his essay "Gold in the Bug," he warns the reader not to obliterate a literary text by searching for extratextual referents: "It is not hard to imagine to what extent every detail of geographic locality in a piece of fiction can have the effect of satisfying naturalistic dogma: thus localist, fictitious space seems to provide a faithful copy of familiar daily experience" (33). But far from simply creating a textual universe, Poe correlates his newly deserted island with the myth of the discovery of America as an untouched, unpopulated, virgin territory in the sea.

American Notes

There are hardly any traces of historical island life to be found on Sullivan's Island today, but modern homes did not simply replace summer houses on this and the adjoining islands facing the city of Charleston. The reputation of Sullivan's Island was built not just by its fort and its summer accommodations. The Charleston area served as an early and significant emporium for the slave trade, and slaves from West Africa were imported from there to South Carolina plantations, as well as to Georgia and elsewhere.

Nearly half of the Africans who reached the American continent from 1700 to the end of the colonial period probably came through historical Charles Town. Ships ready to enter the bay, however, landed at Sullivan's Island first. In 1707, a brick building known as the "lazaretto," or pest house, was established on the island, and before entering the city's port, ships deposited their human cargo there. Any slaves who had caught a disease on board or even before their journey commenced were supposed to let it run its course on this island first, rather than infect the citizens of the wealthy merchant town five miles across the cove. Thus, Sullivan's Island became the first landing place by law as a site of quarantine for Africans imported from across the sea. After a period of from ten days to three weeks, newly arrived Africans were examined by a health inspector, who approved them for further travel. Those who died en route were thrown overboard, at times close to the island itself, and there were incidents of corpses washing ashore in the bay. Those who found their death on Sullivan's Island were committed to a mass grave (Ball, 89). The port physician described the smell on board the ships as "most offensive and noisome, what for Filth, putrid Air, and putrid Dysenteries,"[2] due to the number of corpses. Sullivan's Island's pest house must have been little better.

In his study of colonial Carolina, Peter H. Wood has called Sullivan's Island the "Ellis Island of black Americans" (xiv).[3] The black population, briefly sequestered on Sullivan's Island, was brought there by force, however, and expected death rather than any form of new American "freedom." These Africans had already seen many of their comrades die even before their embarkation, or later at sea or at the landing point (Weir, 177). Thus, even life in slavery may have come as a surprise to many. At first, ships reached Sullivan's Island year-round, and many Africans died because of the harsh winter conditions on the island. In later years, as voyage schedules were adjusted, Africans arrived mostly during the summer months. Thus, they were also immediately ready to cultivate plantations and prepare for the coming harvest (Weir, 177).

After their stay on Sullivan's Island, these new immigrants were sold at the Charleston slave market, often to Carolina planters and merchants. About seventy-five thousand slaves remained in South Carolina, where they formed more than half of this colony's population. The slave trade ended in South Carolina in 1788, sealed by a prohibition that initially lasted five years and was soon extended for a longer period. In 1803, however, South Carolina resumed the trade. From December 1803 on, until a lasting prohibition took effect in 1807, about forty thousand new slaves entered the state. Some came to the Charleston area directly from Africa, but most arrived at the Carolina port via England, Rhode Island, or even France (H. Thomas, 544–45).

Perhaps the greatest danger of a slave insurrection occurred in 1775, at the time of the American Revolution. The governor of Virginia, John Murray, earl of Dunmore, had promised to grant freedom to all slaves who would take the British side. The new royal governor to South Carolina, Lord William Campbell, arrived in Charleston in the summer of 1775 and reported home to England about the white citizens' anxieties about weapons possibly stored by blacks on a nearby ship: "Words . . . cannot express the flame that this occasioned amongst all ranks and degrees; the cruelty and savage barbarity of the scheme was the conversation of all companies" (Ball, 219). A council of safety was formed to evacuate the islands in the case of an approach of the enemy—the American colonials—but by September, Campbell could not hold his stand. He formed a flotilla of three ships close to Sullivan's Island, which now constituted the king's last domain in the Charleston area. Many slaves who had heard about Murray's declaration now fled to Sullivan's Island and took over the pest house, recruited new arrivals there, and tried to reach the ships. By December 1775, five hundred slaves had fled to the island and built their own village. The chair of Charleston's council of safety, Henry Laurens, demanded that Colonel William Moultrie, after whom Sullivan's Fort would later be named, seize and apprehend the fugitive slaves and burn the pest house. Disguised as Native Americans with feathers and face paint, fifty-four soliders entered the island on 19 December, killing many fugitives and burning their houses. Shortly after this violent invasion, Campbell departed for England, carrying on his ships a number of freed slaves (Ball, 210–21). For a few months, the Sullivan's Island pest house became a symbol of black freedom, but this freedom ceased even before the American Declaration of Independence. The young soldier Poe, stationed in Moultrie's fort many decades later, must have learned of the pest house's history and the soldiers' "heroic" act.

While Sullivan's Island changed in the 1790s from a forced summer quarantine for blacks to a voluntary summer retreat for whites, the islands elsewhere in the Charleston area flourished agriculturally. With the farms and plantations established on them, the islands near the city acquired their own distinct history. Until the end of the seventeenth century, Africans had been in a minority on the island plantations where they provided labor for the white colonists. Around 1700, these Africans numbered about 3,000 compared with 3,800 Europeans; in 1708, the numbers were almost equal: 4,100 Africans against 4,080 Europeans. The figures of the African population grew decisively, however, in the following years. By 1720, there were 11,828 Africans compared with 6,525 Europeans, and by 1740, 39,155 to 20,000 (Wood; Mufwene, "Africanisms in Gullah," 160–61). The expansion of the African population was largely due to the increased importation of slaves, rather than natural population growth (Mufwene, "Africanisms in Gullah," 163). The plantation owners, who came mostly from England's South, imported Scotch and Irish laborers as well, however.

When South Carolina became a crown colony in 1720, segregation became institutionalized (Mufwene, "Africanisms in Gullah," 161). After 1740, the importation of African slaves was reduced, and more and more European workers were brought in—among other reasons, to provide a balance to the African majority. But the plantations developed more and more into institutions that were populated largely by blacks from specific West African regions, and this majority could preserve traces of West African and Mande languages and traditions perhaps better on the islands than anywhere else. It advanced its own culture (Mufwene, "Africanisms in Gullah," 164).[4] White landowners who moved away to other properties left plantations behind that were soon run by blacks who viewed the Sea Islands as their own "free" territory. The customs of the islands' population derived from those of its white and black laborers, as did the Gullah language, still spoken by some island inhabitants today.

For the authors of Fort Moultrie's tourist map and brochure, the history of Sullivan's Island emerges separate from the culture of these other islands; the island itself is described as an uninhabited space, to be frequented by Charlestonians during the summertime. These citizens, presumably, were at least moderately wealthy, and they possessed linen, table silver, and substantial leisure time. The same characteristics of privilege are also notable for the hero of Poe's story "The Gold-Bug," even though the landscape its hero is eager to enter appears as an utter wilderness. Far from being a slave port or a summer residence for wealthy citizens, Poe's island emerges as a place for adventure, and it offers housing for a world-weary hermit of illustrious lineage, William Legrand.

Story Time

At first, therefore, history is inscribed not in the landscape but in the protagonist's genealogy. Legrand seems to be socially acceptable, a member of an "ancient Huguenot family" (Mabbott, 3:806) that unfortunately had lost its wealth. Considering the historical circumstances, Legrand does not appear to be an unusual figure for many wealthy descendents of Huguenot families populated the Charleston area in the eighteenth century. Henry Laurens, the dominant slave trader of the mid–eighteenth century and the erstwhile chair of Charleston's security council was of Huguenot descent. A colorful figure who in later years withdrew from active slaving, he entered politics, became president of the Continental Congress, and finally, during the Revolutionary years, was peace commissioner in Paris (H. Thomas, 268–70).

Indeed, Legrand resembles one of Poe's other characters, the Parisian aristocrat C. Auguste Dupin, who is praised in the author's "tales of ratiocination" for the reasoning power and imagination with which he solves mysteries. Legrand's "greatness," in turn, is reflected by his name, "Le-grand." He never travels without a servant, an "old negro" (Mabbott, 3:807) and former slave, whose name seemingly signifies greatness as well. The servant is called Jupiter, like the omnipotent god of Roman and Western mythology. Poe thereby alludes to the condescending practice of giving slaves imposing names, thus introducing an element of the burlesque.[5] Jupiter not only obeys his "Massa Will" (Mabbott, 3:807) but is also employed by Legrand's family to serve as a kind of guardian to his master, who is afflicted by melancholy. Legrand, who favors the isolation of "natural" surroundings, moves to Sullivan's Island as a result of his depressions and also to seek remedy. Wilderness, as a place beyond language and history, offers a return if not to innocence, then to an imagined presocial origin of mankind.

That life in isolation includes a servant, however. Jupiter accompanies his master and lives with him in an improvised hut. They discover a pe-

culiar golden bug, as well as a piece of paper that reveals, largely by acci-
dent, a drawing of a skull rendered in invisible (though if exposed to
heat, black) ink. Added to the drawing is a message written in cryptographic script that Legrand deciphers as the location of a secret treasure.
The drawing of a goat—a kid—hints at the person who hid this treasure
many years ago. Is this the pictographic signature of the famous pirate
Captain Kidd? Legrand discovers a rock from which a skull in a tree becomes visible, and he asks Jupiter to climb the tree and drop the bug
through one of the skull's eye holes. After measuring a calculated cir-
cumference from that point of impact on the ground (and after digging
once in vain), Legrand discovers a chest filled with jewelry and gold.
French, Spanish, German, and English coins—no American ones—are
gathered here like foreign tongues, familiar to the discoverer and reader
only because of their common material value.

Legrand's obsession with the beetle, the drawings, and the cryptographic script and his roamings through the island's wilderness have left
doubts in the narrator's as well as Jupiter's mind in regard to Legrand's
sanity. His discovery of the treasure, on the other hand, inspires a new
respect for his ingenuity. Captain Kidd's stolen goods restore Legrand to
wealth, and wealth is returned to its "proper" owner. After having been
reduced to doing his own digging, Legrand can now abandon all labor
and become a proper—that is, rich and nonworking—master again.

In Legrand's search for this treasure, and the translation of the code
into the island's geography, Jupiter serves as a commentator, critic, and
comic figure whose own wit questions Legrand's readings but also discovers clues. Jupiter's words and the narrator's attempt to capture them
serve as a counterexample to cryptography. Jupiter's language, too, is a
repertoire of codes, to be deciphered not only by Legrand or the narrator but also by the reader. Jupiter's dialect and turns of phrase match
Captain Kidd's endeavors and reveal, moreover, their meaning. The
heavy and rare gold bug, Legrand's prize find, turns thus, for example,
into a "goole bug" and a ghoulish monster:

> "Yes, massa, Jup climb any tree he ebber see in he life."
> "Then up with you as soon as possible, for it will soon be too
> dark to see what we are about."
> "How far mus go up, massa?" inquired Jupiter.
> "Get up the main trunk first, and then I will tell you which way
> to go—and here—stop! take this beetle with you."
> "De bug, Massa Will!—de goole bug!" cried the negro, drawing
> back in dismay—"what for mus tote de bug way up de tree?—
> d——n if I do!"

"If you are afraid, Jup, a great big negro like you, to take hold
of a harmless little dead beetle, why you can carry it up by this
string—but, if you do not take it up with you in some way, I shall
be under the necessity of breaking your head with this shovel."

"What de matter now, massa?" said Jup, evidently shamed into
compliance; "always want for to raise fuss wid old nigger. Was
only funnin any how. *Me* feered de bug! what I keer for de bug?"
Here he took cautiously hold of the extreme end of the string,
and, maintaining the insect as far from his person as circumstances would permit, prepared to ascend the tree. (Mabbott,
3:818)

The bug aids the fortune hunt mainly by its physical weight and by the
mere association with a golden treasure. Its ghoulish nature may indeed
be part of a joke. The gold bug is of uncertain value; it is a surplus not
really needed to gain wealth in the end. But while Captain Kidd's cryptography provides a riddle that has to be solved, Jupiter's revelatory
speech turns the story into a comedy in which Legrand responds in slap-
stick manner only. The narrator is made to realize the difference between
Sein and *Schein*, between the "big negro's" statements and his fear and
trembling. Jupiter has to be taken at his word and, at the same time,
should not be taken at his word. His body betrays his assertions. The
punishment of this body serves as a response to Jupiter's resistance or
unwelcome statements, just as Jupiter would threaten to beat Legrand if
he appeared insane:

"Keeps a syphon wid de figgurs on de slate—de queerest figurs
I ebber did see. Ise gitting to be skeered, I tell you. Hab for to
keep mighty tight eye pon him noovers. Todder day he giv me slip
fore de sun up and was gone de whole ob de blessed day. I had a
big stick ready cut for to gib him d——d good beating when he
did come—but Ise sich a fool dat I hadn't de heart arter all—he
look so berry poorly." (Mabbott, 3:812)

In what can only be described as a carnivalesque reversal, here the slave
assumes the position and pose of a master. That position—the imitation
of a masterly act that is no "proper" behavior for a (former) slave—
appears at the core of another one of Poe's tales, "The Murders in the
Rue Morgue," where the threat of imitation is turned into "reality." In
that gruesome story, the position of the slave as master is taken by an
ape, whose language, more so than even Jupiter's speech, baffles all listeners as "foreign."[6] Words, not coins, are collected here. They are com-

mented upon in newspaper accounts as testimony about the perpetrator's speech, and they evoke a babel of tongues—although they also serve the solution of the crime. The ape, who is thought by each witness to speak a different language unknown to him or her, proves to be a foreigner to the human race itself.

At the time Poe's story "The Gold-Bug" was published in the *Dollar Newspaper* in 1843, the depiction of black servants in fiction or drama was certainly no novelty. But while blacks had become "visible" in texts, these texts did not usually document a servant's words. Servants, and perhaps especially black ones, were marked by their silence. Their actions or utterances were translated and reported by others. Documenting a black servant's voice could appear in itself as a subversive act, introducing an agent who was otherwise doomed to silence. In "The Gold-Bug," as in many other tales of this time, this voice was not strong enough to guide the plot but rather was intended to fill out spaces, to provide comic relief, to add an additional layer of signification. These servants did not just look different; their blackness also entered their speech, reducing the potential threat of their appearance.

In Poe's body of work, "The Gold-Bug" occupies a unique position because of its extended rendering of a black person's voice. Still, Poe was probably quite aware of previous literary examples. In his reviews, he referred to the works of William Gilmore Simms, who may have been the first American writer to represent a black person's speech in a short story.[7] Simms's first such tale appeared in 1833 and was followed by several others.[8] His black characters come from the same area in which Poe locates his black servant, and they speak the Gullah language (Gonzales, 166; Morris, "Gullah in Simms").

In his study of colonial South Carolina, Wood refers to Poe's tale and describes Poe's Jupiter as a "believable Gullah speaker" (170). Other critics disagree, however. "He was never gifted at the management of dialect," writes the literary critic Killis Campbell, who expands his argument to encompass the entire American scene: "In fact dialect was slow to gain a foothold in America, and certainly there is little in Poe's use of it to commend it" ("Poe's Treatment of the Negro Dialect," 112). But while Campbell's peculiar generalization may excuse the author's failure, he describes Poe's verbal puns simply as "badly managed" speech and as Poe's comments on the "negro's" "exceptional stupidity." Campbell reflects the racial discourse of the 1930s in which his essay was written as he adds: "I can't find anything particularly Charlestonian in the negro's speech in the passage in 'The Gold Bug.' The dialect, such as it is, doubtless is based on the speech of the darky slave as Poe knew him in Richmond and in Goochland County (at 'the Byrd')" (113).

Several linguists question the accuracy of Jupiter's dialect as well. In his study of Gullah, Reed Smith writes: "The peculiar genius that could create 'Ulalume' and 'The Fall of the House of Usher' was not fitted to depict a Negro successfully. Jupiter's characterization, however, is better done than his dialect, which is not so bad for Gullah as it would be if it were an attempt at the upland dialect" (15). Ambrose E. Gonzales is more critical, comparing Jupiter's words not just with those of the island population but also with those of Charleston's inhabitants: "Poe, in 'The Goldbug,' put into the mouth of a Charleston Negro such vocables as might have been used by a black sailor on an English ship a hundred years ago, or on the minstrel stage, but were never current on the South Carolina coast" (12–13). In short, Jupiter's dialect designates him as different, but it does not ground its speaker in a specific geographic and cultural setting.

This may, however, be precisely the point. Poe not only turns an island into a wilderness but also erases all traces of an island population, although he finds a person who is knowledgeable enough to show the narrator a rock that would correspond to an "obsolete word" (Mabbott, 3:840) in Captain Kidd's cryptographic message. In contrast to Campbell's reading,[9] this person does not live on the island, though:

> I was on the point of extending my sphere of search, and proceeding in a more systematic manner, when, one morning, it entered into my head, quite suddenly, that this "Bishop's Hostel" might have some reference to an old family, of the name of Bessop, which, time out of mind, had held possession of an ancient manor-house, about four miles to the northward of the Island. I accordingly went over to the plantation, and re-instituted my inquiries among the older negroes of the place. At length one of the most aged of the women said that she had heard of such a place as *Bessop's Castle*, and thought that she could guide me to it, but that it was not a castle, nor a tavern, but a high rock.
>
> I offered to pay her well for her trouble, and, after some demur, she consented to accompany me to the spot. We found it without much difficulty, when, dismissing her, I proceeded to examine the place. (Mabbott, 3:840–41)

Thus, the island that "consists of little else than the sea sand" (Mabbot, 3:806) acquires not only a peculiarly hilly landscape but also, if only briefly, a history that is preserved in African American memory. Turned into a temporary servant, the nameless and (for the reader) silent old woman remembers, points at a place, and then leaves it to Legrand's scholarly examination. For a short but crucial moment, a woman has entered this tale of adventure, but thereafter, the island is Legrand's again. The woman's recollections, the memory that she preserves, are once more replaced with Legrand's search for Captain Kidd's story—that of a white pirate who used the island as his temporary landing spot and hiding place for stolen treasure, a place presumably valued for its desolation.

Like Kidd, Legrand flees civilization, albeit for a different reason, and on the island itself he and Jupiter find no signs of the "older negroes," just a pirate's mark. Jupiter is newly manumitted and views the island as a territory waiting to be discovered anew. Thus, women have no real place in this adventure tale, in which it suffices to explore, invade, and conquer a virginal landscape. But master and servant have more in common than their gender. Both Legrand, a member of a French immigrant family, and his servant Jupiter are oddly dislocated. Jupiter's particular "dislocation," however, returns him to a ground that must have been familiar to the story's readers, namely, to the tradition of the minstrel show. Jupiter serves to please and amuse his white master, the presumably white narrator, and his presumably white readers. And while some critics have been eager to read Poe's tale as a cryptographic exercise to decipher Kidd's message as a code for gold (Whalen, "Code for Gold"; Rosenheim, *Cryptographic Imagination*) or—as Marc Shell aptly points out—a critique of a new economic system that would eschew solid gold for paper money of dubious value (5–23), the story's other colors have largely been neglected. "The Gold-Bug" is, however, a story not only about a hidden treasure but also about the narrator, Legrand, and his former slave. Incongruously, this slave seems to mimic white behavior and assume the name of a powerful figure in Western, "white" civilization, while playing the role of the black for the white Southerner's imagination.

North And South

Poe's "Gold-Bug" may refer to a specific town and island, but far from just creating referents to an American landscape, the story is also part of a particular American literary tradition of popular stories of adventure. "The Gold Bug" resonates quite obviously with Washington Irving's *Tales of a Traveller*, first published in 1824. Poe refers to Irving's stories in his well-known review of Nathaniel Hawthorne's *Twice-Told Tales* as "graceful and impressive narratives" (Harrison, 11:153–54) and as a "rare exception," namely, as "American tales of real merit."[10] Poe's early reviews of Hawthorne's tales were published in 1842, the year he wrote "The Gold-Bug."

The fourth part of Irving's *Tales*, entitled "The Money-Diggers. Found among the Papers of the Late Diedrich Knickerbocker," relates the story of Captain Kidd and his presumed treasure, buried somewhere under a tree near Massachusetts' Charles Bay (not South Carolina's Charles Town). Many years later, Tom Walker looks for this treasure. He is a fearless loner, and, like Legrand, he discovers a skull that may prove to reveal a secret, or may also simply be a graveyard find. But his kicking the skull calls forth a rather peculiar apparition, who is first identified by his voice:

> "Let that skull alone!" said a gruff voice. Tom lifted up his eyes, and beheld a great black man seated directly opposite him, on the stump of a tree. He was exceedingly surprised, having neither heard nor seen any one approach; and he was still more perplexed on observing, as well as the gathering gloom would permit, that the stranger was neither negro nor Indian. It is true that he was dressed in a rude half Indian garb, and had a red belt or sash swathed round his body; but his face was neither black nor copper-color, but swarthy and dingy, and begrimed with soot, as if he had been accustomed to toil among fires and forges. He had a shock of coarse black hair, that stood out from his head in all directions, and bore an axe on his shoulder. (Irving, *Tales of a Traveller*, 453)

This "black man" who is, indeed, not properly black, proves to be the devil. While Tom is unable to find Captain Kidd's treasure, he also resists one of this devil's temptations: "He proposed, therefore, that Tom should employ [the money] in the black traffic; that is to say, that he should fit out a slave-ship. This, however, Tom resolutely refused: he was bad enough in all conscience; but the devil himself could not tempt him to turn slave-trader" (461). Tom becomes a usurer instead.

Irving's *Tales* follow the fate of a second person as well, the Manhattan burgher Wolfert Webber, who also becomes obsessed with the treasure hunt. He pursues Black Sam, "the old negro fisherman" (503) who may still remember the place where a group of murderers buried their loot. Black Sam guides Wolfert and a German doctor, who was supposed to treat him for delusions, to a mysterious place underneath a rock. But after they discover a chest, they disperse in panic, afraid to become victims of bandits who seemed to be on their trail. The happy ending of this story is provided not by any treasure hidden in the soil but by the soil itself:

Before many months had elapsed, a great bustling street passed through the very centre of the Webber garden, just where Wolfert had dreamed of finding a treasure. His golden dream was accomplished; he did indeed find an unlooked-for source of wealth; for, when his paternal lands were distributed into building-lots, and rented out to safe tenants, instead of producing a paltry crop of cabbages, they returned him an abundant crop of rent; insomuch that on quarter-day it was a goodly sight to see his tenants knocking at the door, from morning till night, each with a little round-bellied bag of money, a golden produce of the soil. (546)

Indeed, Manhattan differs from Sullivan's Island, and Wolfert's mostly silent Black Sam is needed neither to till the soil nor to dig for gold. In Irving's tale of capital, the soil itself becomes part of an alchemist venture in real estate speculation.

While Irving's *Tales of a Traveller* may have served as only one possible source for Poe's narrative (Mabbott, 3:800), the similarities, as well as the differences, between them are important. Both Irving's and Poe's heroes search for Captain Kidd's treasure, but Irving relies on the common man. His hunting grounds—the Charles River Bay, Manhattan Island—are not untouched landscapes but areas in which settlers already reside. Wolfert's Dutch cabbage patch affirms no aristocratic lineage, only his bourgeois labor. Irving's venture of turning soil into gold arouses little anxiety about the new capitalist economy; much to the contrary, real estate speculation supports a colonial idyll and the traditional values of a Dutch-American bourgeois life.

Thus, at first the differences between Irving's story and Poe's tale seem quite striking. While Wolfert starts out poor, Legrand simply restores his family's wealth with the help of a pirate's treasure and the labor of a former slave. Neither pirate nor slave quite fits into Wolfert's comfortable picture of family life. In turning the letter into gold, in finding what is already there and buried, Legrand stands firmly outside the economic process. Capitalism, however, may seem more miraculous to Wolfert than the decipherment of cryptograms. Thus, for Wolfert, too, his life assumes a fairy-tale-like turn, and his plot of land functions like a paper bill of exchange, the value of which would be open to outside determination.

In September 1836, Poe reviewed yet another book in the *Southern Literary Messenger* that deals with a presumed treasure hidden by Captain Kidd, Robert M. Bird's *Sheppard Lee: Written by Himself*. The novel's hero, Sheppard Lee, is born and educated in New Jersey. Deprived of his wealth by a dishonest overseer of his fortune, he is left with only a little property and a Negro servant, Jim Jumble, who was deeded to him in his father's will. Lee, who does not want to hold a slave, decides to let him free, but this meets with Jim Jumble's protest. He insists that Lee "is his master and shall take care of him."[11] This servant is soon responsible for one of Lee's most peculiar adventures:

> Jim Jumble conceives that money has been buried by Captain Kidd, in a certain ugly swamp, called the Owl-Roost, not many rods from an old church. The stories of the negro affect his master to such a degree that he dreams three nights in succession of finding a treasure at the foot of a beech-tree in the swamp. He resolves to dig for it in good earnest, choosing mid-night, at the full of the moon, as the moment of commencing operations. (282)

Lee, however, does not share Legrand's success. He encounters spirits in the old church's graveyard and kills himself, more or less accidentally, at the very tree where the treasure was supposed to rest. Separated from his body, Lee's soul continues to transmigrate to other bodies in a more and more fantastic series of events, in which he is able to earn his own "treasure" through usury and other means. Briefly, Poe's review touches on yet another character in Bird's tale of great adventures and on another servant who is named just Tom:

> In his character of Nigger Tom, Mr. Lee gives us some very excellent chapters upon abolition and the exciting effects of incendiary pamphlets and pictures, among our slaves in the South. This part of the narrative closes with a spirited picture of a negro insurrection, and with the hanging of Nigger Tom. (285)

Enter Friday

There is certainly no danger of Jim Jumble's insurrection; he is a humble servant who insists on remaining a slave. There is no need to fear insurrection from Black Sam, a free fisherman who merely serves as a witness. In the early nineteenth century, the historical Charleston area did not have to fear insurrection, either, as it hoped to have followed all precautions. Slaves were imported from Africa only, not from the West Indies, where blacks had gained a reputation for violent protest. Poe's implicit references to the story lines of Irving and Byrd may have been politically reassuring, moreover; not much danger can be expected from a black person who fulfills a comic function.

Poe's own character, Jupiter, seems to resemble Jim Jumble; he is a former slave who continues to care for his master. And if we unearth the archaeological layers of characters and stories that may have provided first models for Poe's narrative, the account of possible sources would hardly be complete without a reference to Daniel Defoe's master text about a servant-master relationship. Indeed, Poe perhaps even more than Irving or Byrd seems to have been influenced by this English colonial narrative that pairs a story of adventure with a lesson of domination. Defoe's hero does not choose an island existence because of any melancholy disposition; he is, instead, stranded on an island without any viable alternative. At first, he does not seem to be the master of his own fate. Survival itself becomes a measure of success.

For Legrand, the drawing of a goat as a "kid" on his rescued piece of paper served as a signature for the pirate Captain Kidd. On Defoe's island, goats roam to be captured by his hero (141). For a while, Defoe's hero, Robinson Crusoe, ransacks the wreck of the ship that brought him to the island and tries to tame his own part of the wilderness. His treasures are found on a shipwreck that proved to hold a cargo of liquor, food, and clothing, as well as money and gold: "[W]hen I came to the Till in the Chest, I found there three great Bags of Pieces of Eight, which held about eleven hundred Pieces in all; and in one of them, wrapt up in a Paper, six Doubloons of Gold, and some small Bars or Wedges of Gold; I suppose they might all weigh near a Pound" (150). All of this would not make a rich man of Crusoe, who cherished the food and clothing on his deserted island more than money or gold, which would be of no use.

But Crusoe's island does not remain deserted for long. First he notices a footprint in the sand (121), only to discover that natives have landed on the other side of the island. Crusoe's anxieties about these "Savages" inspire a new plan for domination:

> Besides, I fancied my self able to manage One, nay, Two or Three Savages, if I had them, so as to make them entirely Slaves to me, to do whatever I should direct them, and to prevent their being able at any time to do me any Hurt. It was a great while, that I pleas'd my self with this Affair, but nothing still presented; all my Fancies and Schemes came to nothing, for no Savages came near me for a great while. (156)

While Poe's "Gold-Bug" features a newly freed slave (who still behaves subserviently), Defoe's novel focuses on the making of a slave. The opportunity to acquire a "Savage" presents itself to Crusoe shortly after he documents these thoughts. He is able to rescue one of the "Savages" who is pursued by others, and before Crusoe is even able to make him a slave, this stranger turns him into a master:

> [T]he poor Savage fled, but had stopp'd; though he saw both his Enemies fallen, and kill'd, as he thought; yet was so frighted with the Fire, and Noise of my Piece; that he stood Stock still, and neither came forward or went backward, tho' he seem'd rather enclin'd to fly still, than to come on; I hollow'd again to him, and made Signs to come forward, which he easily understood, and came a little way, then stopp'd again, and then a little further, and stopp'd again, and I cou'd then perceive that he stood trembling, as if he had been taken Prisoner, and had just been to be kill'd, as his two Enemies were. I beckon'd him again to come to me, and gave him all the Signs of Encouragement that I could think of, and he came nearer and nearer, kneeling down every Ten or Twelve steps in token of acknowledgment for my saving his Life: I smil'd at him, and look'd pleasantly, and beckon'd to him to come still nearer, at length he came close to me, and then he kneel'd down again, kiss'd the Ground, and laid his Head upon the Ground, and taking me by the Foot, set my Foot upon his Head; this seems was in token of swearing to be my Slave for ever; I took him up, and made much of him, and encourag'd him all I could. (159)

Language is encouraged only within limits here, as his first words were "Yes," "No," and "Master," a seemingly sufficient vocabulary. Crusoe names his slave Friday after the day of the week of their encounter, and he shows little curiosity to learn about any other possible name, his servant's interests, or his history. A person who seems to be his father appears and disappears. Little is made of the customs of Friday's people that seem—as a litter of bones and skulls documents—quite barbaric.

In contrast to the Englishman, the "Savage" who should be tamed as a slave is described as an "Indian" (160), somebody whose looks mediate between the darkness of the Africans and the aesthetically pleasing features of the European:

> He was a comely handsome Fellow, perfectly well made; with straight strong Limbs, not too large; tall and well shap'd, and as I reckon, about twenty six Years of Age. He had a very good Countenance, not a fierce and surly Aspect; but seem'd to have something very manly in his Face, and yet he had all the Sweetness and

Softness of an *European* in his Countenance too, especially when
he smil'd. His Hair was long and black, not curl'd like Wool; his
Forehead very high, and large, and a great Vivacity and sparkling
Sharpness in his Eyes. The Colour of his Skin was not quite black,
but very tawny; and yet not of an ugly yellow nauseous tawny, as
the *Brasilians*, and *Virginians*, and other Natives of *America* are; but
of a bright kind of a dun olive Colour, that had in it something
very agreeable; tho' not very easy to describe. His Face was round,
and plump; his Nose small, not flat like the Negroes, a very good
Mouth, thin Lips, and his fine Teeth well set, and white as Ivory.
(160)

Friday may not be English, but he is not African, either. Unlike Jupiter,
he is able to smile subtly and does not burst into comedic laughter. In
simply being different (also from the "Negroes"), he offers Crusoe
something new, while the island itself is conversely familiar, part of his
home territory. He does not have to learn about a new geographic place,
just about his place in a newly formed relationship.

In his study on the figure of the servant in literature, Bruce Robbins
remarks on a peculiar linguistic confusion. "Place" does not only denote
the locale where people live, or a geographic location that is open for description. "According to common usage," Robbins writes, "servants did
not look for work, like other members of their class, but for a place (53).
Defoe's description abounds with references to the "Place" (e.g. 114),
the geographic site in which Crusoe happens to find himself. Friday, in
turn, does not search for a "Place" of service. Instead, the geographi-
cally familiar locus turns into the metaphorical one of the slave. He, too,
suddenly finds himself in this peculiar relationship. But while Crusoe
may have found his footprints threatening, Friday proceeds to pose his
master's foot upon his head, in an act of clear subservience.

The master-slave relationship—already imagined by Crusoe, perhaps
already known to Friday, too—is a complicated one. Friday is named and
educated by the newly arrived Englishman, but his native wit provides
for this man's survival. Crusoe may act as an imperial master, but he is
dependent on his servant for life itself. This master-servant relationship
is played out in Poe's narrative as well. In denying Jupiter any pleasing
European look, however, Poe relocates the colonial experience and as-
cribes the lack of power more strongly to an inferior servant's body. At
the same time, however, Poe also highlights a mutual dependence.
Jupiter has to obey Legrand, but he verbally threatens to whip him as
well. Both men are dependent on each other. In her discussion of Poe's
fiction, Toni Morrison comments on Jupiter's comic behavior, his

dialect, and his looks that seem to mark points of difference from the description of his master. Nevertheless, for Morrison, Jupiter seems to turn the tables and assert a dominant position—just as Friday did before him—in a radical and telling slip:

> We can look to "The Gold-Bug" and "How to Write a Blackwood Article" (as well as *Pym*) for samples of the desperate need of this writer for "othering" so common to American literature: estranging language, metaphoric condensation, fetishizing strategies, the economy of stereotype, allegorical foreclosure; strategies employed to secure his characters' (and his readers') identity. But there are unmanageable slips. The black slave Jupiter is said to whip his master in "The Gold-Bug"; the black servant Pompey stands mute and judgmental at the antics of his mistress in "A Blackwood Article." And Pym engages in cannibalism *before* he meets the black savages; when he escapes from them and witnesses the death of a black man, he drifts toward the silence of an impenetrable, inarticulate whiteness. (*Playing in the Dark,* 58)

Thus, Poe writes not only about the servant's inferiority but also about his implicit power over his master, both in reality and in imagination. While establishing the other as an object for domination, Poe marks the limits of the master's authority and offers a description of racial anxiety.

And, as for Robbins's servants or for Crusoe who constructs his "Castle," place is important for Poe as well. It is a marker for a relationship of power, but not a geographic one of retreat and defense. "Through the use of Africanism," Morrison writes, "Poe meditates on place as a means of containing the fear of borderlessness and trespass, but also as a means of releasing and exploring the desire for a limitless empty frontier" (51). Poe's Sullivan's Island may just be that: a simile of frontier life, of the pursuit of that peculiar American dream of exploring and conquering the unknown, those "white" places on the map that are so seemingly unpopulated and are awaiting their "white" domination.

Black Servants

Legrand's freed slave is a stranger to the island much as his master is. Whereas Friday has to lose his father, family, and friends to share his life with his master, none of Jupiter's friends or relatives appear. Thus, Legrand assumes the position of a father figure, a paternal master, from the very beginning. Poe transforms Crusoe's dream of mastery into a dream of pioneer life as boyhood adventure. This is how Poe read Defoe's novel, too. In a review published in the *Southern Literary Messenger* in January 1836, several years before the publication of his own tale of island adventure, Poe describes *The Life and Surprising Adventures of Robinson Crusoe, of York, Mariner* as an "invaluable work" that does honor to the country (presumably, Defoe's England).[12] And while the old woman in "The Gold-Bug" is needed because she remembers the rock from which Legrand can spot the right tree, reading Defoe's tale relates in Poe's review to a notion of memory, which is now a matter of effect. The (male) reader is made to remember his own boyhood. Poe refers to his experiences with Defoe's book as if a later reading would uncover the first one, recapturing his youth as a matter of course, like a newly discovered treasure:

> How fondly do we recur, in memory, to those enchanted days of
> our boyhood when we first learned to grow serious over Robinson
> Crusoe!—when we first found the spirit of wild adventure enkin-
> dling within us; as by the dim fire light, we labored out, line by
> line, the marvellous import of those pages, and hung breathless
> and trembling with eagerness over their absorbing—over their en-
> chaining interest! (98)

The book turns here if not into an educational program then at least into an instrument for a boy's *Bildung*.[13] For Poe, the experience of adventure, voluntarily assumed, becomes as important for the adolescent as it seems necessary for Robinson Crusoe. And, indeed, Poe describes a reading experience that lives by identification:

> Men do not look upon [the book] in the light of a literary perform-
> ance. Defoe has none of their thoughts—Robinson all. The powers
> which have wrought the wonder have been thrown into obscurity
> by the very stupendousness of the wonder they have wrought! We
> read, and become perfect abstractions in the intensity of our inter-
> est—we close the book, and are quite satisfied that we could have
> written as well ourselves. All this is effected by the potent magic of
> verisimilitude. Indeed the author of Crusoe must have possessed,
> above all other faculties, what has been termed the faculty of *identifi-
> cation*—that dominion exercised by volition over imagination which
> enables the mind to lose its own, in a fictitious, individuality. (98)

Perhaps it is just because of this similarity between the reading process and the master-slave relationship, between any boy's experience and Defoe's tale of adventure, that the issue of race is not mentioned here.

In her discussion of Poe's tale, Morrison refers to Jupiter's plan to whip Legrand as a telling "slippage" in that master-slave relationship. But in Poe's review of Defoe's novel, yet another accidental revelation occurs. According to Poe, the reader who identifies himself with Crusoe has to remember himself as a young boy; he can become like Crusoe only when being bound to the book that contains his story. He is "enchained." The book assumes a place of mastery; it is an object that subjects. The process of reading—as a boy—puts the reader in a fixed position of dependency that Crusoe desires for his "Savage," whom he would nevertheless like to "civilize" and educate. Reading, it seems, educates masters while producing slaves. The process turns the reader into an ambiguous figure who encompasses the full dialectics of the master-slave relationship.

In his review, however, Poe does not concentrate on the reading process so much as on the question of the text's "verisimilitude." Defoe's story becomes one of the past, and not just because reading has to be remembered as a boyhood experience. The very islands that provide the laboratory for the master-slave relationship are no longer available as places of discovery and adventure:

> Alas! the days of desolate islands are no more! "Nothing farther," as Vapid says, "can be done in that line." Wo, henceforward, to the Defoe who shall prate to us of "undiscovered bournes." There is positively not a square inch of new ground for any future Selkirk. Neither in the Indian, in the Pacific, nor in the Atlantic, has he a shadow of hope. The Southern Ocean has been incontinently ransacked, and in the North—Scoresby, Franklin, Parry, Ross & Co. have been little better than so many salt water Paul Prys. (98)[14]

Poe's statement serves as an ironic comment on many of his own tales of adventure and exploration, like his *Narrative of Arthur Gordon Pym* or the adventures of *Julius Rodman*, which claim precisely the existence of undiscovered lands.[15] And in his own tale of an island adventure, "The Gold-Bug," Poe strives, indeed, to describe a place that is at least temporarily deserted; it is a wilderness, yet one with a history of settlement that can be recaptured by a black woman's memory or a white pirate's cryptographic script. Thus, there are no virgin lands, though perhaps they can be re-created by emptying an island of its previous inhabitants, by changing the plot to one that would import the servant with his master. While Poe lends his servant-character a voice, his Jupiter becomes doubly disowned: he is a servant, and he has no geographic "home."

In his review, Poe already projects his own revision of the island story into his reading of Defoe's tale. Crusoe's island resembles Legrand's depopulated wilderness and lacks any inhabitants, either Native Americans or Gullah blacks. But by turning Defoe's Indian into a former slave, Poe performs a move that has been influential and often imitated. Most strikingly, it is repeated in Morrison's reading of Defoe's tale.

In her essay "Friday on the Potomac," which introduces a volume of reflections on the confirmation hearings of Supreme Court Justice Clarence Thomas and Anita Hill's testimony, Morrison attempts a more detailed reading of *Robinson Crusoe*. She describes Friday as the black slave par excellence whose story provides a telling metaphor for a behavior expected of all free blacks as well. His education as a proper slave becomes the example for acculturation to white "civilization." "Crusoe's narrative is a success story, one in which a socially, culturally, and biologically handicapped black man is civilized and Christianized—taught, in other words, to be like a white one," Morrison writes (xxiii). Friday learns to think and behave as Crusoe does.

While this Indian-as-black can acculturate only by showing submission to his master, Poe's Jumble Jim–as–Southern black can be viewed as only a limited success. Jupiter speaks more than three words, but in "improper" English; he also never fully seems to understand what everything is about. In Poe, he is deprived of his home and of the possibility of white acculturation, which can only be viewed as a carnivalesque undertaking. Paradoxically, not just Poe's many layerings of Legrand's story but also specifically his rendering of a boyhood dream that would turn Defoe's native "Indian" into a former slave make this tale such a particularly American enterprise; it is not just about a black servant but about the making of a black. Poe's American dream lives both by the decyphering of cryptograms and by the constantly renewed inscription of a landscape constructed not by history but by memories. Poe remembers his white boyhood's reading, as Legrand in the tale seems dependent both on the body of a black servant and on the memory of a black mother figure. In writing his own tale, Poe thus celebrates the complexity of Legrand's mind and his talents for ratiocination while also documenting the scene of detection as one of repression, thus offering us a dialectics that is very much with us even today.

Indeed, the archaeological strata that can be uncovered by studying Poe's tale resemble those of the actual island itself. Sullivan's Island, too, appears like a layered mount for which Fort Moultrie may serve as a symbol (figure 5.7). Elsewhere on the Charleston area islands, hotels, shops, and restaurants advertise a "Gullah" culture that excludes any white settlers' history. On Sullivan's Island and the adjacent Isle of

FIGURE 5.7. Sullivan's Island, Fort Moultrie

Palms, however, black history is repressed. These are islands that live by the reputation of Fort Moultrie, and in advertisements blacks appear as comic figures only and offer an oddly exotic touch (figures 5.8 and 5.9). The fort itself displays a narrative that excludes all black involvement in its past. But the question of race cannot be avoided. In the center court of the fort, the Seminole leader Osceola lies buried (figure 5.10). The *National Park Handbook*, issued by the fort, depicts him as the hero of his tribe, a man who "vigorously opposed U.S. Government efforts to remove his people from their ancestral lands" for two years.[16] But as he failed, he turned also into a theatrical figure, reminiscent of Poe's ex-slave Jupiter. And after a discussion of Poe's stay on the island, and his "Balloon Hoax"—a story that mentions Fort Moultrie as well but was, indeed, written in 1844—the *Handbook* treats Osceola as a similar, and perhaps curiously imitative, hoax:

> Another break in the tedium of post life came a decade later, when the Seminole war leader Osceola was captured by American forces and taken to Fort Moultrie in January 1838. He was confined here only a few weeks before he died from quinsy, a severe throat infection. Throughout his captivity Osceola received courteous treatment and even became a local celebrity. At the fort, he sometimes made fun of the U.S. Army's "mode of warfare, and gave an excellent pantomine . . . of the manner of the white man and the Indian loading and firing." Osceola was "at liberty within the walls, and roamed about at pleasure," and many

FIGURE 5.8. Isle of Palms, sushi bar

FIGURE 5.9. Isle of Palms, music shop

FIGURE 5.10. Sullivan's Island, grave of Osceola, Fort Moultrie

Charlestonians took the opportunity to visit him. On January 6 Osceola and four Seminole chiefs attended Charleston's New Theatre production of "Honey Moon." The event inspired a five-verse poem entitled "Osceola at the Charleston Theater." When Osceola died, the garrison at Fort Moultrie buried him with military honors near the fort entrance. (41)

During his brief confinement, here described as pleasurable, Osceola was displayed, asked to produce pantomines, and invited to meet some fellow actors. Thus, he was allowed to become a mere interruption of tedious post life, and one that remains unknown to many of the island's visitors today. None of the island's streets are named after him, while the author of the earlier-mentioned hoax and the titles of his works appear on the local library, on street signs, and in commercial displays. Thus, Poe's fiction and the island's current self-representation differ slightly. Poe may have rewritten the island's history in "The Gold-Bug," but Sullivan's Island now actively uses Poe to efface its own past. Not Fort Moultrie and the pest house, but Fort Moultrie and the "The Gold-Bug" constitute the history that the island's inhabitants want to remember, thus turning Poe into a patriotic poet who would help celebrate the pioneering spirit of domination.

Notes

All photographs of Sullivan's Island and the Isle of Palms are by Liliane Weissberg.

1. Text accompanying a tourist map distributed by the Fort Moultrie gift shop, 1997.

2. The physician, paradoxically called Alexander Garden, is quoted in Berkeley and Berkeley, 124, and also in Ball, 90.

3. Compare also Weir, 173.

4. See also Mufwene, "Investigating Gullah: Difficulties in Ensuring 'Authenticity,'" especially 178–79, as well as the anthology edited by Michael Montgomery, *The Crucible of Carolina: Essays in the Development of Gullah Language and Culture.*

5. See also Poe's black character Pompey in his tale "How to Write a Blackwood Article."

6. There is no place here to compare both stories in more detail, but in regard to the implicit discourse on race, I would like to refer to Elise V. Lemire's reading of "The Murders in the Rue Morgue" (see chapter 7, this volume). See also Harrowitz.

7. See, for example, Poe's review, "Tale-Writing—Nathaniel Hawthorne—Twice-Told Tales. By Nathaniel Hawthorne.—Mosses From an Old Manse. By Nathaniel Hawthorne": "Of skillfully-constructed tales—I speak now without reference to other points, some of them more important than construction—there are very few American specimens. I am acquainted with no better one, upon the whole, than the 'Murder Will Out' of Mr. Simms, and this has some glaring defects" (Harrison, 11:153). This review appeared in *Godey's Lady's Book* in November 1847.

8. See William Gilmore Simms, *Martin Faber: The Story of a Criminal* and his *Tales of the South,* as well as other books. See J. Allen Morris, "The Stories of William Gilmore Simms," especially 29. A more general survey is given by Marcia Marvin Lavely's dissertation, "A Study of American Literature Which Incorporates the Use of the Gullah Dialect."

9. "He also introduced the negro into the later scenes of 'The Gold Bug,' having looked for Bessop's Castle among the older negroes of Sullivan's Island" (Campbell, "Poe's Treatment," 110). "He" may refer to Poe as well as to his story's character, Legrand.

10. Poe, review of "Twice-Told Tales. By Nathaniel Hawthorne" (Harrison, 11:102. This review appeared in *Graham's Magazine* in April and May 1842.

11. Poe, review of "Sheppard Lee, Written by Himself" (*CW,* 5:282). The review appeared in the *Southern Literary Messenger* in September 1836.

12. Poe, review of "The Life and Surprising Adventures of Robinson Crusoe" (*CW,* 5:98). This review was published in the *Southern Literary Messenger* in January 1836. See also Pollin, "Poe and Daniel Defoe."

13. This contrasts peculiarly with the evaluation of Poe's own works by many late nineteenth-century and early twentieth-century American critics who would refer to it as adolescent literature, one that perhaps encourages an arrested development. See the brief summary and bibliography of Poe's reception in the United States in Weissberg, *Edgar Allan Poe,* 163–69.

14. Defoe's book was inspired by the adventures of Alexander Selkirk.

15. Early chapters of *The Narrative of Arthur Gordon Pym* appeared in serial form in 1837, preceding publication of the book in 1838; *The Journal of Julius Rodman* was first published in incomplete serial form in 1840. See also Weissberg, "Editing Adventures: Writing the Text of *Julius Rodman*."

16. Stokeley, picture caption 41.

CHAPTER 6

Presence of Mind

Detection and Racialization in "The Murders in the Rue Morgue"

LINDON BARRETT

The misadventures that constitute Edgar Allan Poe's *Narrative of Arthur Gordon Pym* end with, what seems to Poe's mind, the most horrible and unthinkable of misadventures, encountering a "body of savages . . . [who] appeared to be the most wicked hypocritical, vindictive, bloodthirsty, and altogether fiendish race of men upon the face of the globe" (*CW*, 1:201). In landscapes, in seascapes, as well as in human anatomies, the closing details of the narrative contrast images of blackness and whiteness, marking out a world of irreconcilable divisions fixed ultimately as the clash of peoples and civilizations. These closing images and sentiments affirm that issues of race, as much as or more than any other issue, are integral to the narrative. In *Playing in the Dark*, Toni Morrison discusses these closing images in elaborating a figurative "darkness from which our early literature seemed unable to extricate itself, suggest[ing] the complex and contradictory [racial] situation in which American writers found themselves" (33). Morrison believes that no early U.S. writer is more important to this situation than Poe, a comment that is rare in a critical conversation around Poe that seems, at best, circumspect concerning race and, at worst, disingenuous.

Although Morrison highlights some of the most patent racial features of Poe's work in making this point, some of the premises of *Playing in the Dark* suggest that patent acknowledgments of race may not be the most

compelling element of customary treatments of race in U.S. culture. At
the outset Morrison posits that mechanisms of denial, indirection, and
erasure rule U.S. racial thought—denial, indirection, and erasure not at
all intended to challenge racial meanings themselves but devoted to
maintaining them as unobstrusively as possible. Morrison understands
that patent reflection on race (or an "Africanist presence," in her terms)
is by no means the singular or even paramount sign of the influence of
race or racialized thought in U.S. culture and literature and, thus, she dis-
regards prevalent knowledge, which holds

> that traditional, canonical American literature [and culture] is free
> of, uninformed, and unshaped by the four-hundred-year-old pres-
> ence of, first, Africans and then African-Americans in the United
> States. It assumes that this presence—which shaped the body
> politic, the Constitution, and the entire history of the culture—
> has had no significant place or consequence in the origin and de-
> velopment of that culture's literature. Moreover, such knowledge
> assumes that the characteristics of our national literature [and cul-
> ture] emanate from a particular "Americanness" that is separate
> from and unaccountable to this presence. (4–5)

One of the integral components of U.S. racial thought, in other
words, is the *unreasonable* effort to mask or overlook the systemic racial
differentiation and subordination cultivated in the United States. In what
manner are issues of race integral not only to openly Gothic and brood-
ing elements of Poe's canon but also to narratives seemingly far afield of
open considerations of race? The response to this question presented
here assumes that racialization may be a more telling or provocative
component of Poe's "Murders in the Rue Morgue" than *The Narrative
of Arthur Gordon Pym* precisely because of its seeming irrelevance or
invisibility.

The first of Poe's famed trilogy of detective stories, "The Murders in
the Rue Morgue" aims, as does the entire trilogy, to document and stand
as a monument to Reason itself—at its most sophisticated. The story
presents its protagonist's extraordinary powers of apprehension, and the
terms on which Reason itself is posed prove instrumental to uncovering
issues of race and racialization. For "[r]ace and the various exclusions it
license[s] became naturalized in the Eurocentered vision of itself and its
self-defined others, in its sense of *Reason and rational direction*" (Goldberg,
10; emphasis added). Modern Eurocentric Reason and rational direction
provide effective, elaborate justifications for political, economic, social,
and psychic systems of racial order guaranteeing that racially "distribu-

tive management of bodies . . . [results in] the massive generation and redeployment of surplus value" (Goldberg, 53).

The issues of racialization integral to "The Murders in the Rue Morgue" are signaled by three details crucial to its denouement confirming extreme powers of Reason in Dupin, its protagonist: first, the seemingly irresolvable controversy concerning the language of the murderer; second, the invocation of the French naturalist Georges Cuvier; and, third, references to distant and exotic Borneo. These details yield the identity of the murderer (the deceptively humanlike ape), as well as underwrite incontestable proof of Dupin's ingenious and exemplary mind. The duality or duplicity of this outcome is key, because two figures are paramount by the end of the narrative, one merely mimicking and, therefore, mistaken as human, the other figuring the zenith of human potential. The capacity for thought marks the distance between these figures as nadir and zenith, and insofar as these pairings resolve the mystery of detection in the narrative, they also redact entrenched figurations of the racial animus of "blackness" and "whiteness."

That reason, formidably so, becomes the figure of *race* in the West is a peculiarity evident in both learned and popular traditions. Recently, for example, Ronald Judy, in *(Dis)Forming the American Canon,* confronts Kant over his offhanded equation of racial blackness with stupidity in *Observations on the Feeling of the Beautiful and the Sublime*—Kant being only one leading figure of the venerated Western intellectual tradition in which the equation is so routine that it never warrants careful exposition or expostulation. What and who stand beyond the pale of Reason in the West is, for some, so plain that the question never seems openly to bear reasoning itself. Similar traditions exist popularly and less formally. In the antebellum United States, both North and South, open dismissals of blackness in this particular vein are all too easy to document. Writing in 1858, in the decade after Poe's death, Ralph Butterfield, M.D., for instance, puts the matter starkly when he states the following in *American Cotton Planter and Soil of the South*:

Everybody knows that negroes are deficient in reason, judgment and forecast—that they are improvident, and thoughtless of the future, and contented and happy in the enjoyment of the mere animal pleasures of the present moment. If negroes can have plenty to eat and to wear, if they can freely indulge their amorous animal propensities, and then if to these are added a liberal allowance of whiskey and tobacco, they are indeed supremely blessed, and they sigh for no higher or brighter state of existence. (212)

The belief in an inverse relation between racial blackness and Reason is emphatic. In terms of the cultural logic of the United States, to speak of Reason is already to a very significant degree to make a racially exclusive move. The valence of the gesture is especially intriguing in the era of the escalating debate concerning the U.S. meaning of racial blackness taking place in Poe's lifetime.

It bears repeating that the circumspection around questions of race in the work of Poe is disingenuous, because the very contours of the culture in which Poe finds himself and the terms of subjection open to him are defined by highly consequential notions of race and racial blackness, influences virtually impossible to escape, and from which escape would be marked, no doubt, by unequivocal announcements of repudiation on Poe's part—of which there are none. In the same way that, without explicit evidence to prove otherwise, one must assume that Poe is a *native* speaker of English given the culture he lived in, one must assume that, given the culture he lived in, Poe necessarily refracts notions of racial hierarchy in which racial whiteness is privileged extraordinarily over racial blackness. It cannot be surprising that Poe imagines and refracts the culture in which he is steeped. In the words of social historian David Roediger, the imagined and legislated "pleasures of whiteness . . . [effectively] function as a 'wage'" (13), or apparent boon, in the United States, for even the most dispossessed of those certified racially white, nonetheless pursue opportunities to become acknowledged cultural figures. Restated, the contention is that the exemplary presence and life of the mind central to "The Murders in the Rue Morgue" iterate and reflect the oppositions of racial blackness and whiteness established *as Reason* by the cultural logic of the United States and the West. If racial opposition is absent, so is Reason.

One might say that the focus in "The Murders in the Rue Morgue" on the measured, urbane, and exclusive display of Reason functions as an analogue of the images of "impenetrable whiteness" Morrison examines in *The Narrative of Arthur Gordon Pym*:

> These images of impenetrable whiteness need contextualizing to explain their extraordinary power, pattern, and consistency. Because they appear almost always in conjunction with representations of black or Africanist people who are dead, impotent, or under complete control, these images of blinding whiteness seem to function as both antidote for and meditation on the shadow that is companion to this whiteness—a dark and abiding presence that moves the hearts and texts of American literature with fear and longing. (33)

According to Morrison, meditations or representations of whiteness are conjoined to their antithesis at the very point of their articulation. This claim constitutes one of the many restatements in *Playing in the Dark* that race insinuates itself into the fabric of the U.S. literary imaginary in the most circumspect of ways.

The approach of historian Alexander Saxton in exploring the racial attitudes of the young John Quincy Adams is very much to the point here. In explaining how his analysis will proceed in *The Rise and Fall of the White Republic: Class Politics and Mass Culture in Nineteenth-Century America*, Saxton writes: "The first of the sections that follow reconstructs the ideas and attitudes about race available to John Quincy Adams in the milieu of his youth, and presumably accessible to other young men of his class and generation" (25). Saxton re-creates what must have been the racial universe of the youthful Adams by assessing the racial circumstances and attitudes of Adams's family and acquaintances as well as those fostered and disseminated in the public domain. Saxton infers, in the absence of any direct statements on the part of Adams here or later contradicting this social and cultural inheritance, that he shares these views defining his age and culture. Indeed, evidence from subsequent years demonstrates "Adams modifying and adjusting those [racial] ideas and attitudes to suit the strategic needs, as he perceived them, of the class coalition that was moving him forward as a leader" (25). The same principles are pertinent to issues of race insinuated in "The Murders in the Rue Morgue." What evidence exists in the narrative, one must ask, that confirms or belies the racial attitudes of the culture in which Poe lived?

It would be mistaken, however, to suggest that the critical conversation on Poe completely circumvents open discussion of matters of race. Dana Nelson, in *The Word in Black and White*, recounts the long-standing controversy concerning whether Poe held pro- or antislavery sentiments. Spanning decades, these exchanges debate whether Poe is, in fact, the author of an unsigned proslavery book review published in April 1836 in the *Southern Literary Messenger*, a journal for which he served as editor at that time. In detailing this intellectual history, Nelson carefully states her wish to avoid narrow concerns about intentionality and Poe; she wishes, rather, to consider "the racist dimension of Poe's work . . . [and] the cultural work performed *now* by masking that aspect of his work" (92; emphasis in original). She proposes the issue of settling the authorship of the single book review as less than relevant because it makes little sense to imagine that issues of race in Poe's literary work should rest foremost on the question of the authorship of a tangential document. She claims it much more productive to see that complexities of race reside in Poe's texts themselves and in the cultural systems those texts both reflect and participate in. In brief, the question of Poe's personal dispositions may be interesting but is not in fact crucial. What is crucial for a sound investigation of the racial exigencies of his canon is gauging his relation to a U.S. national imaginary continually playing in the dark, in Morrison's apt phrase.

John Carlos Rowe, in "Poe, Antebellum Slavery, and Modern Criticism," puts the matter well when he points out that one cannot reasonably overlook the fact that "Poe's prose and poetry is, of course, full of abused, murdered, dismembered women, of native peoples represented as the embodiment of primitive evil, of visionary aristocrats, of royalty 'saved' by poetic manipulation, of the hateful 'masses'" (136). Poe's work is so steeped in the material intrigues of cultural power and political control that it makes little sense to imagine that the significance of its racial issues turns on determining the authorship of an isolated declaration of political sentiment. Rowe, even more so than Nelson, reminds readers that the incidents and relations set out in Poe's works ineluctably engage the "materiality of history" (126) and culture—as one must suspect of all literature. Even as the tales (and perhaps especially the detective fiction) work to present the "argument that language, the essence of reason, is the basis of all reality and thus the only proper 'property,'" they profess as strenuously, though more surreptitiously, that "[a]s the 'enlightened ruler' of language, the essence of reason, its rational governor, the poet works to recontain that savagery—the mob, the black, the lunatic—within poetic form" (127). Rowe presumes along with Nelson that the question rests, rather than simply with declared or documentable political allegiances, in imaginative configurations found in the literature itself.

However, Rowe, like Morrison and Nelson, looks foremost to *The Narrative of Arthur Gordon Pym* to make the case for the significance of race and racialization in Poe's work. Allegorizing aspects of the narrative in terms of dynamics of the antebellum South, Rowe writes, for instance: "Like Nat Turner, the Black Cook [in *Pym*] strikes his victims on the head, testifying to the symbolic danger to reason posed by the emergence of the irrational savagery so many Southern whites imagined would accompany slave rebellion or even legal emancipation" (128). Rowe suggests the great importance of the conflation of blackness and irrationality to both the allegorized terms of Poe's imagination and the historical terms of the moment in which Poe lives. The threat of racial blackness takes the form of a threat to rational conduct and to social organization, and, although Rowe questions the role of reason in the detective narratives, he never openly proposes that the same dynamics of reason so evident in *Pym* might also be crucial to the detective narratives in which the display of reason is paramount.

David Van Leer, in "Detecting Truth: The World of the Dupin Tales," makes the opposite gesture. While Van Leer does query the exemplary display of Reason in Poe's detective fiction, he never imagines or poses any conjunction between matters of Reason and matters of racialization. His ultimate concern is the peculiarity that in the fictive world of these tales the reasoning presented is finally specious because it posits "no difference between seeming and being" (68). Like Rowe, Van Leer implies that it is the question of representation—who holds the authority to represent, as well as representational strategies themselves—that is at stake. Both Van Leer and Rowe understand reason as tied to processes of the construction and elaboration of what is forged as visible and comprehensible, rather than to any primary access to "truth." Van Leer presents extended suspicions concerning the "bravada demonstration of Dupin's ability to predict his friends' thoughts" (68) that opens "The Murders in the Rue Morgue." While this demonstration would stand ideally as a preface to more astounding displays of Dupin's genius to follow, displays of genius that will solve the mystery of the unfathomable murders, Van Leer dismantles the display as follows:

> Such an analytic tour de force is . . . not truly ingenious. Yet it does suggest how Dupin's method deduces its conclusions from generalized concepts rather than inducing them from observed reality. The outside world barely intrudes on Dupin's analysis: The narrator murmurs a word, looks up to heaven, smiles, and stops stooping. Not arising from an exact observation of details, Dupin's reasoning depends on the logical inevitability of any thought process. The narrator "could not say" a word "without being brought" to think of another word. Once thinking that second word he "could not avoid" looking upward or fail to associate the constellation he sees with yet another word. "From certain pungencies" (which Dupin forbears to enumerate) the narrator necessarily relates this Latin word to its use in a hostile review of the actor. Thought, by this account, is merely a passive review of the actor. Though Dupin claims to have "correctly followed" his friend's thoughts, he actually anticipates them. There is nothing in the passage that counts as evidence. Most of the narrator's actions—his skyward glance, smile, and posture—corroborate what Dupin has already concluded to be the necessary train of his thoughts. (70–71)

In sum, Van Leer closely analyzes what Poe represents as Reason; he considers what features pass for Reason (with its access to truth) in Poe's fictive world.

The narrative would ostensibly have it otherwise, but one recognizes at last not simply individual genius at its center but also a system of racial stratification in the prodigious display of mindfulness. Whereas Van Leer probes the suspect Reason of Poe's tales, and Nelson and Rowe emphasize the relevance of race to Poe's work, the interest here is to uncover the ineluctable co-implication of Reason and race.

The disinterested capacity for human genius recorded in "The Murders in the Rue Morgue" is occasioned by a violent central crime that is a disturbing and puzzling antithesis to any world of perceptual order and mental acuity. If night and simulated darkness stand as the preferred element for the narrator and his friend Dupin in indulging their "souls in dreams—reading, writing, or conversing" (Mabbott, 2:533), then, as it turns out, this preferred environment for their radical immersion in the life of the mind proves equally the cloak for bizarre and disconcerting events. The darkness of night, insofar as it is the preferred element for the life of the mind in the narrative, seems concomitantly the very seat of the unreasonable, for what makes the murders of Madame L'Espanaye and her daughter so bizarre and disconcerting is not simply their extreme, macabre violence but the fact that they seem to defy all logical or reasonable explanation. Dupin's self-appointed charge to isolate, penetrate, vanquish what, as it turns out, is only *apparently* unreasonable reasserts the supremacy of the life of the mind. Only to those with powers of reasoning unequal to Dupin's do the murders ultimately seem unreasonable, and to underscore the point, the tale ends with Dupin musing over the lesser powers of the prefect of police, whom he overshadows with his spectacular solution to the murders:

> I am satisfied with having defeated him in his own castle. Nevertheless, that he failed in the solution of this mystery, is by no means that matter for wonder which he supposes it; for, in truth, our friend the Prefect is somewhat too cunning to be profound. In his wisdom is no *stamen*. It is all head and no body, like the pictures of the goddess Laverna,—or, at best, all head and shoulders, like a codfish. (Mabbott, 2:568; emphasis in original)

Predictably, Dupin's intervention into the macabre, baffling events begins with his digesting all available information. However, although there are abundant clues at the scene of the crime, as well as an abundance of reports from witnesses who were within earshot of the crime, all this information seems to point only to its own oddity or to prove contradictory. One of the most salient pieces of evidence investigators have to work with, the series of voices overheard by witnesses during the fatal altercation, amounts to only irreconcilable reports. Two voices other than the women's are heard, and, while there is a fairly stable consensus among witnesses that one of the two voices heard during the altercation was that of a Frenchman, there is absolutely no agreement on the language of the very unusual second voice also heard in the apartments. The singular point of corroboration by the witnesses is that it was a "shrill voice [which] was that of a foreigner" (Mabbott, 2:540). The confusion is remarkable: a gendarme on the scene believes the peculiar voice was Spanish; a neighbor thinks the voice Italian; a restaurateur, native to Amsterdam, believes it belonged to a Frenchman; an English tailor believes the voice to be German; an undertaker, native to Spain, deposes the voice was English; an Italian confectioner believes the voice was Russian. Each witness names a language he does not speak or understand, so that their collective testimony registers, in essence, only the absolute alienness of what was heard.

What is truly alien, of course, according to the terrain the depositions mark out is all that lies outside the geography of the leading European powers. Each of the witnesses names a European language with which they are unfamiliar as the language of the unidentifiable voice. Deftly, Dupin fathoms that the mistake each witness makes is to draw the scope of their reckoning much too narrowly. To each witness the "foreign" is that which is unfamiliar within the parameters of Europe, while, opposingly, an important measure of Dupin's brilliance rests on the fact that he fully recognizes that what is most strange, peculiar, and unfamiliar lies, with certainty, without rather than within European geographies. All but Dupin overlook the fact that attempts to identify the second voice may be so baffling precisely because those paradigms against which it is measured are themselves overly familiar, rather than aberrant or extraordinary. Dupin remarks:

> [E]ach spoke of [the voice] as that *of a foreigner*. Each is sure that it was not the voice of one of his own countrymen. Each likens it— not to the voice of an individual of any nation with whose language he is conversant—but the converse. . . . Now, how strangely unusual must that voice have really been about which such testimony as this *could* have been elicited!—in whose *tones*, even, denizens of the five great divisions of Europe could recognise nothing familiar! (Mabbott, 2:549; emphasis in original)

The matter in question must be profoundly outré to exceed "the five great divisions of Europe." All that is truly reasonable or reckonable must be legible within the terms set out by at least one of these five great divisions, Dupin's logic seems to run.

Hence, what will turn out to be the triumphant logic articulates a vast world map, one with a patent center and with all lying beyond this center unmistakably suggestive of the bizarre or virtually unthinkable. The racialized imperative of this logic is not as bald, however, as it at first seems, for the culprit, of course, turns out to be not an otherwise racialized (i.e., non-European) person but a frenzied orangutan. Indeed, Dupin quickly dismisses the possibility of any "Asiatic" or "African" being the culprit: "You will say that it might have been the voice of an Asiatic—of an African. Neither Asiatics nor Africans abound in Paris; but, *without denying the inference*, I will now merely call your attention to three points" (Mabbott, 2:550; emphasis added). He does not so much remove suspicion—and ultimately culpability—from "Asiatics" or "Africans" as move it through racially distinct peoples. He proclaims that one is perfectly right in imagining that the unrecognizably strange voice might be that of an Asiatic or an African. The inclinations are correct but the odds are against it, he reasons, and even as he undermines this line of speculation, he nonetheless equates the bizarre and unfathomable with these "exotic" cultures and peoples. Dupin, in other words, is never quite willing to dispel or dismiss the insight even as he proceeds to point out evidence that will lead him not to "Asiatics" or "Africans" but to the actual culprit.

Suggestively, Dupin's preeminent reasoning finally reveals the bizarre and fatal intrusion into the apparently orderly world of modern urban life to be a threat from without in the form of a volatile, foreign agent unfit by nature for unrestrained civil intercourse. Such reasoning is precisely at the center of the escalating debate concerning the meaning of racial blackness in the antebellum United States. The trajectory of Dupin's triumphant exposition in significant measure resembles widespread notions in U.S. culture of African Americans as a lurking "pathogen" (10)—to use a telling term employed by historian Clarence Walker. Walker writes:

> In the eyes of these statesmen [Thomas Jefferson, John C. Calhoun, William Lowndes Yancey, and Alexander Stephens] and the people they represented, Negroes were primitive, comical outsiders who were governed more by appetite than reason. . . . To most nineteenth-century white Americans the Negroes' racial difference and inferiority were not mere abstractions. Race was a physical fact. (5)

By marshaling evidence to represent popular nineteenth-century U.S. sentiment in his essay "How Many Niggers Did Karl Marx Know? Or, a Peculiarity of the Americans," Walker mounts a challenge to U.S. historiography of slavery and race relations invested primarily in analyses of class to the negligence of the fact that "[t]o most nineteenth-century white Americans . . . racial difference and inferiority were not mere abstractions" (8). As both learned and popular sentiment make plain, to live with Africans and African descendants in one's midst is to live in extreme proximity to the dangers of a foreign and primitive presence understood, as Walker argues, as no less than pathogenic. Moreover, in the West, in both the learned and the popular mind, the wild primitive state of the orangutan remains an important analogue for the natural condition of Africans and their descendants:

> If Negroes were likened to beasts, there was in Africa a beast which was likened to men. It was a strange and eventually tragic happenstance that Africa was the habitat of the animal which in appearance most resembles man. The animal called "orang-outang" by contemporaries (actually the chimpanzee) was native to those parts of western Africa where the early slave trade was heavily concentrated. Though Englishmen were acquainted (for the most part vicariously) with monkeys and baboons, they were unfamiliar with tail-less apes who walked about like men. Accordingly, it happened that Englishmen were introduced to the anthropoid apes and to Negroes at the same time and in the same place. The startling human appearance and movements of the "ape"—a generic term though often used as a synonym for the "orang-outang"—aroused some curious speculations. (Jordan, *The White Man's Burden*, 15)

What Dupin seems to insinuate with his equivocation is a subtle though inviolable connection between whatever lies beyond the wards of Europe and its five great divisions and what, in solving the murder mystery, is eventually revealed as the bestial. It is important to note, however, that this co-implication of the non-European and the bestial remains suggestive above all at this point in the narrative, for as yet there is no reasonable or reasoned figure in which and by which such a co-implication is confirmed. Ultimately, of course, this figure will be Dupin in his exposition of the guilty orangutan, its temperament, mimicry of human behavior, and origins.

Dupin's subsequent references to naturalist Georges Cuvier in elaborating his solution to the murders invokes these curious speculations much more directly. Both in terms of intellectual notoriety and in assuming the co-implication of the bestial and the non-European, Cuvier stands in the narrative as the figure of reason who precedes and in many ways validates the triumphant figure of Dupin. A leading European naturalist of the early nineteenth century, Georges Cuvier was also "regarded by contemporaries as the arch place-man, the greatest manipulator of patronage in science and in some branches of the administration, notably those of education and the Conseil d'Etat, of his day" (Outram, 5). A leading scientific and public figure, Cuvier, "[t]hrough studying the various structural means by which animals carried out the major processes of life, . . . believed he could establish rational criteria for a 'natural system' of classification" (Appel, 4). This certainty extended, furthermore, into considerations of the ostensible varieties of humankind, and one of Cuvier's most famous associations, that with southern African native Sarjte Bartmann (also known as the "Hottentot Venus"), underscores this point, as well as his position as both scientist and public figure: as part of the lucrative nineteenth-century vogue for "the exhibition of unusual humans . . . in both upper-class salons and in the street-side stalls" (Gould, 20), twenty-year-old Sarjte Bartmann was brought from southern Africa to Europe and displayed to eager audiences in both London and France from 1810 until her death in 1815. Drawing intense interest and large crowds for her embodiment of "steatopygia, or protruding buttocks, . . . which captured the eye of early European travelers [to Africa]" (Gilman, 232), Bartmann proved as fascinating in death as in life. The young woman's autopsy "was written up by Henri de Blainville in 1816 and then, in its most famous version, by Cuvier in 1817," a version "[r]eprinted at least twice during the next decade" (Gilman, 232). Emphasizing "any point of superficial similarity [of Bartmann] with an ape or monkey" (Gould, 22),[1] Cuvier's report reveals sensibilities and intentions plainly in line with enduring but specious speculations proposing the subhumanity, or inferior developmental or evolutionary state, of Africans and their descendants. Bartmann's dissected genitalia remain in the back reaches of the Musée de l'homme in France, a trophy testifying to unabashed nineteenth-century efforts to "define the great scale of human progress, from chimp to Caucasian" (Gould, 20).

This is to say that, if one can point to a figure in "The Murders in the Rue Morgue" for whom Africans and their descendants undoubtedly hold "a grim fascination, not as a missing link in a later evolutionary sense, but as . . . creature[s] who straddled that dreaded boundary between human and animal" (Gould, 22) and for whom this assumption underwrites an exhibition of intellectual prowess, it is certainly Georges

Cuvier—who, as it turns out, is key to Dupin's comprehension of the baffling events in the apartments of Madame L'Espanaye. In sum, one man of preeminent learning and perception executes his skills of apprehension by taking his cue from another. The figure of Cuvier represents a form of genius reiterated in Dupin and his deductions, since, as Dupin himself openly acknowledges, his recognition of the solution to the mystery of the murders turns on Cuvier. Having solved the mystery for himself, Dupin asks the narrator to read a passage from Cuvier's work that:

> was a minute anatomical and generally descriptive account of the large fulvous Ourang-Outang of the East Indian Islands. The gigantic stature, the prodigious strength and activity, the wild ferocity, and the imitative propensities of these mammalia are sufficiently well known to all. I understood the full horrors of the murder at once. (Mabbott 2:559)

The full horrors have to do with the bestial nature of the threat now understood by the narrator to be in their midst—a bestial nature that Cuvier in his career does not confine to wild animals, a presumption Dupin, in referencing Cuvier, reiterates at least implicitly. In all its suggestiveness, the pivotal reference to Cuvier does more than echo and reinforce the schemes of racialization implicit in Dupin's earlier equivocal comments concerning the language of the assailant. Allusions to the figure of Cuvier signal in substantial ways that schemes of racialization dismissive of "Asiatics" or "Africans" are themselves unquestionable signs of Reason. These particular signs are instrumental to Cuvier's notoriety, so that part of what constitutes the public knowledge on which Dupin draws is a racially stratified notion of intellect itself.

Summarily or directly stated, Dupin and Poe share Cuvier: in the fictive nineteenth-century world of Dupin, Cuvier is a notable international figure, as he also is in the nineteenth-century United States of Poe. Stated differently still, insofar as Poe labors for verisimilitude, he fixes instrumental elements of that verisimilitude on an internationally known celebrity who posits Africans to be "the most degraded of human races, whose form approaches that of the beast and whose intelligence is nowhere great enough to arrive at regular government" (Cuvier, *Recherches,* 105). These ideas, of course, are central to U.S. national identity and policy—official and unofficial:

> In the United States of the mid–nineteenth century, racial prejudice was all but universal. Belief in black inferiority formed a cen-

tral tenet of the southern defense of slavery, and in the North too, many who were undecided on the merits of the peculiar institution, and even those who disapproved of it, believed that the Negro was *by nature* destined to occupy a subordinate position in society. (Foner, *Politics,* 77; emphasis added)

In the absence of contravening references and in conjunction with other collaborating details, the pivotal reference to Cuvier succinctly suggests that the racial assumptions of the narrative remain strictly in line with the social and cultural inheritance informing quotidian U.S. notions of race.

Emphatically, the contention here is not that "The Murders in the Rue Morgue" is about U.S. slavery or in any way *directly* about the position of Africans and African descendants in U.S. society. The point is that the "materiality of history," to borrow the phrase of John Carlos Rowe, directly impinges on the narrative by characterizing its exposition and celebration of extraordinary reason in widespread (international) racist formulations proposing subordinate evolutionary, social, and intellectual positions to nonwhite peoples. Mental apprehension of the offending orangutan in many ways supplants the need for open declarations about race, or might in itself signal such a declaration. No dark-skinned person or persons need be singled out as guilty, and the reference to Cuvier subtly and with calculated verisimilitude substantiates this knowledge.

Still, beyond the key position of Georges Cuvier in the intellectual drama, the disclosure of the origins of the offending orangutan in Borneo is a further important element in the narrative's understated meditation on race. The "third largest island in the world after Greenland and New Guinea," Borneo is "one of numerous islands in the humid tropics of Asia which are scattered around the southern and eastern rim of the South China sea" (King, 7). Encircled by the South China Sea, the Java Sea, and the Celebes Sea, Borneo rests southeast of Malaysia and directly east of Sumatra. While the island fell mainly within the sphere of Dutch imperial power in the seventeenth century, the nineteenth century ushered in the island's primary period of colonization, which took place under the British rather than the Dutch; accordingly, the exotic location, landscape, and peoples of Borneo proved a catalyst for ardent Western imaginations in the nineteenth century, which "saw Borneo natives as living in a state of nature, closely in tune with their natural environment. In some cases, the European imagination merged humans and animals" (King, 10). The orangutan, as it happens, was conceived to be the primary figure of such a merger. For instance, "Englishman Capt. Daniel

Beeckman following his visit to southern Borneo . . . was the first to portray the forest ape, the *orang utan* (Pongo pymaeus) as a creature of fable" (King, 10–11; emphasis in original), and Norwegian Carl Bock ventured to Borneo "in search of the 'missing link': living creatures with combined human and animal characteristics" (King, 13).

As a result of falling increasingly under the sway of Western imperialism, Borneo in the nineteenth century serves as a point on the globe that marks for the West a hotbed of primitivism, exotic adventure, and encounters with startling, dangerous beasts. It is an enticing locale for both popular fiction and travelogues, such as *The Expedition to Borneo of H.M.S. Dido for the Suppression of Piracy: With Extracts from the Journal of James Brooke, Esq. of Sarawack (Now Agent for the British Government in Borneo)* published by Harper and Brothers in 1846 and written by Captain the Hon. Henry Keppel, R.N. In sum, "crossed by the equator a little below its center, so that about two thirds of its area lie in the northern and one third lies in the southern hemisphere" (Hose and McDougall, 1), Borneo furnishes an ample and remarkable arena for reveries of racial superiority, as the African interior similarly would once it became fully accessible to European explorers in the latter half of the nineteenth century (as Thomas Pakenham closely documents in his extensive study *The Scramble for Africa*). Both in the Western popular imagination and in "The Murders in the Rue Morgue," the enormous compass of Borneo—several times larger than England and "from the sea-coast to the summits of the highest mountains . . . covered with a dense forest" (Hose and McDougall, 5–6)—represents the antithesis of the Western metropole and serves as a compelling site for aggrandizing fantasies.

The importance Borneo holds in Dupin's solution documents Poe's familiarity with the popular meanings of distant geographies associated with "Asiatics" and "Africans." Further, it ideally fixes as the occasion for the murders the force of alien brutality eluding civilized restraint. Differently, the reason there seems to be *no* explanation for the murders is because there is no *reasonable* explanation. The murders are so alien not only in physical circumstances but also in possible motive that they *make no sense*. The force behind them is the chance and irrational brutality of a primitive agent. And the incontrovertible sign that this alien force stands *without* reason is the neglected economic windfall of the fatal ecounter. For, although it was fairly well known that Madame L'Espanaye and her daughter "lived an exceedingly retired life—[and] were reputed to have money" (Mabbott, 2:539), and although three days before the murders Madame L'Espanaye "took out in person the sum of 4000 francs, . . . which was paid in gold, and a clerk sent home with the money" (Mabbott, 2:541), the money was not stolen during the fatal altercation. All of Paris is left puzzling over the incident and musing: "why did [the perpetrator] abandon four thousand francs in gold to encumber himself with a bundle of linen? The gold was abandoned. Nearly the whole sum mentioned by Monsieur Mignaud, the banker, was discovered, in bags, upon the floor" (Mabbott, 2:556). In one instance, one might "imagine the perpetrator to be so vacillating an idiot as to have abandoned his gold and his motive together" (Mabbott, 2:556). The perpetrator, however, is beyond idiocy and *foreign* to the principles of economic exchange and accumulation understood profoundly as the hallmark of civilized and rational social being.

Even the wayward sailor, a member of the abundant lower classes, who is indirectly responsible for the murders through illicit ownership of the orangutan, is patently guided by principles of economic self-interest. In his unfolding mastery of the convoluted circumstances, Dupin places a false newspaper report of the capture of the beast, certain the sailor will appear to claim the animal because he "will reason thus:—'I am innocent; I am poor; my Ourang-Outang is of great value—to one in my circumstances a fortune of itself—why should I lose it through idle apprehensions of danger?'" (Mabbott, 2:561). He attributes economic motives to the sailor's ill-fated stewardship of the beast in the first place. That is, the desperate and unwise actions of the lower orders are eminently comprehensible (even if misguided), whereas the unfettered "intractable ferocity" of the inhabitants of foreign wards well beyond the geography of Europe is governed by no such recognizable principles of reason. Dupin's genius rests on providing an account of the unquestionably and unimaginable other—which is, as gingerly outlined as it may be, sketched in nineteenth-century codes of racialization. The prodigious intellectual powers of Dupin, then, reach beyond the limits of reason itself to provide most unexpectedly a logical account of circumstances seeming to defy all logic.

Dupin's duel here is with principles of unreason that are articulated through subtle markers of race. As much as the offending orangutan represents a principle of unreason, it also connotes in nineteenth-century cultural parlance signifiers of race: linguistic, anatomical, physiognomic, geographic. Oblique invocations of non-European racialization as a principle of violent unreason are at the center of Dupin's ruminations, and it is imperative to note that this is not an aberration. The larger principle at work here is one of exclusion and exclusiveness, one establishing the singular claims of racial "whiteness" to sites of value and acclamation by evacuating racial otherness from the conceptual field in question. This is the principle the fictive world of Dupin closely shares with the antebellum world of Poe. Eric Foner's redaction of the charged political concepts increasingly dominating the U.S. cultural conversation in the decades prior to the Civil War underscores this commonality, for "[i]n a nation in which slavery was a recent memory in the North and an overwhelming presence in the South; whose westward expansion (the guarantee of equal opportunity) required the removal of Indians and the conquest of lands held by Mexicans, it was inevitable that the language of politics . . . would come to be defined in racial terms" ("Free Labor," xxvii). Just as racial others are discharged from the condition and exposition of reason in "The Murders in the Rue Morgue," nonwhites are excluded, in fact, from ironically universalist rhetoric in the antebellum United States: "Despite its universalist vocabulary, the [triumphant republican] idea of free labor had little bearing on the actual conditions of nonwhites in nineteenth-century America" ("Free Labor," xxvii). It is not open declarations of racial sentiments on the part of Poe that are so telling but, rather, the continuity between his work and widespread racial and racist constructions.

In the essay "Amorous Bondage: Poe, Ladies, and Slaves," Joan Dayan makes a similar proposal in a relatively broad survey of Poe's work. She interrogates the way in which, "[w]ithout mentioning blacks, Poe applies the accepted argument on the 'nature' of negroes and the 'spirit' of women—both feeling, not thinking things—to the white men usually excluded from such categorizations" (119). She believes that "for Poe the cultivation of romance and the facts of slavery are inextricably linked" (110) and that his "gothic is crucial to our understanding of the entangled metaphysics of romance and servitude" (111). Dayan sets out to interpret the obliquely evident racial imperatives of Poe's imaginative world and proceeds by often reading Poe's work allegorically or by referring to aspects of his personal history—for instance, his "relationships with the leading pro-slavery advocates in Virginia" or the fact that his "guardians, the Allans, had at least three servants (all slaves, but at least one of these was owned by someone else and bonded to Mr. Allan)" (134).

Equally, one might disclose powerful correspondences between Poe's imaginative vision and the cultural vision of his society, as well as the terms that conjoin them. How is it possible, in a culture in which an antipathy between racial blackness and whiteness stands as a rudimentary principle, for one to understand oneself as a racial subject, a U.S. social subject, or a literary subject outside of the psychic as well as the legislated denigration of racial blackness? Racial taxonomies form a set of social knowledges virtually impossible to elude or not to imbibe, which codify and advertise African Americans as confined by nature to bodily existences having little or nothing to do with the life of the mind and its representation. In the absence of evidence that Poe stood far outside these cultural assumptions, it would be absolutely misguided not to conceive *as a matter of course* that such attitudes inform his delineations of great mindfulness, reason, and ingenuity—and, indeed, his entire canon. The burden of proof, it seems, rests with the opposing position. Literacy, for instance, is a primary issue through which the dynamics of racial blackness are emphatically played out in the cultural moment of the antebellum United States. Cultural fiats surrounding literacy[2] point out that the body within the ideologies of the dominant U.S. community holds the ultimate terms of identity for African Americans.[3] As the dominant community would have it, the identity of African Americans is bound up primarily, if not exclusively, with the terms of the body, a signal identification, since in European philosophizing the body is restricted to being the object of thought and never its subject. Literacy provides manifest testimony of the mind's ability to extend itself beyond the constricted limits and conditions of the body, so that to enter into literacy is to gain important skills for extending oneself beyond the condition and geography of the body. In other words, because literacy provides the most manifest formalization of the life of the mind, it is indispensable to this elaborate cultural construct.

Granting this perspective even tentatively in the case of "The Murders in the Rue Morgue," one begins to "see that the cool analytical rigor of Dupin's solutions, their masterly appropriation of the forms of scientific induction, might also serve to mask an underlying web of prejudices, received opinions, and unfounded ideological presumptions, lending them at second-hand, as it were, respectability and seemingly impeccable intellectual credentials" (Nygaard, 253). More generally, the conviction that Poe operated within, rather than substantially without, the terms of the antebellum culture in which he lived is to a significant degree shared by Dayan: "When we note varying denigrations of blacks in Poe's early works, it becomes even more unsettling that issues of race, like those of gender, have not figured significantly in Poe criticism" ("Amorous Bondage," 256). A gulf between Poe and normative U.S. racial ideology is an unlikely proposition, one in which, given its unlikeliness, the burden of proof rests with those subscribing to it.

Nonetheless, if Reason is conflated subtly with whiteness in "The Murders in the Rue Morgue," how might one account for the final disposition of its central characters, all of whom are white, but only one of whom, Dupin, stands confirmed fully by the logic of the narrative? John Bryant, in "Poe's Ape of UnReason: Humor, Ritual, and Culture," addresses this issue indirectly in an analysis that argues for Poe's "comic development" (52). According to Bryant, the dynamic from which Poe wrings his humor is one in which "the irrational (a human function intimately conjoined with sexuality) allows for a tentative spiritual connection to Beauty and Ideality, but that same irrationality, when manifested artistically in the grotesque of the imp of the perverse, debases, or even denies regenerative human faculties" (29). In reconstructing this humor, Bryant also acknowledges the speciousness of Dupin's triumphant reasoning: "Dupin knows the murderer is just an ape but has us rehearse the case so that we will conclude falsely that the perpetrator is a madman and hence that, by association, Dupin too is mad. But he fingers the Ape before we can draw such conclusions, thereby demolishing any implications of his actual irrationality" (33). The joke seems to be that there are two apes in the narrative—Dupin in his performance of an "ape of Un-Reason," being the second. The pun confirms the long-standing principle that if racial opposition is absent, so, too, is Reason, since the competing figurative and literal uses of "ape" only reiterate the diacritical relations (nadir and zenith) drawing together in the tale language, Cuvier, and Borneo.

Insofar as whiteness is vulnerable to bizarre intrusions into its apparently orderly world in the form of volatile, foreign agents (or impulses) unfit by nature for unrestrained civil intercourse, Dupin plays with—thereby signaling his mastery of—the threat. This singular mastery places Dupin in the most authoritative and advantageous position in the narrative. He sees the inexplicable horror beyond the scope or reach of the prefect, the horror that his friend, the narrator, recognizes only through proximity to Dupin, and which consumes two innocent white female victims. Dupin understands Reason, the analogue of whiteness, in ways that none of the other racially white characters do but, significantly, in ways that almost blur the distinction on which the terms of Reason—by racial fiat—rest. Dupin, in his closer mental proximity to the profoundly foreign intrusion, maintains, to his advantage, the full terms of his racial whiteness. In this paradox, the narrative returns its readers to peculiarities well articulated by Toni Morrison: "What does positing one's writerly self, in the wholly racialized society that is the United States, as unraced and all others as raced entail? . . . How do embedded assumptions of racial (not racist) language work in the literary enterprise that hopes and sometimes claims to be 'humanistic'?" (*Playing in the Dark*, xii). In effect, there is more than one alarming puzzle offered by Poe's narrative of individual brilliance, since Dupin's triumph documents that the truly white person always looks necessarily and intently beyond Europe and whiteness.

Notes

I gratefully acknowledge the many suggestions of the editors, as well as an unknown reader for Oxford University Press, concerning this chapter.

1. Gould adds parenthetically: "I hardly need to mention that since people vary so much, each group must be closer than others to some feature of some other primate, without implying anything about genealogy or aptitude" (22).

2. See, for example, Cornelius.

3. See my article "African American Slave Narrative: Literacy, the Body, Authority."

CHAPTER 7

"The Murders in the Rue Morgue"

*Amalgamation Discourses and the
Race Riots of 1838 in Poe's Philadelphia*

ELISE LEMIRE

Edgar Allan Poe's younger contemporary and fellow Philadelphian Charles Godfrey Leland (1824–1903) wrote in his *Memoirs* (1893) that "Whoever shall write a history of Philadelphia from the Thirties to the era of the Fifties will record a popular period of turbulence and outrages so extensive as to now appear almost incredible" (216). Leland was referring to a time when many whites felt compelled to shape social life as they saw fit and by whatever means required, no matter how violent. On numerous occasions and in response to various perceived outrages, white mobs took to the streets of Philadelphia and other cities, wrecking buildings and other personal property and attacking—and sometimes killing—the human subjects of their wrath.[1] Free blacks and white abolitionists were frequent targets, undergoing numerous assaults across the Northeast, particularly in the 1830s.[2] One of Philadelphia's worst riots occurred in May 1838, during the second Anti-Slavery Convention of American Women. Antiabolitionist whites attacked and burned the Friends Shelter for Colored Orphans, a black church, and the Pennsylvania Hall for Free Discussion, the city's newest and largest building and the site of the convention. Poe lived in Philadelphia at the time of this riot; he had moved there sometime in early 1838 and stayed until 1844.[3] Following the riot, he wrote what has come to be recognized as the first detective story, "The Murders in the Rue Morgue," in which a runaway orangutan wielding a barber's razor violently kills two white women in their upstairs apartment. The story appeared in the April 1841 issue of Philadelphia's *Graham's Magazine*. Recently, after years of eliciting what critic Shawn Rosenheim calls "bad Freudian readings," "Murders" has begun to receive the attention of scholars interested in placing Poe and his work within U.S. social and cultural history ("Detective Fiction," 167).[4] I show here that the specific anxieties about race that culminated in the May riot go a long way toward explaining both what may have prompted Poe to place a murderous orangutan in the bedroom of two white women as well as how his contemporary readers would have read the violent encounter.

The narrator of "Murders" makes it clear that the mystery's solution makes sense only if one is familiar with orangutans. After gentleman detective C. Auguste Dupin has solved the mystery for himself, he asks his companion, the tale's narrator, to read a passage from the work of French naturalist Frederick Cuvier (1769–1832) about which the companion says:

> It was a minute anatomical and generally descriptive account of the large fulvous Ourang-Outang of the East Indian Islands. The gigantic stature, the prodigious strength and activity, the wild ferocity, and the imitative propensities of these mammalia are sufficiently well known to all. I understood the full horrors of the murder at once. (Mabbott, 2:559)

The characteristics of the orangutan that "at once" illuminate the murders were "sufficiently well known to all" because the writings of Cuvier and other naturalists were reproduced widely during the first half of the nineteenth century to feed the burgeoning interest in natural history.[5] The American middle and upper classes were enthusiastic purchasers of natural history in the form of magazine articles, school textbooks, laymen's science books, engravings, newspaper reports, encyclopedia entries, and exhibits in museums and elsewhere.[6] Poe had attempted to capitalize on this interest, and had thus familiarized himself with Cuvier, when he contributed to *The Conchologist's First Book* (1839) and helped write Thomas Wyatt's *Synopsis of Natural History* (1839), shortly before penning "Murders." According to Poe, for *The Conchologist's First Book*, he "translated from Cuvier . . . the accounts of the animals" (quoted in D. Thomas, "Poe in Philadelphia," 950). And the *Synopsis*, as stated on its title page, included substantial "additions from the work of Cuvier."[7]

Of all the creatures in the natural world, monkeys and apes were—and continue to be—of particular interest to naturalists and laymen alike because of their many similarities to humans.[8] In 1735, Linnaeus (1707–78), the Swedish scientist who developed the modern system of biological classification, put humans in the same taxonomic order as simians, later arguing that he could "discover scarcely any mark by which man can be distinguished from the apes. . . . Neither in the face nor in the feet, nor in the upright gait, nor in any other aspect of his external structure does man differ from the apes" (66). Simians thereby seemed to confirm that the animal kingdom is hierarchical and continuous. Monkeys were viewed as the link between humans and animals and were studied accordingly. And so it was that, on 1 July 1839, when a nonhuman primate (variously called an "Ourang Outang" and a chimpanzee) arrived in Philadelphia from Liberia, the newspapers were enthusiastic about this chance to see an animal so much like a human:

NOW exhibiting at the Masonic Hall, Chestnut street, from 8 o'clock, AM. to 6 o'clock, PM., the only living CHIMPANZEE, lately brought from Africa[.] This animal is the genuine "Troglodytes Niger" of Naturalists, or "Wild Man of the Woods," and is the finest specimen ever seen in this country. It bears a most striking resemblance to the human form, and in natural sagacity far exceeds the description of Naturalists.

Admittance 25 cents; Children half price. Tickets to be had at the door. (*Philadelphia Gazette*, 20 August 1839)[9]

As critics have often noted, this particular primate may have served as Poe's inspiration for "Murders."[10] More important than a particular primate's presence, however, is that, as the newspaper articles about it reveal, many people were already interested in and somewhat knowledgeable about primates from having read the work of naturalists. Clearly Poe felt he could count on precisely that knowledge.

The simian characteristics to which Dupin refers as "well known"— "gigantic stature," "prodigious strength," "wild ferocity," and "imitative propensities"—are all used in Poe's story with a great degree of specificity at first to mystify and ultimately to account for the orangutan's escape from its owner's quarters, then its seemingly impossible ascension to the fourth-flour apartment of Madam L'Espanaye and her daughter, and finally its incredibly violent destruction of them. When Dupin asks his companion to attempt to fit his own hands into a to-scale tracing of the marks left on Mademoiselle's L'Espanaye's neck, for example, his companion "made the attempt in vain" and infers that "[t]his . . . is the mark of no human hand" (Mabbott, 2:559). That an orangutan's "stature" was so great—and therefore that its hands would be very large—was popularly known. In an 1833 compilation entitled *A Natural History of the Globe, of Man, and of Quadrupeds; From the Writings of Buffon, Cuvier . . . and Other Eminent Naturalists*, for example, it was noted that "[Andrew] Battel [*sic*] assures us . . . the Pongo [a Europeanization of a native name for orangutan] is . . . as tall (he says) as a giant" (2:252).

In *Bingley's Natural History*, another book from the period with excerpts from Cuvier, Battell is also noted to have described orangutans as "so powerful . . . that ten men would not have strength enough to hold one of them" (Bingley, 34).[11] Another such account marvels that, as one large orangutan approached a tree, its strength "was shown in a high degree, for with one spring he gained a very lofty bough and bounded from it with the ease of smaller animals of his kind" (*New-England Galaxy*, 10 June 1825). Thus, when the L'Espanaye apartment is found in disarray, Dupin reasons that only someone with this kind of massive strength could have thrown the furniture about, stuffed the daughter's corpse up the chimney, and thrown the mother's body out the window (Mabbott, 2:549). Of the clumps of hair remaining, Dupin marvels at "the prodigious power which had been exerted in uprooting perhaps half a million of hairs at a time" (Mabbott, 2:557). Poe's readers would have been ready to concur that only the strength of the mighty orangutan was adequate for such a task.

Primates were also known for their agility. The following passage excerpted in *Bingley's Natural History* is typical in the terms it employs, terms which match those used by Poe: "Its agility was almost incredible. . . . Sometimes, suspended by one arm, it would poise itself, and then suddenly turn round upon a rope, with nearly as much quickness as a wheel or a sling. Sometimes it would slide down one of the ropes, and would again ascend with astonishing agility" (39). In the same book, another orangutan, having escaped its chains, is said to have been "seen to ascend, with wonderful agility, the beams and oblique rafters of the building" (37). Such tales are deemed notable for the amount of awe the animal's agility inspires. Their prowess is termed "incredible," "astonishing," and "wonderful" (39, 37). Although the narrator of "Murders" does not mention the simian characteristic of agility in his summary of the passage from Cuvier, Dupin carefully references that trait in his solution of the mystery:

> I wish you to bear especially in mind that I have spoken of a *very* unusual degree of activity as requisite to success in so hazardous and so difficult a feat. It is my design to show you, first, that the thing might possibly have been accomplished:— but, secondly and *chiefly*, I wish to impress upon your understanding the *very*

extraordinary—the almost praeternatural character of that agility which could have accomplished it. (Mabbott, 2:555; emphasis in original)

We are eventually told by the orangutan's owner that the animal escaped the sailor's apartment by springing "at once through the door of the chamber, down the stairs, and thence, through a window . . . into the street" (Mabbott, 2:565). After being chased into the Rue Morgue, "it perceived the lightning-rod, clambered up with inconceivable agility, grasped the shutter, which was thrown fully back against the wall, and, by this means, swung itself directly upon the headboard of the bed. The whole feat did not occupy a minute" (Mabbott, 2:565).

But Poe was far from done with his employment of the orangutan's various traits. He and his readers were well aware that popular accounts of the orangutan's strength often stressed how it was employed for ferocious ends, although Cuvier's work did not. Readers of natural history were told repeatedly that, despite their usual placidity, an orangutan, as stated in *Bingley's*, "could be excited to violent rage" (42). Indeed, the first sentence of the entry on orangutans in the encyclopedia available to the young Poe in the Allan home notes, "These animals will attack and kill the negroes who wander in the woods; drive away the elephants, beating them with their fists or clubs; and throw stones at people who offend them" (*Dr. Rees's New Cyclopaedia* 1, part 2). *Bingley's* points to the account of an eighteenth-century French navigator whose cabin boy was attacked when he "refused to answer . . . [two orangutans'] demands. . . . [T]hey sometimes became enraged, caught him by the arm, bit and threw him down" (35). In each case, the animal's actions are interpreted as anger that its desires are not being met; people who "offend them" are stoned, and boys who do not meet their "demands" are seized, bitten, and thrown down. Likewise, in "Murders," Poe's orangutan becomes enraged when its desires are thwarted. Only then does it use its brute strength to wreak destruction on human lives:

> The screams and struggles of the old lady (during which the
> hair was torn from her head) had the effect of changing the prob-
> ably pacific purposes of the Ourang-Outang into those of wrath.
> With one determined sweep of its muscular arm it nearly severed
> her head from her body. The sight of blood inflamed its anger
> into phrenzy. Gnashing its teeth, and flashing fire from its eyes, it
> flew upon the body of the girl, and imbedded its fearful talons
> in her throat, retaining its grasp until she expired. (Mabbott,
> 2:566–67)

As in the popular accounts, although the orangutan in "Murders" "probably" has "pacific purposes," it quickly becomes enraged when Madame L'Espanaye attempts to escape.

Natural history accounts also marveled at the degree to which primates could act like humans, another trait cited by Poe's narrator after perusing Cuvier and one central to the story's plot. The following account of an imitative orangutan from Le Comte Georges Buffon (1707–88) was cited in just about every antebellum book on the animal kingdom. This particular version is taken from the same entry on orangutans in the encyclopedia owned by the Allans, cited earlier:

> Buffon relates, that he had seen this animal offer its hand to those who came to see him, and walk with them; as if he had been one of the company; that he has seen him sit at table, unfold his napkin, wipe his lips, make use of his knife and fork, pour out his drink into a glass, take his cup and saucer, put in sugar, pour out the tea, and stir it, in order to let it cool; and that he has done this not only at the command of his master, but often without bidding. (*Dr. Rees's New Cyclopaedia* 1, part 2)

Like the orangutan described by Buffon, the animal in Poe's story wants to imitate its owner and even escapes from a locked closet to do so. The sailor explains, as recounted by the narrator:

> Returning home from some sailors' frolic on the night, or rather in the morning of the murder, he found the beast occupying his own bed-room, into which it had broken from a closet adjoining, where it had been, as was thought, securely confined. Razor in hand, and fully lathered, it was sitting before a looking-glass, attempting the operation of shaving, in which it had no doubt previously watched its master through the key-hole of the closet. (Mabbott, 2:564–65)

Poe's orangutan here goes one step further than Buffon's, trying to look like its so-called master. For although the animal's use of a mirror can be construed as merely further imitation—indeed, it is said only to sit before the glass, not necessarily to be looking in it—the use of the mirror can also be read as the sign of the animal's desire to emulate and even become a man. For the orangutan imitates that particular ritual whereby men rid themselves of that facial hair which, left in its natural state, would more closely ally men with hairy or furry creatures. Indeed, less than twenty-five years later, Abraham Lincoln would be widely lambasted for growing a beard, with many anti-Lincoln men referring to the author of the Emancipation Proclamation as the "Illinois Ape" and "the baboon."[12]

The same razor used in this scene as a means of imitation plays a key role in the murders. The orangutan's owner reports, as narrated by Dupin's companion: "As . . . [he] looked in [to the L'Espanaye apartment], the gigantic animal had seized Madame L'Espanaye by the hair, (which was loose, as she had been combing it,) and was flourishing the razor about her face, in imitation of the motions of a barber" (Mabbott, 2:566). But if the orangutan once sat before a looking glass attempting to imitate an act "it had no doubt previously watched," here it is said to "imitate" a profession it seems to have never seen, at least so far as the reader knows. Even more remarkably, these same barbering attempts, a seeming narrative inconsistency, result in Madame's slit throat.

This barbering primate would have been less puzzling to local readers, for, at the time Poe's tale was published in Philadelphia, the city's own Peale's Museum displayed stuffed monkeys dressed and arranged so as to depict the life of a barbershop.[13] In his *Memoirs*, Charles Godfrey Leland noted of his boyhood in 1830s Philadelphia, "I owe so very much . . . to old Peale's Museum. . . . How often have I paused in its dark galleries in awe before the tremendous skeleton of the Mammoth. . . . And the stuffed monkeys—one shaving another—what exquisite humour, which never palled upon us!" (38–39). Such an exhibit might have served to remind viewers of the oft-noted similarities between monkeys and humans. That Leland found the monkeys humorous, however, indicates that the museum was not necessarily prompting serious philosophical consideration of what, if anything, distinguishes humans from other animals. What, then, was the purpose of displaying barbering monkeys?

In the antebellum period, the tending of white men's hair and beards was typically done by blacks, for whom such labor was considered "natural." In his study *The Colored Aristocracy of St. Louis* (1858), Cyprian Clamorgan asserts that "a mulatto takes to razors and soap as naturally as a young duck to a pool of water . . . ; they certainly make the best barbers in the world, and were doubtless intended by nature for the art. In its exercise, they take white men by the nose without giving offense, and without causing an effusion of blood" (18). Fifteen years after Poe published "The Murders in the Rue Morgue," Herman Melville has his protagonist in "Benito Cereno" (1856) voice sentiments similar to Clamorgan's about the naturalness of black barbering skills. On board the *San Dominick*, Captain Amasa Delano comforts himself that nothing is amiss when he watches the Negro Babo shave his master, Don Benito. The scene is described by Delano as follows: "There is something in the Negro which, in a peculiar way, fits him for avocations about one's person. Most Negroes are natural valets and hairdressers, taking to the comb and brush congenially as to the castanets, and flourishing them apparently with almost equal satisfaction" (185). For Delano, "seeing the colored servant, napkin on arm, so debonair about his master, in a business so familiar as that of shaving too, all his old weakness for Negroes returned" (186). But if Delano envisions barbers as content servants or slaves, Clamorgan makes it clear that barbering was the chosen profession of those free blacks who wanted to rise. He notes that "a majority of our colored aristocracy [in St. Louis] belong to the tonsorial profession" (18). Of the thirty-one men whom Clamorgan describes as being of this aristocracy, census materials indicate that as many as eleven were barbers at some time. The next most prevalent job among this set is that of steward, of which only four of the thirty-one men worked as such.

There was a wealthy tier of blacks in Philadelphia as well. Of the fifteen thousand blacks who lived there in 1830, one thousand held a substantial amount of wealth by the period's standards (E. Lapsansky, 57). And although the total number of blacks in Philadelphia constituted less than 10 percent of the city's total population, there had been a 30 percent increase in the black population since 1820, which gave many whites the impression that the city's population, as well as its economy was shifting drastically. In his landmark work, *The Philadelphia Negro: A Social Study* (1899), W. E. B. Du Bois cites an 1849 study in which barbers are said to make up roughly 5 percent of the total black workforce in Philadelphia. Many blacks were undoubtedly attracted to the entrepreneurial nature of the barbering business. Historian Roger Lane explains that "barbers could be classified as either skilled workingmen, if they worked for others, or as small capitalist entrepreneurs if they were in business for themselves. The line between the two was slight and often artificial. . . . [I]t is appropriate to think of black tradesmen more as real or potential entrepreneurs than as wage-earners" (115). In short, Leland and other visitors to Peale's Museum would have read the monkeys there as parodies of black barbers, an ambitious and fairly large group about whom, as we will see, whites felt no little anxiety and therefore might have drawn comfort from mocking them.

Of course, the connection made at Peale's museum between black barbers and monkeys was made possible by the common perception in Poe's day that simians are related to humans and to blacks in particular. One Dr. John Jeffries explained in "Some Account of the Dissection of a Simia Satyrus, Ourang Outang, or Wild Man of the Woods," published in the *Boston Journal of Philosophy and the Arts* in 1825, that the orangutan "forms, in the chain of created beings, the connecting link of brutes to man" (570), making an obvious reference to the concept of the Chain of Being, a posited hierarchy of beings from God down to the lowliest of the animals, the conceptualization of which reached full flower in the eighteenth century.[14] Because most whites believed, however, in a hierarchy of the human races as well, and because, as Winthrop Jordan notes, black Africans and the animals called "orang-outangs" (actually chimpanzees) were first encountered by whites at the same time and in proximate areas, "orang-outangs" were viewed by whites as more closely related to blacks than to themselves (Jordan, *White Over Black,* 29). In the eighteenth century, scientists sought to substantiate these perceived relationships. The Dutch anatomist Pieter Camper (1722–89), for example, argued that the hierarchical relationship between whites, blacks, and nonhuman primates was evidenced by, among other things, race- and species-specific *linea facialis,* or "facial lines." In his dissertation on this topic, translated into English in 1794, he explained that "a line, drawn along the forehead and upper lip [of a person or animal in profile] . . . pointed out the degree of similarity between a negroe and the ape" (9).[15] For, according to him, blacks, on average, have a facial angle of seventy degrees and apes of forty-two to fifty degrees, whereas the profile of whites approaches a vertical line. Many natural historians in the United States, including Jeffries in his *Boston Journal* article, drew similar conclusions from their own measurements of facial angles in the first half of the nineteenth century, prompting historian Londa Schiebinger to conclude that Camper's drawings of facial angles became "the central visual icon of all subsequent racism . . . in the nineteenth century" (149–50).[16] Blacks were repeatedly drawn in profile with exaggerated facial angles by scientists and artists alike in order to denigrate them for their supposed relationship to nonhuman primates.

Belief in a relationship between blacks and orangutans led to all kinds of comparisons in the nineteenth century between the two and even the insistence that orangutans could be mistaken for blacks. An 1825 article in the *Saturday Evening Post* noted of an orangutan that the "unwillingness to part with his cup of tea was testified in the expressive glances of an old negro" (4 June 1825). We are also informed by Jeffries in the article cited earlier from the *Boston Journal of Philosophy and the Arts* that the captain of the ship who transported the animal under study, "While sitting at breakfast, . . . heard some one enter a door behind, and found a hand placed familiarly on his shoulder; on turning round, he was not a little surprised to find a hairy negro making such an unceremonious acquaintance" (571–72). If this orangutan can surprise, it is not only because it is thought to look like a "hairy negro" but also because it lacks the attributes of gentility; it is the fact of its "unceremonious acquaintance" that initially startles the captain. The description of the scene depends not only on the supposition that nonhuman primates and blacks look alike but also on the realization that the orangutan has reached beyond a station defined as lowly by its very proximity to the station of Negroes. Similarly, in his own employment of a barbering and therefore overreaching orangutan, Poe also insists that the reader draw comparisons between blacks and simians, even as he does not explicitly evoke the imagined similarity in his list from Cuvier of the characteristics of orangutans. And by making a barbering razor the chief murder weapon, Poe draws on perceived similarities precisely to invoke the frightening and dangerous possibility of black upward mobility that black barbering signaled for so many whites.

Clamorgan also reveals the nature of the black barber's terrible power, despite insisting that black barbers can take white men by the nose "without giving offense":

> When one of these gossiping knights of the razor gets his customer under his hands, it would seem that his tongue keeps pace with his razor; they are dumb as mutes until they get a man's head thrown back on a level with his breast, his face, and especially his mouth, besmeared with a thick coating of lather, and the glittering steel flourishing in *terrorem* over his throat. (17)

The white customer is immobilized by the lather, by the blade "flourishing in *terrorem*" over his throat, and by the black man's voice, usually silenced in American life but liberated here by his position as an entrepreneurial businessman. Again, it was the economic element of the black barbering profession in particular that made it a great source of anxiety for whites. As Clamorgan and Du Bois demonstrate, barbering was the most visible profession of the propertied black class. This alone would account for the fact that it was singled out as a point over which whites felt it necessary to fret. Because barbering was an entrepreneurial and thus potentially white job and because the backbone of the barbering business was shaving beards, the barbershop put the bared necks of white clients in fearful proximity with aspiring blacks both literally and metaphorically.

So, too, in a lithograph by Anthony Imbert (ca. 1829–30), created as the wrapper illustration for a series of 1820s cartoons entitled *Life in Philadelphia* by Philadelphian Edward W. Clay (1799–1857), is a white client of a black barber shown in a vulnerable position (figure 7.1).[17] The *Life in Philadelphia* series mocked the class aspirations of the blacks

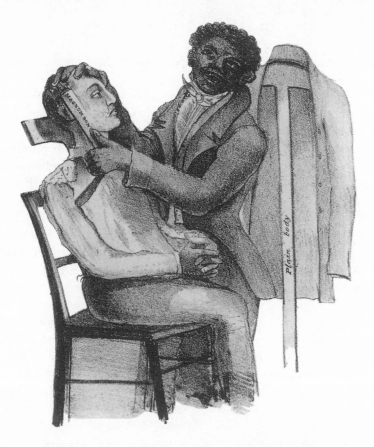

Lithograph of Imbert.

FIGURE 7.1. Anthony Imbert. Wrapper illustration for "Life in Philadelphia" (ca. 1829-30). Courtesy, The Historical Society of Pennsylvania

of the city by depicting attempts at proper dress and manners as misguided and laughable. Immensely popular and even copied overseas, the title of the series became a recognized shorthand way of referring to black ambition throughout the 1820s and 1830s and thus served to remind white Philadelphians that the blacks of their city were a particularly striving bunch. In Imbert's contribution to the series, the white client's head is held firmly in place, and he is unable to see the long razor blade posed to scrape clean his cheek. The barber sports the various accoutrements he perceives to signal affluence: an ornate collar and a fancy coat. Imbert labels the barber's razor "Magnum Don," or great gentleman, to underscore the barber's pretension in his dress and, perhaps too, in his choice of an entrepreneurial profession. In contrast, the white client wears simple garments. The rack supporting his equally unostentatious coat is clearly labeled "Plain body." The Quaker-like garb and the white man's calm, even devotional, gaze at the barber indicate that Imbert may have wanted to portray the client as an abolitionist. In that case, the abolitionist's desire for equality—political, economic, and otherwise—would have paved the way for his own economic and perhaps literal bloodletting. Either way, Imbert associates the economic striving of free blacks in Philadelphia with both cultural and economic poaching on white society and connects that poaching with possible white extinction.

So, too, in "Benito Cereno" does the potential for murder lurk in the barber's razor. Babo lathers only those areas of his master that do not sport a beard, "the upper lip and low down under the throat," the latter a decidedly vulnerable spot. In the barber's chair, Don Benito does not manifest the same comfort expressed by Delano upon witnessing the barbering scene: "Not unaffected by the close sight of the gleaming steel, Don Benito nervously shuddered" (186–87). Delano does not fail to notice this response, "nor, as he saw the two thus postured, could he resist the vagary that in the black he saw a headsman, and in the white a man at the block" (187). Benito shudders again when the knife touches his throat: "No sword drawn before James the First of England, no assassination in that timid king's presence, could have produced a more terrified aspect than was now presented by Don Benito" (188). Babo nicks him but draws only a small amount of blood. Later, Melville justifies the white men's unease about the black barber by revealing that Don Benito was Babo's captive.

So when Poe has the orangutan in "Murders" attempt to shave Madame in what will result in her beheading, he has stepped into the terms set up by Peale's Museum whereby monkeys are black barbers and thus barbering blacks are bestial. And yet, in doing so, he is not "humorous" (Leland's term for describing the museum) but instead plays out the anxiety at the heart of Imbert's barber print and "Benito Cereno"; throats are slit and blood shed. This is not to say that Poe allows the orangutan to function in a fully allegorical manner. For, at the end, when the sailor is allowed to sell his orangutan "for . . . a very large sum at the *Jardin des Plantes*" (Mabbott, 2:568), Poe, in effect, returns the orangutan to Cuvier and to the realm of natural history more generally where it is less easily allowed to function as a symbol. In this way, Poe ultimately disavows any connection in his tale between orangutans and blacks, and it is this disavowal that has long made "The Murders in the Rue Morgue" seem so very distant from the historical context that shaped it. Rather, Poe continually draws on the perceived similarities between blacks and nonhuman primates to create a comparison between the two in the reader's mind.

Poe's readers would have perceived one other way in which Poe invokes the orangutan's supposed relationship to blacks: the way in which he makes speech a central component of the mystery in the Rue Morgue. Whereas the possibility of orangutan speech was once thought to prove kinship between simians and humans, eighteenth- and nine-teenth-century naturalists insisted that nonhuman primates do not have the capacity for speech.[18] In *Dr. Rees's New Cyclopaedia*, Camper is noted for "having dissected the whole organ of voice in the orang, in apes, and several monkeys." This work apparently offers "the most evident proof of the incapacity of orangs, apes, and monkeys, to utter any modulated voice, as indeed they have never been observed to do." Of course, such experiments indicate that the question of orangutan speech was still a nagging one.

In "Murders," during the police investigation, as depicted in the newspaper, everyone reports hearing on the night of the murder the voice of a Frenchperson and another voice, which each assumes is of a European language different than his own. Dupin concludes:

"Each likens it—not to the voice of an individual of any nation
with whose language he is conversant—but the converse. . . .
Now, how strangely unusual must that voice have really been,
about which such testimony as this *could* have been elicited—in
whose *tones*, even, denizens of the five great divisions of Europe
could recognize nothing familiar! You will say that it might have
been the voice of an Asiatic—of an African. Neither Asiatics nor
Africans abound in Paris; but, without denying the inference, I will
now merely call your attention to three points." (Mabbott,
2:549–50; emphasis in original)

The three points are enumerated—the harshness of the voice, its quick tempo, and the fact that no words were distinguishable—after which Dupin moves on to a discussion of the murderer's means of egress. By even momentarily leaving open the possibility that the voice might have been that of an African or Asiatic—Dupin proceeds "without denying the inference"—the three points link African and Asian speech to inde-cipherable babble and thus ultimately to that of the animal that some be-lieved could not "utter any modulated voice" and others believed possi-bly could speak, however rudimentary that speech probably would be: the orangutan. Poe thereby implies again that there is a kinship between Africans or blacks and nonhuman primates.

But if orangutans were thought to look, act, and sound like blacks and even to be related to them, nothing made the two seem more similar than the type of desire they each supposedly had for the women above them in the Chain of Being. The perception that orangutans sought to mate with African women originated in the late sixteenth and early seventeenth centuries and was still going strong years later. Consider that, in 1795, the frontispiece of Linnaeus's *Genuine and Universal System of Natural History* shows an orangutan snatching an African woman from her human mate.[19] The white belief that black men were also lascivious began in the seventeenth century when travelers turned their various anxieties about Africa into reports that African men had "large Propagators" (quoted in Jordan, *White Over Black,* 34). Shakespeare drew on this commonplace in *Othello* (1604-5), in which Iago suspects the "lusty Moor" of having been "twixt [his] sheets" and convinces Brabantio that "an old black ram / Is tupping [his] white ewe." In Poe's day, the play was a popular one, giving John Quincy Adams in 1835, and presumably others, a welcomed reason to declare the interracial marriage it depicted "a gross outrage upon the law of Nature" (438), even as he and others flocked to performances.[20] That white Americans linked their conception of black male sexuality with black kinship to nonhuman primates is best evidenced by Thomas Jefferson's argument in his *Notes on the State of Virginia* (1785), the most widely read "scientific" book on blacks until the mid–nineteenth century, that blacks "prefer" whites "as uniformly as is the preference of the Oranootan for the black women over those of his own species" (265).[21] Jefferson was so sure that orangutans desired black women that he used that purported fact to prove that blacks desire whites. The supposed kinship between blacks and orangutans is not referenced overtly here but makes Jefferson's comparison possible.

Many natural history texts of the nineteenth century repeated the popular myth about orangutans and women. *A Natural History of the Globe, of Man, and of Quadrupeds* (1833) insisted that orangutans "are passionately fond of women. . . . [T]here is no safety for them in passing through the woods they inhabit, as these animals immediately attack and injure them" (2:253). Indeed, any reference to primates instantly conjured up notions of interspecies rape. And, as often as not, the race of the endangered woman was no longer specified, which meant that she was now assumed to be white. In 1859, Poe's great admirer Charles Baudelaire (1821–67) commented on a sculpture called "Ourang Outang Carrying Off a Woman Deep into the Woods":

> Why not a crocodile, a tiger, or any other beast that might eat a woman? Because it's not a question of mastication but of violation. For the ape alone, the gigantic ape—at the same time more and less than a man—has sometimes demonstrated a human ap-

petite for women. And in this the artist finds the means to astonish his viewer. (quoted in Ambrogio, 135)

According to Baudelaire, the artifact in question constitutes a coherent
narrative only if the viewer knows that orangutans have "sometimes
demonstrated a human appetite for women." And that a woman might
be sexually violated by this animal, "at the same time more and less a
man," was a horror beyond all others, especially if the woman was white.

Edward W. Clay hoped to capitalize on this fear of interspecies sex in
a series of lithographs he made in the late 1830s aimed at denigrating the
immediate abolitionists and abolitionist women in particular.[22] And
while Clay had moved to New York after completing his *Life in Philadelphia* series, his prints would have been viewed as an extension of that
earlier, very popular work. The first print in Clay's series, *Johnny Q, Introducing the Haytien Ambassador to the Ladies of Lynn, Mass.* (1839), is dedicated to "Miss Caroline [*sic*] Augusta Chase & the 500 ladies of Lynn
who wish to marry Black Husbands" (figure 7.2). In February 1839, Aro-
line Chase led the Lynn (Massachusetts) Female Anti-Slavery Society in
garnering signatures for a petition they presented to the Massachusetts
legislature in support of repealing the law in effect since 1705 that nulli-
fied interracial marriages and fined those who performed them.[23] In the
first several months of the *Liberator*, in 1831, William Lloyd Garrison
had repeatedly reprinted the law, arguing alongside it that "the law in
question violates one of the principles of our Constitution . . . the
right of every individual to seek happiness" (29 January 1831). Lydia
Maria Child had also cited the law in her *Appeal in Favor of That Class of
Americans Called Africans* (1833) as the first "evidence" of racial prejudice
in the North (187). Even as their own racism kept them from encouraging whites to actually intermarry, especially when pressed on the point,
Garrison, Child, and Chase realized the central role that the prohibition
against interracial marriage played in creating an exploitative race-based
society.[24] The abolitionists finally succeeded in having the law repealed
in 1843.

Like the many newspaper reports on the women of Lynn, such as one
in the *Boston Post* which asserted that they "despair of having a white
offer and so are willing to try *de colored race*," Clay depicts them as eager
quite literally to embrace the ambassador from the only black republic
(quoted in Sterling, 78; emphasis in original). One white woman is made
to remark, "How I should like to kiss his balmy lips!" In Clay's mind,
abolitionist women were motivated solely by such interracial desires and
should, of course, be shunned for it and their political work aborted.
This view was a popular one. In his April 1845 review in the *Aristidean* of

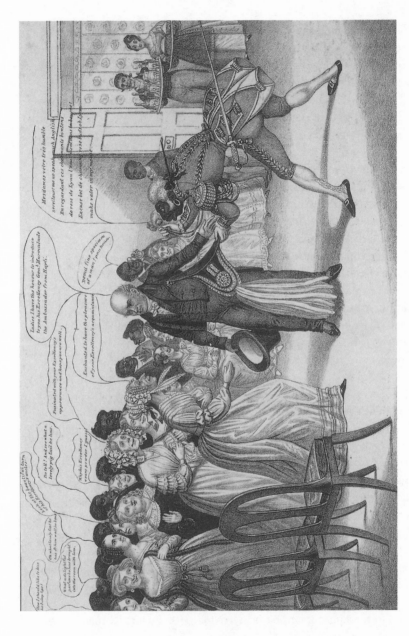

FIGURE 7.2. Edward W. Clay, *Johnny Q, Introducing the Haytien Ambassador to the Ladies of Lynn, Mass.* (1839). Courtesy, The Library Company of Philadelphia

Henry Wadsworth Longfellow's *Poems on Slavery* (1842), Poe supposes that the volume "is intended for the especial use of those negrophilic old ladies of the north, who form so large a part of Mr. Longfellow's friends" (*Essays*, 762). It is not that these so-called antiabolitionists did not oppose slavery; they usually did. But they favored a gradual and voluntary end to it and certainly did not go so far as to champion the right to intermarry. The antiabolitionists wanted the world to continue on as before, just eventually without slavery, whereas Garrison's followers espoused the need for a radically new world, even as most of them never fully embraced that vision themselves.

In Clay's print, the ambassador's own arousal by his proximity to these eager white women is evidenced by his distended buttocks and his insistence, albeit garbled, that the abolitionist ladies of Lynn "make vater in my mouse." More than this, the exaggeration of the ambassador's facial angle would have raised the possibility that the ambassador will act on his stated desires and that, when he does, the resulting coupling will be an unnatural and indeed monstrous one. For, as we have seen, it was a commonplace of comparative anatomy that the angle of one's jaw signified one's place in the Chain of Being and that the facial angle of blacks placed them in direct proximity with nonhuman primates. That the abolitionist women supposedly desired such simian beasts made them all the more worthy of condemnation.

The belief in the right of blacks and whites to intermarry shared by the women of Lynn and the other most radical abolitionists in New England led their opponents to castigate them as "amalgamationists." (The word we hear today to refer to interracial sex and marriage, *miscegenation*, was not coined until 1864).[25] The charge was used to lambaste all of the other abolitionists as well. Since the early 1830s, immediate abolitionists had separated themselves from the colonizationists by clamoring not only for immediate black emancipation but also for the end of race prejudice in the North.[26] And their own actions were meant as a first step. They formed racially integrated societies, held racially integrated meetings, and, in many cases, formed interracial friendships.[27] By the middle of the decade, some white women, such as Angelina and Sarah Grimké, stood up publicly behind the antislavery lectern from which they addressed men as well as women, whites as well as blacks, at a time when speaking from the platform was considered defeminizing. And some white women, such as Abby Kelley Foster, traveled on the abolitionist circuit with black men (Pease, 61). If the abolitionists wanted to free all blacks, and if they were willing to socialize and work with them, then they must want to marry them, or so the antiabolitionists would have the public believe.

During Poe's stay in Philadelphia, revulsion for the immediate abolitionists reached a boiling point. On 15 May 1838, the second Anti-
Slavery Convention of American Women was held in Philadelphia at the
newly built Pennsylvania Hall for Free Discussion, where, just the day
before, two days of dedicatory activity had begun with an address by
abolitionist David Paul Brown, a black lawyer. The convention was likewise a racially integrated meeting. Two black women were elected officers: Susan Paul as one of ten vice presidents and Sarah M. Douglass as
treasurer. Grace Douglass, Sarah's mother, and Harriet Purvis, another
black woman, also attended. There was no separate black gallery as there
would have been at the time in theaters and churches. For, as one abolitionist reported later, "[W]e should have been false to our principles if
we had refused to admit men of every sect, rank, and color, on terms of
equality" (quoted in Webb, 154). Also meeting in the first two days of
the Hall's existence was the Pennsylvania State Anti-Slavery Society for
the Eastern District.

These racially integrated meetings of two antislavery organizations
and the fact that Garrison spoke at the hall on 15 May infuriated many of
the whites in the city. On the evening of the fifteenth, placards were
posted throughout Philadelphia calling on "all citizens" to gather the
next morning at eleven o'clock at the hall, where they would "interfere,
forcibly if they *must*" (quoted in Webb, 136; emphasis in original). A
rumor also began to circulate that, on the evening of the sixteenth, a
white woman who had married a black man would give a lecture on abolition (Webb, 167–68). One newspaper reported of the rumor that it
"was too much, and more than the high-spirited Philadelphians could
bear" (quoted in Webb, 167–68). And so it was that twenty to fifty people were seen prowling about at the appointed time, although the mob
did not turn riotous. It was further incensed, however, when whites
linked arms with black women upon exiting the hall as a means of
shielding the latter from the mob's ire. This was construed as a sure sign
that amalgamation would be next. As an eyewitness reported in a letter
to a Georgia paper dated 17 May:

> Yesterday, in the broad light of day, I saw many pairs and trios of
> different hues, from "jetty black to snowy white," arm in arm,
> emerge from its [Philadelphia's] spacious halls. There, sir, was the
> descendant of Ham or of Africa, linked, side by side, with some
> of the fairest and wealthiest daughters of Philadelphia, conversing
> as they went, no doubt strengthening each other in *the faith*, by
> their warm expressions of mutual assurance and hope that the pe-

riod would soon arrive when they might become sisters-in-law. (quoted in Webb, 169; emphasis in original)

That evening, during the keynote address by Angelina Grimké, the mob threw brickbats and other objects through the new glass windows. Grimké had married another white abolitionist, Theodore Weld, only days before. Several blacks had attended by invitation, and one of the two officiating clergymen, Theodore S. Wright, was black. It seems this was so shocking to many whites that it might as well have been an interracial marriage; rumors about the wedding were thus shaped accordingly and with great success in motivating the mob to attack Grimké during her address. The next day, on the evening of the seventeenth, a mob convened at six o'clock and lit the building on fire. The hall was allowed to burn to the ground as the fire companies watched idly, only bothering to keep nearby buildings hosed down.

In the days and months that followed, those who participated in or supported the mob continued to explain their anger and their actions in terms of the perceived threat of amalgamation. One paper dubbed Pennsylvania Hall a "Temple of Amalgamation." And a lithograph of the hall, *The Evening before the Conflagration,* followed suit, depicting it as an interracial brothel. Interracial couples embrace in each window, and others link arms and more in the street (reprinted in P. Lapsansky, 228). Another paper clearly linked these impressions to the mob violence, insisting that blacks and whites sitting together "in amalgamated ease" would bring "disgrace and degradation to the whites of better morals" unless "these maniacs could be checked in their mad course" (quoted in Webb, 167–68).

Poe's 1841 tale, like Clay's prints and the rioters at Pennsylvania Hall, raises the specter of interracial sex. The orangutan kills the two women not just while they are in their bedroom but as they are making preparations to retire for the evening. The sailor is careful to recall that the women were "habited in their night clothes" (Mabbott, 2:566). Further, as literary critic Judith Fetterley notes, "One of the bodies has been forcibly thrust up a chimney, an image evocative of rape; hair, traditionally associated with feminine sexuality and allure, and described in the newspaper accounts of the event as 'tresses,' has been pulled from the head of one of the women" (156). At a time when abolitionist women were reviled for interacting socially and perhaps sexually with black men, white readers would have read the orangutan's assault as not merely typical of orangutans but as a point of comparison to interracial rape. White women were at risk when in proximity to black men because these men were animals who, like the animal to whom they were supposedly related, had monstrous sexual desires.

After *Johnny Q,* Clay went on to create six more prints that depict the assumed interracial desires of white abolitionist women and black men, all but one of which were published in 1839. Most had the words "Practical Amalgamation" in the title to remind whites that abolitionists believed both in the right to intermarry and that only a concerted and organized effort on every white person's part to socialize with blacks could end the racial division at the heart of U.S. society. For Clay and other antiabolitionists, this abolitionist directive to socially interact with blacks was really a directive to "amalgamate." Two of Clay's prints detail scenes of interracial socializing between abolitionists, marked by their plain dress, and blacks: *Practical Amalgamation (Musical Soirée)* (1839) and *An Amalgamation Waltz* (1839). These evenings lead directly to the scene depicted in a print called simply *Practical Amalgamation* (1839). A black man and woman, next to each other on a settee, flirt with and lasciviously embrace not each other but their respective white lovers. This was followed by *Practical Amalgamation (The Wedding)* (1839), in which the abolitionism and interracial socializing of the previous prints culminate in the marriage of a white woman to a black man in front of a racially mixed crowd. (This was undoubtedly another reference to the wedding of Grimké and Weld.) In addition to depicting the black men in these prints as primates by exaggerating their facial angles, Clay puts them in lavish dress and wealthy settings, thereby yoking sexual and economic ambitions.

Clay's print *The Fruits of Amalgamation* (1839; figure 7.3) depicts the culmination, or "fruits," of that interracial marriage as successful procreation specifically in the middle or upper class. The black husband is in elaborate dress reclining on a sofa and reading the abolitionist newspaper the *Emancipator* while an ornately framed picture of Garrison hangs on the wall. The man's rise from the lower classes and his attainment of a white wife are thus linked, as in Clay's previous prints in the series, to the efforts of abolitionists. His white servant enters the room to serve tea to him and his guests, another interracial couple. Clay's rendering of the body of the white wife, deliberately placed under a picture of "Othello and Desdemona," again links social to sexual transgression. She breastfeeds their baby, rendered particularly dark by Clay. Its dark hand rests conspicuously on her bared white breast as she simultaneously supports her husband's feet on her lap. If the black hand on her breast violates her female purity in racialized sexual terms, the feet of her black husband further indicate that she has become the sexual welcome mat for black entrance into the middle and upper classes when she should have served as the gatekeeper. Clearly, white womanhood has desecrated middle- and

FIGURE 7.3. Edward W. Clay. *The Fruits of Amalgamation* (1839). Courtesy, American Antiquarian Society

upper-class sanctity by admitting these sexual predators specifically into the parlor. To use Kathryn Kish Sklar's terms, this room was supposed to serve as a woman's "cultural podium" from which she could exert her moral beneficence on American society (137). Karen Halttunen adds, "The parlor was the arena within which the aspiring middle classes worked to establish their claims to social status, to that elusive quality of 'gentility'" (60). That the parlor in particular has been polluted makes the specific point that abolitionism's threat to whites is a class threat as well as a race threat and, indeed, that the two are inextricable in the United States.

It is possible that Clay may have wanted viewers to see the parlors he depicts as belonging to members of the black middle class. An anonymous writer, thought by historian Emma E. Lapsansky to be a black Philadelphian named Joseph Willson, in 1841 described the parlors of "the higher classes of colored society." They were "carpeted and furnished with sofas, sideboards, cardtables, mirrors, . . . and in many instances, . . . a piano forte" (quoted in E. Lapsansky, 70). If the parlors Clay depicts belong to blacks, then white women have taken up with them in their abodes, thus changing the focus of middle-class prosperity from the white to the black race where whites work as servants to their new black masters. But whether Clay means the parlors to belong to white or black families, in either case, according to him, abolitionism would place bestial black men—there is the exaggerated facial angle again in this print—in the heart of domesticity, where they would corrupt and soil the very angel of the house whose purity was supposed to consolidate middle-class virtue and thus middle-class cultural and economic power. Clay's prints thus make the point that economic and class fears were never entirely separate from sexual ones. In them, familial and social reproduction are inextricably linked.

Also like Clay, Poe links the possibility of black upward mobility to the specter of amalgamation when he has the instrument of that mobility for many free blacks, the barber's razor, serve as the means of violating the bodies of two cloistered white women. And in carrying the Imbert scene to a bloody conclusion, Poe not only plays on the very fears circulating in antebellum Philadelphia in the wake of immediate abolitionism but also attempts to heighten them, thus potentially exacerbating those very tensions that had earlier erupted in mob violence at Pennsylvania Hall.

Well aware of what motivated the violence against them in May 1838 and wishing to stop further violence, the abolitionists denied vehemently in the Pennsylvania papers and other publications any desire to promote intermarriages, thereby attempting to distinguish themselves from the more radical Garrisonians.[28] Indeed, such denials had been pouring in to the press ever since the New York antiabolitionist riots in the summer of

1834. Arthur Tappan and other leaders of the New York–based American Anti-Slavery Society filled the pages of their *Emancipator* and more mainstream papers as well with denials that amalgamation was currently one of their agenda items and with assertions that, because they, too, felt interracial marriage to be unnatural and distasteful, amalgamation would certainly not ever be one of their agenda items in the future either.[29] In short, the antiabolitionists were successful in forcing a compromise between themselves and most of the immediatists; antiabolitionist rioting ensured that any desire to radically refashion U.S. (white) society, however compromised that plan was, would be abandoned by the abolitionists.[30] Indeed, the repeal of the Massachusetts law prohibiting interracial marriage was ultimately a national aberration. Such laws remained in effect in many states until 1967.[31] Literature such as "Murders" must have had its small part in solidifying this compromise.

But Clay's prints and Poe's tale are not simply attacks on free blacks and white abolitionists. The sexual content of Clay's work also must have provided titillating entertainment. And although the white bared breast and the amorous embraces he depicts would have undoubtedly provided certain pleasures without the added racial elements, such pleasures were only heightened when black men, the most sexualized men of all for white culture, were placed in physical proximity to white women.[32] In fact, it is the proximity of black men that provides the occasion for depicting the bared breast and amorous embraces in the first place. The irony of the prints, then, is that in visually rendering antiabolition sentiments, Clay provided his audience with a form of pornography, literally that which stages sex and thereby might elicit sexual arousal.

Poe's tale, much as it offered a stern warning, provides a similar erotic spectacle. The detective genre, which Poe is credited with inventing here, serves to keep the scene of sexualized violence center stage, providing the reader with various accounts of it as Dupin and others discuss the crime. And when the sailor finally provides an eyewitness account of the attack, it is from the position of the window, the classic position of the voyeur and one the reader is made to share with the sailor. The detective genre also ensures that the reader, the sailor, and Dupin will never have to confront their own involvement in the violent and erotic spectacle from which they cannot avert their eyes. For in solving the mystery of who murdered the two women, Dupin absolves the reader, the sailor, and himself for indulging the titillation that presumably kept all riveted to the scene. And if it is all the orangutan's fault, then those desires can go unexamined and even unacknowledged. Readers can maintain their respectability because a surrogate has been found to both enact and take the blame for their titillation.[33] It seems hardly surprising that Poe developed such a prurient and violent, but ultimately conservative, genre at a time when charges of amalgamation mobilized many whites into violent mobs, even as they snatched up lithographic prints that portrayed inter-racial sex in titillating fashion.

Notes

This chapter is part of a forthcoming book on the discourses of interracial sex and marriage in the United States from 1776 to 1865. Research for the project was conducted at the American Antiquarian Society and made possible by a Kate B. and Hall J. Peterson Fellowship there. A Charlotte W. Newcombe Doc-toral Dissertation Fellowship from the Woodrow Wilson National Fellowship Foundation supported the writing of an earlier version of the project, and a Fel-lowship for College Teachers and Independent Scholars from the National En-dowment for the Humanities allowed me to complete it. For their suggestions and comments, I thank Donald Gibson, Myra Jehlen, Brian Roberts, Michael Warner, and especially Audrey Fisch and Jim Taylor.

1. On the range of issues that led to Jacksonian rioting, including "ethnic hatred; religious animosities; class tensions; racial hatred; economic grievances; moral fears over drinking, gaming, and prostitution; political struggles, [and] the albatross of slavery" (364), as well as the "widely held assumptions about the re-lation of the individual to social control" (361–62) that seemed to justify each riot, see Grimsted.

2. On the number and location of the antiabolitionist and other race riots in the 1830s, see Richards. For descriptions of the Philadelphia riots in particular, see Du Bois, 26–30, and Warner, 125–50; for explorations of their causes, see E. Lapsansky, Runcie, and Richards.

3. The exact date of Poe's arrival in Philadelphia is not known. In "Poe in Philadelphia, 1838–1844: A Documentary Record" (1978), which provides more detail than his later book *The Poe Log*, Dwight Rembert Thomas notes:

> Traditionally, Edgar Allan Poe is said to have moved from New York City to Philadelphia during "the summer of 1838," but there are appar-ently no documents to support this dating. Poe had arrived in New York by February 28, 1837, and he was still in this city on May 27 of that year. On July 19, 1838, he was in Philadelphia, writing James Kirke Paulding, then Secretary of the Navy, to request a clerkship. Between June, 1837, and July, 1838, there is no precise evidence of his location. No items of his correspondence are known to survive, and no mention of him in the contemporary newspapers or in the correspondence of his acquain-tances has been discovered. In all probability, Poe remained in New York until late 1837 or early 1838. (1)

Of course, Poe may have arrived slightly after the riot in 1838, but discussions and debates about it would still have been echoing throughout the local press.

4. Historical readings of "Murders" have only recently begun to appear. See, for example, Dayan "Amorous Bondage," and Whalen "Edgar Allan Poe and the Horrid Laws of Political Economy." Such readings come in the long wake of Poe's dismissal by F. O. Matthiessen and others who, like Vernon Parrington, believed "The problem of Poe . . . lies quite outside the main current of American thought" (58).

5. Cuvier's work was translated into English and published in New York in 1832 as *The Animal Kingdom, arranged in conformity with its organization. By the Baron Cuvier. . . . Translated from the French, and abridged for the use of schools, &c, by H. M'Murtrie* [*sic*], a work in which the orangutan is noted for its similarities to humans, its climbing abilities, its red hair, and its Bornean origins, all elements that Poe employs in his tale. There was also a sixteen-volume English edition of Cuvier published in London in 1827–35. Most natural history books of the period, however, were compilations of the translated remarks of noted naturalists, among which Cuvier ranked prominently.

6. See Barber on the popularity of natural history in the nineteenth century.

7. Poe's full remarks about *The Conchologist's First Book* (1839) read as follows:

I wrote it, in conjunction with Professor Thomas Wyatt, and Professor McMurtrie of Pha—my name being put to the work, as best known and most likely to aid its circulation. I wrote the Preface and Introduction, and translated from Cuvier, the accounts of the animals etc. *All* schoolbooks are necessarily made in a similar way. The very title-page acknowledges that the animals are given "according to Cuvier." (quoted in D. Thomas, "Poe in Philadelphia," 950; emphasis in original)

Poe also must have read Cuvier's *Animal Kingdom* in English, particularly insofar as he claimed to have written *The Conchologist's First Book* with the translator, McMurtrie. Charles F. Heartman and James R. Canny include Wyatt's *Synopsis* in their *Biography of First Printings of the Writings of Edgar Allan Poe*, 45–46.

8. On the fascination with nonhuman primates in the eighteenth century, see Schiebinger. On the interest in and politics of modern primatology, see Haraway.

9. Other announcements read similarly. The local *Public Ledger* ran the following announcement on 1 July:

A CURIOSITY—A ship Sabulda, which arrived at this port on Friday last from Liberia, Africa, has brought a living and healthy female "Ourang Outang," which approaches probably, in form and action, nearer the human race, than any specimen that has been exhibited in this country. It belongs to a gentleman who came passenger in the ship—he has also the skeleton of another Ourang Outang, which stood five feet some inches high, and when shot weighed 170 pounds.

The *Pennsylvania Inquirer* reported on the same day: "An Ourang Outang. An animal of this species, and of a truly extraordinary character, has just arrived at this port, in the ship Saluda [*sic*], from Africa.—We are told that it is more perfect in its proportions, and in its resemblance to the human form, than any specimen of the kind, ever seen in this country" (quoted in D. Thomas, "Poe in Philadelphia," 50–51). The primate's arrival was also discussed by the *Saturday Courier*, 6 July p. 3, col. 2, and by other Philadelphia newspapers.

10. Thomas muses, for example, that "When Poe selected an ourang outang as a protagonist for 'The Murders in the Rue Morgue,' he was almost certainly mindful of the popular sensation caused by the exhibition of this chimpanzee in August and September, 1839" ("Poe in Philadelphia," 51). More recently, Jeffrey Meyers argues in *Edgar Allan Poe: His Life and Legacy* (1992) that "[t]he murderer was undoubtedly inspired by the huge, hairy, red ourang-outang that was exhibited before astonished crowds at the Masonic Hall in Philadelphia in July 1839" (123). Neither Thomas nor Meyers, however, ponders the precise nature of the public's fascination and thus, by extension, what might have prompted Poe to use this animal. Whalen, one of the few who sees the story's connection to antebellum race ideologies, also notes the exhibition of the "orangutan" at Masonic Hall ("Horrid Laws," 415 n. 53). Richard Kopley notes that Poe may have been inspired by an earlier report of an orangutan, in the *Saturday News* on 26 May 1838 (7).

11. There were several earlier editions of Bingley than the one I was able to locate and cite here from 1872. Bingley died in 1823.

12. Lincoln was called the "Illinois Ape" in the *Richmond Examiner* on 23 April 1861. See Randall on this and other such nicknames for Lincoln (65–66).

13. On this and other exhibits of monkeys at Peale's Museum, see Sellers, 207.

14. On the Chain of Being, see Lovejoy.

15. Camper's drawings of black, white, and simian facial angles are reproduced in Honour, 15, and in Schiebinger, 151.

16. William Dandridge Peck, professor of natural history at Harvard, was one such nineteenth-century scholar who measured facial angles. See Smallwood, 302–4.

17. On Clay and his work, see N. Davidson.

18. On the interest in orangutan speech in the eighteenth century, see Schiebinger, 81–84.

19. This image is reprinted in Schiebinger, 97.

20. On the ways in which American productions of *Othello* "dramatized some of this country's racial reality and its racial fantasies," see Edelstein.

21. On the popularity of *Notes*, see Jordan, *White Over Black,* 429.

22. Unlike Clay's *Life in Philadelphia* lithographs (1828–30), which consisted of fourteen numbered plates, the antiabolitionist prints were introduced as single-sheet caricatures, which were not numbered. But their common theme of flirtation and romance across racial lines indicates that they constituted a series and must be considered as such. Of the seven prints related to interracial romance, six published in 1839 and one in 1845, six include the term *amalgamation* in the title, three of which are further linked by their titles "practical amalgama-

tion." *Johnny Q* is related to the series, if not perhaps a part of it, by its direct reference to interracial sex in the dedication to "Miss. Caroline Augusta Chase, & the 500 ladies of Lynn, who wish to marry Black husbands." Further evidence that Clay came to consider all these prints, including *Johnny Q*, a series or at least a themed group is a line below the title of *Practical Amalgamation (The Wedding)*. There Clay notes, "Also. Just Published—The Amalgamation Waltz—The Courtship—The Fruits—Johnny Q.—& Black Cut—." (This last print has not been identified.)

23. Clay misspells Chase's first name to avoid charges of libel. Several newspaper reports on the Lynn petition were reprinted in the *Liberator* on 22 February 1839, including many that Chase and her fellow signers wanted to marry black men. The report from the House of Representatives on the petition was reprinted in the *Liberator* on 15 March 1839.

24. Garrison dodged the question of whether he would mind if his own daughter married a black man. See the *Liberator* on 5 February 1831. And Child assured her readers that "none but those whose condition in life is too low . . . will form such alliances" (187).

25. On the coining of the term *miscegenation,* see Bloch; S. Kaplan, "The Miscegenation Issue"; and Lemire. One of the first accusations that the abolitionists supported amalgamation appeared in the *Methodist Magazine and Quarterly Review of New York* in January 1833.

26. On the colonization movement, see Staudenraus.

27. On racial integration in the abolitionist movement, see Quarles, 23–41.

28. Webb wrote in 1838 after the burning of the hall:

It has been alleged . . . that it is part of the design of the abolitionists to promote intermarriages between whites and colored people; and the false and absurd charge of advocating amalgamation, has been used perhaps more effectually than any other, in exciting and arraying against us the passions, prejudice, and fury of the mob. This charge has been so often denied, and from its first presentation has stood so entirely on the bare assertion of our calumniators, unsupported by proof, that nothing but its vociferous reiteration at the present time, and its injurious influence on the minds of the ignorant and misinformed, would induce us again to allude to it, as we now do, for the purpose of once more recording against it our explicit denial. (154)

29. See, for example, the *Emancipator* issues of 29 July 1834; 5 August 1834; and 19 August 1834. See, too, all of the New York daily papers for the month of July 1834.

30. On the common stance taken against interracial sex and marriage by abolitionists and antiabolitionists alike in the wake of the widespread rioting in the 1830s, see my forthcoming book.

31. On the history of so-called antimiscegenation legislation, see Martin.

32. Bared white breasts were considered shocking at the time. Consider that,

in the 1840s, Hiram Power's statue *The Greek Slave* created a ruckus in part because the general public was not ready to see a bare-breasted white woman. See Herbert; Yellin, 99–124.

33. On the detective's role "in annihilating the libidinal possibility, the 'inner' truth that each in the group might have been the murderer," see Zizek, 59.

CHAPTER 8

Poe's Philosophy of Amalgamation
Reading Racism in the Tales

LELAND S. PERSON

Emphasizing the "horror, and thick gloom, and a black sweltering desert of ebony," as well as the "southward" drift of his ship, the narrator of Poe's early story "Ms. Found in a Bottle" (1833) discovers "black stupendous seas" swelling above him and then a gigantic ship, whose "huge hull" is a "deep dingy black," bearing down upon him (Mabbott, 2:139, 140). When he is hurled from his own ship to the other, he quickly secretes himself in the hold because, he says, "I was unwilling to trust myself with a race of people who had offered, to the cursory glance I had taken, so many points of vague novelty, doubt, and apprehension" (Mabbott, 2:141). As he becomes convinced that his new, "terrible," ship is doomed, he finds himself on deck, "unwittingly" daubing with a black tar brush upon the "edges of a neatly-folded studding-sail." When it is unfurled, he reports, the black-on-white message he has unwittingly written reads "DISCOVERY" (Mabbott, 2:142).

Toni Morrison has recently challenged American literary scholars to discover a racial presence even in texts from which race seems absent. "Explicit or implicit," argues Morrison, "the Africanist presence informs in compelling and inescapable ways the texture of American literature. It is a dark and abiding presence, there for the literary imagination as both a visible and an invisible mediating force. Even, and especially, when American texts are not 'about' Africanist presences or characters or narrative or idiom, the shadow hovers in implication, in sign, in line of de-

marcation" (*Playing in the Dark,* 46–47).[1] Poe scholars such as John Carlos Rowe and Sam Worley have analyzed race and racism in *The Narrative
of Arthur Gordon Pym*; both have situated that text within its antebellum
cultural and political context. Louis Rubin and Joan Dayan have gone
furthest in reading race in other works that do not seem to be "about"
race. Dayan in particular brilliantly decodes some of the tales, including
"Ligeia," to disclose what Morrison calls an Africanist presence. In this
chapter I want to go further still in reading several of Poe's tales within a
discursive context of race and race differences. Specifically, I want to
create a conversation between Poe's short fiction and its historical and
cultural context to determine (if not overdetermine) the function rather
than simply the presence of race and racism. Color and race differences
fascinated eighteenth- and nineteenth-century Americans, and I think
Poe inscribes such fascination in those tales, such as "Ligeia," "The Murders in the Rue Morgue," and "The Black Cat," that feature black and
white exchanges and triangulated, arguably racial relationships. I want to
trace an evolutionary line, in fact, through those three tales to "Hop-
Frog" (1849), Poe's last tale and his most obvious drama of racism and
racial revenge. In short, I want to explore the white imagination Poe represents in selected tales and to discover the significance, to return to the
narrator of "Ms. Found in a Bottle," of black and white color coding.

Evidence has accumulated over the years to indicate that, regardless
of whether he wrote the infamous Paulding-Drayton review for the
Southern Literary Messenger in 1836, Poe sympathized with proslavery
rhetoric. Bernard Rosenthal effectively made that case even without relying on the Paulding-Drayton text. Poe himself, of course, hardly engraved invitations to his readers to recognize the racial significance of
his tales. Like the buried corpses in "The Cask of Amontillado," "The
Tell-Tale Heart," and "The Black Cat," race lurks behind walls and
screens in Poe's writing. Part of the challenge of recovering racial signifiers from Poe's fiction, in fact, is trying to coordinate racial content with
other features of his writing that seem to discourage the discovery of
racial or any other particular cultural meaning. David Reynolds and John
Carlos Rowe address this issue from very different perspectives. Both re-
situate Poe's writing within its cultural context, but both argue that aspects of Poe's fictional project work against each other. In Reynolds's
view, Poe tried to exploit the market for sensational fiction even as he
censured its excesses; the complex aesthetic surface of his fiction dis-
tanced it from the rich undercurrent of event. The result is a kind of
double-headed fiction, characterized by "apolitical irrationalism" that
becomes "simultaneously a full enactment of the popular Subversive
imagination and a careful containment of it" (230). Poe's first-person

narrators in particular, Reynolds asserts, provide a "firm device for controlling the sensational" (237). Rowe unequivocally considers Poe a "proslavery Southerner" (117), but he points out that the deconstructive tendencies of Poe's writing (or at least poststructuralist analyses of it) have the ironic effect of "complementing" Poe's "racist strategy of literary production" (118) by realizing precisely what Poe himself had hoped: "the substitution of an immaterial world for the threatening world of material history" (121). The challenge I wish to pose for myself in this chapter, then, is coordinating Poe's racial content (however indirectly signified) with both his playful, deconstructive impulse and his exploitation of first-person psychological romance. Indeed, I want to argue, first-person psychological romance in the Gothic or sensational mode represented an ideal vehicle for representing and destabilizing the psychological constructs of white male racism.[2]

Vitiligo and the Slippery Slope of Racism

As numerous scholars have established, color immediately became the primary criterion for instituting racial differences and a racial hierarchy in American culture. For obvious reasons, including amalgamation, color simultaneously became a slippery marker of difference. Virginia authorities tried to police miscegenation from the beginning, severely punishing miscegenators as early as 1630 and prohibiting it by law in 1662 (Williamson, 7, 8). But in 1785 Virginia defined a Negro as a person with a black parent or grandparent, thus defining as "white" any person with less than one-fourth black "blood" (Williamson, 13). Williamson claims, in fact, that this legal definition "became a sore upon the social body of Virginia and remained such for half a century"—leading, among other things, to cases of "passing," as some "blacks" "rushed to claim the privileges of whiteness" (14). It was not until after Poe's death, during the 1850 census, that mulattoes were counted as a separate category of people. In that year, the census listed 406,000 people as mulatto out of a Negro population of 3,639,000 (11.2 percent) and a total U.S. population of over 22 million; 80,000 mulattoes were counted in Virginia (Williamson 24, 25).

In *Notes on the State of Virginia* (1787), Thomas Jefferson describes an "anomaly of nature"—albino "blacks," including a

negro man within my own knowledge, born black, and of black parents; on whose chin, when a boy, a white spot appeared. This continued to increase till he became a man, by which time it had

extended over his chin, lips, one cheek, the under jaw and neck on
that side. It is of the Albino white, without any mixture of red,
and has for several years been stationary. He is robust and healthy,
and the change of colour was not accompanied with any sensible
disease, either general or topical. (71)

Jefferson reveals his fascination not only with color but also with vitilgo,
or spontaneous color changes in the skin.[3] He disassociates color and
racial identity, and he curtails the "plot" of this brief story before a total
eclipse of blackness can occur that might make racial identification more
difficult. "The first difference which strikes us is that of colour," Jefferson announces. "Whether the black of the negro resides in the reticular
membrane between the skin and scarf-skin, or in the scarf-skin itself;
whether it proceeds from the colour of the blood, the colour of the bile,
or from that of some other secretion, the difference is fixed in nature,
and is as real as if its seat and cause were better known to us" (138). Jefferson's treatment of color and race exemplifies the quasi-scientific discourse of racial differences of the eighteenth and nineteenth centuries,
especially the desire to "fix" racial differences "in nature" and to affix
them to color. Whether inherent or acquired and regardless of its
source, Jefferson suggests, color represents the "first difference"—
constituting a kind of optical essentialism. At the same time, Jefferson
does not rest easy behind the lines of difference. "I tremble for my
country," he admits, "when I reflect that God is just: that his justice cannot sleep for ever: that considering numbers, nature and natural means
only, a revolution of the wheel of fortune, *an exchange of situations*, is
among possible events: that it may become probable by supernatural interference!" (163; emphasis added).[4] Jefferson was hardly alone in trembling with fear as well as fascination at the prospect of color change,
"revolution," and an "exchange of situation." Even a cursory study of
American popular culture reveals numerous examples of color and racial
"anomalies of nature."

Eighteenth- and nineteenth-century American fascination with color
and color differences underwrote public exhibition and spectacle, especially of cases that tested racial differences. P. T. Barnum displayed a
"leopard child" in his American Museum, as well as two albino Negro
girls, "Pure White, with White Wool and Pink Eyes," beside their black
mother and baby sister (Saxon, 101). Charles Willson Peale was so fascinated by his discovery (on his honeymoon) of a mulatto slave in Somer-
set County, Maryland, whose skin had changed color from dark brown
to "paper-white," that he painted the portrait of James, a "White
Negro," and hung it in his Philadelphia museum (Sellers, 53). Peale be-

lieved that "the Negro lacked only an equal advantage of education," that "only ignorance and skin color set the race apart" (Sellers, 53), so the social and political potential of vitiligo intrigued him. Whitening might eliminate race and race-based inequalities, or so Barnum certainly thought. M. R. Werner notes that in August 1850 a "negro came to New York who claimed to have discovered a weed that would turn negroes white." Barnum exhibited him at his American Museum and "hailed" him and his magic weed as the "solution of the slavery problem, contending in his advertisements that if all the negroes could be turned white the problem of slavery would disappear with their color" (Werner, 204).[5] Such erasure of racial difference figures prominently in the most famous case of vitiligo in late-eighteenth-century America.

Ira Berlin notes that freedom created some unusual opportunities for former slaves; in the late eighteenth century the South was "invaded by black vaudevillians," including Henry Moss, a "Negro turned White as Snow" (62). Moss traveled to Philadelphia in 1796, advertised himself as "A Great Curiosity," and charged an admission fee of "one Quarter of a Dollar each person," using the money he earned to purchase his freedom (Stanton, 6).[6] Fascinated with Henry Moss, who had fought in the Revolution as a member of the Continental Army (Stanton, 6), Samuel Stanhope Smith, professor of moral philosophy at the College of New Jersey, used him to underwrite a different "revolution" and to substantiate his claim that color differences were superficial—the effect of climate and other environmental conditions (Stanton, 5).[7] Smith's account of Moss's entrepreneurial hoax in his celebrated *Essay on the Causes of the Variety of Complexion and Figure in the Human Species* is worth quoting in full:

Henry Moss, a negro in the state of Maryland, began, upwards of twenty years ago to undergo a change in the colour of his skin, from a deep black, to a clear and healthy white. The change commenced about the abdomen, and gradually extended over different parts of the body, till, at the end of seven years, the period at which I saw him, the white had already overspread the greater portion of his skin. It had nothing of the appearance of a sickly or albino hue, as if it had been the effect of disease. He was a vigorous and active man; and had never suffered any disease either at the commencement, or during the progress of the change. The white complexion did not advance by regularly spreading from a single center over the whole surface. But soon after it made its first appearance on the abdomen, it began to shew itself on various parts of the body, nearly at the same time, whence it gradually *encroached* in different directions on the original colour till, at

length, the black was left only here and there in spots of various
sizes, and shapes. These spots were largest and most frequent,
where the body, from the nakedness of the parts or the ragged-
ness of his clothing, was most exposed to the rays of the sun.
This extraordinary change did not proceed by gradually and
equably diluting the intensity of the shades of black colour over
the whole person at once; but the original black, reduced to spots,
when I saw it, by the *encroachments* of the white, *resembled dark clouds
insensibly melting away at their edges.* The back of his hands, and his
face, retained a larger proportion of the black than other parts of
his body; of these, however, the greater portion was changed. And
the white colour had extended itself to a considerable distance under the
hair. Wherever this took place, the woolly substance entirely disap-
peared, and a fine, straight hair, of silky softness succeeded in its
room. (58; emphasis added)

This narrative description, in which amalgamation is already emplot-
ted as an encroaching color change, stands ready-made for romance and
already resembles one of Poe's narratives in its scientific detail and acute
observation. Smith's metaphors colonize the black body, allegorizing
and nationalizing Henry Moss as a kind of black—then white—Uncle
Sam. Registering the hope or fear that amalgamation would spread—
spreading with it the erasure of color and racial difference—Smith creates a kind of "cradle" of amalgamation in Moss's abdomen, even
though he promulgates a polygenetic rather than single-origin theory of
vitiligo. Although Smith comments that he lost track of Moss, who "removed into the State of Virginia," he concludes Moss's story very differently from the way Thomas Jefferson abridged his tale of vitiligo—with
the information, provided "by respectable authority," that the "whitening process was soon afterwards completed, and that, in his appearance,
he could not be distinguished from a native Anglo-American" (59). As
William Stanton observes, Smith argued for the unity of the human
species, monogenesis rather than polygenesis (despite the polygenetic
coloration he described on Henry Moss), and he wished to "explain
away the many differences that defined the races" (5). In this brief
"plot," it seems to me, he uncannily illustrates a philosophy of amalgamation that anticipates Poe's. Accelerating the multigenerational process
of "reversion," Smith inscribes the possibility that the color and racial
foundation of (political) difference would become indistinguishable and
disappear from an individual black body, which thereby offers a physical
site for a potentially national phenomenon—a thoroughly amalgamated
society in which racial differences can no longer be grounded in color.

In making color the primary sign of race differences (and "blood" the primary source of color), Americans created more problems than they solved. Dayan points out that the "law of reversion" in the South and the Caribbean "certified the futility in trying to remove blackness, even the least molecules of black blood, by successive alliances with whites." In fact, the "concept of blackness had to be reinforced, made absolute and unchangeable against the prima facie evidence of fading color, and the strategy was to call this idea *blood*" ("Amorous Bondage," 201–2). Poe seems acutely aware of this law of reversion in stories such as "Ligeia" and "The Black Cat," but he pushes the logic of color and color (inter)-change to the breaking point—deconstructing color as a reliable signifier of racial difference and refusing to ground racial differences stably in differences of appearance. Dana Nelson observes that *The Narrative of Arthur Gordon Pym* "reveals the general failure of Pym and his colonial epistemology to represent Otherness as 'radical,' to inscribe a stable opposition between 'black' and 'white' as well as between 'art' and 'nature' which would support colonial knowledge" (101).[8] Certainly "Ligeia" offers an object lesson in such instability, as dark and light change positions in a hallucinatory montage that calls their difference into question.

It will strike many readers as a leap of logic to connect Poe's obvious color coding in a story such as "Ligeia" with nineteenth-century race relations. As Winthrop Jordan reminds us, however, "Blackness had become so thoroughly entangled with the basest status in American society that at least by the beginning of the eighteenth century it was almost indecipherably coded into American language and literature." It is easy to understand the racial drama of *Othello*, Jordan concludes; it is "less easy to comprehend the cryptogram of a great white whale" (*White over Black,* 258). In other words, chiaroscuro color coding was so deeply ingrained in the American imagination that its particular reference to race could be repressed. My argument in this chapter, therefore, does not depend on the allegorical claim that Ligeia or the orangutan or the black cat *is* a black person but on the view that those characters and especially their functions within their respective stories can support racially relevant readings. Louis Rubin suggests dismissing the "notion of conscious intention or one-for-one allegorical relationships" in a search for connections between Poe and race or slavery in favor of examining Poe's writing for suggestive imagery and dramatic situations (177). Sam Worley has cogently situated *The Narrative of Arthur Gordon Pym* within the context of increasingly strident pro- and antislavery rhetoric of the late 1830s. He also notes the repressive climate in which Poe wrote—reflected most significantly in the passage of a radically suppressive censorship statute by the Virginia legislature in 1836 (238).[9] To write about race from anything but a proslavery perspective would have been extremely precarious after 1836, when Poe of course began to write his most famous tales. Poe may not have written plantation romances or directly engaged issues of slavery and racial difference in his tales, but he understood the symbolic value of color, and he clearly embedded dramas of color in his psychological romances. The dynamic function of racially encoded signs within Poe's texts resonates within a context of racial discourse and must have resonated at some level for nineteenth-century readers. In the process, I think, Poe ingeniously represented the workings of white racist psychology.

Poe's Topsy-Turvy Tales

In analyzing the confluence of race and gender, abolitionism and feminism, Shirley Samuels and Karen Sánchez-Eppler both note the popularity of topsy-turvy dolls in nineteenth-century America. As Sánchez-Eppler explains, the "topsy-turvy doll is two dolls in one: when the long skirts of the elegant white girl are flipped over her head, where her feet should be there grins instead the stereotyped image of a wide-eyed pickaninny." "Always either one color or the other," she goes on, "the topsy-turvy doll enacts the binary structure of difference, emblematizing a nation governed by the logical dualism of segregation" and standing "as a cultural sign of the ways in which antebellum America conjoined racial issues with sexual ones" (133). I think it can be argued, especially in "Ligeia," that Poe has literalized and narrativized the topsy-turvy doll, inscribing a topsy-turvy plot that turns on the optical illusion of exchange and displacement the doll so efficiently enacts. The "hideous drama of revivification" (Mabbott, 2:328) in "Ligeia," moreover, can be reinterpreted in the context of antebellum fascination with color and color changes as a drama of amalgamation—of color and racial confusion. This is not to say that Ligeia herself is really "black," but the "unspeakable horrors" that arise "from the region of the ebony bed" (Mabbott, 2:238) do make her, in Dayan's terms, the "site for a crisis of racial identity" ("Amorous Bondage," 200).[10] With her ivory skin and raven hair Ligeia is already an amalgamated figure, the narrator's "amalga-mate," and as a figure of extraordinary learning she poses a problem for the narrator similar to the one Phillis Wheatley posed for Jefferson.[11]

Dayan ingeniously suggests that the "three or four large drops of a brilliant and ruby colored fluid" that fall into Rowena's cup toward the end of the story (Mabbott, 2:325) can be read as blood, "the sign by which the spectral presence of race becomes incarnate as an ineradicable stain" ("Amorous Bondage," 201). Jefferson had noted that, when freed, the African American would be "removed beyond the reach of mixture" (*Notes*, 143), but in "Ligeia" the "contamination" or poisoning of the white female body with dark "blood" issues forth in a nightmarish amalgamation: not a subtle case of vitiligo but the exchange of light woman for dark, the total eclipse of whiteness by blackness—a massive "encroachment" (to recall Smith's term) by "huge masses of long and dishevelled hair . . . *blacker than the wings of the midnight*" and "the full, and the black, and the wild eyes—of my lost love—of the lady—of the LADY LIGEIA" (Mabbott, 2:330).[12]

Although Louis Rubin claims that C. Auguste Dupin's discovery that an orangutan committed the brutal murders in "The Murders in the Rue Morgue" (1841) renders them "literally meaningless"—"there is no motive, no crime, no villain, but only helpless victims" (142)—appreciating the racial connections in this tale restores a particular cultural meaning to the murders. Winthrop Jordan discusses the persistent linkage of African Americans and apes, especially orangutans, as well as the common belief that apes assaulted and even mated with women (*White over Black*, 31).[13] Dayan cites colonial historian Edward Long's *History of Jamaica* and his assertion that the orangutan "has in form a much nearer resemblance to the Negro race, than the latter bear to white men" ("Romance and Race," 103) to emphasize the necessary dehumanization of blacks on which white racism depends. Given the racist link between apes and blacks, the murders of two women in "The Murders in the Rue Morgue" ingeniously test the conceptual lines between species and between races. Offering a "glimpse," in Harry Levin's terms, of an "old Southern bugbear: the fear of exposing a mother or a sister to the suspected brutality of a darker race" (141), the murders seem rooted in white racist fears of black uprisings—especially as those uprisings would register on the bodies of white women.[14] Furthermore, in depicting "something *excessively outré*—something altogether irreconcilable with our common notions of human action, even when we suppose the actors the most depraved of men" (Mabbott, 2:557)—Poe seems not only to restore the lines of difference he had blurred in "Ligeia" but also to inscribe the common rationalization of species difference that often buttressed white racism.[15] In his verbal sketch of the murderer, Dupin combines "the ideas of an agility astounding, a strength superhuman, a ferocity brutal, a butchery without motive, a *grotesquerie* in horror absolutely alien from humanity, and a voice foreign in tone to the ears of men of many nations, and devoid of all distinct or intelligible syllabification" (Mabbott, 2:558). Indeed, only by interpreting the barbarity as the

work not of a "madman" (the narrator's guess) but of a different species
can Dupin solve the crime. At the same time, he and the narrator test the
structures of difference in the white imagination. For example, Dupin
makes a facsimile drawing of the marks found on Mademoiselle L'Espanaye's throat; he invites the narrator to place his fingers "in the respective impressions" and then try to wrap the drawing around a "billet" of
wood approximately the size of the woman's neck (Mabbott, 2:559).
This ironic reenactment places the narrator in the murderer's position
while it exempts him from occupying that position. He concludes that
this "is the mark of no human hand" (Mabbott, 2:559) even as he tries
out and thus humanizes the subject position of the murderer.

"The Murders in the Rue Morgue," in fact, turns on the paradox that,
to solve the crime, the detective, the narrator, and reader must identify
with and thus humanize even the most *"excessively outré"* act of butchery—if only to attribute the crime to some "other" being. Furthermore,
Poe clearly demonstrates that the orangutan's act represents a learned
behavior. It has simply imitated its sailor-owner, who discovered it one
day, razor in hand, "sitting before a looking-glass, attempting the operation of shaving, in which it had no doubt previously watched its master
through the key-hole of the closet" (Mabbott, 2:565). When the sailor attempts to quiet the creature "by the use of a whip" (Mabbott, 2:565), it
flees, only to end up in the Rue Morgue and in the bedroom of Madame
L'Espanaye and her daughter. "As the sailor looked in, the gigantic animal had seized Madame L'Espanaye by the hair, (which was loose, as she
had been combing it,) and was flourishing the razor about her face, in
imitation of the motions of a barber" (Mabbott, 2:566). Nearly severing
the woman's head from her body with "one determined sweep of its
muscular arm," "flashing fire from its eyes," and then embedding its
"fearful talons" in the daughter's throat, the orangutan happens to notice
its master in the window. Indeed, its "wandering and wild glances fell at
this moment upon the head of the bed, over which the face of its master, rigid with horror, was just discernible" (Mabbott, 2:567). This reciprocal gaze of owner and animal—across the bed (and sexuality) of white
womanhood—triangulates desire and violence in a possessive, murderous relationship between master and slave that becomes displaced upon
the body of the white woman. Without necessarily adopting the Oedipal
model that Joel Kovel employs in his analysis of white racism, we can
still observe another instance of Poe's purposeful triangulation.[16] Unlike
the triangle in "Ligeia," however, in which the male narrator found himself positioned between women, the narrator (as well as the sailor) in
"The Murders in the Rue Morgue" finds himself witnessing racially encoded, male-on-female violence. Male power and the male gaze are be-

tween men, Poe suggests, until their inherent violence issues forth in a psycho-logic of violent murder. Ostensibly a spectator at this scene of inhuman, unmotivated violence, the sailor is ultimately revealed to be the source of violence—the orangutan only the agent he has set in motion. Jefferson had noted:

> The whole commerce between master and slave is a perpetual ex-
> ercise of the most boisterous passions, the most unremitting des-
> potism on the one part, and degrading submissions on the other.
> Our children see this, and learn to imitate it; for man is an imita-
> tive animal. This quality is the germ of all education in him. From
> the cradle to the grave he is learning to do what he sees others do.
> If a parent could find no motive either in his philanthropy or his
> self-love, for restraining the intemperance of passion towards his
> slave, it should always be a sufficient one that his child is present.
> But generally it is not sufficient. The parent storms, the child
> looks on, catches the lineaments of wrath, puts on the same airs
> in the circle of smaller slaves, gives loose to his worst of passions,
> and thus nursed, educated, and daily exercised in tyranny, cannot
> but be stamped by it with odious peculiarities. The man must be a
> prodigy who can retain his manners and morals undepraved by
> such circumstances. (*Notes on the State of Virginia*, 162)

Poe goes one obvious step further, tracing the roots of white racist fears to white racist behavior—to the unwitting education of slaves, through the "use of a whip," in the possession and murder of women. Under the gaze of its master, Poe notes, "the fury of the beast, *who no doubt bore still in mind the dreaded whip*, was instantly converted into fear" (Mabbott, 2:567; emphasis added), and the animal sets about trying to conceal the two women's dead bodies. In that action, as Poe's readers will recognize, the orangutan acts humanly and rationally—at least as humanly as the murderer-narrators of such tales as "The Tell-Tale Heart," "The Black Cat," and "The Cask of Amontillado."

Also featuring an intimate relationship between man and beast, "The Black Cat" challenges readers to discover "the Africanist presence" even as it obscures racial connections. "Supporters of slavery struggled to explain why slaves were running away (besides the obvious explanation)," notes Robert V. Guthrie, and in an 1851 article one nineteenth-century physician, Samuel Cartwright, diagnosed such "unnatural" behavior as a mental disorder called *drapetomania*, "which he said was common to Blacks *and to cats*" (Guthrie, 116; emphasis added). Without suggesting that the cat in Poe's tale "The Black Cat" *is* a surrogate black *person*, it is fair to note the similarity between the narrator's attitude toward the cat and the attitudes of many slaveholders. Like Melville's Amasa Delano, who takes to "negroes, not philanthropically, but genially, just as other men to Newfoundland dogs" (*Piazza Tales,* 84), the narrator appreciates the "unselfish and self-sacrificing love of a brute" whom he also admires as a "remarkably large and beautiful animal, entirely black, and sagacious to an astonishing degree" (Mabbott, 3:850).[17] Initially, Pluto acts like a faithful house cat. He "attended me wherever I went about the house," the narrator comments. "It was even with difficulty that I could prevent him from following me through the streets" (Mabbott, 3:851). Like Cartwright's "drapetomaniacs," however, Poe's black cat finally offends his master by avoiding his presence and then biting his hand (Mabbott, 3:851). Whether or not they performed a racially allegorical reading of the tale, nineteenth-century readers would have recognized and perhaps identified with the psychology of power that Poe dramatizes in this gruesome incident. Lesley Ginsberg in fact considers "The Black Cat" a Gothic reenactment of Nat Turner's 1831 revolt. If the South was "haunted by Turner," she suggests, "the gothic exaggerations of the narrator's drama with a dark animal whom he owns allows his story to be read as the nightmarish return of the South's inescapable repressions" (117). Influenced though it is by alcoholism, the narrator's enjoyment of absolute power over the black cat mirrors the absolute power of slave ownership. Indulging himself in the capricious violence that power enables, the narrator even "deliberately" cuts one of the cat's eyes "from the socket" after the animal bites his hand (Mabbott, 3:851). Although the wound heals, the cat does not forgive his master. He flees "in extreme terror," in fact, whenever the narrator approaches (Mabbott, 3:852). In effect, the narrator has created a "drapetomaniac."

"The Black Cat" represents one of Poe's best treatments of what he calls the "spirit of PERVERSENESS" (Mabbott, 3:852), but I think that spirit has a more particular reference. Without reducing the tale to a racial allegory, we can appreciate its analogical relevance to the "perverseness" of the master-slave relationship, especially when the narrator's self-confessed perverseness leads him to lynch the black cat by hanging it "in cool blood" from the limb of a tree (Mabbott, 3:852). While Poe stresses the ethical dimensions of this murderous act by defining perverseness as the "unfathomable longing of the soul *to vex itself*" and by ascribing the narrator's motives to his desire to commit a sin (Mabbott, 3:852), it is difficult to miss the cultural and political cross-references: the psychology of a white supremacy that recoils upon itself as the most intense fear and guilt. Even without consciously making the connection, readers are effectively forced in this first-person narrative to identify with a psychology of power (over women and beautiful black animals) that under-girds white male racism. At the same time, Poe destabilizes that psy-chology by reversing the lines of power he has established and, for the rest of the story, effectively placing his narrator in the slave's position—a "revolution" in the wheel of fortune and an "exchange of situation" that turns, as it had in "Ligeia," on a change in color.

In North Carolina, Winthrop Jordan notes, a "tradition was inaugurated at the turn of the century when lynching parties burned a Negro for rape and castrated a slave for remarking that he was going to have some white woman" (*White over Black,* 473). Poe's narrator first mutilates the black cat before hanging it, but he notes afterward (and after his house has burned down) that the cat's image has been transcribed on his chamber wall. "I ap-proached and saw, as if graven in *bas relief* upon the white surface, the figure of a gigantic *cat,*" he reveals. "The impression was given with an accuracy truly marvelous. There was a rope about the animal's neck" (Mabbott, 3:853). Deftly putting the reader's attention at the mercy of the narrator's "impression," Poe emphasizes the "white surface" and the inscriptive power of the black presence—a truly perverse testament to paranoid vio-lence, rationalized as vigilante justice. This black-on-white inscription be-comes reversed in the second part of the tale, however, as the black body of a second cat forms the surface on which Poe inscribes white writing.

In this topsy-turvy tale, I want to argue, Poe examines the effects of such murderous white racism (reinscribed logically in the racist mind as cruelty to animals). Like Smith's narrative of Henry Moss, Poe's narra-tive of murder and revenge—as well as the seemingly extraordinary *indi-vidual* psychology that seems to be the tale's focus—can be generalized to the nation at large. "For months," the narrator confesses, "I could not rid myself of the phantasm of the cat" (Mabbott, 3:853). When a sec-ond, almost identical black cat appears and quickly becomes a "great fa-vorite" with his wife, he feels "unutterable loathing" (Mabbott, 3:854). Despite its uncanny resemblance to Pluto, the second cat is not the ghost of the first; for Pluto "had not a white hair upon any portion of his body; but this cat had a large, although indefinite splotch of white, covering nearly the whole region of the breast" (Mabbott, 3:854). Like the "white spot" Thomas Jefferson described, this splotch of white, which "constituted the sole visible difference" between the two cats (Mabbott, 3:855), resonates loudly within the context of color-coded race differences. Surely nineteenth-century readers would have felt the similarity to popular instances of vitiligo, if not directly to someone like Henry Moss. They might also have suspected amalgamation, racial crossbreeding that, by initiating the "whitening" process, portends the erasure of visible color differences. Instead of simply spreading over the cat's body, as in most cases of vitiligo, the white spot on the cat's breast grows more distinct, ultimately forming the "image of a hideous—of a ghastly thing—of the GALLOWS!" (Mabbott, 3:855). Attributing a kind of intentionality to this white mark, Poe ironically thematizes the progress of vitiligo not as a sign of racial "encroachment" or erasure but as a sign of white racial guilt and black revenge. "And now was I wretched beyond the wretchedness of mere Humanity," the narrator confesses (Mabbott, 3:855), and his situation—his exchange of situation— anticipates Benito Cereno's in its reversal of fortune. Used to enjoying absolute power over his "domestic pets," he now finds himself at the mercy of a "brute beast" and thus struggling to maintain the absolute species difference on which his authority depends. "And *a brute beast*," he says incredulously, "whose fellow I had contemptuously destroyed—*a brute beast* to work out for *me*—for me a man, fashioned in the image of the High God—so much of insufferable wo!" (Mabbott, 3:855–56). Like the dehumanizing language of difference in "The Murders in the Rue Morgue," the narrator's disbelief reflects at least analogically the race-based logic of white racism in which African Americans figure as some lesser species—not human at all—and white Americans can deify themselves as "fashioned in the image of the High God."

Poe adroitly complicates the narrator's arguable master-slave relationship with the black cat, furthermore, by triangulating it, much as he had in "The Murders in the Rue Morgue," through the body of the white woman. In the climax of the tale, after all, when the narrator exasperatedly tries to kill the cat with an ax, only to have the blow "arrested" by his wife, he buries the ax in her brain instead (Mabbott, 3:856). Employing the same "logic" as the orangutan in "The Murders in the Rue Morgue," he then attempts to bury the evidence of the murder by walling his wife up in the cellar—only to have her location revealed by the screams, "half of horror and half of triumph," of the cat he has inadvertently walled up with her (Mabbott, 3:859). Poe's topsy-turvy plot of racial "exchange" ends up toppling the narrator.

In an even more gruesome scene of black revenge, Poe's last published tale, "Hop-Frog" (1849), depends on a racially charged exchange of positions and features another topsy-turvy plot that imbrutes and punishes the "master" race. More like the ingenious Babo in "Benito Cereno" than like the orangutan or black cat, Hop-Frog carefully crafts a counterplot to reveal and then revenge himself upon white racists who have abused and insulted both him and his female friend Trippetta. Hop-Frog stages a topsy-turvy scene in which the king and his seven counselors come to occupy the positions of servants, or slaves. Given Hop-Frog's ingenious decision to dress the king and his ministers as

orangutans and the common nineteenth-century association of orangutans with African Americans, the racial dimensions of this revenge plot
become obvious. Hop-Frog himself need not be construed as a black
man. His "otherness" resides primarily in his dwarfism, a condition he
shares with such nonwhite characters in Poe's fiction as Dirk Peters in
The Narrative of Arthur Gordon Pym and the three-foot-tall Pompey in
"How to Write a Blackwood Article" (1838).[18] Characterized by "prodigious muscular power" and "wonderful dexterity" that makes him resemble a squirrel or a "small monkey" (Mabbott, 3:1346), Hop-Frog also
shows little tolerance for alcohol, which quickly excites him "almost to
madness" (Mabbott, 3:1347). The "work of vengeance" (Mabbott,
3:1354), moreover, obviously plays into, even as it plays with, white racial
fears. Twice, for example, Poe emphasizes that women become especially frightened by orangutans (Mabbott, 3:1350, 1352). In tarring the
king and his ministers and covering them with flax, chaining them together, hanging them en masse from the ceiling, and then burning them
to a "fetid, blackened, hideous, and indistinguishable mass" (Mabbott,
3:1354), Hop-Frog clearly marks this performance of a lynching with
color and racial signifiers.[19] As it had in "The Black Cat," black revenge
inscribes itself on the white body in an ironic reversal of vitiligo—white
bodies turning black. As Dayan puts it, the "epidemic curse—the fatality
of being black or blackened—has been visited on the master race" ("Romance and Race," 104). As in "Ligeia," "The Murders in the Rue
Morgue," and "The Black Cat," furthermore, Poe uses the white female
body as a medium for vengeful racial exchange. The deaths of Rowena,
Madame L'Espanaye and her daughter, and the narrator's wife and the
insult to Trippetta provoke black-on-white vengeance that violently subverts color categories in the white racist imagination. Although the
orangutan masquerade has its origins in Hop-Frog's native culture, he
converts that country "frolic" to vengeful purpose only after the king in-
sults Trippetta. "I cannot tell what was the association of idea," he tells
the king, "but *just after* your majesty had struck the girl and thrown wine
in her face . . . there came into my mind a capital diversion—one of
my own country frolics—often enacted among us, at our masquerades"
(Mabbott, 3:1349–50). Like Melville's Babo or the orangutan in "The
Murders in the Rue Morgue," Hop-Frog learns violence from his master.

White Racism and Black Revenge

Regarding a similarly violent murder in *The Narrative of Arthur Gordon Pym*, John Carlos Rowe connects the demonic black cook's serial

braining of the sailors he throws overboard to Nat Turner's gory use of a broadax to murder his master and the master's wife during his "Southampton Insurrection" ("Poe, Antebellum Slavery," 127–28). "Hop-Frog," like "Ligeia," "The Murders in the Rue Morgue," and "The Black Cat," seems to act out nightmarish fantasies of slave revolt and black-on-white vengeance, but the traces of racial and racist discourses that I have discovered in these selected tales make it difficult to conclude that Poe was simply a "proslavery Southerner," as Rowe suggests ("Poe, Antebellum Slavery," 117). Without speculating on Poe's intentions, I think these tales reveal complicated patterns of racism and antiracist sympathy, a recognition on Poe's part that racial signifiers are inherently unstable, while racism and racist efforts to ascribe fixed racial identities lead inevitably to revenge.

In light of contemporaneous interest in vitiligo, "white Negroes," and topsy-turvy dolls, Poe's color symbolism in "Ligeia" gains a complex significance. Ligeia's rebellion, her displacement of the fair Rowena (if only in the narrator's imagination), plays to fears of amalgamation, black insurrection, and (in Jefferson's phrase) an "exchange" of racial "situations," but the ending of the tale also suggests the impossibility of suppressing or repressing blackness, however "disheveled" the "masses" of black hair may be. The racially encoded murders in "The Murders in the Rue Morgue" play obviously upon the same fears of uncontrollable black violence, but by locating the source of violence in *white* behavior, Poe refuses to maintain the popular Southern boundary between white civility and black barbarism. Poe works an obvious "exchange of situation" in "The Black Cat," and he uses vitiligo and the black body on which it appears to inscribe a provocative symbol (the gallows) of white-on-black violence that the rest of the tale bears out—a nightmarish vision of uncontrollable *white* violence visited upon black male and white female bodies alike. Only the posthumous alliance of black "cat" and white woman, on top of whose body the narrator has effectively installed the black male body, can bring the white male murderer to justice. "Hop-Frog" radically reverses the spontaneous whitening associated with vitiligo, as well as the strategic imbrutement associated with white racism, as if the "masses" of disheveled black hair Poe had described at the end of "Ligeia" have become a blackened "mass" of formerly white orangutans. Leaving the kingdom with the (presumably black) woman he has saved from white assault, Hop-Frog leaves a mass of morally (and genetically) blackened white folks—a perverse fulfillment of amalgamated nightmare.

Recognizing an "Africanist presence" in Poe's tales means reading race and racism in deeply encoded symbolism that obviously signifies on many other levels. Critics such as Louis Rubin, John Carlos Rowe, and especially Joan Dayan have certainly begun the process of resituating Poe's writing in the material conditions of its production, including nineteenth-century discourses of slavery, race, and racism. The tales I have discussed, it seems to me, reflect more than scattered traces of racial discourse. They cohere around particular images, ideas, and patterns—around what I have called a philosophy of amalgamation particularly and representatively situated in white male psychology. In representing race within the subject position most readily available to him, however, Poe did not transparently inscribe white racist ideology. Coordinating embedded (it is tempting to say repressed) racial discourse with first-person narratives of psychopathology, Poe inevitably represented the fault lines of racist psychology. Dana Nelson argues that *The Narrative of Arthur Gordon Pym*, while a "racist text" on one level, also "counters racist colonial ideology and the racialist scientific knowledge structure" (92), and I think the same can be said for "Ligeia," "The Black Cat," "The Murders in the Rue Morgue," and "Hop-Frog." Deconstructions of black essentialism, these four tales also posit the revenge of blackness as a critical fascination of white psychology. Poe's philosophy of amalgamation turns on a psychology of white male racism, but it turns out to produce a perverse, topsy-turvy reversal of racial differences—a nightmare of amalgamation, reversed racism, and ironic vigilante justice.

Notes

1. Henry Louis Gates Jr. adds that the "themes of black and white, common to the bipolar moment in which the slave narratives and the plantation novel oscillate, inform the very structuring principles of the great gothic works of Hawthorne, Melville, and Poe" (50–51).

2. David Leverenz makes a related point when he argues that "Poe inhabits and undermines gentry fictions of mastery, not least by exposing the gentleman as a fiction." Poe "constructs, then deconstructs," the private lives of gentlemen, Leverenz says, "by transgressing the great social divide between public displays of mastery and an inwardness felt as alien to oneself. Arabesques of public leisure become grotesque enslavements to obsessions" (212).

3. For additional accounts of "white negroes" during the seventeenth, eighteenth, and nineteenth centuries, see Winthrop Jordan's *White over Black*, 249–52. Jordan points out that ethnocentrism and the widespread belief that blacks were utterly different militated against anyone's connecting white Negroes and albino Europeans as products of a "single physiological peculiarity" (252).

4. Louis Rubin cites this passage for its relevance to "The Fall of the House of Usher"—as if it forecast Roderick Usher's enslavement to terror and the col-

lapse of the Southern slaveholding aristocracy as figured in the fall of the house (159–60).

5. According to William M. Ramsey, Melville based one of the confidence man's disguises on Barnum's hoax: John Ringman, the "man with the weed." Eric Lott discusses Barnum's racial exhibits and his penchant for performing in blackface (76–77). According to Lott, such "instances of imaginary racial transmutation literalize one train of thought responsible for the minstrel show. They are less articulations of difference than speculations about it. They imagine race to be mutable; very briefly they throw off the burden of its construction, blurring the line between self and other, white workingman and black" (77).

6. William Stanton quotes the following advertisement:

> There is a black man at present at Mr. LEECH's Tavern, the sign of the BLACK HORSE, in Market-Street, who was born entirely black, and remained so for thirty-eight years, after which his natural colour began to rub off, which has continued till his body has become as white and as fair as any white person, except some small parts, which are changing very fast; his face attains more to the natural colour than any other part; his wool also is coming off his head, legs and arms, and in its place is growing straight hair, similar to that of a white person. The sight is really worthy of the attention of the curious, and opens a wide field of amusement for the philosophic genius. (*The Leopard's Spots*, 6)

7. As George M. Fredrickson points out, however, this environmentalist philosophy, which was "characteristic of Enlightenment thinking about human differences," was beginning to erode by 1810, paving the way in the middle of the 1800s for essentialist "scientific" studies of racial differences and inferiority: "For its full growth intellectual and ideological racism required a body of 'scientific' and cultural thought which would give credence to the notion that the blacks were, for unalterable reasons of race, morally and intellectually inferior to whites, and, more importantly, it required a historical context which would make such an ideology seem necessary for the effective defense of Negro slavery or other forms of white supremacy" (2).

8. Sam Worley makes a similar point in arguing that Poe's use of the proslavery argument toward the Tsalalians "exceeds the apologists' case in ways that bring the contradictions of proslavery to the forefront" (235).

9. "Given the intensity of the ideological struggle," Worley comments, "the suggestion that *Pym* bears marks of the debate seems not so unlikely as the suggestion that it somehow might have escaped such concerns" (223). The case for inevitable inscription is harder to make for tales like "Ligeia" and "The Black Cat," but Worley's point offers a valuable starting premise.

10. Dayan anatomizes Ligeia's character, noting her wildness and passion, her lack of paternal name, her eyes (in the narrator's words) "far larger than the ordinary eyes of our own race" (Mabbott, 2:313), in order to claim that she suggests a "racial heritage that would indeed be suspect." Even Ligeia's ivory skin "links her further to women of color," because the "epistemology of white-

ness" depended "for its effect on the detection of blackness" ("Amorous Bondage," 201).

11. Jefferson had famously noted that "[r]eligion indeed has produced a Phyllis Whately [sic]; but it could not produce a poet. The compositions published under her name are below the dignity of criticism." Jefferson used Wheatley to exemplify his claim that he could never "find that a black had uttered a thought above the level of plain narration; never see even an elementary trait of painting or sculpture" (*Notes on the State of Virginia*, ed. Peden, 140).

12. In her study of nineteenth-century Circassian beauties, Linda Frost notes that all the women whose pictures she found had one thing in common: their "huge, bushy hair" (257). Even though Circassian women epitomized whiteness and Victorian womanhood, she concludes, their bushy hair "would have resonated for contemporary audiences with images of African and tribal women circulating in the culture" (259).

13. Jordan emphasizes the "sexual link between Negroes and apes" that enabled Englishmen to express "their feelings that Negroes were a lewd, lascivious, and wanton people" (*White over Black*, 32).

14. Louis Rubin argues that the "fear of servile revolt must have played a role in the highly active imagination of an impressionable youth growing up in Richmond" (162), where Gabriel Prosser's insurrection had occurred in 1800. Rubin also notes that the "shock waves" of Nat Turner's revolt in 1831 reached Poe's home in Baltimore "very quickly," amplified by Thomas Gray's publication of Turner's "confessions," including its "lurid account of women and children being hacked to death in their beds" (163).

15. George Fredrickson notes that by the middle of the 1830s proslavery spokesmen increasingly made the case for the "unambiguous concept of inherent Negro inferiority" (46), and Winthrop Jordan points out that, even though rational science insisted that "the Negro belonged to the species of man," the notion of species difference stayed alive. One of the most crucial components of this "irrational logic," Jordan says, was the myth of Negro-ape "connection" (*White over Black*, 236).

16. Analyzing the "basically sexualized nature of racist psychology" (67), Kovel argues that only the theory of the Oedipus complex—"enlarged into a cultural apparatus that defines and binds real roles even as it apportions fantasies amongst the players of these roles—will account for this variety of phenomena." Racist psychology thereby becomes largely a white male psychology. "Black man, white man, black woman, white woman—each realizes some aspect of the oedipal situation" (from the white male point of view). The black man, for example, represents both father and son "in their destructive aspects"; the "Southern white male simultaneously resolves both sides of the conflict by keeping the black man submissive, and by castrating him when submission fails" (71). Similarly, white male psychology projects radically different qualities (icelike purity, excessive sexuality) on white and black women, respectively, while fears of black male rape of white women act out unconscious fantasies those stereotypes were consciously designed to repress.

17. Without analyzing the tale, Dayan compares the relationship between the black cat and the narrator to that between slave and master. Poe wrote the tale, she suggests, "to demonstrate how destructive is the illusion of mastery" ("Amorous Bondage," 192).

18. After Psyche Zenobia has punished Pompey for stumbling into her by tearing out large clumps of his hair, Pompey gets his revenge when Psyche Zenobia finds herself pinned down by the hand of the belfry clock. "I screamed to Pompey for aid," she notes, "but he said that I had hurt his feelings by calling him 'an ignorant old squint eye'" (Mabbott, 2:353).

19. Poe works a similar reversal using apes in "The System of Doctor Tarr and Professor Fether" (1844), one of his most transparently racial tales, as Louis Rubin has perceptively shown. Having been displaced and locked up by the inmates (after being tarred and feathered), the former keepers of the lunatic asylum burst forth at the end of the tale; they appear as a "perfect army" of "Chimpanzees, Ourang-Outangs, or big black baboons of the Cape of Good Hope" (Mabbott, 3:1021).

CHAPTER 9

"Trust No Man"

Poe, Douglass, and the Culture of Slavery

J. GERALD KENNEDY

Despite obvious differences in their spheres of achievement—not to mention differences of racial self-identification, education, and ideology—both Edgar Allan Poe and Frederick Douglass grew to manhood in the upper South and for about two years (ca. April 1831–March 1833) inhabited the same Baltimore neighborhood, only a few blocks from each other. For the record, Poe lived with his aunt, Mrs. Clemm, in "Mechanics Row" on Wilks Street, a short walk from 37 Philpot Street, where young Fred Bailey—as Douglass was then called—lived with the Hugh Auld family. The Aulds, in fact, attended a Methodist Episcopal church on Wilks Street (figure 9.1).[1] Whether or not Poe and Douglass ever crossed paths in the Fell's Point area, their lives present surprising parallels. As orphans who never knew their fathers and who became separated from their mothers in early childhood, both experienced rejection by surrogate father figures, endured privation, and savored public notice as compensation for early humiliations.[2] Without ignoring the markedly different circumstances of a free white man and a black slave, we may note that both wrote about cruelty, brutality, and terror, and both published texts in 1845 that made them famous: "The Raven" and *Narrative of the Life of Frederick Douglass*, respectively. While their works appear together in all current anthologies of American literature, there has been no previous comparative discussion. By rereading Poe's *Narrative of Arthur Gordon Pym* (1838) alongside Douglass's *Narrative* and by situating both works in the social context of

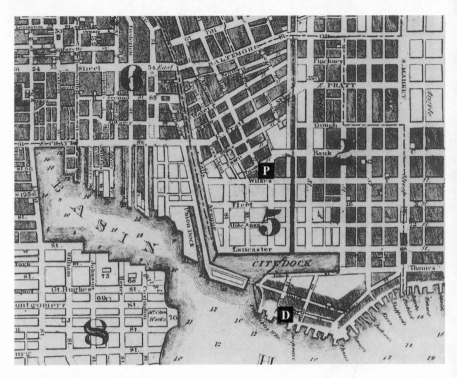

FIGURE 9.1. J. M. Matchett's 1832 map of Baltimore. Detail of Fell's Point area with Wilkes Street (above the number 5) and Philpot Street (below the number, closer to the harbor). Map shows the residence of Poe (P) on Mechanic's Row, Wilkes Street, and the address of Douglass (D), then (as Fred Bailey) living with the Hugh Auld family on Philpot Street. Photo courtesy of Maryland Department, Enoch Pratt Free Library.

the 1830s—a decade marked by new challenges to slavery, especially as practiced in cities of the upper South—we can see how these very different books carry the imprint of a common culture pervaded by racial hostility and deception. This comparison also reveals how each writer saw—and saw through—cultural constructions of race.

In *Figures in Black*, Henry Louis Gates Jr. provides another rationale for pairing these disparate texts when he suggests that like the sentimental novel, the American picaresque "pseudo-autobiography" had a "profound effect" on the shape and rhetoric of the slave narrative (81). Gates traces this genealogy to show that, like the picaro, narrators of slave memoirs deliver their critique of society as outsiders whose estrangement from established authority ensures an ironic perspective on the events they narrate. The picaro's marginal position predisposes him or her to question the codes and social practices that legitimate established authority. Both the slave and the picaro, Gates points out, "move horizontally through space and vertically through society" (82), commenting on or parodying all that they observe. More broadly, both the American picaresque pseudo-autobiography (exemplified by *Pym*) and the slave autobiography (epitomized by Douglass's *Narrative*) emerged from the eighteenth-century "true story," a purportedly veridical narrative by someone who has played a singular role or survived an extraordinary adventure. The genre introduced by Defoe in *Robinson Crusoe* evolved into a confessional form congenial to both fiction and autobiography, and it is worth noting here that certain conventions from *Crusoe*—the tone of piety, the rhetoric of extremity, and the foregrounding of spiritual tests illustrating the work of Providence—persisted well into the nineteenth century, enabling writers as different as Poe and Douglass to appeal to the same white, sentimentalist, middle-class Christian audience.

Placing Poe's *Pym* and Douglass's *Narrative* within a common literary tradition does not, of course, imply a commonality of purpose, nor does it erase important distinctions between a wholly fabricated adventure tale and an autobiography rooted in verifiable experience. Clearly, Poe concocted his novel to meet a publisher's blunt demand for a "single and connected story" of one or two volumes in length (Thomas and Jackson, 212). To manifest his authorial disdain, Poe—who advocated tales readable at a single sitting—tried to hoax or mystify a credulous American reading public into accepting as autobiography an extended, fabulous narrative whose ambiguous ending left his audience literally in a fog. His narrator, Arthur Gordon Pym, consequently insists in the preface on the "truth" of his account, as Poe—influenced by Defoe—invokes the "potent magic of verisimilitude" (*Essays*, 202) to beguile an audience awaiting the departure of the Wilkes expedition in 1838 and eager for revelations about the South Seas and Antarctica. To judge from contemporary reviews (Pollin, "*Pym* and Contemporary Reviewers"; "Poe Viewed"), the ruse largely failed, but Poe folded into the story of Pym's voyage a number of symbolically evocative motifs and culturally suggestive episodes that now sustain critical interest in a work that flaunts its portrayal of "mutiny and atrocious butchery," "shipwreck and horrible sufferings," "massacre," and "distressing calamity" (*CW*, 1:53).

Douglass, too, recounted "atrocious butchery" and "horrible sufferings" but claimed the sanctity of truth to stir the national conscience. Urged by Wendell Phillips and other abolitionist leaders to compose his life story, he began in late 1844 to draw upon memories and recollections to reconstruct his formative experiences. Exactly how he learned the conventions of autobiography remains uncertain; surely some declamatory passages, such as the apostrophe to the ships (*Narrative*, 59–60), were inspired by his earliest reader, *The Columbian Orator*. Other rhetorical devices—his use, for example, of stock epithets like "the gory lash"—suggest the influence of contemporary abolitionist writing. Whatever his autobiographical touchstones might have been, Douglass was one of the earliest ex-slaves to compose his own story and to demonstrate thereby the power of literacy.[3] Producing an eyewitness account of degradation, brutality, and injustice, Douglass supplied the reform movement with a compelling exposé of the dehumanizing nature of slavery. Asserting that he wrote to throw "light on the American slave system" and to hasten "the glad day of deliverance to the millions of [his] brethren in bonds" (*Narrative*, 102), Douglass embraced the autobiographical mode not to sell books but to change minds, not to mystify but to expose the evils of chattel slavery and to advocate its elimination.

Pursuing what appear to be radically different ends, then, the two authors nonetheless adopted similar narrative strategies—even, at times, similar language—to construct stories about restless young American males who defy paternalistic authority through acts of rebellious escape, who negotiate a terrifying world fraught with bloodshed and duplicity, who discover the life-or-death importance of reading and writing, who undergo violent, racialized encounters with a treacherous other, and who experience symbolic death and rebirth. If these thematic parallels point generally toward an overarching national metanarrative (and one thinks here of the "regeneration through violence" described by Richard Slotkin), they refer specifically, I would argue, to the social and political conditions from which these two narratives emerged: the explosiveness developing in the urban upper South in the 1830s around the practice of slaveholding.

Douglass's narrative represents the slave system of his day in ways that seem obvious enough: he characterizes the crude living conditions, painful family separations, and physical cruelties endured by slaves, as well as the deceitful relationships that developed between slaves and overseers. He foregrounds the suppression of literacy—which became a veritable obsession in the South during the 1830s—and compares slavery on the plantation with bondage in the city (an important distinction to be noted later). He alludes, moreover, to the special dangers attending the slave's escape to freedom and anxious underground existence in a supposedly free state. Poe's references in *Pym* to the slavery crisis of the 1830s have seemed likewise self-evident. Forty years ago Sidney Kaplan suggested that the novel's depiction of the black natives of Tsalal amounts to "an allegorical and didactic damning of the Negro from the beginning to the end of time" (Introduction, xxiii). Placing the novel in historical context, Kaplan remarks: "In the decade of the founding of Garrison's *Liberator*, of Nat Turner's conspiracy, of the formation of the American Anti-Slavery Society, of Theodore Weld's *The Bible against Slav-*

ery, [Poe] felt called upon to say a more basic piece—to show that slave masters 'violated no law divine or human,' to defend pigmentocracy in his own way" (xxv).[4] Clearly the Southampton slave insurrection and Southern reaction to the abolitionist movement influenced the novel's conception, but Poe's response to slavery and racial difference was—as we shall see—a good deal more ambiguous than Kaplan judged, just as his projection in *Pym* of the slavery crisis is more extensive and complex than heretofore suspected.

Suffice it to say that from markedly different social and racial positions, Douglass and Poe were both embroiled in the controversy developing around slavery in the 1830s, and a brief examination of the historical moment reveals new dimensions of social mimesis in their writings. Kaplan's summary (provided earlier) cites several crucial events in a decade that saw slavery come under relentless questioning that unsettled the status quo. In January 1831, William Lloyd Garrison founded his newspaper, launched the abolitionist movement in the North, and excited fury in the South, where apologists for slavery were quick to attribute the August 1831 rebellion led by Nat Turner to Yankee meddling and provocation. Turner and his cohorts massacred fifty-five whites, mostly women and children, and produced a retaliatory wave of lynchings that continued long after the trial and execution of "General Nat." Alison Goodyear Freehling has commented that the episode

> rekindled fears, long dormant, that any slave, in any neighborhood, might be a Nat Turner. The greatest danger, white Virginians recognized, was not of *general* insurrection, but of *individual* acts of violence. Slave domestics could always poison whites' food, murder sleeping slave holders and their families. Locked doors and bolted windows could not protect against insurgent blacks within the house. (9–10)

The rebellion generated terror in Tidewater Virginia and adjacent North Carolina, and its effects rippled throughout the South. As Freehling suggests, it destabilized all master-slave relationships and evoked pandemic mistrust by exposing the precarious nature of a social order based on racial slavery. In Baltimore, as Richard C. Wade notes, white citizens braced for a massive uprising by black inhabitants (227). The event also provoked fierce legislative debate in Virginia in 1831–32 over the need for emancipation, thus reawakening an old quarrel and exposing the politically divided nature of the populace.

Despite broad acknowledgment of the inconsistency between slavery and the principles of the Declaration of Independence, most Virginians viewed slaveholding as an irksome economic problem rather than a moral wrong, but they differed fiercely about the need for its elimination. Southern abolitionists of the "gradualist" school gained partial victory in Richmond with a compromise plan exploring state-assisted colonization in Liberia; Freehling suggests that a pervasive "Negrophobia" united the white population in its support of colonizing slaves and free blacks (177). The legislature never enacted the plan, however, because free blacks resisted the idea of deportation; the impasse caused lawmakers to suspend discussion of whether and how to eliminate slavery. But when the American Anti-Slavery Society met in Philadelphia in 1833 and promulgated its Declaration of Sentiments, indignant slaveholders began to construct proslavery arguments to counter rhetorical attacks. Even in Northern cities like Philadelphia, crowds gathered to denounce the antislavery movement, and as Sam Worley has noted, abolitionist propaganda sparked riots in the South, as well as swift countermeasures to quash public opposition to slavery: "Not only were abolitionist materials censored, but with the virtual codification of strategies that posed slavery as a positive good, even those defenders of slavery whose logic drew on the argument of 'necessary evil' from previous decades were also silenced" (Worley, 222).

Poe and Douglass inevitably felt the effects of the slavery controversy in Baltimore, where both were living at the time of the Nat Turner rebellion. Biographer William McFeely indeed speculates that Douglass may have been sent back to the Lloyd plantation on the Eastern Shore in 1833 as a result of the uprising:

> The revolt had taken place not all that far down the Chesapeake Bay, in Virginia. Turner had been [much like Douglass himself] a too-bright slave, hired out and not under a master's direct discipline and, what is more, a preacher, self-educated and eloquent. His insurrection failed, but it left young black men like Frederick with new hope, and in great jeopardy. (McFeely, 37)

In the eyes of many, Baltimore represented a volatile contact zone on the margins of Southern culture, and, as Barbara Jeanne Fields points out, most slaveholders viewed the city as "unsound" on the question of slavery: "Baltimore, the metropolis of a border state whose most vigorous region was more closely integrated with the world of free labor than with that of slaves, occupied just such [an unstable] margin. The large slave holders of Maryland never lost sight of that fact, nor of the potential it contained for the subversion of their interests" (Fields, 57). Proximity to the North also complicated the regime of slavery by providing shorter escape routes and an abundance of nearby sympathizers willing to assist fugitives. Moreover, it brought to Baltimore a steady stream of Northern transients importing ideas of abolition and emancipation, such as the Irish immigrants whom Douglass encountered one day on the docks: "They both advised me," he recalled, "to run away to the north; that I should find friends there, and that I should be free" (*Narrative*, 44).

Slavery had also become complicated in Baltimore by the presence of a significant population of free blacks, and, as Fields observes, "the simultaneous growth of a free black population hopelessly entangled with the slaves lodged a conspicuous anomaly in the heart of the slave order" (xi). Those who regarded slavery as the natural condition of black people confronted the contradictory evidence of an industrious and self-sufficient free black citizenry. The commingling of slaves and free blacks inevitably excited the desire for freedom among those in bondage, even as it created local safe havens and opportunities for gaining information about methods of escape. In a city built upon industry, slaves also had many more opportunities to find gainful employment by which to purchase their eventual freedom. This labor pattern, as T. Stephen Whitman has shown, forced many city slaveholders to modify the terms of bondage and finally—as Douglass's later relationship with Hugh Auld suggests—to concede that slavery was inherently incompatible with an urban, industrial milieu (163–65).

Douglass's experience in the city—in contrast to his stint from 1833 to 1836 mostly as a field hand in Talbot County—presents a virtual paradigm of the urban devolution of slavery. "I had resided but a short time in Baltimore," he wrote, "before I observed a marked difference in the treatment of slaves, from that which I had witnessed in the country. A city slave is almost a freeman, compared with a slave on the plantation. He is much better fed and clothed, and enjoys privileges altogether unknown to the slave on the plantation" (*Narrative*, 38). The relative freedom that Douglass exercised as an urban slave—in his role as guardian and playmate of a young white boy—produced a concomitant anxiety in his nominal master, Hugh Auld, the brother of Douglass's owner, Thomas Auld. The famous scene in Douglass's *Narrative* when Hugh Auld intervenes to suspend the spelling and reading lessons offered by his wife, Sophia, exemplifies the putative master's concern about maintaining authority and control over a slave likely to be made "unmanageable" by literacy. Although forbidden to continue his studies, Douglass nevertheless enjoys sufficient liberty of movement and activity to pursue his lessons covertly with neighborhood boys. This subversion of the structure of dominance through an act of dissimulation became, especially during the 1830s, an increasingly pervasive strategy among slaves of the upper South who experienced both closer surveillance after the Nat Turner rebellion and more rigid discipline on the part of nervous slaveholders.

These tensions were particularly sharp in cities like Baltimore, where the environment itself militated against strict control. Douglass suggests that the proximity of neighbors tended to suppress the whippings by which plantation overseers subjugated slaves, and the manifold opportunities for employment encouraged the practice of hiring out slaves for profit rather than consigning them to unpaid domestic toil. Whitman notes that the growing capacity of bondsmen to perform skilled labor and to influence the local economy forced many slaveholders to make promises of manumission, which became "part and parcel of strategies to employ slave labor successfully in an increasingly hostile environment in Baltimore" (115). When Douglass returned to the city in 1836, Hugh Auld (a ship's carpenter) found a position for him as a caulker in the shipyard in order to pocket his slave's weekly wages. Gradually, though, Douglass developed both skill and autonomy: "After learning how to calk, I sought my own employment, made my own contracts, and collected the money which I earned" (*Narrative*, 83). When Auld continued to garnish his wages, however, Douglass became incensed, and, facing five more years of labor before gaining the manumission promised by Thomas Auld, he escaped bondage in September 1838, capping a personal struggle that epitomized the unraveling of the slave system in the "hostile environment" of the urban upper South.

Many of the same conditions existed in Richmond, where Poe had been reared as a young man of privilege in the 1820s and whence he returned in 1835 as a fledgling magazinist. While Agnes Bondurant's *Poe's Richmond* (1942) skirts questions of race or slavery, a more recent study portrays African American life in antebellum Richmond and corroborates the difficulties of controlling an urban slave population. Marie Tyler-McGraw and Gregg D. Kimball remark that beginning about 1830, slaves found more opportunities for making money as the city's "business and industry expanded and diversified" (63). Pointing out that the tobacco industry relied exclusively on the labor of slaves who boarded out, they observe: "The practice of giving board money to hired slaves and to slaves owned by the factory grew throughout the antebellum period; combined with the practice of paying for overtime, it helped create a very fluid and ungovernable situation in which slaves with money roamed the city more or less at will after work" (Tyler-McGraw and Kimball, 23). As in Baltimore, blacks possessed economic leverage: "The ultimate power of slaves and free blacks was that Richmond could not function without their labor—which meant that varying degrees of illegal activities or socially unacceptable behavior were often tolerated for the sake of productivity and profit" (Tyler-McGraw and Kimball, 63). Racial tensions in Richmond escalated after the Nat Turner rebellion of 1831—which prompted the outlawing of black schools and the teaching of reading to slaves—and the Virginia slavery debate of 1831–32 exposed deep anxieties in the white population. Tyler-McGraw and Kimball thus characterize a protracted dilemma:

> In the entire period between the Revolution and the Civil War, Richmond was never able to adequately monitor and control black access to and use of literacy, money, religious and political concepts, and space. That they tried is evidenced by the mounting body of laws and statutes passed on the subject. That they failed is witnessed by the same massive body and by the organization of private Richmond societies which illustrate both the level of concern over slavery and the changing attitude toward it. It was the failure of Richmond to either control slavery or abolish it which led to an increasing rigidity and reactiveness toward it. (64)

As in Baltimore, the presence of a significant free black population complicated the management of urban slaves in Richmond, and, as Tyler-McGraw and Kimball note, "sometimes local whites and northern sea captains aided slaves in their escape attempts" (69). In a detail pertinent to Arthur Gordon Pym's fictional flight from home, convention, and paternal authority, they add that "the most common form of escape from Richmond involved hiding out in the storage spaces of a ship" (69).

Until he began his one year at the University of Virginia in early 1826, Poe had spent most of his youth in this milieu of bustling commerce, a city sustained by an increasingly restive slave population. With his foster parents, John and Frances Allan, Poe had visited nearby plantations for vacations and holidays. According to anecdotal sources, Poe had a devoted black "mammy" and grew up playing with slave children (Weiss, 17–19; Phillips, 109–10). Allan, a merchant born in Scotland, had for years owned a few domestic slaves, and the young Poe apparently developed a friendship with at least one of them, Armistead Gordon, who told him frightening stories about premature burial (Mabbott, xiv). Allan's fortunes changed dramatically in 1825 when he inherited from an uncle, John Galt, "three landed estates . . . with the slaves, stocks, and property of all kinds belonging thereto" (Thomas and Jackson, 63–64). Shortly thereafter, Allan bought a Richmond mansion to signal his new affluence, and his adolescent foster son likely began to fancy himself the eventual heir of a great house with slaves. During his brief sojourn at Charlottesville, Poe—like all students at Mr. Jefferson's university—hired a personal servant, probably a slave, from a local hotel keeper (Thomas and Jackson, 80). Yet his only known comment about living among slaves came in a letter of March 1827, protesting to Allan the harsh treatment he had received at home since his forced withdrawal from the university: "You suffer me to be subjected to the whims & caprice, not only of your white family, but the complete authority of the blacks—these grievances I could not submit to; and I am gone" (*Letters*, 1:8). Poe here presents his compulsory subjugation to "the blacks" as the final insult, the precipitating cause of his own flight in 1827—the exact year of Pym's departure—from Allan's paternal authority. That he should portray the fictional Pym hiding like a runaway slave beneath the decks of the *Grampus* adds suggestive irony to the connection implied by his fictional chronology. For Poe's break with Allan in 1827 and his subsequent disinheritance effectively ended his prospect of becoming a Southern slaveholder and barred him from the genteel caste to which he aspired.[5]

Poe's other dealings with slaves and free blacks, prior to the composition of *Pym* in 1836–37, remain equally sketchy. In December 1829, during a stay in Baltimore with his aunt, Maria Clemm, he apparently acted as her agent in the transfer of a slave named Edwin to a certain Henry Ridgway for a term of nine years. (figure 9.2).[6] Returning to Baltimore in 1831 after his brief, disastrous career as a West Point cadet, Poe lived with Mrs. Clemm on Wilks Street (near the Auld home), and making the rounds in futile search of employment, Poe daily must have encountered slaves and free blacks circulating about the Fell's Point area near the city dock. The pitiful entreaties for cash made by Poe and his aunt to John Allan and others during this period make it highly unlikely that Mrs. Clemm still held domestic slaves in the early 1830s (Thomas and Jackson, 123, 124). All evidence suggests, rather, that Poe, his aunt, and his cousin Virginia lived in dismal poverty during this period.

When he returned to Richmond in late 1835 as editorial assistant to Thomas W. White, owner of the *Southern Literary Messenger*, Poe found himself suddenly thrust into the current debate over slavery. Mainly through the mistaken attribution of an April 1836 *Messenger* review of two books on slavery, he has been stigmatized by several recent critics as a virulent racist and staunch apologist for slavery (see especially Rosenthal and Rowe ["Poe, Antebellum Slavery, and Modern Criticism"]). The "Paulding-Drayton" review equates slaveholding with fundamental property rights, and it emphasizes the slave's helplessness and utter dependence on the white master. Terence Whalen has now shown con-

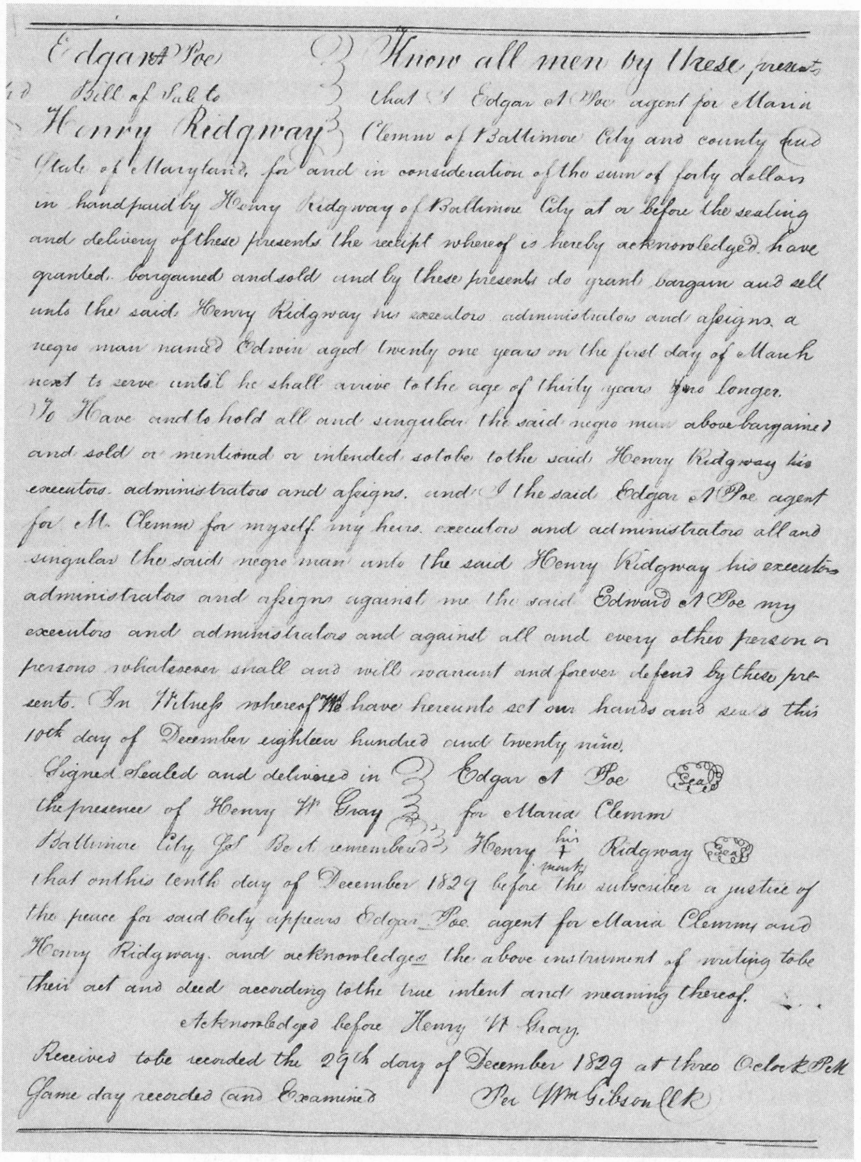

Edgar A Poe
Bill of Sale to
Henry Ridgway

Know all men by these presents that I Edgar A Poe agent for Maria Clemm of Baltimore City and county and State of Maryland, for and in consideration of the sum of forty dollars in hand paid by Henry Ridgway of Baltimore City at or before the sealing and delivery of these presents the receipt whereof is hereby acknowledged, have granted, bargained and sold and by these presents do grant bargain and sell unto the said Henry Ridgway his executors administrators and assigns, a negro man named Edwin aged twenty one years on the first day of March next to serve until he shall arrive to the age of thirty years & no longer. To Have and to hold all and singular the said negro man above bargained and sold or mentioned or intended so to be to the said Henry Ridgway his executors administrators and assigns. and I the said Edgar A Poe agent for M. Clemm for myself my heirs executors and administrators all and singular the said negro man unto the said Henry Ridgway his executors administrators and assigns against me the said Edward A Poe my executors and administrators and against all and every other person or persons whatsoever shall and will warrant and forever defend by these presents. In Witness whereof We have hereunto set our hands and seals this 10th day of December eighteen hundred and twenty nine.

Signed Sealed and delivered in the presence of Henry W Gray — Edgar A Poe (Seal) for Maria Clemm

Henry his + mark Ridgway (Seal)

Baltimore City Sct. Be it remembered that on this tenth day of December 1829 before the subscriber a justice of the peace for said City appears Edgar Poe agent for Maria Clemm and Henry Ridgway and acknowledges the above instrument of writing to be their act and deed according to the true intent and meaning thereof.

Acknowledged before Henry W Gray.

Received to be recorded the 29th day of December 1829 at three O'clock P.M. Same day recorded and Examined Per Wm Gibson Clk

FIGURE 9.2. Letter of conveyance, identifying Edgar Allan Poe as the representative of Mrs. Clemm in the sale of a slave. Thanks to Jeffrey Savoye for locating this document.

vincingly, however, that Poe did not write the controversial essay and that, eager to appeal to a national audience, he discreetly avoided aligning himself in print with proslavery advocates like Nathaniel Beverley Tucker, the actual author of the disputed *Messenger* review. Instead, Poe cultivated—in reviews and fiction—what Whalen calls an "average racism," a "strategic construction" of ideas about race and slavery "de-

signed to overcome political dissension in the emerging mass audience"
(Whalen, *Edgar Allan Poe and the Masses,* 112). That is, Poe's views were
fairly typical of white attitudes on both sides of the Mason-Dixon Line
at a time when, as Stanley Harrold has observed, "racism permeated all
sections of antebellum white society" (23). As an assistant in Richmond,
Poe found himself in an awkward position, trying to hew an editorial
line that would offend neither Southern nor Northern readers. His January 1836 review of Joseph Holt Ingraham's book *The South-West* observes
patronizingly that the slave's degraded condition leaves him unable "to
feel the *moral* galling of his chains," and Poe praises Ingraham, a Northerner, for "smoothing down" misconceptions about slavery and refusing
to "pervert [the South's] misfortunes into crimes—or to distort its
necessities into sins of volition" (122). These comments—virtually
Poe's only public remarks about slavery per se during his stint with the
Messenger—indicate that he viewed slavery not as an institution beneficial
to blacks (a position advanced by apologists) but as a lamentable system
upon which the economy of the South had come to depend. That is, Poe
articulated the general misgivings of most white Virginians on the subject of bondage.

From the evidence of such short stories as "A Predicament," "The
Man That Was Used Up," and "The Gold Bug"—each of which
includes a Pompey or a Jupiter in the stereotypical role of a black
servant—Poe also understood and presumably shared widespread white
attitudes about the racial inferiority of blacks. Such assumptions so thoroughly pervaded American culture in that era as to render superfluous
current efforts to identify and castigate individual purveyors of literary
racism. The entire culture was, from a late twentieth-century perspective,
fundamentally racist. Such sentiment surfaces in the writings of Emerson and Whitman and even among the remarks of Northern antislavery
reformers; Douglass observes pointedly in *My Bondage and My Freedom*
that, just as slaves were rarely accorded the dignity of a last name in the
South, so "abolitionists make very little of the surname of a negro"
(164). On the lecture circuit, he notes, he was "generally introduced as a
'chattel'—a *'thing'*—a piece of southern *'property'*—the chairman assuring
the audience that *it* could speak" (366). He hints that such condescending references implied a kind of proprietary attitude not unlike that of a
slave master. Then and now, North and South, racist slurs betrayed both
arrogance and unconscious insecurity. Poe was not immune to the cheap
reassurance of a racist joke, and indeed his expulsion from the home of
a wealthy Richmond slaveholder, which consigned him to lifelong
penury, may have predisposed him to racist humor. But Poe was also an
outcast from the culture of slaveholding who had become contemptu-

ous of paternalistic authority figures like John Allan and Thomas W. White, and he felt himself wronged by such men often enough to possess at least potential empathy for those in bondage.

Thus it was that in 1836, under threat of dismissal at the *Messenger*, as Poe began to write *The Narrative of Arthur Gordon Pym*, he contrived a richly ambiguous story brimming with defiance and replete with scenes of rebellion and treachery. It was a potboiler novel that mirrored not only the "Negrophobia" and fear of insurrection abroad in the South in the 1830s but also, as filtered through Poe's personal indignation, the explosiveness of a culture built upon wealth, exploitation, and betrayal. As the author constructed a mutinous vision of the upper South, he also perceived the emergence of a violent national schism that threatened the ship of state. A reexamination of Douglass's more direct critique of antebellum America allows us to see better the complexity of Poe's social mimesis in *Pym*.

In this cross-reading James C. Scott provides a revealing theoretical perspective on the cultural milieu with his elaboration of the "hidden transcripts" inherent in oppressive socioeconomic systems.[7] Scott explains how "the greater the disparity of power between the dominant and the subordinate," the more public behavior of overseers and workers tends to reflect a ritualized concealment of true feelings. As Scott succinctly remarks, "the more menacing the power, the thicker the mask" (3). As opposed to the "public transcript"—the apparent display of authority and deference—the hidden transcript often consists on the one hand of latent suspicion or anxiety and on the other of covert indignation. Particularly among subordinate groups, the hidden transcript contains a subversive code by which secret sentiments may be communicated. Scott sees subservience as a performance rich in manipulative possibilities, as a discipline for controlling violent rage, and as a tactic of political resistance. His work both confirms and complicates Bertram Wyatt-Brown's discussion of "the mask of obedience," the guise of servility and "shamelessness" adopted by slaves to avoid the "excesses of . . . victimization" (133).

Scott's study has obvious relevance to American slavery, from which he draws many telling examples. His analysis suggests that surveillance and concealment, the mirroring strategies of master and slave, respectively, arose directly from the violent tensions of subjugation. To endure bondage, slaves developed "a whole range of practices"—jokes, folktales, songs, and sayings—to transmit private sentiments without arousing alarm (Scott 14), and they devised clever subterfuges to conceal proscribed activities. Slaveholders and overseers likewise developed a repertoire of tricks to maintain psychological and physical control over a more numerous and often more physically imposing slave population. In the South of the 1830s, these reciprocal strategies of deceit produced a culture unusually rife with deception—a deception always charged by the palpable threat of brutality and death.

Douglass's *Narrative* provides rich insight into this dynamic of mutual duplicity. He introduces his life story by raising the vexed issue of his own biracial identity, which itself testifies to the gross deception by which white slaveholders concealed their paternity of slave children by flogging, neglecting, and even selling them. Covert relations with slave women produced marital duplicities and secret siblings; unspeakable jealousies sometimes erupted in sexual violence, as Douglass illustrates by the bloody whipping of Aunt Hester (or Esther), a "woman of noble form, and of graceful proportions" (19). But the master-slave relationship not only generated incidental deceptions; it also fostered a general climate of treachery defining everyday life. Douglass tells elsewhere about Colonel Lloyd's seemingly benign questioning of the slave he meets on the road, who, when asked to whom he belongs and how he is treated, complains of ill use and hard work. Not realizing that he has been talking to his master, the man thus finds himself two weeks later chained, handcuffed, and sold to a Georgia slave trader. The scene of interrogation is exemplary: slaveholding required constant vigilance and elaborate strategies of control, which in turn taught slaves deviousness. Douglass describes slave owners' widespread use of informants, as well as the consequent disinformation evoked by this practice:

> The slave holders have been known to send in spies among their slaves, to ascertain their views and feelings in regard to their condition. . . . [The slaves] suppress the truth rather than take the consequences of telling it, and in doing so prove themselves a part of the human family. If they have anything to say of their masters, it is generally in their masters' favor especially when speaking to an untried man. (27–28)

Douglass suggests how the use of domestic surveillance created an atmosphere of suspicion in which dissimulation became crucial to survival. Even secretiveness, though, does not ensure the success of Douglass's first "run-away plot." The disclosure of a "betrayer"—tentatively identified in *My Bondage and My Freedom* as his friend Sandy Jenkins—dramatizes the insidiousness of espionage on the plantation (321).

Amid the mutuality of deceit fostered by slavery, the figure of the overseer epitomized the duplicitousness of the system. About the aptly named Austin Gore, who shoots a slave named Demby for refusing to

come out of a creek, Douglass remarks that he was "artful enough to de-
scend to the lowest trickery" (29). Although not an overseer, Thomas
Auld proves unsuccessful as a slaveholder because "he possessed all the
disposition to deceive, but wanted the power" (51). The redoubtable
"slave breaker" Edward Covey—whom Douglass later engages in a
memorable fight—seems in contrast a master of deception: "He seldom
approached the spot where we were at work openly, if he could do it secretly. He always aimed at taking us by surprise. Such was his cunning
that we used to call him, among ourselves, 'the snake'" (56). So powerful
is Covey's guile that he seems ubiquitous: "He appeared to us as being
ever at hand. He was under every tree, behind every stump, in every
bush, and at every window, on the plantation" (57). In an astute analysis
of the ultimate effects of deceit, Douglass remarks that duplicity informed the overseer's manner and consciousness:

> Mr. Covey's *forte* consisted in his power to deceive. His life was
> devoted to planning and perpetrating the grossest deceptions.
> Every thing he possessed in the shape of learning or religion, he
> made to conform to his disposition to deceive. He seemed to
> think himself equal to deceiving the Almighty. . . . Poor man!
> Such was his disposition, and success at deceiving, I do verily be-
> lieve that he sometimes deceived himself into the solemn belief
> that he was a sincere worshiper of the most high God. (57)

Covey personifies the ironic, corrupting effect of oppression upon the
oppressor—a major theme for Douglass—and figures as the ultimate
victim of his own deceptions.

In response to such deviousness, those in bondage developed their
own strategies of concealment. Douglass speaks of the double language
of slave songs, perceived by white listeners as evidence of the "content-
ment and happiness" of the singers, while those within the slave community expressed with every tone "a testimony against slavery and a
prayer to God for deliverance from chains" (24). Retrospectively aware
of this doubleness, Douglass admits that he did not perceive the subversive, coded nature of the songs because for him the "hidden transcript"
was so self-evident. He writes: "I did not, when a slave, understand the
deep meaning of those rude and apparently incoherent songs. I was myself within the circle; so that I neither saw nor heard as those without
might see and hear" (24). Douglass notes that as a boy living in Baltimore with the Aulds, he was "compelled to resort to various stratagems"
to achieve literacy (39). Forbidden from reading, he created a secret
cache of books and newspapers; on errands he carried a concealed book

and bribed neighborhood boys to tutor him. Later, Douglass practices secrecy when he holds his Sunday school classes to teach other slaves to read. And when he conspires to escape slavery by forging "protections" for himself and four friends, Douglass permits us to glimpse a clandestine conspiracy. But he maintains secrecy in the *Narrative* about the details of his eventual escape in 1838, refusing to provide any details that would "induce greater vigilance on the part of slave holders" (84).

Deception begets deception, and perhaps Douglass's most acute insight into the culture of slavery is lodged in his comment on the tactic of allowing slaves to get hopelessly drunk at the Christmas holidays to "disgust" them with an illusory "freedom": "This mode of treatment," he observes, "is part of the whole system of fraud and inhumanity of slavery" (67). This formulation implies a reciprocal relationship between "fraud" and "inhumanity," between deception and brutality. Something like the charade of the King and the Duke in *The Adventures of Huckleberry Finn*, slavery itself rests, he suggests, on an originary act of imposture, a fraudulent presumption of superiority. "Inhumanity" thus imposes itself by a systematic deceit that its victims eventually learn to mirror and manipulate for their own ends. That is, the recurrent scenes of cruelty that compose the history of slavery—the individual acts of physical domination, the whippings, beatings, and shootings—provoke and indeed guarantee strategies of resistance that range from feigned servility and coded language to petty larceny and covert conspiracies. The reciprocity corroborates Scott's basic thesis that "the practice of domination *creates* the hidden transcript" (27). The reign of violent oppression enforces a doubleness in all relations between masters and slaves. It further introduces deceit into relations between unfaithful slaveholders and their wives, between masters and overseers (who must always conceal their failures), and at times between defiant slaves and servile spies willing to trade information for leniency.

The crucial yet unstable relationship between deception and violence likewise informs the climactic episode in Douglass's *Narrative*—the author's ferocious fight with Covey that marks "the turning-point in [his] career as a slave" (65). Insofar as Covey personifies duplicity—and, indeed, the larger "fraud" of slaveholding—he succeeds briefly in transforming Douglass into something inhuman, into "a brute" who is "broken in body, soul, and spirit" (58). Covey's strategies of deception evoke terror by insinuating a superhuman power capable of sudden, fatal violence. In Douglass's version of the Southern Gothic, Covey is a demonic presence whose treacheries help to explain the perplexing subjugation under slavery of blacks by whites.[8] Yet as Douglass discovers when he defies Covey and tests his mettle, that supremacy is illusory: "the snake" is tamed, held at bay in hand-to-hand conflict, and thus demystified. The "fraud" of Covey's trickery conceals his relative powerlessness, and with this breakthrough, Douglass experiences "a glorious resurrection, from the tomb of slavery to the heaven of freedom" (65). Appositely, Scott comments that "the most explosive realm of politics is the rupture of the political *cordon sanitaire* between the hidden and the public transcript" (19). By fighting Covey, regaining his humanity, and protecting himself from further beatings, Douglass breaks the cordon sanitaire separating the semblance of Covey's power from the fact of his cowardice. At the same time, Douglass destroys the illusion of his own brutish servility and reestablishes his strength and manhood. But although he successfully faces down one frightening embodiment of the "fraud" of slaveholding, he finds it more difficult to extricate himself from the endemic deceptions of the culture itself.

On two occasions in the *Narrative,* Douglass alludes to the pervasive anxiety of betrayal that shaped the experience of slavery. Just after he learns the word *abolition* and begins to envision a life of freedom, he meets the aforementioned Irishmen on the wharf who commiserate with him and advise him to flee to the North. But his response exposes the fear of duplicity to which slaves were prone: "I pretended not to be interested in what they said, and treated them as if I did not understand them; for I feared they might be treacherous. White men have been known to encourage slaves to escape, and then, to get the reward, catch them and return them to their masters" (44). Later, after he has escaped from Baltimore, Douglass portrays himself as lost in the city, still gripped by the terror of betrayal despite his arrival in the "free" state of New York:

> I was afraid to speak to any one for fear of speaking to the wrong one, and thereby falling into the hands of money loving kidnappers, whose business it was to lie in wait for the panting fugitive, as the ferocious beasts of the forest lie in wait for their prey. The motto which I adopted when I started from slavery was this— "Trust no man!" I saw in every white man an enemy, and in almost every colored man cause for distrust. (90)

The salient point here about the culture of slavery is that even in the relative security of New York, Douglass experiences something very like paranoia. While it is no doubt true (as Scott argues) that deceit informs power relationships in all cultures, slavery imposed such a gulf between the free and enslaved populations that mistrust generated ubiquitous treachery. Douglass's motto—"Trust no man!"—epitomizes not only the anxiety of the runaway slave but also, in a larger sense, the precarious nature of many social relations in a culture built upon systematic racial oppression. For just as all black-white relationships were underwritten by "hidden transcripts," so, too, were many white-white and black-black relations apt to be marked by uncertainties about the other's complicity with or opposition to race-based slavery. In much the same way that the war in Vietnam posed the political litmus test of the 1960s, slavery represented the raw, dividing issue of the decade when Douglass fled to the North. On the eastern seaboard between New York and Richmond, in the intermediate cities of Philadelphia, Baltimore, and Washington, questions about the fate of slavery and the future of black people in bondage provoked outrage and suspicion. Especially in New York, where strong proslavery and abolitionist sentiment festered simultaneously, where "cooperative" free blacks betrayed fugitive slaves, and where opportunistic slave catchers lurked everywhere, Douglass had reason to trust no one. In this moment of radical uncertainty, "afraid to speak to any one for fear of speaking to the wrong one," Douglass precisely articulates a social predicament pervasive in the 1830s.

The motto adopted by Douglass in escaping slavery might well serve as the inscription to Poe's *Pym*, a novel shot through with duplicities of plot and narration. On one level, *Pym* fed directly into proslavery discourse: amid the many scenes of rebellion and deception that traverse the narrative, the massacre on Tsalal of a British crew by apparently friendly natives seems to reinforce stereotypical notions of black treachery and brutality. Poe's narrator comments pointedly: "From everything I could see of these wretches, they appeared to be the most wicked, hypocritical, vindictive, bloodthirsty, and altogether fiendish race of men upon the face of the globe" (201). For certain critics from Kaplan to Rowe, the Tsalal episode has thus presented incontrovertible evidence of Poe's specifically Southern racism. In this reading, the nearby island whose rock ledge resembles "corded bales of cotton" (1133) tells us all we need to know about the novel's symbolic geography, and Pym's demonizing of the black-skinned natives makes plain Poe's own unbridled bigotry (S. Kaplan, "Introduction to *Pym*," xxv; Rowe, "Poe, Antebellum Slavery and Modern Crtiticism," 127–38). The same critics read the atrocity on Tsalal as a transparent rendering of Poe's white, Southern anxiety about a general slave insurrection, and Kaplan, at least, construes the concluding philological speculations as evidence of Poe's acceptance of the biblical curse on Ham as a divine sanction for slavery (xxi–xxiii).

Poe's relentless attention in the closing chapters to race and his narrator's condescending, contemptuous depiction of the "jet black" natives with "thick and long wooly hair" (*CW*, 1:168) indeed seem to confirm an inveterate prejudice. One cannot deny the racial fear and loathing embedded in the story of the massacre. Like the mystery of the purloined letter, however, Poe's racism seems on closer inspection both simple and odd. It is simple (or "average," in Whalen's phrase) insofar as the attitude of Anglo-Saxon superiority informing Pym's pseudo-ethnography of the black "savages" would have been shared by most white readers, North or South, in the 1830s. Poe drew many anthropological details, in fact, from Benjamin Morrell's *Narrative of Four Voyages*, a widely read travel account that assumes—as did virtually all contemporary Anglo-American narratives of exploration—the inherent inferiority and simplicity of darker skinned peoples.

But Poe's racism also seems "odd" insofar as he ironizes the position of his own picaresque narrator by flaunting Pym's bafflement at native reactions to whiteness. Early in the cross-cultural encounter the narrator perceives a salient fact about the natives: "It was quite evident that they had never before seen any of the white race—from whose complexion, indeed, they appeared to recoil" (*CW*, 1:169). But unlike Melville's Ishmael, Pym cannot conceive of whiteness as a source of terror and so remains flummoxed by the natives' behavior: "We could not get them to approach several very harmless objects—such as the schooner's sails, an egg, an open book, or a pan of flour" (*CW*, 1:170). Pym's obliviousness to the native taboo evoked by white objects—or white-skinned intruders—persists to the end of the narrative. Drifting toward the South Pole with his companion Dirk Peters and a black hostage named Nu-Nu, Pym notes a revealing incident without comprehending its meaning:

> To-day, with a view of widening our sail . . . I took from my coat pocket a white handkerchief. Nu-Nu was seated at my elbow, and the linen accidentally flaring in his face, he became violently affected with convulsions. These were succeeded by drowsiness and stupor, and low murmurings of Tekeli-li, Tekeli-li. (204)

As most readers deduce from textual hints, the word *Tekeli-li* refers to the native taboo associated with whiteness. The narrator, however, remains clueless, a point that Dana Nelson emphasizes in suggesting that Poe delivers in *Pym* a cultural critique exposing the blindness of white "colonial knowledge" (*The Word in Black and White*, 98–100, 107–8). Worley makes a similar point in his examination of language and hierarchy in *Pym*, asserting that the novel "manages to undermine the very proslavery arguments that inform it" (242). What Nelson and Worley both notice but never entirely explain is that, in puzzling yet unmistakable ways, Poe works against the grain of his own racial prejudices, producing a novel that both enforces and subverts conventional white attitudes about race.

This narrative aporia deserves reconsideration. Without denying the "Negrophobia" of the Tsalal episode, we may observe that *Pym* both affirms and questions Anglo-Saxon racial hegemony. Apposite to Poe's representation of menacing blacks, Toni Morrison recounts her discovery about the Africanist presence in white American literature: "I came to realize the obvious: the subject of the dream is the dreamer. The fabrication of an Africanist persona is reflexive, an extraordinary meditation on the self; a powerful exploration of the fears and desires that reside in the writerly conscious" (*Playing in the Dark,* 17). The implications for Poe and *Pym* are instantly obvious: although the novel unfolds from the subject position of a young white American horrified in the final chapters by the murderous behavior of black "savages," the narrator is nevertheless (as we see in the opening chapters) in revolt himself against wealth, property, and trade—against the same commercial forces that the natives repulse by their actions. That is, Poe the "dreamer" of Tsalal (whatever his appropriations from Morrell) projects both his fear of blacks and, conversely, his desire for revenge against the white, paternalistic hierarchy from which he has been expelled.[9] When we consider that Pym goes to sea hidden in a crate like an escaping slave and that Poe likely named Arthur Gordon Pym after his black friend Armistead Gordon—reputedly "the most interesting man he ever talked to"—we begin to discern the layered complications beneath the novel's blatant representations of race.[10] Morrison argues that "no early American writer is more important to the concept of American Africanism than Poe," because in *Pym* he explores—indeed fixates upon—the cultural signification of white and black (*Playing in the Dark,* 32). His relentless association of the natives with blackness and the Anglo-American sailors with whiteness marks an important moment in American constructions of race. But Poe conducts this semiosis within a larger dialectic, that of civilization and savagery, which problematizes still further his negotiations of race. He accomplishes this through the motif of deception—a sign of the slavery crisis of the 1830s—in a way that paradoxically emphasizes distinctions between the civilized and the primitive in order to erase them.

Critics of *Pym* have established two seemingly inconsistent facts: the novel was written in four distinct phases, producing a patchwork effect with multiple incongruities of tone and detail (Ridgely, "Growth of the Text"); yet the narrative as a whole is so traversed by themes of revolt and deception as to suggest a deliberate design (E. Davidson, 164–71; P. Quinn, 176–77). From the adolescent prankishness of the opening episode recounting the wreck of Pym's sailboat, the *Ariel,* Poe under-scores the relationship between duplicity and violence in much the same way that Douglass associates "fraud" and "inhumanity." Pym and his friend Augustus Barnard barely escape death during a wild nocturnal ad-venture at sea yet manage to conceal the fact from their parents because, as Poe explains, "schoolboys . . . can accomplish wonders in the way of deception" (*CW,* 1:64). Just as Frederick Douglass forges "protec-tions" to sail up Chesapeake Bay, Augustus writes a false letter—an invi-tation to visit a friend—that liberates Pym from the world of genteel respectability limned by the novel's opening sentences. The narrator gladly leaves his humdrum, civilized life to experience (as Augustus has) "adventures in the South Pacific Ocean" and encounters with "the na-tives of the Island of Tinian" (*CW,* 1:57). Like the rambunctious Huck Finn, Pym feels stifled by civilization and yearns for the primitive: "My visions were of shipwreck and famine; of death or captivity among bar-barian hordes; of a lifetime dragged out in sorrow and tears, upon some gray and desolate rock, in an ocean unapproachable and unknown. Such visions or desires—for they amounted to desires—are common, I have since been assured, to the whole numerous race of the melancholy among men" (*CW,* 1:65). In a suggestive rewriting of Poe's own life script, a disguised Pym en route to the wharf mocks his maternal grand-father—who swears to cut Pym off "with a shilling" if he but mentions going to sea—and thus renounces the substantial "property" he expects to inherit. As if scorning the patrimony of John Allan, Poe thus figures a repudiation of chattel ownership: Pym defiantly frees himself from family obligation and the patriarchal structure of nineteenth-century mercantile capitalism.[11]

The narrator's experience aboard the ill-fated *Grampus* literalizes his romantic desire for "shipwreck and famine," producing a rapid transi-tion from the civilized to the savage. Ironically, Pym the would-be rebel settles himself in his "little apartment"—an oversized packing crate con-cealed beneath the deck—with "feelings of higher satisfaction . . . than any monarch ever experienced upon entering a new palace" (*CW,* 1:69). Surrounded by food, drink, and books, he peruses the history of the Lewis and Clark expedition, digesting a narrative of colonial explo-ration. Yet even as he reads about the advance of putatively "civilized" men into the "savage" West, a mutiny above decks overthrows Captain Barnard's authority (derived from the ship's owners, Lloyd and Vreden-burgh) and produces a scene of slaughter. Mounting the revolt is a mot-ley gang that includes two racially differentiated figures, a black cook named Seymour and a "ferocious-looking" man of mixed white and In-dian blood, the aforementioned Dirk Peters (*CW,* 1:87). Both superficially personify the savage: the black cook proves himself a "perfect demon" (*CW*, 1:86), dispatching more than twenty sailors loyal to the captain by dashing their brains out with an ax. Although one of the "less blood thirsty" mutineers, Peters combines brutishness with deformity; Poe explains the "ferocity" of his appearance by noting his long, protruding teeth, bowed arms and legs, and immense yet entirely bald head, indented in a way that Pym likens suggestively to "the head of most negroes" (*CW*, 1:86, 87). Although the mutineers are mostly white, their rebellion against capital, law, and property rights—instigated, as we learn, by "a private pique of the chief mate's against Captain Barnard" (*CW*, 1:93)—marks an important step in the dismantling of social authority figured by the fate of the *Grampus*. As Nathaniel Beverley Tucker's controversial *Messenger* review reveals, proslavery arguments depended on the claim that property ownership (i.e., slavery) was the basis of all civilized institutions. In *Pym*, Poe initially affirms that thesis by showing that a revolt—partly fomented by men of color—against an authority based on property rights produces anarchy and shipwreck.

But as is so often the case in this perversely ambiguous novel, the issue proves more complicated. For shortly after Pym emerges from his hiding place in the hold, he joins forces with Augustus and Dirk Peters (by now a beneficent, protective figure) to stage a countermutiny against the gang led by the first mate and the black cook. Performing a kind of minstrel show in reverse, Pym dons whiteface, impersonating a corpse streaked with blood to help his cohorts overwhelm the hostile group and kill all but one of them. The symbolic implications of this development are worth considering, for the countermutiny itself patently signifies a restoration of order and ownership: Peters rejects the plan of piracy advocated by the first mate and intends to surrender the vessel at the first port (*CW*, 1:104). Curiously, in becoming the guardian of Pym and Augustus and the unlikely defender of property rights, Peters sheds the frightening racialized identity assigned at the outset and becomes simply "the hybrid" (*CW*, 1:117). Allying himself with Augustus, the captain's patrilineal successor, he puts down the insurrection by fraud and deception: he applies chalk to Pym's face to simulate the pallor of death and thereby evokes the terror of whiteness. The trick allows the trio to become "masters of the brig" (*CW*, 1:113), yet the decimation of the crew leaves them unable to manage the vessel, and a great storm soon reduces the ship to a floating hulk. By killing the black cook and the rest of the rebellious crew to protect an implicit theory of capital and property, if not maritime slavery, Peters and his confederates (a word I use deliberately, if anachronistically) achieve a hollow victory, for the *Grampus* has become a worthless wreck. As a metaphor for national destiny, then, the destruction of the ship may ultimately represent Poe's own profound pessimism about the fate of a country riven by the issue of chattel slavery.

In the days that follow, the four survivors—Pym, Peters, Augustus, and a surviving mutineer named Parker—lose all vestiges of civilized behavior. "Raving with horror and despair," they beg to be rescued by a passing ship littered with rotting corpses (*CW,* 1:124). Their movement toward the ostensibly primitive culminates in cannibalism, an atrocity prefigured when a seagull deposits a "horrid morsel" of flesh from the death ship at Parker's feet (*CW,* 1:125). The image suggests a thought that Pym refuses to name, but soon thereafter Parker (the eventual victim) proposes the unspeakable: that one of the group must die to sustain the others. Pym here admits, "I had, for some time past, dwelt upon the prospect of our being reduced to this last horrible extremity, and had secretly made up my mind to suffer death in any shape or under any circumstances rather than resort to such a course" (*CW,* 1:132). That is, Pym prefers death to barbarism, for cannibalism is "the most horrible alternative that can enter into the mind of man" (*CW,* 1:132)—and there is no doubt here that Pym means a civilized *white* man. Travel narratives of the period typically associated cannibalism with "primitive," dark-skinned tribes—Native Americans, Pacific Islanders, Indians, or Africans—living in places remote from Western civilization, and published accounts of such practices evoked Anglo-American anxieties, as Melville well understood when he wrote *Typee* (1846). For the stranded survivors, the horrific lottery and subsequent slaughter and consumption of Parker mark a descent into what they regard as savagery, into the heart of a moral darkness conceived by the white colonial mind as racially marked. Significantly, Pym can bring himself to report the event only in summary. He explains that he "must not dwell upon the fearful repast which immediately ensued" (*CW,* 1:135), presumably because the very narration defies a genteel taboo. The real scandal of the account, however, lies in Poe's suggestion that the difference between the civilized and the savage is contingent, superficial, and unrelated to race. In a shocking scene often interpreted as a communion ritual, Pym, Peters, and Augustus consume the body and blood of Parker, tossing his hands, feet, and head into the ocean in a gesture of gruesome fastidiousness. Pym's dream of "shipwreck and famine" thus culminates in an act so degrading, so thoroughly associated with dark-skinned "primitive" peoples, that he can barely bring himself to confess it.

Having reached the nadir of inhumanity, however, Pym promptly forgets the episode and devotes the rest of his truncated narrative to reconstructing an absolute demarcation between the civilized and the savage.

Shortly after Augustus dies, a British schooner, the *Jane Guy,* rescues Peters and Pym, and here (as scholars and critics have often noted) the narrator undergoes a transformation of voice and personality, becoming the epitome of scientific reason and colonial self-interest. Pym indeed rationalizes his own forgetting:

> In about a fortnight, during which time we continued steering to the southeast, with gentle breezes and fine weather, both Peters and myself recovered entirely from the effects of our late privation and dreadful suffering, and we began to remember what had passed rather as a frightful dream, from which we had been happily awakened, than as events which had taken place in sober and naked reality. (*CW,* 1:148)

By dismissing his participation in cannibalism as a bad dream, Pym represses a reality that could unsettle his new pretensions to civilized gentility. He now appeals to the "well regulated human intellect" (*CW,* 1:153), discoursing knowledgeably—and aridly—about island geography, flora and fauna, and the history of South Seas exploration. Nelson places Pym's narrative of exploration aboard the *Jane Guy* in an "expansionist, Anglo-Saxon ideological context" (*The Word in Black and White,* 93) and reveals the implicit motives of economic exploitation suggested by the narrator's documentary observations. Becoming a champion of commercial exploitation, Pym reclaims his birthright as the scion of wealthy investors. After experiencing savagery, shipwreck, and famine— once the objects of his adolescent longing—he assumes the role of the "civilized," white colonial scientist as if to save himself from his own romantic fancies.

Once the *Jane Guy* reaches Tsalal, Pym's patronizing characterization of the natives underlines his need to distance himself from the primitive, and, like slavery advocates of the era, he portrays the black islanders alternately as "bloodthirsty savages and compliant children" (Worley, 230). For Pym, however, they are always different, always other than Anglo-Saxon; he regards their language as "jabbering" (*CW,* 1:168) and sees their animistic reactions to a gash in the ship's deck as proof of "ignorance" (*CW,* 1:169). From a position of assumed cultural superiority, he observes their amusing reactions to mirrors and to the "harmless" white objects noted earlier. Yet while Pym imagines that his Western scientific knowledge allows him to understand the blacks, he also registers uncertainties: when the well-armed whites march toward the native village, he notices the systematic appearance of "detachments" of natives along the way and feels "distrust" (*CW,* 1:172). His suspicions are later confirmed when the natives engineer a massive rockslide that kills all the crew except Peters and Pym. For the narrator, the massacre confirms the "savage" nature of the natives and reveals their deceitfulness: all their expressions of hospitality and friendliness in retrospect bear witness to their treachery.

Pym here expresses a white racial fear common in the South after the Nat Turner insurrection (and the earlier, abortive uprising led by Denmark Vesey), but his commentary on native duplicity also reveals as much about his need to sanitize white motives as to expose black deceptions:

> I believe that not one of us had at this time the slightest suspicion of the good faith of the savages. They had uniformly behaved with the greatest decorum, aiding us with alacrity in our work, offering us their commodities frequently without price, and never, in any instance, pilfering a single article. . . . Upon the whole, we should have been the most suspicious of human beings had we entertained a single thought of perfidy on the part of a people who treated us so well. A very short while sufficed to prove that this apparent kindness of disposition was only the result of a deeply-laid plan for our destruction, and that the islanders for whom we entertained such inordinate feelings of esteem were among the most barbarous, subtle, and bloodthirsty wretches that ever contaminated the face of the globe. (*CW*, 1:179–80)

The "decorum," helpfulness, and "apparent kindness" of the natives constitute part of what Scott calls the "hidden transcript" in power relations, and, as we see in Douglass's discussion of slave songs, such tactics masked the actual response to subjugation and exploitation in the culture of slavery from which *Pym* emerged. What seems most remarkable here, though, is Pym's insistence on the innocence of the colonial project. After an earlier visit to the native village to determine "what were the chief productions of the country and whether any of them could be turned to profit" (*CW*, 1:176), the white men have begun clearing the land (disregarding native reactions to tree cutting) to establish an industrial site for the curing and export of locally harvested sea cucumbers. Like Peter Stuyvesant on Manhattan Island, they have arrived with trinkets to appropriate land and resources from a darker skinned people presumed to be ignorant and uncivilized. Without a twinge of shame, Pym speaks of colonizing "work," of native "commodities" accepted without compensation, and of the "inordinate feelings of esteem" that the white men have for the blacks. As we perceive, however, they express their "eternal friendship and good-will" (*CW,* 1:175) to the natives purely as a strategy of exploitation: as Poe well understood about business relations, feigned friendliness (a "grin") is essential to "diddling" (*CW,* 3:870).

Here and elsewhere in the final chapters of *Pym,* Poe exposes the reciprocal duplicities of domination. He allows us to see that the white men, too, practice deception on Tsalal not only in the friendship they affect for the natives but also in their pretense of openness and trust. Whatever they do, however, they rely on their weapons for security: Pym observes that in preparing to visit the native village, the white men "took care to be well armed, yet without evincing any distrust" (*CW,* 1:171). Later, protected by firepower, they simulate honest trade: "We established a regular market on shore, *just under the guns of the schooner,* where our barterings were carried on with every *appearance* of good faith" (*CW,* 1:177; emphasis added). On their second trip to the native village they set out "armed to the teeth" with "muskets, pistols, and cutlasses" (*CW,* 1:180), despite Pym's adamant insistence (in the longer passage cited earlier) that none of the whites harbor "the slightest suspicion" about the goodwill of the natives. The contradictions of Pym's account allow us to see that although the whites "evince" trust and good faith, in reality they possess none, for they have come to Tsalal bearing the same assumptions of Anglo-Saxon racial superiority that for almost two centuries sustained the African slave trade, and they cannot set aside the arms that alone ensure their domination over the black people. Commenting on the willingness of the natives to abandon their weapons, the wily chief Too-wit remarks: "*Mattee non we pa pa si*—meaning that there was no need of arms where all were brothers" (*CW,* 1:180). Because this unilateral disarmament is part of a strategy to deceive and massacre the sailors, Too-wit's comment represents a cynical ploy, a part of the hidden transcript underwriting black-white relations on Tsalal. On another level, however, his remark is a critique of the obvious bad faith of white men who will not set aside their weapons: there is no brotherhood possible with men who carry guns. On yet another level, Too-wit's observation is a utopian assertion of the basis of civilized relations: where all persons treat each other with respect and consideration, weapons are unnecessary.

When the natives trigger the rockslide that buries the men of the *Jane Guy,* they rupture the cordon sanitaire (in Scott's phrase) between public demeanor and private feeling, between surface appearance and underlying reality. The scene parallels Douglass's fight with Covey insofar as it exposes a determination to resist racial dominance sustained by fraud and force. Predictably, Pym excoriates the "infamous wretches" who orchestrate the disaster, and then (as if to signify further his contempt for the natives) he magnanimously recalculates Peters's racial status, observing that "we were the only living white men upon the island" (*CW*, 1:185). Exposing naked racial hostility, the narrator exults that the explosion of the *Jane Guy* kills "perhaps a thousand" natives and leaves a similar number "desperately mangled" (*CW*, 1:190). Yet Pym's wildly racist condemnation of the "savages" should not obscure the difference between his perspective and Poe's, for even at the height of the uprising the author takes pains to remind us of the native taboo and to demonstrate again Pym's utter incapacity to imagine whiteness as a source of fear and loathing. When the Tsalalians find the carcass of a white animal with scarlet claws, they cry "Tekeli-li" and build a fence around the totemic object, leaving the colonial ethnographer to remark vacuously: "Why it had occasioned so much concern among the savages was more than we could comprehend" (*CW*, 1:190).

Just as he fails to understand the taboo, Pym fails to appreciate the subtlety of the strategy by which the natives disarm themselves to destroy their potential oppressors. As Nelson notes, "The Tsalalians manage to dupe the crewmen by turning their sense of security against them" (*The Word in Black and White*, 99). Poe's tendency throughout his fiction to fetishize intellectual strategy (one thinks of "Mystification" or "The Purloined Letter") and to assume the subject position of the avenger is worth recalling. In "The Cask of Amontillado," Montresor discloses the intricacies of his plan to redress the "thousand injuries" of Fortunato by exploiting the latter's pride in his vast knowledge of wines. In "Hop-Frog" he imagines the clever revenge exacted by a "dwarf and a cripple" from "some barbarous region" (Mabbott, 3:899–900) upon a king and his seven ministers. The grotesque jester (who resembles no one so much as Dirk Peters) persuades the monarch and his ministers to masquerade as orangutans—flaunting their power through implicit racial parody—before they are put to the torch by the dwarf. In effect the massacre on Tsalal prefigures the revenge of Hop-Frog, and although tainted by Pym's blatant "Negrophobia," the episode also dramatizes the eruption of Poe's subversive imagination, or what Joan Dayan calls his "envisioned revenge for the national sin of slavery" ("Amorous Bondage," 197). Pym's insistence on the distinction between the civilized and the primitive—endlessly reiterated in the word *savages*—at last exposes the crux of his inability to grasp the taboo of whiteness, for in his Anglo-American, colonial consciousness, terror can derive only from the darkness or blackness associated with the savage. Because he imagines the difference between the civilized and the primitive to be as absolute as the difference between black and white, he cannot conceive of alternate cultural values in which whiteness evokes the terror of the *unheimlich*, the

alien, or the barbarian.[12] *We* see this difference, however, by virtue of
the picaresque irony of Pym's obtuseness, which is the sign, I would
argue, of Poe's conflicted relationship to the culture of slavery.

In his preface to *Tales of the Grotesque and Arabesque* (1839), Poe dis-
counted the influence of German romanticism and remarked: "If in
many of my productions terror has been the thesis, I maintain that terror is not of Germany but of the soul" (Mabbott, 2:473). Clearly, however, the terror of Tsalal came not from the soul but from Richmond,
Baltimore, and the slavery of the upper South, just as many other horrors in *Pym* derived ultimately from Poe's sense of social crisis—from
the unresolvable, tragic dilemma confronting the young republic in the
1830s. If the wreck of the *Grampus*, as I have already argued, meta-
phorizes the looming national disaster over slavery, the fiery destruction
of the *Jane Guy* perhaps prefigures the devastation of the South as a result of its dependence on slavery. In what seems an innocuous observation early in the novel, Poe mentions the dire result of fully packing a
ship with a well-known Southern commodity: "A load of cotton, . . .
tightly screwed while in certain conditions, has been known, through the
expansion of its bulk, to rend a vessel asunder at sea" (*CW*, 1:97). Might
Poe's ultimate point of reference here be the slave economy of the
South? Is *Pym*, as Dayan nearly suggests, finally an antislavery jeremiad?
Does that last, cryptic sentence of the concluding "Note" indeed refer
to God's ultimate vengeance for "the *known* offense of slavery," por-
tending an "inevitable catastrophe" for the South (Dayan, "Romance
and Race," 109)? For some critics, the novel's final image—of a colossal
polar figure whose skin is "of the perfect whiteness of the snow" (*CW*,
1:206)—identifies Poe as a Southern bigot in quest of racial purity. But
the novel authorizes a contrary, subversive reading, for as Pym approaches his own textual vanishing point, this emissary of supposed
enlightenment is literally in the same boat with a "savage" and a "half
breed Indian" (*CW*, 1:55). That is, the American picaro cannot at
last avoid the multicultural nature of social experience; the destiny of
Pym, the white man, cannot be dissociated from that of the black and
the red.

As Douglass's *Narrative* so trenchantly reveals, the practice of slaveholding contaminated virtually all relations of racial difference and fostered an ethos of mutual deception as a way of channeling the latent
violence of subjugation. That climate of deceit, sustained by "the whole
system of fraud and inhumanity of slavery," marked both the life story
that Douglass had to tell and the "tragical-mythical-satirical-hoaxical"
novel Poe eventually produced (Ridgely, "Tragical-Mythical"). The fact
that both narratives incorporate urgent scenes of reading—Douglass

perusing the story in the *Columbian Orator* of a slave arguing for his freedom and Pym rubbing phosphorus on a note to glimpse a warning written in blood—reminds us of the crucial relationship between literacy and survival in the slave South of the 1830s. Who could write and what could be written—especially about slavery—were matters of intense controversy in the South during the decade in which Poe wrote *Pym* and Douglass underwent the ordeals recounted in his *Narrative*. Worley describes the reciprocity between an emergent "hierarchy of writing" in the South and "the actual power relations of antebellum southern society": "By simultaneously censoring writing on the one hand and producing and distributing proslavery and states' rights arguments on the other, the South mirrored its longstanding social hegemony in a hierarchy of information controlled by a master class that kept chattel slavery anchored at the bottom" (Worley, 238–39). Douglass wrote his autobiography, clearly, to disrupt the power relations of the slave South by overturning the hierarchy of writing—by claiming the right to inscribe his story specifically as "an American slave" (as the book's title page insists) and thereby helping to dismantle slavery.[13] Poe's strategy in *Pym* is far less clear, and the novel's surface appeal to racism complicates our contemporary understanding. Early on, as I have suggested, the narrator seems to mirror Poe's own desire for freedom and his hostility toward a mercantile culture. But the aporia signaled by Pym's later interpretive failures points to Poe's semiconscious rejection of the capitalist exploitation and cultural blindness that his narrator represents. Although Poe, like most white Americans in the 1830s, arguably shared Pym's sense of racial superiority, internal evidence nevertheless suggests that his novel, begun in Richmond but largely composed on the other side of the Mason-Dixon Line in New York in 1837, ultimately questions the Anglo-Saxon prejudices of his narrator, thus implicitly defying the political censorship of the antebellum South.

External evidence supports this reading as well. If Poe's position on race can be linked with any *Messenger* article published under his editorship, it seems most congruent with the review of "Liberian Literature" published in February 1836 by Lucian Minor. As did Poe himself, Minor supported the recolonization of blacks as a way of eliminating slavery, and his essay celebrates the aspects of "English" civilization now to be found in Liberia, where so recently "the tangled and pathless forest frowned in a silence unbroken save by the roar of wild beasts, the fury of the tornado, the whoop of the man-stealer, or the agonizing shrieks of his victims on being torn from their homes to brave the horrors of the Middle Passage and of the West Indies" (Minor, 158). For Minor, the issue of race dominated his portrait of Liberian prosperity:

> What heightens—indeed what *constitutes* the wonder—is, that the
> main *operatives* in this great change are *not white men*. The printer
> and the editor of the newspaper—the merchants—most of the
> teachers and all of the pupils—the owners and cultivators of
> the farms—the officers and soldiers in the military companies—
> the throng in the churches—are all *colored people*. (158)

The patronizing aspect of Minor's "wonder" notwithstanding, this essay
(published under Poe's aegis two months before the infamous Paulding-
Drayton review) illustrates the persistence in the upper South of an oppositional ideology that forthrightly condemned the slave trade, advocated recolonization as a means of ending slavery, and accepted the
capacity of blacks to become literate, self-reliant citizens. In a letter to
Minor, Poe reported about the article, "Lauded by all men of sense, it
has excited animadversion from the Augusta Chronicle. The scoundrel
says it is sheer abolitionism" (*Letters,* 1:87). Walking an editorial
tightrope, Poe was emphatically neither an abolitionist nor a proslavery
apologist: he edited Minor's essay to eliminate "all passages . . . at
which offence could, by any possibility, be taken" (*Letters,* 1:83), yet he let
stand the searing references to slave stealing and the Middle Passage, implicitly counting himself among the "men of sense" supporting Minor's
position. While the expedient of deportation offends the contemporary
conscience, Minor, Poe, and other Southern supporters of "colonization" sought a peaceful, pragmatic solution to the slavery crisis as they
rejected proslavery assumptions about the helplessness and ineducability
of blacks. Indeed, by dismantling the racist notion that civilization is a
by-product of whiteness while savagery is a symptom of blackness,
Minor's rhapsody on "the march of Liberia to prosperity and civilization" (158) carries out much the same cultural work performed by Poe's
multiple ironies in *Pym*.

When Harper and Brothers published *Pym* in New York in 1838—five
weeks before Douglass arrived in the city—the novel created a momen-
tary stir as a hoax but produced no discernible political impact. The
satire implied by the narrator's racist stupidity was far too oblique and
the concluding philological speculations entirely too esoteric to move a
mass audience to reconsider its prejudices. Caught between positions on
slavery that he regarded as extreme and surrounded (in both Richmond
and New York) by the tensions, brutalities, and deceptions of a culture
profoundly conflicted by the practice of slaveholding, Poe constructed a
fable of escape from the troubled new republic, a fable that figures revolt first as a quixotic gesture and then as a menacing sign of class and
racial conflict. Ironically, his narrator travels halfway around the world,

away from Nantucket—soon a hotbed of abolitionism and the site of Douglass's debut as a public speaker—only to succumb to the blandishments of racial domination and colonial exploitation on the island of Tsalal. There is absolutely no evidence that the fugitive Douglass noticed *Pym*, nor is there much likelihood that his uneasy sojourn in Gotham afforded the leisure of browsing in bookstores. Neither is there any evidence or likelihood that Poe read Douglass's *Narrative* when it appeared in 1845, although he probably noticed Margaret Fuller's review of the book in the *New York Tribune*. Unless they met each other on the streets of Baltimore in the early 1830s (and there is a scene well worth imagining), Poe and Douglass took no cognizance of each other as they pursued their different dreams of American freedom—Poe toiling to liberate himself from the "magazine prison house" (*Essays*, 1036–38) and Douglass struggling to dismantle the "prison-house of bondage." But a century and a half later, we can see what denizens of the mid–nineteenth century could not: that Douglass's narrative illuminates the hidden transcript—and ironic protest—in Poe's novel by exposing the mutual deceptions of an era when no man could be trusted.

Notes

For helpful readings of this chapter in manuscript I wish to thank Richard Kopley, Terry Whalen, Scott Peeples, and my colleagues Pat McGee, Angeletta Gourdine, and Bainard Cowan, as well as my wife, Sarah Liggett.

1. The church attended by the Aulds was located approximately five blocks from Mrs. Clemm's house. (My thanks to Richard Kopley for calling attention to this detail.) Mrs. Clemm and her family apparently attended the First Presbyterian Church on East Street where Poe's brother was buried on 2 August 1831.

2. Poe never knew his father, David Poe, who abandoned the family when Poe was an infant. Haunted by the question of his father's identity, Douglass repeated in print and on the lecture platform the rumor that he had been fathered by his white master. As William S. McFeely points out, Douglass liked to fancy himself the son of plantation owner Col. Edward Lloyd; but his first master was actually Aaron Anthony (his most likely progenitor), although other evidence suggests that his second master, Thomas Auld, may have been his father (11–14). After returning from his first sojourn in Baltimore, Douglass developed a "tortured bond" with Thomas Auld that culminated in Auld's protecting Douglass (after his arrest for conspiring to escape) by sending him away, back to Hugh Auld's home in Baltimore, rather than selling him on the auction block (40–41, 56–57). Poe's letters to John Allan, the foster father who disowned him, suggest an analogy to Douglass's love-hate relationship with Thomas Auld.

3. In his definitive study of the slave narrative, William L. Andrews identi-

fies George White as "the first slave narrator to compose and write down his life on his own" in a work published in 1810 (48, 342).

4. The cited phrase comes from the notorious "Paulding-Drayton" review in the *Southern Literary Messenger*, attributed (mistakenly) by Kaplan to Poe. I will return to this crucial issue shortly.

5. David Leverenz has provided a brilliant critique of Poe's conflicted relationship to the Virginia gentry: "Trapped between a phantom gentry culture and the mechanistic demands of urban capitalism, [Poe's] gentlemen-narrators discover that their own poses are as nightmarish as the vulgarian scrambling that has contaminated their world" (233). As will be seen, the remark is applicable as well to a narrator from Nantucket, Arthur Gordon Pym.

6. As T. Stephen Whitman has shown, such term agreements were becoming common in Baltimore and often carried the promise of manumission after a certain number of years (51–52). Poe's involvement in this transaction is noted in Thomas and Jackson, 100.

7. My thanks to Dwight McBride for steering me toward Scott's work and offering a useful early critique of my own project.

8. In a provocative recent study that indirectly links Poe's *Pym* and Douglass's *Narrative*, Teresa A. Goddu shows how "the gothic has served as a useful mode in which to resurrect and resist America's racial history" (*Gothic America*, 153). In her final chapter, Goddu mines Richard Wright's observation that amid the racial oppression of modern America "if Poe were alive, he would not have to invent horror; horror would invent him" (131). She then discusses Gothic "spectacles of horror" in Stowe, Jacobs, and Douglass, focusing (in the last instance) on the whipping of Aunt Hester in the *Narrative* (137–39).

9. Poe had been legally disowned by John Allan, who died in 1833 and left his foster son out of his will. By 1836, when he began composing *Pym*, Poe had already been threatened with dismissal by Thomas W. White and, indeed, lost his job with the *Messenger* before the first installment of the story appeared in the journal.

10. In the year of Poe's death, Henry "Box" Brown published a slave narrative celebrating his escape from Richmond by shipping himself to Philadelphia in a packing crate. Burton R. Pollin suggests the possible influence of Gordon on the naming of Arthur Gordon Pym (*CW*, 1:217 n. 1.1A) and cites the source from which the comment quoted here derives (Mabbott, xiv). I am indebted to Professor Pollin for his kind suggestions about further research on Armistead Gordon.

11. For a more ample consideration of Poe's conflict with the forces of capitalism, see Terence Whalen's chapter "Edgar Allan Poe and the Horrid Laws of Political Economy" (*Edgar Allan Poe and the Masses*, 21–57). Many early readers perceived connections between the fictional "Edgarton" and the Richmond of the 1820s. "Mr. E. Ronald's Academy on the hill" (*CW*, 1:57) corresponds to Joseph H. Clarke's Richmond Academy, which Poe attended in the early 1820s. There was also a "Mr. Ricketts, a gentleman with only one arm" (*CW*, 1:57) who lived in Richmond, according to Mary Phillips, citing

J. H. Whitty (118). As Pollin notes, the original of Augustus Barnard was very likely Ebenezer Burling, a youth who enticed Poe into drinking and who fled Richmond with Poe in March 1827 aboard a departing ship *(CW,* 1:218 n. 1.10).

12. Pym similarly refuses *(CW,* 1:195) to regard the markings within the chasm on Tsalal as writing—a position consistent with his view of the natives as "ignorant islanders" *(CW,* 1:202)—and he likewise rejects the possibility that the "huge tumuli" scattered about the ground might be "the wreck of some gigantic structures of art" *(CW,* 1:198). His need to see the natives as "savages" incapable of intelligent cultural production occludes his interpretive faculties, a blindness Poe himself exposes in the "Note" through the philological commentary of a supposed editor.

13. My colleague James Olney examines the subtle implications of Douglass's title in his essay "The Founding Fathers" (6).

BIBLIOGRAPHY

Adams, John F. "Classical Raven Lore and Poe's 'Raven.'" *Poe Studies* 5 (1972): 53.

Adams, John Quincy. "Misconceptions of Shakspeare [*sic*] upon the Stage." *New-England Magazine* 9, no. 54 (1 December 1835): 435–440.

Allen, Hervey. *Israfel: The Life and Times of Edgar Poe.* 2 vols. London: Brentano's, 1927.

Allen, Theordore W. *The Invention of the White Race.* London: Verso, 1994.

Alterton, Margaret. *Origins of Poe's Critical Theory.* Temecula: Reprint Services, 1992.

Ambrogio, Anthony. "Fay Wray: Horror Films' First Sex Symbol." In *Eros in the Mind's Eye: Sexuality and the Fantastic in Art and Film,* ed. Donald Palumbo, 127–39. New York: Greenwood Press, 1986.

Andrews, William L. *To Tell a Free Story: The First Century of Afro-American Autobiography, 1760–1865,* Urbana, Ill.: University of Illinois Press, 1986.

Appel, Toby A. *The Cuvier-Geoffroy Debate: French Biology in the Decades before Darwin.* New York: Oxford University Press, 1987.

"The Aristidean." *Broadway Journal* 1 (3 May 1845).

Avery v. Everett. 110 N.Y. 317 (1888).

Avins, Alfred. *The Reconstruction amendments' debates; the legislative history and contemporary debates in Congress on the 13th, 14th, and 15th amendments.* Richmond: Virginia Commission on Constitutional Government, 1967.

Bailey & als v. Poindexter's Ex'or. VA 14 Gratt. 148 (1858).

Ball, Edward. *Slaves in the Family.* New York: Farrar, Straus and Giroux, 1998.

Barber, Lynn. *The Heyday of Natural History, 1820–1870.* Garden City, N.Y.: Doubleday, 1980.

Barrett, Lindon. "African American Slave Narrative: Literacy, the Body, Authority." *American Literary History* 7 (fall 1995): 415–442.

Baudelaire, Charles. "Edgar Allan Poe: His Life and Works." In *Baudelaire on Poe: Critical Papers,* eds. Lois and Francis E. Hyslop, 35–86. State College, Pa.: Bald Eagle Press, 1952.

———. "New Notes on Edgar Poe." In *Baudelaire on Poe: Critical Papers,* 119–46.

Beaver, Harold. Introduction. In *The Narrative of Arthur Gordon Pym of Nantucket,* 7–30. New York: Penguin, 1975.

Bell, Derrick. *Faces at the Bottom of the Well: The Permanence of Racism.* New York: Basic Books, 1992.

Benjamin, Walter. *Charles Baudelaire: A Lyric Poet in the Era of High Capitalism,* Trans. Harry Zohn. London: NLB, 1973.

Berkeley, Edmund, and Dorothy Smith Berkeley. *Dr. Alexander Garden of Charles Town.* Chapel Hill: University of North Carolina Press, 1969.

Berlin, Ira. *Slaves without Masters: The Free Negro in the Antebellum South.* New York: Pantheon, 1974.

Bezanson, Walter E. "The Troubled Sleep of Arthur Gordon Pym." In *Essays in Literary History,* ed. Rudolf Kirk and C. F. Main, 149–75. New Brunswick, N.J.: Rutgers University Press, 1960.

Bingley, William. *Bingley's Natural History; exhibiting in a series of delightful anecdotes and descriptions, the characteristics, habits and modes of life of the various beasts, birds, fishes, [and] insects. . . . With large additions from Cuvier, Buffon. . . .* 1872.

Blackford, L. Minor. *Mine Eyes Have Seen the Glory.* Cambridge: Harvard University Press, 1954.

Blackstone, William. *Commentaries on the Laws of England.* 1769. 4 vols. Chicago: University of Chicago Press, 1979.

Bloch, J. M. *Miscegenation, Melaleukation, and Mr. Lincoln's Dog.* New York: Schaum, 1958.

Blum, John M., Edmund S. Morgan, Willie Lee Rose, Arthur M. Schlesinger, Jr., Kenneth M. Stampp, and C. Vann Woodward, eds. *The National Experience: A History of the United States to 1877.* New York: Harcourt Brace Jovanovich, 1981.

Bondurant, Agnes M. *Poe's Richmond.* 1942. Richmond: Poe Associates, 1978.

Brown, William Wells. *My Southern Home. From Fugitive Slave to Free Man: The Autobiographies of William Wells Brown.* Ed. William L. Andrews. New York: Penguin, 1993.

Bryant, John. "Poe's Ape of UnReason: Humor, Ritual, and Culture." *Nineteenth-Century Literature* 51 (1996): 16–52.

Buckingham, J. S. *The Slave States of America.* 2 vols. London: Fisher, Son, and Co., 1842.

Buffon, Georges-Louis Leclerc Comte de. *Histoire naturelle, générale et particulière.* 44 vols. Paris, 1749–1804.

Burke, Edmund. *A Philosophical Enquiry into the Origin of Our Ideas of the Sublime and the Beautiful.* 1757. New York: Oxford University Press, 1990.

Butterfield, Ralph. *American Cotton Planter and Soil of the South* 2 (September 1858): 293–294. Quoted in *Advice among Masters: The Ideal in Slave Management in the Old South*, ed. James O. Breeden, 212. Westport, Conn.: Greenwood Press, 1980.

Campbell, Killis. *The Mind of Poe, and Other Studies.* 1933. New York: Russell and Russell, 1962.

———. "Poe's Treatment of the Negro and the Negro Dialect." *Studies in English* 16 (1936): 106–14.

Camper, Pieter. *The Works of the Late Professor Camper, on the Connexion between the Science of Anatomy and the Arts of Drawing, Painting, Statuary, &c. in Two Books. Containing a Treatise on the Natural Difference in Features in Persons of Different Countries and Period of Life.* 1791. Trans. Thomas Cogan. London, 1794.

Carey, John L. *Some Thoughts Concerning Domestic Slavery.* 2d ed. Baltimore: Joseph N. Lewis, 1838.

Carlson, Eric W., ed. *The Recognition of Edgar Allan Poe: Selected Criticism since 1829.* Ann Arbor: University of Michigan Press, 1966.

Carr, Leslie G. *"Color-Blind" Racism.* Thousand Oaks, Calif.: Sage, 1997.

Carter, Robert. "The Broadway Journal." *Boston Liberator* 23 (March 1845).

Cash, W. J. *The Mind of the South.* New York: Knopf, 1941.

Ceplair, Larry. Introduction. In *The Public Years of Sarah and Angelina Grimké: Selected Writings, 1835–1839*, 1–10. New York: Columbia University Press, 1989.

Césaire, Aimé. *Discourse on Colonialism.* 1955. Trans. Joan Pinkham. New York: Monthy Review Press, 1972.

Charvat, William. *The Profession of Authorship in America, 1800–1870.* Ed. Matthew J. Bruccoli. Columbus: Ohio State University Press, 1968.

Child, Lydia Maria. *An Appeal in Favor of That Class of Americans Called Africans.* 1833. Amherst: University of Massachusetts Press, 1996.

Clamorgan, Cyprian. *The Colored Aristocracy of St. Louis.* 1858. Reprinted in *Bulletin of the Missouri Historical Society* 31, no. 1 (October 1974): 9–31.

Cornelius, Janet Duitsman. *When I Can Read My Title Clear: Literacy, Slavery, and Religion in the Antebellum South.* Columbia: University of South Carolina Press, 1991.

Coues, Elliott, ed. "A New Edition" of Biddle's *History of the Expedition under the Command of Lewis and Clark to the Sources of the Missouri River, thence across the Rocky Mountains and down the Columbia River to the Pacific Ocean, performed during the Years 1804–5–6, by Order of the Government of the United States.* 1814. 2 vols. New York: F. P. Harper, 1893.

Cover, Robert M. *Justice Accused: Antislavery and the Judicial Process.* New Haven: Yale University Press, 1975.

Creswell's Executor v. Walker. 37 Alabama 233 (1861).

Cuvier, Baron Georges. *The Animal Kingdom, Arranged after its Organization; Forming a Natural History of Animals and an Introduction to Comparative Anatomy.* Trans. W. B. Carpenter and J. O. Westwood. London: Henry G. Bohn, 1863.

———. *The Animal Kingdom arranged according to its organization . . .* Ed. and trans. H. McMurtrie. London: Orr and Smith, 1834.

———. *Recherches sur les ossemens fossiles.* Vol. 1. Paris: Deterville, 1812. Quoted in Stephen Jay Gould. *The Mismeasure of Man,* 36. New York: Norton, 1981.

d'Auberteuil, Hilliard. *Considérations sur l'état présent de la colonie française de Saint-Domingue.* 2 vols. Paris: Grangé, 1776–77.

Davidson, Edward. *Poe: A Critical Study.* Cambridge: Harvard University Press, 1957.

Davidson, Nancy Reynolds. "E. W. Clay: American Political Caricaturist of the Jacksonian Era." Ph. D. diss., University of Michigan, 1980.

Dayan, Joan. "Amorous Bondage: Poe, Ladies, and Slaves." *American Literature* 66 (June 1994): 239–73. Reprinted in *Subjects and Citizens: Nation, Race, and Gender from Oroonoko to Anita Hill,* ed. Michael Moon and Cathy N. Davidson, 223–65. Durham: Duke University Press, 1995; and in *The American Face of Edgar Allan Poe,* ed. Shawn Rosenheim and Stephen Rachman, 179–209. Baltimore: Johns Hopkins University Press, 1995.

———. *Fables of Mind: An Inquiry into Poe's Fiction.* New York: Oxford University Press, 1987.

———. *Haiti, History, and the Gods.* Berkeley: University of California Press, 1998.

———. "Romance and Race."In *The Columbia History of the American Novel,* ed. Emory Elliott, 89–109. New York: Columbia University Press, 1991.

DeCamp, David. "African Day-Names in Jamaica." *Language* 43 (1967): 139–49.

Defoe, Daniel. *Robinson Crusoe.* Ed. Michael Shinagel. New York: Norton, 1975.

Depestre, René. *Bonjour et adieu à la négritude.* Paris: Editions Robert Laffont, 1980.

Dew, Thomas R. "Abolition of Negro Slavery." *American Quarterly Review* 12 (1832): 189–265. Reprinted in Thomas W. White. *Review of the Debate in the Virginia Legislature of 1831–1832.* Richmond: T. W. White, 1832; in *The Proslavery Argument.* Charleston: Walker, Richards & Co., 1852; and in *The Ideology of Slavery: Proslavery Thought in the Antebellum South, 1830–1860,* ed. Drew Gilpin Faust, 23–77. Baton Rouge: Louisiana State University Press, 1981.

———. "An Address." *Southern Literary Messenger* 2 (November 1836): 765.

Dickens, Charles. *American Notes and Pictures from Italy.* 1842. Introduction, Sacheverell Sitwell. New York: Oxford University Press, 1957.

Donald, David Herbert. "The Proslavery Argument Reconsidered." *Journal of Southern History* 37 (February 1971): 3–18.

Douglass, Frederick. *My Bondage and My Freedom.* 1855. In *Autobiographies,* ed. Henry Louis Gates Jr., 103–452. New York: Library of America, 1994.

———. *Narrative of the Life of Frederick Douglass, an American Slave.* 1845. In *Autobiographies,* ed. Henry Louis Gates Jr., 1–102. New York: Library of America, 1994.

Dr. Rees's New Cyclopaedia. Philadelphia, 1806–21.

Dred Scott v. Sanford. 60 U.S. 19 How. 393 (1857).

Du Bois, W. E. B. *The Philadelphia Negro: A Social Study.* Philadelphia, 1899.

Dumm, Thomas. *Democracy and Punishment: Disciplinary Origins of the United States.* Madison: University of Wisconsin Press, 1987.

Dyson, Michael Eric. *Race Rules: Navigating the Color Line.* Reading, Mass.: Addison-Wesley, 1996.

Eagleton, Terry. *The Ideology of the Aesthetic.* Oxford: Blackwell, 1990.

Edelstein, Tilden G. "*Othello* in America: The Drama of Racial Intermarriage." In *Region, Race, and Reconstruction: Essays in Honor of C. Vann Woodward,* ed. J. Morgan Kousser and James M. McPherson, 179–97. New York: Oxford University Press, 1982.

Eliot, T. S. *From Poe to Valéry.* New York: Harcourt Brace, 1948.

Ellison, Ralph. *Invisible Man.* New York: Random House, 1952.

Emerson, Ralph Waldo. *Essays and Lectures.* Ed, Joel Porte. New York: Library of America, 1993.

———. *The Journals and Miscellaneous Notebooks of Ralph Waldo Emerson,* ed. William H. Gilman et al. 16 vols. Cambridge: Belknap Press of Harvard University Press, 1960–82.

Emerson v. Howland et al. 8 Massachusetts 636 (1816).

Fanon, Frantz. *Black Skin, White Masks.* 1952. Trans. Charles Lam Markmann. New York: Grove, 1967.

Faust, Drew Gilpin. "A Southern Stewardship: The Intellectual and the Proslavery Argument." *American Quarterly* 31 (spring 1979): 63-80.

Fetterley, Judith. "Reading about Reading: 'A Jury of Her Peers,' 'The Murders in the Rue Morgue,' and 'The Yellow Wallpaper.'"In *Gender and Reading: Essays on Readers, Texts, and Contexts,* ed. Elizabeth A. Flynn and Patrocinio P. Schweickart, 147–64. Baltimore: Johns Hopkins University Press, 1986.

Fiedler, Leslie. *Love and Death in the American Novel.* New York: Criterion Books, 1960.

Fields, Barbara Jeanne. *Slavery and Freedom on the Middle Ground: Maryland during the Nineteenth Century.* New Haven: Yale University Press, 1985.

Fishkin, Shelley Fisher. *Was Huck Black? Mark Twain and African-American Voices.* New York: Oxford University Press, 1993.

Foner, Eric. "The Idea of Free Labor in Nineteenth-Century America." In *Free Soil, Free Labor, Free Men: The Ideology of the Republican Party before the Civil War,* ix–xxxix. New York: Oxford University Press, 1995.

———. *Politics and Ideology in the Age of the Civil War.* New York: Oxford University Press, 1980.

Frederickson, George M. *The Black Image in the White Mind: The Debate on Afro-American Character and Destiny, 1817–1914.* New York: Harper and Row, 1971.

"Free Democratic." Handbill. Reprinted in Roger Burns and William Fraley. "'Old Gunny': Abolitionist in a Slave City." *Maryland Historical Magazine* 68(winter 1973): 369–82.

Freehling, Alison Goodyear. *Drift toward Dissolution: The Virginia Slavery Debate of 1831–1832.* Baton Rouge: Louisiana State University Press, 1982.

Freimarck, Vincent, and Bernard Rosenthal, eds. Introduction. In *Race and the American Romantics,* 1–21. New York: Schocken Books, 1971.

Frost, Linda. "The Circassian Beauty and the Circassian Slave: Gender, Imperialism, and American Popular Entertainment." In *Freakery: Cultural Spectacles of the Extraordinary Body,* ed. Rosemarie Garland Thompson, 248–62. New York: New York University Press, 1996.

Gates, Henry Louis, Jr. *Figures in Black: Words, Signs, and the "Racial" Self.* New York: Oxford University Press, 1987.

Genovese, Eugene D. *Roll, Jordan, Roll: The World the Slaves Made.* New York: Vintage, 1976.

Gilman, Sander. "Black Bodies, White Bodies: Toward an Iconography of Female Sexuality in Late Nineteenth-Century Art, Medicine, and Literature." In *"Race," Writing, and Difference,* ed. Henry Louis Gates Jr., 223–61. Chicago: University of Chicago Press, 1986.

Ginsberg, Lesley. "Slavery and the Gothic Horror of Poe's 'The Black Cat.'" In *American Gothic: New Interventions in a National Narrative,* ed. Robert K. Martin and Eric Savoy, 99–128. Iowa City: University of Iowa Press, 1998.

Goddu, Teresa A. "The Ghost of Race: Edgar Allan Poe and the Southern Gothic." In *Criticism and the Color Line: Desegregating American Literary Studies,* ed. Henry B. Wonham, 230–50. New Brunswick, N.J.: Rutgers University Press, 1996.

————. *Gothic America: Narrative, History, and Nation.* New York: Columbia University Press, 1997.

Goldberg, David Theo. *Racist Culture: Philosophy and the Politics of Meaning.* Cambridge: Blackwell, 1993.

Gonzales, Ambrose E. *The Black Border: Gullah Stories of the Carolina Coast.* Columbia, S.C.: The State Co., 1922.

Gould, Stephen Jay. "The Hottentot Venus: A Sensation from Picadilly to Paris, She Drew Crowds from All Classes, Including Scientists." *Natural History* 91, no. 10 (October 1982): 20–27.

Graham, Howard Jay. "The Early Antislavery Backgrounds of the Fourteenth Amendment." *Wisconsin Law Review* (May 1950): 479–507.

Granucci, Anthony F. "'Nor Cruel and Unusual Punishments Inflicted': The Original Meaning." *California Law Review* 57 (1969): 863.

Gray, Thomas R. *The Confession, Trial, and Execution of Nat Turner, The Negro Insurrectionist.* 1831. Dictated to Thomas R. Gray. New York: AMS Press, 1975.

Greenblatt, Stephen. *Shakespearean Negotiations: The Circulation of Social Energy in Renaissance England.* Berkeley: University of California Press, 1988.

Grimsted, David. "Rioting in Its Jacksonian Setting." *American Historical Review* 77 (April 1972): 361–397.

Griswold, Rufus Wilmot. "The 'Ludwig' Article." *New York Daily Tribune* 9 October 1849. Reprinted in *The Recognition of Edgar Allan Poe: Selected Criticism since 1829,* ed. Eric W. Carlson. Ann Arbor: University of Michigan Press, 1966.

Guthrie, Robert V. *Even the Rat Was White: A Historical View of Psychology.* New York: Allyn and Bacon, 1998.

Hall, Kim F. "'Troubling Doubles': Apes, Africans and Blackface in *Mr. Moore's Revels.*" In *Race, Ethnicity, and Power in the Renaissance,* ed. Joyce Green MacDonald, 120–44. Cranbury, N.J.: Associated University Presses, 1997.

Halttunen, Karen. *Confidence Men and Painted Women: A Study of Middle-Class Culture in America, 1830–1870*. New Haven: Yale University Press, 1982.

Haraway, Donna. *Primate Visions: Gender, Race, and Nature in the World of Modern Science*. New York: Routledge, 1989.

Harris, Cheryl. "Whiteness as Property." *Harvard Law Review* 106 (1993): 1710–91.

Harrold, Stanley. *The Abolitionists and the South, 1831–1861*. Lexington: University Press of Kentucky, 1995.

Harrowitz, Nancy. "Criminality and Poe's Orangutan: The Question of Race in Detection." In *Agonistics: Arenas of Creative Contest*, ed. Janet Lungstrum and Elizabeth Sauer, 177–95. Albany: State University of New York Press, 1997.

Heartman, Charles F., and James R. Canny. *Bibliography of First Printings of the Writings of Edgar Allan Poe*. 1943. New York: Kraus Reprint Co., 1972.

[Heath, James]. "Editorial Remarks." *Southern Literary Messenger* 1 (January 1935): 254.

Hegel, Georg Wilhelm Friedrich. *Aesthetics: Lectures on Fine Art*. Trans. T. M. Knox. 2 vols. Oxford: Oxford University Press, 1975.

Herbert, T. Walter. "The Erotics of Purity: *The Marble Faun* and the Victorian Construction of Sexuality." *Representations* 36 (fall 1991): 114–32.

Hershberg, Theodore. "Free Blacks in Antebellum Philadelphia: A Study of Ex-Slaves, Freeborn Blacks, and Socioeconomic Decline." *Journal of Social History* 5 (winter 1971–72): 183–209.

Hirst, Henry B. "The Ruined Tavern." *Sartain's Magazine* 10 (May 1852): 434.

Honour, Hugh. *The Image of the Black in Western Art*. Vol 4, *From the American Revolution to World War I*. Houston: Menil Foundation, 1989.

Horsman, Reginald. *Race and Manifest Destiny: The Origins of American Racial Anglo-Saxonism*. Cambridge: Harvard University Press, 1981.

Hose, Charles, and William McDougall. *The Pagan Tribes of Borneo*. New York: Barnes and Noble, 1966.

Hovey, Kenneth Alan. "Critical Provincialism: Poe's Poetic Principle in Antebellum Context." *American Quarterly* 4 (1987): 341–54.

Hubbell, Jay B. "Edgar Allan Poe." In *Eight American Authors: A Review of Research and Criticism*, ed. James Woodress, 3–36. Rev. ed. New York: Norton, 1972.

Hull, William Doyle, II. "A Canon of the Critical Works of Edgar Allan Poe with a Study of Poe as Editor and Reviewer." Ph.D. diss., University of Virginia, 1941.

Hume, David. "Of National Characters." 1748. In *David Hume: Political Essays*, ed. Knud Haakonssen, 78–92. New York: Cambridge University Press, 1994.

Ingraham, Joseph Holt. *The South-West. By a Yankee*. 2 vols. New York: Harper and Brothers, 1835; Ann Arbor: University Microfilms (1966): 1:190–91.

Irving, Washington. *Astoria*. 1836. Portland, Ore.: Binfords and Mort, 1967.

———. *Tales of a Traveller*. 1824. Rev. ed. Hudson edition. 1 vol. New York: G. P. Putnam's Sons, 1890.

Jackson, David K. Continuation of "Some Unpublished Letters of T. W. White to Lucian Minor." *Tyler's Quarterly Historical and Genealogical Magazine* 18 (July 1936): 32–49.

———. *Poe and the "Southern Literary Messenger."* Richmond, Va.: Dietz Press, 1934.

———. "Some Unpublished Letters of T. W. White to Lucian Minor." *Tyler's Quarterly Historical and Genealogical Magazine* 17 (April 1936): 224–43.

Jacobs, Robert D. "Poe and the Agrarian Critics." *Hopkins Review* 5 (1952): 43–54.

———. *Poe: Journalist and Critic.* Baton Rouge: Louisiana State University Press, 1969.

James, Henry. *French Poets and Novelists.* New York: Macmillan, 1878.

Jefferson, Thomas. "Memoir of Meriwether Lewis." In *The History of the Lewis and Clark Expedition,* ed. Elliott Coues. 3 vols. 1893. New York: Dover, 1950–1989.

———. *Notes on the State of Virginia.* Ed. William Peden. New York: Norton, 1972.

———. *Notes on the State of Virginia. Thomas Jefferson: Writings.* Ed. Merrill D. Peterson, 123–325. New York: Library of America, 1984.

Jeffries, John, M.D. "Some Account of the Dissection of a Simia Satyrus, Ourang Outang, or Wild Man of the Woods." *Boston Journal of Philosophy and the Arts* (1825): 570–580.

Johnston, Norman, Kenneth Finkel, and Jeffrey A. Cohen. *Eastern State Penitentiary: Crucible of Good Intentions.* Philadelphia: Philadelphia Museum of Art, 1994.

Jordan, Winthrop D. *The White Man's Burden: Historical Origins of Racism in the United States.* New York: Oxford University Press, 1974.

———. *White over Black: American Attitudes toward the Negro, 1550–1812.* New York: Norton, 1977.

Judy, Ronald. *(Dis)Forming the American Canon.* Minneapolis: University of Minnesota Press, 1993.

Kant, Immanuel. *Observations on the Feeling of the Beautiful and the Sublime.* 1764. Trans. John T. Goldthwait. Berkeley: University of California Press, 1960.

Kaplan, Amy. "'Left Alone with America': The Absence of Empire in the Study of American Culture." In *Cultures of United States Imperialism,* ed. Amy Kaplan and Donald Pease, 3–21. Durham: Duke University Press, 1993.

Kaplan, Sidney. Introduction. In *The Narrative of Arthur Gordon Pym,* vii–xxv. New York: Hill and Wang, 1960.

———. "Introduction to *Pym*." In *Poe: A Collection of Critical Essays,* ed. Robert Regan, 145–63. Englewood Cliffs, N.J.: Prentice-Hall, 1967.

———. "The Miscegenation Issue in the Election of 1864." *Journal of Negro History* 34 (July 1949): 274-343.

Kennedy, J. Gerald. *The Narrative of Arthur Gordon Pym and the Abyss of Interpretation.* New York: Twayne, 1995.

———. *Poe, Death, and the Life of Writing.* New Haven: Yale University Press, 1987.

Kime, Wayne. "Poe's Use of Irving's *Astoria* in 'The Journal of Julius Rodman.'" *American Literature* 40 (May 1968): 215–22.

King, Victor T. *The Peoples of Borneo.* Oxford: Blackwell, 1993.

Kopley, Richard. *Edgar Allan Poe and "The Philadelphia Saturday News."* Baltimore: Enoch Pratt Library, 1991.

Kovel, Joel. *White Racism: A Psychohistory.* New York: Vintage, 1970.

Lane, Roger. *William Dorsey's Philadelphia and Ours: On the Past and Future of the Black City in America.* New York: Oxford University Press, 1991.

Lapsansky, Emma Jones. "'Since They Got Those Separate Churches': Afro-Americans and Racism in Jacksonian Philadelphia." *American Quarterly* 32 (1980): 54–78.

Lapsansky, Phillip. "Graphic Discord: Abolitionists and Antiabolitionist Images." In *The Abolitionist Sisterhood: Women's Political Culture in Antebellum America,* ed. Jean Fagan Yellin and John C. Van Horne, 201–230. Ithaca: Cornell University Press, 1994.

Laser, Marvin. "The Growth and Structure of Poe's Concept of Beauty." *ELH* 15 (1948): 9–84.

Lavely, Marcia Marvin. "A Study of American Literature Which Incorporates the Use of the Gullah Dialect." Ph.D. diss., University of Mississippi, 1991.

Lee, Kun Jong. "Ellison's Invisible Man: Emersonianism Revisited." *PMLA* 107 (March 1992): 331–44.

Lee, A. Robert. "'Impudent and Ingenious Fiction': Poe's *The Narrative of Arthur Gordon Pym of Nantucket.*" In *Edgar Allan Poe: The Design of Order,* 112–34. New York: Barnes and Noble, 1987.

Leland, Charles Godfrey. *Memoirs.* New York, 1893.

Lemire, Elise V. "Making Miscegenation: Discourses of Interracial Sex and Marriage in the United States, 1790–1865." Ph.D. diss., Rutgers University, 1996.

Leverenz, David. "Poe and Gentry Virginia." In *The American Face of Edgar Allan Poe,* ed. Shawn Rosenheim and Stephen Rachman, 210–36. Baltimore: Johns Hopkins University Press, 1995.

Levin, Harry. *The Power of Blackness: Hawthorne, Poe, Melville.* New York: Knopf, 1970.

Lewis, Matthew Gregory. "To the Reader." In *The Castle Spectre.* London: Joseph Bell, 1798.

Linnaeus, Carl. "Anthropomorpha." Respondent C. E. Hoppius. Vol. 6. *Amoenitates academicae.* 1760. Erlangen, 1787.

Long, Edward. *The History of Jamaica, or the General Survey of the Ancient and Modern State of That Island.* 3 vols. London, 1774. New York: Arno, 1972.

Lott, Eric. *Love and Theft: Blackface Minstrelsy and the American Working Class.* New York: Oxford University Press, 1993.

Lovejoy, Arthur O. *The Great Chain of Being: A Study of the History of an Idea.* 1936. Cambridge: Harvard University Press, 1960.

Mabbott, T. O. *Selected Poetry and Prose of Edgar Allan Poe.* New York: Rinehart, 1951.

Mallarmé, Stéphane. *Oeuvres complètes.* Ed. Henri Mondor and G. Jean-Aubry. Paris: Gallimard, 1945.

————. *Les Poèmes d'Edgar Poe, traduits par Stéphane Mallarmé.* Paris: Gallimard, 1928.

Marchand, Ernest. "Poe as Social Critic." *American Literature* 6 (1934): 28–43.

Martin, Byron Curtis. "Racism in the United States: A History of Anti-miscegenation Legislation and Litigation." 3 vols. Ph.D. diss., University of Southern California, 1979.

Matthiessen, F. O. *American Renaissance: Art and Expression in the Age of Emerson and Whitman.* New York: Oxford University Press, 1941.

McFeely, William S. *Frederick Douglass.* New York: Simon and Schuster, 1991.

McNutt, Donald. "Fictions of Confinement: Poe, Dickens, and Eastern State Penitentiary." Unpublished ms.

Melville, Herman. "Benito Cereno." In *Billy Budd, Sailor and Other Stories,* 144–223. New York: Signet Classics, 1979.

————. *The Piazza Tales and Other Prose Pieces, 1839–1860.* Vol. 9 of *The Writings of Herman Melville.* Ed. Harrison Hayford, Alma A. MacDougall, and G. Thomas Tanselle. Chicago: Northwestern-Newberry, 1987.

Methodist Magazine and Quarterly Review of New York, 15 (January 1833): 111–16.

Meyers, Jeffrey. *Edgar Allan Poe: His Life and Legacy.* New York: Charles Scribner's Sons, 1992.

Miller, John C. "Did Edgar Poe Really Sell a Slave?" *Poe Studies* 9 (1976): 52–53.

Minor, Lucian. "Liberian Literature." *Southern Literary Messenger* 2 (February 1836): 158–59.

Mommsen, Wolfgang J. *Theories of Imperialism.* Trans. P. J. Falla. Chicago: University of Chicago Press, 1980.

Mondor, Henri. *Vie de Mallarmé.* Paris: Gallimard, 1941.

Montgomery, Michael, ed. *The Crucible of Carolina: Essays in the Development of Gullah Language and Culture.* Athens: University of Georgia Press, 1994.

Morris, J. Allen. "Gullah in the Stories and Novels of William Gilmore Simms." *American Speech* 22 (1947): 46–53.

————. "The Stories of William Gilmore Simms." *American Literature* 14 (1942): 20–35.

Morrison, Toni. *Beloved.* New York: New American Library, 1987.

————. "Introduction: Friday on the Potomac." In *Race-ing Justice, En-gendering Power: Essays on Anita Hill, Clarence Thomas, and the Construction of Social Reality,* vii–xxx. New York: Pantheon, 1992.

————. *Playing in the Dark: Whiteness and the Literary Imagination.* Cambridge: Harvard University Press, 1992.

Mufwene, Salikoko S. "Africanisms in Gullah: A Re-examination of the Issues." In *Old English and New: Studies in Language and Linguistics in Honor of Frederic G. Cassidy,* ed. Nick Doane, Joan H. Hall, and Dick Ringler, 156–82. New York: Garland, 1992.

————. "Investigating Gullah: Difficulties in Ensuring 'Authenticity.'" In *Language Variation in North American English: Research and Teaching,* ed. A. Wayne

Glowka and Donald M. Lance, 178–90. New York: Modern Language Association of America, 1993.

Nash, Gary. *Forging Freedom: The Formation of Philadelphia's Black Community, 1720–1840.* Cambridge: Harvard University Press, 1991.

A Natural History of the Globe, of Man, and of Quadrupeds; From the Writings of Buffon, Cuvier . . . and Other Eminent Naturalists. 2 vols. New York, 1833.

Nelson, Dana. *The Word in Black and White: Reading "Race" in American Literature, 1638–1867.* New York: Oxford University Press, 1993.

Nygaard, Loisa. "Winning the Game: Inductive Reasoning in Poe's 'Murders in the Rue Morgue.'" *Studies in Romanticism* 33 (summer 1994): 223–54.

"Observations on the Ourang Outang." *Boston Journal of Philosophy and the Arts.* Reprinted in *Miscellaneous Cabinet* 16 (August 1823): 44–45.

Olney, James. "The Founding Fathers: Frederick Douglass and Booker T. Washington." In *Slavery and the Literary Imagination,* ed. Deborah E. McDowell and Arnold Rampersad, 1–24. Baltimore: Johns Hopkins University Press, 1989.

Omans, Glen A. "Intellect, Taste, and the Moral Sense: Poe's Debt to Kant." *Studies in the American Renaissance* (1980): 123–68.

O'Sullivan, John. "Annexation." *United States and Democratic Review* 17 (July–August 1845): 5.

Outram, Dorinda. *Georges Cuvier: Vocation, Science, and Authority in Post-revolutionary France.* Manchester: Manchester University Press, 1984.

Pakenham, Thomas. *The Scramble for Africa.* New York: Random House, 1991.

Parrington, Vernon. *Main Currents in American Thought.* 3 vols. New York: Harcourt, Brace, 1927–30.

Patterson, Orlando. *Slavery and Social Death: A Comparative Study.* Cambridge: Harvard University Press, 1982.

[The Paulding-Drayton Review] "Slavery." *Southern Literary Messenger* 2 (April 1836): 336–39. Reprinted in *The Complete Works of Edgar Allan Poe,* ed. James A. Harrison, 8:265–75. New York: Kelmscott Society, 1902.

Paulding, James Kirke. Letter to T. W. White. 3 March 1836. Reprinted in George E. Woodberry. *The Life of Edgar Allan Poe.* 1: 156–60. Boston: Houghton Mifflin, 1909.

Pease, Jane Hanna. "The Freshness of Fanaticism: Abby Kelley Foster, An Essay in Reform." Ph.D. diss., University of Rochester, 1969.

Peck, Louis F. *A Life of Matthew G. Lewis.* Cambridge: Harvard University Press, 1961.

The People, Respondent, v. George W. Hall, Appellant. Supreme Court of California, 4 CA 399 CA Lexis 137 (1854). http://lexis-nexis.com.

Phillips, Mary E. *Edgar Allan Poe, The Man,* 2 vols. Chicago: John C. Winston, 1926.

Pierson, George Wilson. *Tocqueville and Beaumont in America.* Baltimore: Johns Hopkins University Press, 1938.

Pieterse, Jan Nederveen. *White on Black: Images of Africa and Blacks in Western Popular Culture.* New Haven: Yale University Press, 1992.

Platner v. Sherwood. 6 Johns Ch. NY 127 (1822).

Poe, Edgar Allan. *"Ballads and Other Poems.* By Henry Wadsworth Longfellow. Author of 'Voices of the Night,' 'Hyperion,' &c. 2nd edition. John Owen: Cambridge." *Graham's Magazine* 20 (April 1842): 248–51.

———. "Editorial: Right of Instruction." *Southern Literary Messenger* 2 (June 1836): 445.

———. "Letter to B———." *Southern Literary Messenger* 2 (July 1836): 501–3.

———. "Longfellow's Poems." *Aristidean* 1 (April 1845): 130–42.

———. Review of *The South-West,* by Joseph Holt Ingraham. *Southern Literary Messenger* 2 (January 1836): 122–23.

Pollin, Burton R. "Poe and Daniel Defoe: A Significant Relationship." *Topic: A Journal of the Liberal Arts* 16, no. 30 (1976): 3–22.

———. "Poe Viewed and Reviewed: An Annotated Checklist of Contemporary Notices." *Poe Studies* 11 (1980): 17–28.

———. "Poe's *Narrative of Arthur Gordon Pym* and the Contemporary Reviewers." *Studies in American Fiction* 2 (spring 1974): 37–56.

Powers, Richard. *The Gold Bug Variations.* New York: Morrow, 1991.

Quarles, Benjamin. *Black Abolitionists.* New York: Oxford University Press, 1969.

Quinn, Arthur Hobson. *Edgar Allan Poe: A Critical Biography.* New York: D. Appleton-Century, 1941.

Quinn, Patrick F. *The French Face of Edgar Allan Poe.* Carbondale: Southern Illinois University Press, 1957.

Ramsey, William M. "Melville's and Barnum's Man with a Weed." *American Literature* 51 (1979): 101–4.

Randall, J. G. *Lincoln: The Liberal Statesman.* New York: Dodd, Mead, 1947.

Reynolds, David S. *Beneath the American Renaissance: The Subversive Imagination in the Age of Emerson and Melville.* Cambridge: Harvard University Press, 1989.

Ricardou, Jean. "Gold in the Bug." Trans. Frank Towne. *Poe Studies* 9.2 (1976): 33.

Richards, Leonard L. *"Gentlemen of Property and Standing": Anti-abolition Mobs in Jacksonian America.* London: Oxford University Press, 1970.

Richmond Enquirer, 22 May 1835.

Ridgely, Joseph V. "The Authorship of the 'Paulding-Drayton Review.'" *Poe Studies Association Newsletter* 20 (fall 1992): 1–6.

———. "The Growth of the Text." In *The Narrative of Arthur Gordon Pym.* Vol. 1 of *The Collected Writings of Edgar Allan Poe,* ed. Burton Pollin, 29–36. 1981. New York: Gordian, 1994.

———. "Tragical-Mythical-Satirical-Hoaxical: Problems of Genre in *Pym.*" *American Transcendental Quarterly* 24 (fall 1974): 4–9.

Robbins, Bruce. *The Servant's Hand: English Fiction from Below.* New York: Columbia University Press, 1986.

Robinson, Ronald, and John Gallagher. "The Imperialism of Free Trade." *Economic History Review* 6 (1953): 1–15.

Rollason, Christopher. "The Detective Myth in Edgar Allan Poe's Dupin Trilogy." In *American Crime Fiction: Studies in the Genre,* ed. Brian Docherty, 4–22. New York: St. Martin's Press, 1988.

Rosenheim, Shawn J. *The Cryptographic Imagination: Secret Writing from Edgar Poe to the Internet.* Baltimore: Johns Hopkins University Press, 1997.

————. "Detective Fiction, Psychoanalysis, and the Analytic Sublime." In *The American Face of Edgar Allan Poe,* ed. Shawn Rosenheim and Stephen Rachman, 153–78. Baltimore: Johns Hopkins University Press, 1995.

Rosenthal, Bernard. "Poe, Slavery, and the *Southern Literary Messenger:* A Reexamination." *Poe Studies* 7 (December 1974): 29–38.

Rowan, Carl. *The Coming Race War in America.* New York: Little, Brown, 1996.

Rowe, John Carlos. *At Emerson's Tomb: The Politics of Classic American Literature.* New York: Columbia University Press, 1997.

————. "Poe, Antebellum Slavery, and Modern Criticism." In *Poe's Pym: Critical Explorations,* ed. Richard Kopley, 117–38. Durham: Duke University Press, 1992.

Rubin, Louis D., Jr. *The Edge of the Swamp: A Study in the Literature and Society of the Old South.* Baton Rouge: Louisiana State University Press, 1989.

Ruffin v. Commonwealth. 62 VA 21 Gratt. 796 (1871).

Runcie, John. "'Hunting the Nigs' in Philadelphia: The Race Riot of August 1834." *Pennsylvania History* 34 (April 1972): 187–218.

Said, Edward W. *Orientalism.* New York: Random House, 1979.

Sale, George. "A Preliminary Discourse." *The Koran,* trans. George Sale, 1–186. London: J. Wilcox, 1734.

Samuels, Shirley. "The Identity of Slavery." In *The Culture of Sentiment: Race, Gender, and Sentimentality in Nineteenth-Century America,* ed. Shirley Samuels, 571–71. New York: Oxford University Press, 1992.

Sánchez-Eppler, Karen. *Touching Liberty: Abolition, Feminism, and the Politics of the Body.* Berkeley: University of California Press, 1993.

Saxon, A. H. P. T. *Barnum: The Legend and the Man.* New York: Columbia University Press, 1989.

Saxton, Alexander. *The Rise and Fall of the White Republic: Class Politics and Mass Culture in Nineteenth-Century America.* New York: Verso, 1990.

Scheppele, Kim Lane. "Facing Facts in Legal Interpretation." *Representations* 30 (1990): 42–77.

Schiebinger, Londa. *Nature's Body: Gender in the Making of Modern Science.* Boston: Beacon Press, 1993.

Scott, James C. *Domination and the Arts of Resistance: Hidden Transcripts.* New Haven: Yale University Press, 1990.

Sellers, Charles Coleman. *Mr. Peale's Museum: Charles Willson Peale and the First Popular Museum of Natural Science and Art.* New York: Norton, 1980.

Sharpe, Jenny. "'Something Akin to Freedom': The Case of Mary Prince." *Differences: A Journal of Feminist Cultural Studies* 8, no. 1 (1996): 31–56.

Shell, Marc. "The Gold Bug: Introduction to 'the Industry of Letters' in America." In *Money, Language, and Thought: Literary and Philosophical Economies from the Medieval to the Modern Era,* 5–23. Berkeley: University of California Press, 1982.

Silverman, Kenneth. *Edgar A. Poe: Mournful and Never-Ending Remembrance.* New York: HarperCollins, 1991.

Simms, William Gilmore. *Martin Faber: The Story of a Criminal.* New York: J. & J. Harper, 1833.

———. *Tales of the South.* Ed. Mary Ann Wimsatt. Columbia: University of South Carolina Press, 1996.

Sklar, Kathryn Kish. *Catharine Beecher: A Study in American Domesticity.* New Haven: Yale University Press, 1973.

Slotkin, Richard. *Regeneration Through Violence: The Mythology of the American Frontier, 1600–1860.* Middletown, Conn.: Wesleyan University Press, 1973.

Smallwood, William Martin. *Natural History and the American Mind.* New York: Columbia University Press, 1941.

Smith, Douglas G. "Citizenship and the Fourteenth Amendment." *San Diego Law Review* 681 (1997): 682–807.

Smith, Reed. *Gullah: Dedicated to the Memory of Ambrose E. Gonzales.* Columbia: Bureau of Publications, University of South Carolina, 1926.

Smith, Samuel Stanhope. *An Essay on the Causes of the Variety of Complexion and Figure in the Human Species.* 1810. Ed. Winthrop D. Jordan. Cambridge: Harvard University Press, 1965.

Snodgrass, E. Letters to Maria Weston Chapman. 17 March 1846 and 25 November 1846. Boston Public Library, Ms.A.9.2.22: 31, 134.

Spiller, Robert et al., eds. *Literary History of the United States.* 3d. ed. New York: Macmillan, 1963.

Stallybrass, Peter, and Allon White. *The Politics and Poetics of Transgression.* Ithaca: Cornell University Press, 1986.

Stanton, William. *The Leopard's Spots: Scientific Attitudes toward Race in America, 1815–59.* Chicago: University of Chicago Press, 1960.

Staudenraus, P. J. *The African Colonization Movement, 1816–1865.* New York: Columbia University Press, 1961.

Stegner, Wallace. *Beyond the Hundredth Meridian: John Wesley Powell and the Second Opening of the West.* New York: Penguin, 1992.

Sterling, Dorothy. *Ahead of Her Time: Abby Kelley and the Politics of Antislavery.* New York: Norton, 1991.

Stokeley, Jim. *Fort Moultrie: Constant Defender.* Handbook 136. Division of Publications, National Park Services. Washington, D.C.: U.S. Department of the Interior, 1985.

Stone, Albert E. "Identity and Art in Douglass's *Narrative.*" In *Critical Essays on Frederick Douglass,* ed. William L. Andrews, 62–78. Boston: G. K. Hall, 1991.

Stovall, Floyd. *Edgar Poe the Poet: Essays New and Old on the Man and His Work.* Charlottesville: University Press of Virginia, 1969.

Stowe, Harriet Beecher. *Uncle Tom's Cabin; or Life among the Lowly.* Ed. Ann Douglas. Harmondsworth: Penguin Books, 1981.

Summers & al. v. Bean. VA (13 Gratt.) 411. 1856.

Sundquist, Eric. "The Literature of Expansion and Race." In *The Cambridge History of American Literature.* Vol. 2, *Prose Writing, 1820–1865,* ed. Sacvan Bercovitch and Cyrus Patell, 125–328. New York: Cambridge University Press, 1995.

————. *To Wake the Nations: Race in the Making of American Literature.* Cambridge: Harvard University Press, 1993.

Swisshelm, Jane. *Half a Century.* 2d ed. Chicago: Jansen, McClurg & Co., 1880. Reprint, New York: Source Book Press, 1970.

Tate, Allen. "The Angelic Imagination: Poe as God." In *The Forlorn Demon: Didactic and Critical Essays,* 56–78. Chicago: Regnery, 1953.

Thomas, Dwight Rembert. "Poe in Philadelphia, 1838–1844: A Documentary Record." Ph.D. diss., University of Pennsylvania, 1978.

Thomas, Dwight, and David K. Jackson. *The Poe Log: A Documentary Life of Edgar Allan Poe, 1809–1849.* New York: G. K. Hall, 1987.

Thomas, Hugh. *The Slave Trade: The Story of the Atlantic Slave Trade, 1440–1870.* New York: Simon and Schuster, 1997.

Thompson, G. R. "Poe and the Writers of the Old South." In *Columbia Literary History of the United States,* ed. Emory Elliott, 262–77. New York: Columbia University Press, 1988.

Tise, Larry. *Proslavery: A History of the Defense of Slavery in America.* Athens: University of Georgia Press, 1987.

"To Our Friends and Subscribers." *Southern Literary Messenger* (5 January 1839): 1–2.

Tocqueville, Alexis de, and Gustave de Beaumont. *On the Penitentiary System in the United States, and Its Application in France.* Trans. Francis Lieber. Philadelphia: Carey, 1833.

Topsell, Edward. *The Historie of Foure-Footed Beasts.* London: William Iaggard, 1607.

Troup v. Wood. 4 Johns. Ch. NY 299 (1819.13).

Tucker, Nathaniel Beverley. "Bulwer's New Play." *Southern Literary Messenger* 3 (January 1837): 90–95.

————. "A Discourse on the Genius of the Federative System of the United States." *Southern Literary Messenger* 4 (December 1838): 761–69.

————. "An Essay on the Moral and Political Effect of the Relation between the Caucasian Master and the African Slave." *Southern Literary Messenger* 10 (June 1844): 329–39; (August 1844): 470–80.

————. Letter to Duff Green. 20 April 1836. Duff Green Papers. Library of Congress. Typescript in Noma Lee Goodwin "The Published Works of Nathaniel Beverley Tucker, 1784–1851," 212–15. M.A. thesis, Duke University, 1947.

————. "The Nature and Function of the Commercial Profession." *A Series of Lectures on the Science of Government.* 396–415. Philadelphia: Carey and Hart, 1845.

————. "Note to Blackstone's Commentaries. . . ." *Southern Literary Messenger* 1 (January 1835): 227–31.

————. *The Partisan Leader.* Ed. Carl Bridenbaugh. 1836. New York: Knopf, 1933.

————. "The Present State of Europe." *Southern Quarterly Review* 16, no. 32 (January 1850): 277–323.

————. Review of *A History of the United States,* by George Bancroft. *Southern Literary Messenger* 1 (June 1835): 587.

————. Review of "An Oration, delivered before the two Societies of the South Carolina College." *Southern Quarterly Review* 17 (April 1850): 37–48.

————. Review of "An Oration on the Life and Character of Gilbert Motier de Lafayette," by John Quincy Adams, and "Eulogy on La Fayette," by Edward Everett. *Southern Literary Messenger* 1 (February 1835): 307–12.

Tyler-McGraw, Marie, and Gregg D. Kimball. *In Bondage and Freedom: Antebellum Black Life in Richmond, Virginia.* Richmond: Valentine Museum, 1988.

Van Leer, David. "Detecting Truth: The World of the Dupin Tales." In *New Essays on Poe's Major Tales,* ed. Kenneth Silverman, 65–91. New York: Cambridge University Press, 1993.

Vaux, Roberts. "Letter on the Penitentiary System of Pennsylvania, addressed to William Rascoe, Esquire." Philadelphia: Jespar Harding, 1827.

A Virginian [James E. Heath]. *Slavery in Maryland: An Anti-slavery Review.* Baltimore: Saturday Visiter Establishment, 1846.

A Virginian [pseud.]. "Remarks on a Note to Blackstone's Commentaries. Vol. 1. 423." *Southern Literary Messenger* 1 (February 1835). 266–70.

Wade, Richard C. *Slavery in the Cities: The South, 1820–1860.* New York: Oxford University Press, 1964.

Walker, Clarence. *De-romanticizing Black History: Critical Essays and Reappraisals.* Knoxville: University of Tennessee Press, 1991.

Warner, Sam Bass, Jr. *The Private City: Philadelphia in Three Periods of Its Growth.* Philadelphia: University of Pennsylvania Press, 1968.

[Webb, Samuel, ed.] *History of Pennsylvania Hall Which Was Destroyed by a Mob on the 17th of May, 1838.* Philadelphia, 1838.

Webster's an American Dictionary of the English Language. Philadelphia: Lippincott, 1864.

Weidman, Bette S. *"The Broadway Journal* (2): A Casualty of Abolition Politics." *Bulletin of the New York Public Library* 73 (February 1969). 33–113.

Weir, Robert M. *Colonial South Carolina: A History.* Millwood, N.Y.: Kto Press, 1983.

Weiss, Susan Archer. *The Home Life of Poe.* New York: Broadway Publishing, 1907.

Weissberg, Liliane. *Edgar Allan Poe.* Stuttgart: J. B. Metzlersche Verlagsbuchhandlung, 1991.

————. "Editing Adventures: Writing the Text of *Julius Rodman." Modern Fiction Studies* 33 (1987): 413–30.

Werner, M. R. *Barnum.* New York: Harcourt, Brace, 1923.

Whalen, Terence. "Average Racism." *Edgar Allan Poe and the Masses,* 111–46. Princeton, N.J. Princeton University Press, 1999.

————. "The Code for Gold: Edgar Allan Poe and Cryptography." *Representations* 46 (1994): 35–57. Reprinted in *Edgar Allan Poe and the Masses,* 195–224.

————. "Edgar Allan Poe and the Horrid Laws of Political Economy." *American Quarterly* 44 (September 1992): 381–417. Reprinted in *Edgar Allan Poe and the Masses,* 21–57.

————. *Edgar Allan Poe and the Masses: The Political Economy of Literature in Antebellum America*. Princeton: Princeton University Press, 1999.

————. "Subtle Barbarians: Poe, Racism, and the Political Economy of Adventure." In *Styles of Cultural Activism: From Theory and Pedagogy to Women, Indians, and Communism*, ed. Philip Goldstein, 169–83. Newark: University of Delaware Press, 1994.

Whitman, T. Stephen. *The Price of Freedom: Slavery and Manumission in Baltimore and Early National Maryland*. Lexington: University Press of Kentucky, 1997.

Whitman, Walt. "Edgar Poe's Significance." *Complete Poetry and Collected Prose*. Ed. Justin Kaplan, 872–74. New York: Library of America, 1982.

Whitty, James H. "Memoir." In *The Complete Poems of Edgar Allan Poe*. 2d ed., xix–lxxxvi. Boston: Houghton Mifflin, 1917.

Williams, Raymond. *Keywords: A Vocabulary of Culture and Society*. Rev. ed. New York: Oxford University Press, 1983.

Williams, William Appleman. *The Tragedy of American Diplomacy*. Cleveland: World, 1959.

Williamson, Joel. *New People: Miscegenation and Mulattos in the United States*. New York: Free Press, 1980.

Wilson, Edmund. "Poe at Home and Abroad." *New Republic*, 8 December 1926. Reprinted in *The Recognition of Edgar Allan Poe*, ed. Eric W. Carlson, 142–51. Ann Arbor: University of Michigan Press, 1966.

Wilson v. Seiter. 501 U.S. 294 (1991).

Winthrop, John. "A Model of Christian Charity." In *The Norton Anthology of American Literature*, ed. Nina Baym et al. 2d ed. Vol. 1, 37–50. New York: Norton, 1985.

Wood, Peter H. *Black Majority: Negroes in Colonial South Carolina from 1670 through the Stono Rebellion*. New York: Knopf, 1974.

Woodberry, George. *The Life of Edgar Allan Poe*. 2 vols. Boston: Houghton Mifflin, 1909.

Worley, Sam. "*The Narrative of Arthur Gordon Pym* and the Ideology of Slavery." *ESQ* 40 (1994): 219–50.

Wyatt, Thomas. *A Synopsis of Natural History: Embracing the Natural History of Animals, with Human and General Animal Physiology, Botany, Vegetable Physiology and Geology. Translated from the Latest French Edition of C. Lemmonnier. . . . With Additions from the Works of Cuvier, Dumaril, Lacepede, Etc.; And Arranged as a Textbook for Schools*. Philadelphia, 1839.

Wyatt-Brown, Bertram. "The Mask of Obedience: Male Slave Psychology in the Old South." *American Historical Review* 93 (December 1988): 1228–52. Reprinted in *Society and Culture in the Slave South*, ed. J. William Harris, 128–61. London: Routledge, 1992.

Yellin, Jean Fagan. *Women and Sisters: The Anti-slavery Feminists in American Culture*. New Haven: Yale University Press, 1989.

Young v. Burton. 255 South Carolina 162. SC Ct. of Errors (1841).

Zizek, Slavoj. *Looking Awry: An Introduction to Jacques Lacan through Popular Culture*. Cambridge: MIT Press, 1991.

CONTRIBUTORS

LINDON BARRETT is Associate Professor of English and Comparative Literature at the University of California at Irvine. He has published numerous essays in the field of American Studies and is the author of the recently published *Seeing Double: Blackness and Value*, as well as the editor of the forthcoming anthology *Blackness and the Mind/Body Split*.

JOAN DAYAN is Regents Professor of English at the University of Arizona, Tucson. She is the author of *Fables of Mind: An Inquiry into Poe's Fiction* (1987), *Haiti, History, and the Gods* (1995), and numerous articles on North American and Caribbean literature and issues of race.

BETSY ERKKILA is Professor of English and Chair of the English Department at Northwestern University. She is the author of *The Wicked Sisters: Women Poets, Literary History, and Discord* (1992), as well as numerous studies on Walt Whitman. Most recently she edited, together with Jay Grossman, *Breaking Bounds: Whitman and American Cultural Studies* (1996).

J. GERALD KENNEDY is William A. Read Professor of English at Louisiana State University at Baton Rouge, and past Chair of the department. He is the author of numerous books on nineteenth- and twentieth-century American literature, among them *Poe, Death, and the Life of Writing* (1987), *Imagining Paris : Exile, Writing, and American Identity* (1993), and *The Narrative of Arthur Gordon Pym and the Abyss of Interpretation* (1995). He is also editor of the *Oxford Historical Guide to Poe*.

ELISE LEMIRE is Assistant Professor of Literature at the State University of New York at Purchase. She is currently completing a study of the Discourse of Amalgamation in early nineteenth-century America.

LELAND S. PERSON is Professor of English and Chair of the English department at the University of Cincinnati. He has published widely in the field of American literature and is the author of *Aesthetic Headaches: Women and a Masculine Poetics in Poe, Melville, and Hawthorne* (1988).

JOHN CARLOS ROWE is Professor of English at the University of California at Irvine and the author of books on Henry James, Henry Adams, and the Vietnam War. His best-known publications are *Through the Custom-House: Nineteenth-Century American Fiction and Modern Theory* (1982) and *At Emerson's Tomb: The Politics of Classic American Literature* (1997). His study *Literary Culture and U.S. Imperialism*, as well as his anthologies *"Culture" and the Problem of the Disciplines* and *Post-nationalist American Studies*, have recently been published.

LILIANE WEISSBERG is Joseph B. Glossberg Term Professor in the Humanities and Professor of German and Comparative Literature at the University of Pennsylvania, where she is also chair of the Program in Comparative Literature and Literary Theory. She is the author of *Geistersprache: Philosophischer und literarischer Diskurs im späten achtzehnten Jahrhundert* (1990), and a German monograph, *Edgar Allan Poe* (1991), as well as editor of several books, including the American edition of Hannah Arendt's *Rahel Varnhagen* (1997) and *Cultural Memory and the Construction of Identity* (with Dan Ben-Amos, 1999).

TERENCE WHALEN is Associate Professor of English at the University of Illinois, Chicago, He has published numerous articles on Poe and American culture. His book *Edgar Allan Poe and the Masses: The Political Economy of Literature in Antebellum America* was published by Princeton University Press.

INDEX

INDEX

283

nameless black woman in, 140, 141
publication of, 139
reversal of master-slave relations
in, 138, 147–48
role of Jupiter in, 31, 32, 136–138,
141, 151
Gordon, Armistead, 233, 244
Gore, Austin, 238
Gothic fiction, slavery and racial difference in, xv
Gray, Thomas R., 56
Grimké, Angelina, 193
controversial marriage of, 195,
196
Grimké, Sarah, 193
Griswold, Rufus, 58, 67
Gullah language, 135, 139, 140

Haiti, and fictions of color, 120
Harper and Brothers, 29
publication of *Pym* by, 254
Hastings, Warren, 91–93
"Haunted Palace, The"
as allegory of cultural apocalypse,
58
racial meaning of "hideous
throng" in, 58
Hawthorne, Nathaniel, 141
Heath, James, 15, 17, 34
as probable author of anti-slavery
pamphlet, 23
Hirst, Henry B., 58, 59
racialized parody of "The Raven"
by, 59
*History of the Expedition under the Com-
mand of Lewis and Clark* (Biddle),
77
Hood, Thomas, 66
"Hop-Frog," 95, 98, 99, 113, 218–19,
221
and amalgamation nightmare in,
220
conversion of masters into slaves
in, 114
ironic reversal of vitiligo in, 219

master-slave relations in, 219
otherness of title character, 219
racial revenge in, 206, 218–19, 251
topsy-turvy plot of, 218
"How to Write a Blackwood Article,"
dwarfism of Pompey in, 219
Hume, David, 64, 66

I'll Take My Stand, 59
Imbert, Anthony, illustration of black
barber by, 186–88
imperialism, 75–105
and Enlightenment rationality, 98
Indian Removal policy, 46, 48
Jackson's announcement of, 49
Ingraham, Joseph Holt, view of slav-
ery by, 16, 17
"Instinct vs Reason–A Black Cat,"
63
interracial marriage, legal prohibition
of, 199
Invisible Man (Ellison), reference to
Poe in, 49
Irving, Washington, 75, 77, 89, 142
"Israfel," 51

Jackson, Andrew, 45, 48
Jackson, Michael, xiv
James, Henry, opinion of Poe by, 67
Jefferson, Thomas, 41–43, 48, 79,
210, 215, 217
and fear of racial revolution, 208
on freed blacks and racial mixture,
213
interest in skin color by, 208
and Lewis and Clark expedition,
80, 82
and Phyllis Wheatley, 212
and sexual preference of blacks for
whites, 190
Jenkins, Sandy, 238
"Johnny Q" [John Quincy Adams]
(Clay lithograph), and interracial
desire of abolitionist women,
191, 193, 196

AEB - 7442